Thomas Case

Physical Realism

Being an analytical Philosophy from the Physical Objects of Science to the Physical

Data of Sense

Thomas Case

Physical Realism
Being an analytical Philosophy from the Physical Objects of Science to the Physical Data of Sense

ISBN/EAN: 9783337078461

Printed in Europe, USA, Canada, Australia, Japan

Cover: Foto ©ninafisch / pixelio.de

More available books at **www.hansebooks.com**

PHYSICAL REALISM

BEING

AN ANALYTICAL PHILOSOPHY

FROM

THE PHYSICAL OBJECTS OF SCIENCE

TO

THE PHYSICAL DATA OF SENSE

BY

THOMAS CASE, M.A.

FELLOW AND SENIOR TUTOR CORPUS CHRISTI COLLEGE, AND LECTURER AT
CHRIST CHURCH; FORMERLY FELLOW OF BRASENOSE AND
TUTOR OF BALLIOL COLLEGE, OXFORD

ἔστι δ' ἀποδεῖξαι ἐλεγκτικῶς ARISTOTLE

LONDON

LONGMANS, GREEN, AND CO.

AND NEW YORK: 15 EAST 16th STREET

1888

CONTENTS.

PART I.

GENERAL PROOF OF PHYSICAL REALISM.

PART II.

PSYCHOLOGICAL IDEALISM.

GENERAL PROOF OF PHYSICAL REALISM.

' Itaque contemplatio fere desinit cum aspectu ; adeo ut rerum invisibilium exigua aut nulla sit observatio.'

BACON, *Nov. Org.* i. 50.

B

CHAPTER I.

THE PHYSICAL OBJECT OF SCIENCE.

'NATURAL PHILOSOPHY, as now regarded, treats generally of the physical universe, and deals fearlessly alike with quantities too great to be distinctly conceived, and with quantities almost infinitely too small to be perceived even with the most powerful microscopes; such as, for instance, distances through which the light of stars or nebulæ, though moving at the rate of about 186.000 miles per second, takes many years to travel; or the size of the particles of water, whose number in a single drop may, as we have reason to believe, amount to somewhere about 10^{26}, or

$$100,000,000,000,000,000,000,000,000.$$

Yet we successfully inquire not only into the composition of the atmospheres of these distant stars, but into the number and properties of these water-particles; nay. even into the laws by which they act upon one another.'

This quotation from Professor Tait's 'Recent Advances in Physical Science' is a recognition of the reality of the insensible, and of its knowledge by the natural philosopher, as facts. No metaphysical theory of existence can be complete, unless it recognises the known reality of the insensible physical world; and no psychological theory of human knowledge can be accepted as even a probable hypothesis. unless it explains how these scientific objects of human knowledge are known from the original data of sense.

The distinction between the sensible and the scientific, the apparent and the real, the perceptible and the imperceptible, is not only a scientific fact but has become a commonplace in natural philosophy, without having produced any marked effect in mental philosophy. Astronomy has long opposed the real to the apparent motions of celestial bodies; and Sir Isaac Newton carried this contrast so far as to oppose absolute, true and mathematical, to relative, apparent and common, time and space. In physics, apparent size is the room which a body seems to occupy, physical size is the real space taken up by its particles. Not only physics, but chemistry and biology unite in the antithesis of molar and molecular motion, in recognising therefore motions which are for the most part imperceptible, in resolving what seem to our senses to be heterogeneous qualities into mere varieties of imperceptible motion, and in referring these motions to particles which are as imperceptible as the motions themselves. In all these sciences the latent structures and processes of things are opposed to their external appearances and perceptible changes.

I do not mean that these undeniable conclusions, very far removed as they are from the original data of observation and experiment, are at all inconsistent with the sensations, perceptions, observations, or experiences which ordinary men have, and from which the natural philosopher starts. On the contrary, the very untutored senses themselves are best explained—nay, can be only explained—by statements at first sight opposed to them. It is only in appearance that the motion of the earth round the sun contradicts our senses, for, though it contradicts one single appearance, the whole sum of astronomical observations is only to be explained by means of it. Similarly, when it is said that one thing is apparently larger and physically smaller than another, vision is contradicted, but the sense of touch is justified, and our experience as a whole explained. The latent motions of particles, into which sensible qualities are resolved, at first sight contradict but really explain the whole system of our sensations of touch, vision, and hearing.

But though the results of science thus explain the data of sense, it must be remembered that they only explain them, and are not themselves data of sense. No man can make himself see the earth going round the sun, except by standing on the sun itself. No man can see light at the moment when it starts from a distant star years before it reaches his senses. Microscopes can be multiplied in power, but they are millions short of the actual (I do not speak of the potential) divisibility of the particles of things.

Moreover, the natural philosopher gives even greater reality to the imperceptible than to the perceptible. The astronomer not only opposes but prefers real to apparent motion, the physicist physical to apparent size, and all natural philosophers latent structures and molecular processes to masses and their molar motions. It is not too much to say, that the mission of modern as well as of ancient philosophy is to convince mankind that sense is unequal to the subtlety of things : to get behind the scenes and see the machinery of nature at work ; to recognise the insensible as real, yes, and more real, than the sensible. Sense is not science.

Our knowledge is not limited to sensible phœnomena. We are quite as certain of the existence of that which cannot be brought within our sensibility as of that which can, and of objects which we do not experience as of objects of experience itself. Further, we are quite as certain that they exist in space and in time; for if they are not in space they have no size, if they are not in time they have no duration, and that which has neither any size nor any duration is nothing; and, if they are neither in time nor space, they do not move, for motion is change of place in space during time. Space and time are not mere forms of our sensibility, but conditions of things and their motions beyond the range of our sensibility.

We not only know that the imperceptible exists, and that it exists in space and time, but also we know imperceptible attributes both of the perceptible and of the imperceptible. For example, I know that the hour-hand of my watch moves, though I cannot perceive it moving, as well as that the minute-hand moves which I can perceive moving with difficulty, or the second-hand which I can perceive moving with ease. I know that the imperceptible particles of matter gravitate imperceptibly towards one another, as well as I know that their masses gravitate, and that unless gravitation is true of the former, it is not true of the latter. Still more insensible are cohesion and chemical affinity, which are imperceptible motions exerted between imperceptible particles and at imperceptible distances. The whole of modern science is based on the fact that there are numerous latent structures and latent processes which are known to be real attributes of particles themselves latent. He, then, who will venture to assert, as mental philosophers often do assert, that the attributes which we ascribe to things are simply the phænomena or the sensations which they cause in us, must be prepared to deny all

the imperceptible structures and motions which are
recognised as attributes of things in natural philosophy.

Natural philosophy does not stop at the reality and
knowledge of imperceptible things and their imperceptible attributes. It takes one step further : it regards
the imperceptible as not only real but causal.   In the
first place, among imperceptible objects there are latent
processes of cause and effect, no part of which can be
represented by a sensible object.   When, for example,
the physicist declares that the medium called æther
remains fixed in space, while each successive part of it
undulates in consequence of the previous undulation of
another part, in the same manner as water communicates successive waves, he affirms that the whole of this
propagation of undulations through æther is real, though
the whole of it is imperceptible.   Secondly, he affirms
still more ; he affirms that the imperceptible undulations not only cause one another, but finally cause our
sensations of light.   In this instance of light, as well
as in the parallel case of heat, natural philosophy unhesitatingly accepts the conclusion that imperceptible
motions of imperceptible things not only exist but cause
our sensations.   In other words, secondary qualities as
existing in nature are insensible primary qualities which
are causes of secondary qualities, as sensible in us.

Natural philosophy is not a sham.   One or other,
or many, of its propositions, may be untrue.   But its
whole fabric of the physical, but insensible, world
which causes the sensible image of it to arise in us,
cannot be an invention.   There is a thing beyond sense,
a reality beyond phænomena, not only actual in nature,
but known to science.   There is a thing real and known
which is not a sensible phænomenon, because such
things as imperceptible particles are known really to

exist, though they are incapable of becoming sensible.
There are attributes real and known which belong to
this thing, but are not sensations or sensible phænomena, because such attributes as the imperceptible
motions of imperceptible particles are known really to
take place, although they are not capable of becoming
sensible.   Finally, these real things by these real
attributes are real and known causes of human sensations because the imperceptible motions of the imperceptible are known really to cause sensations of light
and other sensations in men, although the latent process, by which an imperceptible motion such as the
undulation of æther produces sensible light, is totally
beyond the reach of sense, which perceives not the
undulation but the sensible result.   Thus real things
and real attributes transcending yet really causing sensations are, in some way or other, known to the natural
philosopher.   The insensible, then, is not a simple
reality, but contains three realities, all insensible : real
substances, real attributes, real causes of sensations.

There are things in themselves.   A thing in itself
might mean a thing out of all relations.   In this sense
nature contains no things in themselves ; it is a system
of related things the universe of which is alone out of
relation as the sum of all relations.   But this is not
what is meant by a thing in itself in philosophy : what
is really meant is not a thing out of all relations, but a
thing distinct from the phænomena it causes in us, a
thing in itself as opposed to its sensible appearance.   In
this meaning, nature contains infinitely more things in
themselves than it contains phænomena ; and man, as a
natural philosopher, knows things in themselves which
are not phænomena, when he knows imperceptible
particles ;   knows not merely the phænomena which

they cause in us, but their real attributes, when he knows imperceptible motions, and knows that the thing in itself, not as an 'unknown cause,' but by its real attributes produces phænomena, when he knows that imperceptible things, by their imperceptible motions, cause human sensations. There are real things known, real attributes known, real causes known, beyond the phænomena of sense. All this knowledge does man as a natural philosopher possess of things in themselves.

Two antitheses have been handed down to us from ancient philosophy, the natural and the supernatural, the visible and the invisible. These distinctions are often treated as convertible; but they are not so. The natural and the visible are not identical; and the supernatural and the invisible are not identical: there is a natural yet invisible world. Between the extremes of visible nature and the invisible supernatural world there is an invisible nature, distinct from both; a world which is neither in heaven nor in man, but in itself. If we combine both the antitheses, they cease to be double, and form this triple division :—

1. The natural and visible, *e.g.* sensible phænomena.

2. The natural and invisible, *e.g.* insensible bodies and imperceptible particles.

3. The supernatural and invisible, *e.g.* God.

Natural philosophy is the science of nature visible and invisible. From the former it infers the latter. But it stops at nature. So far as it is the science of an invisible nature, it is a philosophy of the suprasensible, not a theology of the supernatural. It outruns sense, but walks with reason to knowledge, without flying to faith. That we know invisible nature beyond sense in natural philosophy is a simple fact, explicable by logical

reasoning from sense. Can we in theology further know
the invisible beyond nature as well as beyond sense?
Can we know the supernatural world and God by reasoning from sense? These are questions beyond natural
philosophy. But the theologian may be sure that, on
the one hand, unless we can vindicate our knowledge
of insensible nature, we can hardly hope for a knowledge of an insensible world beyond nature; and that,
on the other hand, reasoning from sense to nature
encourages reasoning from nature to God. Natural
philosophy is the first step beyond sense into the unseen
world, within which natural theology soars heaven-
wards to tell

> Of things invisible to mortal sight.

I will conclude this chapter by quoting, from Sir
John Herschel's 'Discourse on Natural Philosophy,' a
passage which is sufficiently near to the existing state
of science for our present purpose. Its value is that it
groups together a number of scientific conclusions,
which, as it seems to me, cannot be explained by any
theory of reality except realism, or the theory that
there is a real and known world beyond phænomena,
or by any process of knowledge except syllogism, or
deductive inference which carries reason beyond sense.

'What mere assertion will make any man believe,
that in one second of time, in one beat of the pendulum
of a clock, a ray of light travels over 192,000 miles,
and would therefore perform the tour of the world in
about the same time it requires to wink with our eyelids, and in much less than a swift runner occupies in
taking a single stride? What mortal can be made to
believe, without demonstration, that the sun is almost a
million times larger than the earth; and that, although

so remote from us that a cannon-ball shot directly
towards it, and maintaining its full speed, would be
twenty years in reaching it, it yet affects the earth by
its attraction in an inappreciable instant of time? a
closeness of union of which we can form but a feeble
and totally inadequate idea, by comparing it to any
material connection; since the communication of an
impulse to such a distance, by any solid intermedium
we are acquainted with, would require, not moments,
but whole years.   And when with pain and difficulty
we have strained our imagination to conceive a distance
so vast, a force so intense and penetrating, if we are
told that the one dwindles to an insensible point, and
the other is unfelt at the nearest of the fixed stars, from
the mere effect of their remoteness, while among those
very stars are some whose actual splendour exceeds by
many hundred times that of the sun itself, although we
may not deny the truth of the assertion, we cannot but
feel the keenest curiosity to know how such things were
made out.

' The foregoing are amongst those results of scientific
research which, by their magnitude, seem to transcend
our power of conception.   There are others again,
which, from their minuteness, would elude the grasp of
thought, much more of distinct and accurate measure-
ment.   Who would not ask for demonstration, when
told that a gnat's wing in its ordinary flight beats many
hundred times in a second? or that there exist ani-
mated and regularly organised beings, many thousands
of whose bodies laid close together would not extend
an inch?   But what are these to the astonishing truths
which optical inquiries have disclosed, which teach us
that every point of a medium through which a ray of
light passes is affected with a succession of periodical

movements, regularly recurring at equal intervals, no
less than five hundred millions of millions of times in a
single second ; that it is by such movements, communicated to the nerves of our eyes, that we see—nay, more,
that it is the difference in the frequency of the recur-
rence which affects us with the sense of the diversity of
colour ; that, for instance, in acquiring the sensation of
redness our eyes are affected four hundred and eighty-
two millions of millions of times ; of yellowness, five
hundred and forty-two millions of millions of times ;
and of violet, seven hundred and seven millions of
millions of times ?   Do not such things sound more like
the ravings of madmen, than the sober conclusions of
people in their waking senses ?

    ' They are, nevertheless, conclusions to which any
one may most certainly arrive, who will only be at the
trouble of examining the chain of reasoning by which
they have been deduced ; but, in order to do this,
something beyond the mere elements of abstract science
is required. Waiving, however, such instances as these,
which, after all, are rather calculated to surprise and
astound, than for any other purpose, it must be observed that it is not possible to satisfy ourselves completely that we have arrived at a true statement of any
law of nature, until, setting out from such statement,
and making it a foundation of reasoning, we can show,
by strict argument, that the facts observed must follow
from it as necessary logical consequences, and this not
vaguely and generally, but with all possible precision
in time, place, weight, and measure.'

CHAPTER II.

IDEALISM AND REALISM.

THE problem of this essay is to use the insensible world of science as a fact from which to find the nature and origin of knowledge. Science is systematic knowledge. Yet the mental philosopher usually contents himself with endeavouring to explain ordinary knowledge. If he is a mental physiologist, it is true, he also uses natural science to proceed from the organs to the functions of sense. But there is another use of natural science to mental philosophy, which has been too much neglected: the objects of science are as important as the bodily organs to the explanation of knowledge. Natural science should be used to ascertain what we know as well as how we know it. Moreover, the insensible physical world of the natural philosopher ought to prove to the mental philosopher that neither all knowable objects nor all sensible data are psychical, but some are physical. I purpose to show that physical objects of science, being objects of knowledge, require physical data of sense. Hence this essay is called Physical Realism.

We must confront natural with mental philosophy. The former has outstripped the latter. Natural philosophers have long ago discovered to a great extent how physical nature is the *causa essendi* of sensible data: but mental philosophers have failed altogether to show

how sensible data are the *causa cognoscendi* of physical nature. The reason is, the data are mainly unknown. The existing hypotheses of the origin of knowledge do not explain the facts of science, and too often end by denying what they fail to explain. Especially to blame is the hypothesis that all the data of sense are psychical facts, such as sensations and ideas, from which there is no way to insensible but physical objects of scientific knowledge. This vicious hypothesis is psychological idealism. Hence this essay is designed to combat psychological idealism by means of physical realism, and to appeal from the hypothesis of psychical data to the physical objects of science. The physical world of science cannot be explained by the common hypothesis that all sensible data are psychical, nor without the more moderate hypothesis that some are physical.

The motto of all idealism is *ideale prius reale posterius*. But it has many meanings. Anaxagoras founded philosophical idealism by the proposition that the Divine Intelligence is prior to the order of nature; and in adding that soul is also prior to body Plato became its second founder. The Cartesian idealism means that knowledge begins with psychical ideas, and the Kantian idealism that it adds *a priori* mental elements. Of these idealisms two are of supereminent importance in the history of thought; that which places God at the beginning of the world, and that which places psychical ideas at the beginning of knowledge. The former is the belief of the majority of mankind, the latter of most philosophers since Descartes. The former is theological, the latter psychological idealism.

Theological and psychological idealism are not necessarily connected. A philosopher may hold that God causes physical nature and man apprehends it.

He may be theologically an idealist, psychologically a realist. On the other hand, he may suppose that all sensible data are psychical facts, and yet doubt the existence of God. He may be psychologically an idealist, theologically an atheist. The founders of natural theology had no thought of making psychical facts the beginnings of human knowledge. The followers of Hume hardly consider themselves supporters of the doctrine that God created the world. These distinctions are of importance, because there is a crude notion in our times that idealism in mental philosophy is necessary to theology. They are of special bearing on the scope of this essay, which is aimed, not at theological, but solely at psychological idealism.

Psychological idealism began with the supposition of Descartes that all the immediate objects of knowledge are ideas. From Descartes it passed to Locke and Berkeley. But with Hume it changed its terms from ideas to impressions. Kant preferred phænomena, Mill sensations. The most usual terms of the present day are sensations, feelings, psychical phænomena, and states of consciousness. But the hypothesis has not changed its essence, though the idealists have changed their terms,— *Verbum, non animum, mutant.* They at least agree that all sensible data are psychical objects of some kind or other.

The psychological idealists differ widely about the origin of knowledge from these psychical data. Some of them hold that there are *a priori* elements contributed by mind to the psychical data of sense, others that these supposed elements are *a posteriori*. But this difference about the origin does not prevent them from agreeing about the object of sense. which they alike hold to be some kind of psychical fact, whether idea, impression, phænomenon, sensation, feeling or state of consciousness.

There is a further difference among the idealists. Some of them, beginning with Descartes, believe that, though the immediate objects of sense are psychical, reality also includes physical facts. Others, beginning with Berkeley, reply that psychical data cannot yield physical objects, and therefore the psychical is all that is known to be real. The former divide reality into the psychical and the physical, the latter resolve it wholly into the psychical. The former have been called Cosmothetic Idealists, and the latter Absolute or Pure Idealists. But, while they differ only about the objects which can be mediately known, they still agree about the immediate data. Starting from the common hypothesis that all sensible data are psychical, the cosmothetic idealist nevertheless believes in physical realities, but the absolute idealist denies or doubts them.

Cosmothetic idealists further differ among themselves about the physical world. Descartes held that a physical world can be known through the medium of ideas; Locke, in one of his many moods, that it is a cause of ideas, but unknown. This difference is important, because cosmothetic idealism is the usual view of mental physiology in our own time, and it is held in both forms. Mental physiologists have unwarily received from psychologists the hypothesis of psychical data, which they usually call sensations, and have at the same time learnt from nature that the data of sense are effects of physical structures and motions beyond sense. Hence they are cosmothetic idealists. But according as they are rather physiologists or rather psychologists, they lean to Descartes or to Locke. The former hold that, starting from psychical sensations as data, by inference we know their physical causes; the latter, that the psychical sensations are produced by the physical causes, which are nevertheless unknown and unknowable. Their differences, however, do not disturb the consensus that the immediate objects of sense are not physical, but purely psychical.

It may be thought that this consensus of idealism is a proof of truth. But agreement is one of the chief causes of human error, because it tempts men to dispense with further consideration of the question. Moreover, we shall find that the inconsiderate assent to this common proposition is the very reason why opposite schools of idealists cannot conclusively answer one another. Lastly, there are two kinds of consensus: one, assent to a self-evident principle, such as $1+1=2$; the other, agreement in a common hypothesis. Now the proposition that all sensible data are psychical phænomena is not a self-evident principle, but a debatable hypothesis.

Realism is the philosophy of a reality beyond psychical facts. The earliest form in which it was a conscious doctrine was the belief in the reality of universals. Plato thought that there were universal forms existing in themselves, incorporeal and supernatural archetypes, in accordance with which similar individuals are produced in nature. Aristotle agreed that there are real universal forms, and even that they are incorporeal substances. He contended, however, that they exist not in themselves but only as belonging to individual substances, which are concretions of matter and form. In the Middle Ages the disciples of Plato and Aristotle were called Reales, to distinguish them from the Nominales, who either contended that universals were merely general names, or else general

C

conceptions. Those who adopted the latter view were afterwards called Conceptualists.

It is not necessary to be either a Platonist or an Aristotelian. There is a third realism of universals possible; and that, too, without falling into nominalism or conceptualism. The theory of the reality of universals, though overlaid with many errors, contains two important truths. The first is, that science knows of classes which have an indefinite number of similarities, such as triangles, colours, and living beings. The second is, that of these similarities some are fundamental, others derivative; *e.g.* three-sided rectilineal figure is the foundation of innumerable other similarities of triangle; undulations of ether produce the facts of colour, metabolism is the basis of the facts of life. The first truth shows that a natural class, or real kind, is not a name, nor a notion, but a real sum of individuals forming an indefinite number of similarities. The second truth shows that the distinction between essence and property is not a nominal difference depending on the meaning of a name, nor a notional difference depending on the analysis of a notion, but a real distinction depending on the fundamental character of the similarities, on which the rest depend. Without natural classes, whose similarities can be expressed in laws, there would be no science; and without essences, or fundamental similarities of those natural classes on which other similarities depend, we could not have the mathematics of the triangle referring its propositions back to its being a three-sided figure, nor the physics of light, referring all the facts of colour back to the undulation of æther.

A natural class, then, is the sum of individuals possessing an indefinite number of similarities. A real

essence is the fundamental similarities of the individuals
of a natural class. It is easy to make too much of it
or too little. If we follow the nominalist, and make
æthereal undulation the meaning of the name ' light,' or
the conceptualist, and make it the analysis of the
notion, we make too little of it, because the undulation
of æther began before, goes on without, and will last
after, our names and notions. If, on the other hand,
we follow Aristotle, and make it an incorporeal substance coexisting with matter, we make too much of it,
because it is only a motion of matter after all ; while,
if we try to soar with Plato into the supernatural world
and make it a heavenly archetype of earthly light,
we fail to explain the facts and desert science for
mysticism.

The realism of universals, however, is not the
business of this essay. There is another meaning of
realism, which we may call the Realism of Individuals.
This is the theory that there is a physical world of
individuals beyond psychical sensations and ideas. It
may be held with any theory of universals ; the realist
of individuals is not necessarily a realist of universals.
It is also a later product. The realism of universals is
rather a doctrine of ancient, the realism of individuals
rather of modern, philosophers. Not that Aristotle
rejected the distinct reality of physical individuals ;
but it never occurred to him that it needed to be
proved. There was, as Brandis remarked, an unconscious realism in ancient philosophy. It seldom
doubted a world beyond the psychical ; the question
was rather whether there were not three worlds ; natural
individuals, supernatural universals, and psychical in-
telligences. But in modern times the development of
psychological idealism has brought even the physical

world of individuals into question. In opposition to this psychological idealism a conscious realism has arisen, the object of which is to show that there are physical things beyond psychical facts. This realism of physical individuals is part of the business of this essay, and for shortness will in the sequel be called simply Realism.

Realism is constantly misunderstood. It is sometimes supposed to be a synonym for mere Sensualism, or the belief that physical things are as they appear to our senses. But sensualism is only a crude form of realism. There is a realism which goes beyond sense to science, and holds that things are not as they immediately appear to sense, but rather as they are mediately inferred by science. A more serious misunderstanding is the confusion of realism with Materialism. Materialism is a kind of realism; it is also more. It is a double hypothesis: first, that there are physical things; secondly, that they are either the only realities, or at least are prior to psychical realities, whether in nature or in man.

Only the first part of this hypothesis is essential to realism; the second part, which contains, too, the real sting of the materialist, is unnecessary to the realist. A man ceases to be a materialist, but he remains a realist, if he holds that God is the Creator and Governor of the world, while the world is not a psychical fact of God's Intelligence but a physical effort of His Intelligent Will; and that nature is posterior to God though prior to man. The motto of materialism is, *reale prius ideale posterius*: the motto of realism is *reale non est ideale*. In short, it is one thing to affirm a natural world of individual objects beyond sense, another thing to deny a supernatural world beyond nature.

Hence realism is not the exact contrary of all idealism. It is not opposed at all to the idealism of natural theology. It is not even the direct contrary to all psychological idealism. Idealism centres itself on the data, realism on the objects of knowledge. The former says that all sensible data are psychical, the latter that some objects are physical. Hence a difficulty in contrasting them, and even in keeping them distinct. Some idealists, as we have seen, though they regard all data as psychical, admit the independent reality of physical objects. As Hamilton has pointed out, the cosmothetic idealists are also hypothetical, or, as some would say, transfigured realists. The exact contrary of realism is not all idealism but pure or absolute idealism. The pure or absolute idealist denies the reality of aught beyond the psychical world, the realist affirms the reality of the physical.

At the same time realism is not a single body of doctrines. Realists agree only in one position—the reality of physical things. In the foundations of that position, in the sensible data of knowledge, they differ *toto cælo*. It is, therefore, necessary to classify them to prevent confusion, and that sort of *ignoratio elenchi*, which idealism and realism alike have to suffer from their opponents when they are not properly defined.

Of the realism of individuals there are two species recognised among modern philosophers—the Hypothetical Realism of the cosmothetic idealists, and the Intuitive or Natural Realism of the Scotch philosophers, Reid, Stewart, and Hamilton. Agreeing about knowable objects, hypothetical and intuitional realists differ about the data of sense. According to the former, the data are psychical ideas or sensations of the *ego* ; according to the latter, they include the primary qualities of the physical *non-ego*. Agreeing in a physical world, they differ about the way in which it is to be reached, the former holding that it is inferred from psychical data, the latter that it is immediately perceived. Hypothetical or transfigured realism is the hypothesis that our senses present psychical ideas or sensations representing external physical objects; intuitive or natural realism, the hypothesis that the senses present the primary qualities of external physical objects themselves.

Modern philosophy exhibits a constant oscillation between the opposite poles of the *ego* and the *non-ego*; and the two received kinds of realism are opposite currents in this oscillation. The cosmothetic idealist or hypothetical realist, learning from natural philosophy that his senses do not directly perceive external things, takes refuge in the psychical world of his own soul. Dissatisfied with this alternative, and conscious that he somehow apprehends something physical, the intuitional realist flies forward to the direct perception of an external world. Extreme views are usually as untrue as extreme measures are dangerous. Is there a *via media*? I venture to propose a new Realism.

When I consider the objects of science, I am struck by the enormous number of things and attributes entirely beyond the reach of sense and not even corresponding to any sensible object. I refer, especially, to corpuscles, their structures and motions. Secondly, on going further, I find that the whole external world has been discovered by sciences, such as optics, acoustics, and biology, to be insensible, and that nothing is sensible except what has been impressed on the body, and in the body on the nervous system, of a sentient being. Thirdly, I notice that a connection has been scientifically established between external in-

sensible objects and the objects of which I am sensible.
The former are causes of the latter. They are also
found to resemble one another in primary qualities,
such as duration, extension, motion, but not in secondary
qualities, such as light, heat, and sound; for the secondary qualities, as they are in external nature, are
found by corpuscular science to be insensible modes
of primary qualities; light, heat, and sound being all
insensible modes of motion producing a heterogeneous
effect on the senses.

I cannot believe that this whole fabric of insensible
objects can be scientific, yet unknown. But it must be
either physical or psychical. If the objects are psychical, they are either sensations or ideas. But they
are insensible and often inconceivable. Now what is
insensible cannot be a sensation, and what is inconceivable cannot be an idea. Not all objects of science,
then, are either sensations or ideas; therefore they are
not psychical objects at all. It remains that they are
physical objects.

Again, I cannot believe that this whole fabric of
physical objects of science can have been inferred
without sufficient data of sense. I therefore proceed
to inquire what data of sense are required to infer a
physical object of science. This is a question of logic.
Now the rules of logic teach me that whatever is inferred
is inferred from similar data. If I infer that all men
will die, it is because similar men have died. Now, as
we have seen, physical objects are scientifically inferred
from sensible data. It follows that the sensible objects,
which are these data, must also be physical. The
similar can be inferred only from the similar, therefore
the physical can be inferred only from the physical.

This conclusion, however, places me in a dilemma.

Science shows me that the object of sense is internal, logic that it is physical. The former evidence might incline me to cosmothetic idealism, the latter to intuitive realism. Which shall I prefer? Am I to say that the sensible data are psychical objects within me? No, because I require physical data of sense to infer physical objects of science. Am I to say that the sensible data are physical objects without me? No, because no external object is sensible. I can be neither a cosmothetic idealist, because of logic, nor an intuitive realist, because of natural science.

If, then, natural science requires that the object of sense must be within my nervous system in order to be sensible, and logic that it must be physical in order to infer physical objects of science in the external world, how can the sensible object be at once physical and internal? I answer, it is the nervous system itself sensibly affected. The hot felt is the tactile nerves heated, the white seen is the optic nerves so coloured. The sensible object must be distinguished from its external cause on the one hand, and on the other hand from the internal operation of apprehending it: it is the intermediate effect in the nerves produced by the external cause, and apprehended by the operation of sensation. In particular, the operation and the object of sensation must not be confused, because the former may be psychical, the latter is physical. There is some plausibility in saying that the act of consciously touching is psychical, there is none at all in saying that the hot felt is psychical. *Non sequitur.* Vision may be a psychical sensation, but the white seen is a physical object. Nor is there any reason why a psychical operation should not apprehend a physical object. The sensible object then is identical neither with the external cause nor with the internal operation of sensation. It is the effect in the nervous system produced by the one and apprehended by the other. For example, the hot felt and the white seen are produced by external objects and are apprehended by internal sensations of touch and vision, but are themselves respectively the tactile and the optic nerves sensibly affected in the manner apprehended as hot and white.

From such sensible data, internal, as science requires, and physical, as logic requires, man infers physical objects in the external world by parity of reasoning. Men in general begin by inferring that physical objects of sense are produced by physical causes exactly similar. Thus from the hot within we infer a fire without. Such objects, directly inferred to correspond with sensible data, may be called the originals represented by them. They are inferred, but are generally said to be perceived; thus we speak of perceiving the fire though we only infer it. We may, perhaps, say then that the originals of the sensible are insensible objects inferentially perceptible.

Afterwards, scientific men carry on this parity of reasoning, and infer that these originals beyond sense consist of further insensible particles similar to the originals, but not at all represented by sensible data; and that many other objects, such, for example, as the side of the moon always turned from the earth, are incapable of producing sensible objects in us. These unrepresented objects may be said to be not only insensible but imperceptible, and are objects of an inference which may be called transcendental, in the sense of transcending both sensitive and inferential perception.

Lastly, science also finds that in another direction the ordinary man has carried his inferences from

similar data to similar objects too far. Physical objects
are found to be like sensible in their primary, not in
their secondary qualities; for instance, external motion
is like sensible motion, but external heat is an imperceptible mode of motion while sensible heat is not
sensibly a motion at all. How is this inferred?
Because, though at first sight sensible heat would
demand a similar external object, when all the facts
of sensible heat are accumulated they are found to be
the kind of facts that are only produced by motion.
Hence from sensible physical data we scientifically
infer insensible physical objects, like sensible objects in
primary but unlike in secondary qualities.

Such is the realism proposed in this essay. It may
be expressed in two propositions : there are physical
objects of science in the external world; therefore
there are, as data to infer them, physical objects of
sense in the internal nervous system. It is a *via media*
between intuitive realism and the hypothetical realism
of the cosmothetic idealist. As it recognises physical
realities, it is realism. As the objects, which it supposes to be sensible, are not external but internal, it is
not intuitive realism. As the objects of sense, which
it supposes to be the data of inferring an external
physical world, are not psychical but physical, it is
not hypothetical realism. As they are physical data
within, to infer physical objects without, the realism
which I advocate may be called Physical Realism.

There are three realistic ways of explaining our
knowledge of an external physical world. The first is
cosmothetic idealism, which supposes that we are sensible of a psychical, but infer a physical world. This
is against logic, which shows that all inference is by
similarity. The second is intuitive realism, which

supposes that we directly perceive an external physical
world.   This is against natural philosophy, which shows
that we perceive nothing directly but what is propagated
into our nervous system.   The third is physical realism,
which supposes that we sensibly perceive an internal
but physical world, from which we infer an external
and physical world.   This agrees with both natural
philosophy and logic.

Physical Realism must be especially distinguished
from intuitive, or, as it is also called, natural realism.
It is true that the theories have some common points.
This essay owes to Reid the instructive remark on the
'Sentiments of Bishop Berkeley,' that there is no evidence for the doctrine ' that all the objects of knowledge
are ideas in my own mind.'[1]   The rejection of idealism,
the reality of the physical world, the belief in a phy
sical object of sense, and the possibility that a psychical
subject may apprehend a physical object, are all points
in intuitive realism which find a place in physical
realism.   But here the agreement ends.   The intuitive
realist holds an immediate perception of a physical
world outside.   I distinguish the immediate perception
of the physical world within, and the inferential perception of the physical world beyond myself.

The intuitive realist follows the idealist in thinking
too much of the sensible data, and too little of the
insensible objects of science.   He gives too much
weight to consciousness, and too little to science, or
rather too much to the ordinary and too little to the
scientific consciousness.   He appeals to common sense,
which is the problem rather than the solution of philosophy.   He elevates the dicta of consciousness and

---

[1] Reid, *Essays on the Intellectual Powers.* Essay II., chap. x.
p. 283 (ed. Hamilton).

common sense from unanalysed facts into self-evident principles. Hence, in asserting an immediate knowledge of external nature he contradicts science. But we must appeal from common sense to universal science, and from ordinary to scientific realism. The idealist can never be answered by asserting the reality of the sensible world, which he admits, and, if it stood alone, could explain. He must be confronted with the insensible world of science.

The intuitive realists have an impossible theory of the data of sense, comprised of two incompatible extremes. On the one hand, they admit the idealistic position that secondary qualities, as sensible, are psychical sensations; on the other hand, they assert that external primary qualities of the *non-ego* are immediately perceived. The admission is fatal, because the Berkeleian at once points out that primary qualities are apprehended in the same way as secondary, and therefore if one set, as sensible, are psychical sensations, why not the other? The assertion is equally fatal, because scientific analysis shows that nothing external is immediately perceived. Hence I retract the admission and reject the assertion. Whether directed to primary or to secondary qualities, sense apprehends neither a sensation nor an external object, but an internal object in the nervous system. Everything external is inferred.

Perhaps the chief reason of the defect in intuitive realism is the confusion of object and *non-ego*. Object is the *res considerata* apprehended either by sense or by reason. It is not always an external object. In sense, it is always internal, whether it be the hot or the moving, the white or the extended, secondary or primary. In reasoning. it is external, whenever we infer something beyond the sensible object within us. But the intuitive

realists, having confused object and *non-ego*, supposed
that whenever sense has an object it presents the *non-ego*.
Really, sense always apprehends an object distinct from
the operation, but never a *non-ego* distinct from the *ego*,
that is, the man himself. Hence, also, their erroneous
belief that in apprehending a primary quality, as an
object, sense presents a quality of the *non-ego*, and in
not apprehending a secondary quality as it is in the
non-ego, it presents no object. Really, as sensible, both
primary and secondary qualities are apprehended as
objects, but not as external. For example, the sensibly
hot and moving are both apprehended as objects by
sense, but entirely within the sentient being.

The subordination of secondary to primary qualities is not at all in the sensible effects, but in the external
causes. In the external world, secondary qualities are
found by science to be only specific varieties of primary
qualities. In the internal world, all qualities appear
to sense to be equally elementary. As sensible, a
primary quality, such as motion, is not in the *non-ego*,
and a secondary quality, such as heat, is not a mere
sensation; nor are they both sensations; but they are
both sensible objects, both internal to the sentient being,
both physical, both parts of the nervous substance
sensibly affected, both apprehended in the same way as
objects by the operation called ' sensation.' From these
qualities, all apprehended in exactly the same way as
sensible objects in our nervous system, the ordinary
man infers a complete correspondence of qualities outside, the scientific man partly corrects him by reducing
secondary qualities to primary qualities in the external
world.

The relativity of knowledge has become a commonplace. Is it a fact? A sensible effect is the result of

the combination of two causes. As active or efficient cause, the external world produces the sensible effect in the nervous system; as passive or material cause, the nervous system receives this effect according to its susceptibility. Hence the effect is like or unlike to the efficient causes, according to the varying susceptibility of the nervous system. There is a variation in different animals and in different men, and even in the same man at different times. But in all men there is one difference of main importance. The nervous system is far more susceptible of similar effects from primary than from secondary qualities. It is more capable of reflecting the waves of the sea than the undulations of aether. Not that the effect is wholly alike in primary or wholly unlike in secondary qualities. The primary quality of distance is imperfectly reproduced in sense, the secondary quality of aërial vibration is to some small extent represented in the sense of hearing. But, on the whole, there is a general similarity of the sensible to the external in primary, and a general dissimilarity in secondary qualities, because of the inferior susceptibility of the nervous system to receive like effects from the latter qualities in external objects. In the sense, then, that the sensible effect only partly depends on the external efficient cause, and partly also on the matter of the nervous system, there is a relativity of knowledge to the structure of the nerves. There is also an evolution, which consists in the increasing adaptation of the nerves to sustain the effect under the action of the external object.

On the other hand, by the relativity of knowledge it is generally meant that the sensible effect produced is a psychical fact, not partly but wholly heterogeneous to the physical object, if there be one. In this sense

physical realism is opposed to the relativity of knowledge. It is true that red refuses to appear to our
senses as a motion representing the external motion
which produces it. But the cause of this fact is to be
found in the construction of the optic nerve, which,
when acted on by a certain imperceptible motion of
æther, receives a sensible colour apparently unlike
motion, just as oxygen and hydrogen in certain pro-
portions, when acted on by electricity, become water.
In the same way, when a wheel rotates too quickly, the
sensible effect ceases to be a motion, because the nerves
are insusceptible of taking on so rapid a motion in
sense. The sensible effect is similar or dissimilar to
the external object, so far as the nervous system is
capable or incapable of being affected similarly to the
external object. There is no occasion then to resort to
the hypothesis of a psychical relativity : the nervous
element is sufficient.

Moreover, if there were a psychical relativity, it
would be ineradicable, because the sensible effect would
then be completely heterogeneous, and would therefore supply no data of inference to an external physical
cause. Really, sensible effects are partly like and
partly unlike the external causes, because the nerves
are partly fitted and partly unfitted to represent
them. Being partly like, the nervous unfitness to represent secondary qualities as they are in nature is
being constantly eliminated by scientific reasoning.
Thus, sense sometimes presents motion as motion, but
cannot help presenting the hot, the red, &c., as
heterogeneous to motion, because of the structure of
the sensory nerves ; science, by comparing sensible
motion with the sensible facts of the hot, the red, &c.,
infers that the external cause of the latter is really a

mode of motion. In secondary qualities the sensible effect is heterogeneous, but the cause inferred by science is identical with the external object. Not that scientific elimination of the defects of sense ever becomes so complete as to end in absoluteness of knowledge. But there is a constant progress towards making science the mirror of being. Sense starts with physical data partly like and partly unlike external nature ; science, by progressive inferences, tends more and more to discover the external qualities which cause not only the like but the unlike data in the nervous system. The sensible, therefore, is not a psychical effect completely heterogeneous to the external physical cause, but a physical effect partly relative to the nervous system ; and science is perpetually correcting this partial relativity.

It is usual to divide theories of sensation and perception into presentative and representative. There are two presentative theories, respectively characterising the pure idealist and the intuitive realist. The former holds that there is no distinction between sensation and perception : sense, according to him, immediately perceives psychical facts, which are the sum of known existing objects. The latter distinguishes sensation and perception, because he distinguishes the psychical and the physical : sensation, in his view, is limited to psychical sensations, perception immediately apprehends the primary qualities of an external physical world. The pure idealist says, ' What I see is what exists ; ' the intuitive realist, ' What exists I see : ' the former reduces nature to perception, the latter brings perception to nature ; one holds *esse* is *percipi*, the other *esse percipitur*. But the point is that, according to both, the real is the sensible world, which is directly presented, not represented, in perception, without an inference to an external original. The representative theory, on the other hand, distinguishes the data of sense, as presented, from the external world, as represented, in perception. It exists in many forms, according to various theories of the data of sense. But the current form is that of cosmothetic idealism, which holds that sense presents psychical data of some kind, representing physical objects in the external world.

Physical realism must accept the representative theory, but not in its idealistic form. The data presented to sense are internal, yet not psychical. They are physical parts of the nervous system, tactile, optic, auditory, &c., sensibly affected in various manners, representing, but only partly resembling, the external world. Further, in sense, the object is not the operation, the hot is not touch, the white is not vision, the loud is not hearing. From these points I form the following theory of sensation. In that the sensible object is internal, sensation is not the immediate apprehension of an external object. In that the sensible object is physical, sensation is not the immediate apprehension of a psychical fact. In that it is the immediate apprehension of an object, though internal, it is a kind of perception. I should define sensation, or sensitive perception, as the immediate apprehension of an internal physical object within the nervous system of a sentient being.

But perception cannot be confined to sensation. Although it is true that sense feels the hot, and reason infers the fire, everybody talks of perceiving the fire. The philosopher will find it vain to fly in the face of the universal language not only of ordinary life but even of science. He must recognise this perception and analyse it. There is, then, besides sensitive or

immediate perception, inferential or mediate perception.
The former is limited to the internal object of sense, the
latter extends to the external original. Moreover, so
long as we remember that there is an inference in this
latter operation, the term 'perception' not only does no
harm but serves to mark a most important distinction.
We first infer external originals of sensible objects, *e.g.*
the fire, the sea, &c. ; we cannot be said to see, but we
may be said to perceive, these external objects, and also
to observe and experience them, though indirectly.
Afterwards, we go on to infer other external objects not
represented by any sensible object, *e.g.* a corpuscle,
æther : these we cannot be said either to see or perceive : they are not only insensible but imperceptible,
and we infer them by reasoning which transcends perception. In short, we must distinguish sensitive
perception, inferential perception, and transcendental
inference.

Hence the following classification of physical objects
knowable, and of the operations concerned with them :—

1. Internal parts of the nervous system sensibly
affected : sensible data : immediately perceptible, objects
of sense, or of sensitive perception, observation, experience.

E.g. the sensibly moving, the sensibly hot.

2. External parts of the universe : insensible objects :
objects of inference.

(1) Originals represented by sensible objects, and
resembling them in primary not in secondary
qualities : insensible but mediately perceptible
objects of inferential perception, observation,
experience.
E.g. the fire, the waves of the sea.

(2) Objects unrepresented, though causing some
    sensible objects by imperceptible secondary
    qualities: the imperceptible: objects of trans-
    cendental inference.

E.g. corpuscles, the undulations of æther.

This essay contemplates not only a new realistic hypothesis, but a different method from that usually used in
mental philosophy. Every philosophy must have a
beginning. But the beginning must be what is best
known; and in mental philosophy the present objects
of science are better known than the original data
of sense. The method in use takes too direct a way
of getting at the original data. It is true that the
beginnings of human knowledge are sensible data.
But the philosopher does not stand at the beginning of
human knowledge. Philosophy did not begin with the
infancy of the human race. The philosopher cannot
observe his own infancy. The sensible data have long
since been overlaid with an immense mass of inferences.
Hence, though man may have begun once, it is impossible for the philosopher to begin now, with the data.
Yet most books on knowledge begin with the dogmatic
assertion that the immediate objects of the senses are
psychical sensations, from which they proceed to allow
man as much knowledge of nature as can be squeezed
out of the original hypothesis. But the assertion itself
must be proved.

Besides the induction of causation, we may either
reason synthetically from cause to effect, or analytically
from effect to cause. But the latter is the more usual
method, because man knows so much more about
facts than about their causes. Hence the order of
science is usually the reverse of the order of nature.

Nature always proceeds from cause to effect, science usually from effect to cause; so that science becomes an analysis of the synthesis of nature.

Similarly, the order of mental philosophy is the reverse of the order of human knowledge. It is true that the order of human knowledge is from cause to effect in the sense that sensible data are the *causæ cognoscendi* of physical knowledge. We begin with them as children; hence also we are tempted to begin with them again as psychologists. But the procedure is fallacious; we must begin with the more knowable. Now every mental philosopher is an adult man, and every adult man is more certain what he now knows, than how he originally came to know it, of the discoveries of science than of 'the secret springs and principles by which the human mind is actuated in its operation,' of the known objects than of the sensible data. Accordingly, as, in the science of nature, we must generally begin with present facts and go backwards to the *causæ essendi*, so, in the science of knowledge, we must generally begin with the facts of scientific knowledge and go backwards to the *causæ cognoscendi*. Modern philosophers have made the mistake of attempting to repeat the synthesis of knowledge from the original data of the child and the race. But we must rather retrace our steps from the present to the past; instead of trying to follow the synthesis of knowledge from an unknown beginning, we must make an analysis from the present objects of scientific knowledge to the original data of sense. In a word, our method must be an analysis from science to sense.

Hence, I began with attempting to give an outline of the kind of objects recognised in science. This beginning has several advantages. First, science is knowledge; hence to begin with its objects is an appeal not from knowledge to reality, but from the data to the objects of knowledge. It is not a dogmatic assertion of what is, but an historical description of what is known. Secondly, science is knowledge at its widest extent, knowledge proceeding from the sensible through the insensible, but perceptible, to the imperceptible world. Hence we get a more extended view of knowable objects than that usually attained by mental philosophers, who tend to concentrate themselves on the world of sense and perception. Thirdly, science is knowledge at its best, whereas the hypotheses of mental philosophers about sensible data can hardly be called knowledge at all. In appealing from the hypothetical origin of knowledge to what is actually known in science, we are appealing from the less known to the more known. In short, we are getting the facts of knowledge, wherewith to test our hypothesis of its causes.

The next step is analytically to find the sensible data required to cause the knowledge of the objects of science as facts. All theories of the sensible data and of the origin of knowledge, idealistic and realistic, must be treated and compared as hypotheses. We must ask, indeed, what is their direct evidence, but also and mainly whether they account for the knowledge of the objects of science. The general examination of these hypotheses will follow in the next chapter. Afterwards, the various hypotheses of Psychological Idealism will be taken in detail. The elimination of these hypotheses will finally bring us to Physical Realism.

Philosophy began with the external object, which was first of all treated as a pure reality by the Pre-Socratic philosophers. Gradually it came to be regarded as also an object of knowledge, a view which culminated with Aristotle. Aristotle's method was essentially to begin with being as being, then to consider it secondarily as a knowable object, and thus to proceed from the known object to the knowing subject. Objective are generally the foundation of subjective distinctions in his writings. Descartes revolutionised philosophy by beginning with the conscious subject and passing through its conscious operations to the object apprehended. From his time the general order of mental philosophy has been synthetic, from the subjective operations to the objective world. I propose to revert to the old order, and proceed analytically from object to subject, but in a new spirit.

Ancient philosophy rightly began with the object, but considered it too much as being, and too little as known. Consequently, it had a tendency to multiply entities without considering whether they are knowable. Hence the Cartesian revolution and the synthetic method from subject to object. But after the first consciousness, I think, the object is on the whole better known than the subject ; else natural philosophy would not be more advanced than mental philosophy. In order to avoid at once the dogmatism of ancient, and the doubtfulness of modern, philosophy, I propose to begin with the object, not as being, but as known in science, the most perfect form of knowledge. I proceed to ask what sensible objects are required as data for science to know these objects. Of the knowing subject I treat only so far as it bears on the objects known by sense and reason, because, though I know well that I am, I know less what I am than what I know. The ancient method from being to knowing was the right order, though too dogmatic in application. The modern method inaugurated by Descartes, from the subject through the data of sense to the objects of science, was, after its first step, fallacious, because it then proceeded synthetically from the less to the more knowable. The analytic method of physical realism, without neglecting direct evidences of the data, proceeds, on the whole, from the more knowable objects of science to the less knowable data of sense.

TABLE OF IDEALISM AND REALISM.

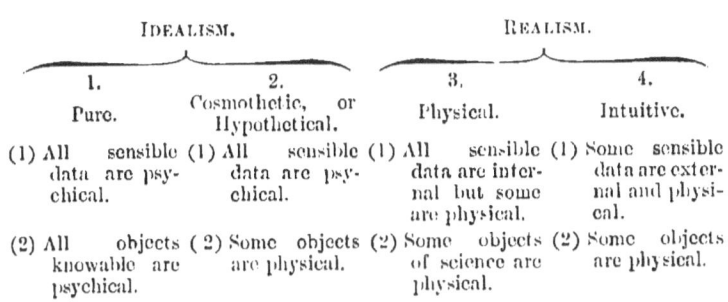

IDEALISM.		REALISM.	
1. Pure.	2. Cosmothetic, or Hypothetical.	3. Physical.	4. Intuitive.
(1) All sensible data are psychical.	(1) All sensible data are psychical.	(1) All sensible data are internal but some are physical.	(1) Some sensible data are external and physical.
(2) All objects knowable are psychical.	(2) Some objects are physical.	(2) Some objects of science are physical.	(2) Some objects are physical.

CHAPTER III.

THE PHYSICAL DATA OF SENSE.

Nihil est in intellectu, quod non prius in sensu. How far is this time-honoured proposition true? As we have seen, it is not true of the objects of science. The whole physical world is beyond the reach of sense, insensible ; the corpuscles, of which it consists, are beyond the reach of inferential perception, imperceptible. It is true that objects of science are similar to sensible objects, but they are not the same. They are objects of intellect which are inferred from sensible objects but have never been in sense. But even this more modest statement must be qualified.

In the first place, it requires Locke's correction that knowledge has two sources—sensation and reflection, outer and inner sense, or sense and consciousness. We immediately apprehend not only the objects of, or rather in, our senses, but also ourselves apprehending those objects, and performing many other conscious operations. Secondly, there is also a simpler source than sensation—the feelings. We immediately feel pleased and pained, and that too without apprehending any object; as in the pain of hunger, the pleasure of nutrition. Sensation is more complex than feeling, because it is the apprehension of an object; touch the apprehension of the hot, vision of the coloured, hearing of the sounding, &c. Frequently we have a feeling and a sensation together; for example, when we feel pleased or pained at the same time as we taste sweet or bitter. But it is of the greatest importance to distinguish feeling as a source of knowledge, especially as it is not at all improbable that it was the original source even of sensation. Even now that feeling and sensation are distinct, feelings are still the raw experiences of volitions, passions the beginnings of actions. We feel pleasure and pain before we will to pursue the one and avoid the other. All knowledge, then, does not begin with sensation, but with feeling, sensation, reflection.

It is true, however, that all knowledge of nature begins with sensation. Yet even this modified proposition must be carefully guarded. In the first place, though physical knowledge begins with the operation of sensation, it does not follow that the object, in apprehending which the operation of sensation consists, is also a sensation. Yet this *non-sequitur* appears in the first few pages of most books of modern philosophy. The causes of the confusion of sensation with its object are to be found partly in the structure of modern languages, which, being far richer in abstract than in concrete terms, tempt philosophers to fall into a loose way of speaking of perceiving a sensation instead of perceiving a sensible object; but mainly in another confusion, that of object and *non-ego*, which makes philosophers shrink from speaking of perceiving a sensible object, lest they should seem to assert an intuition of the external world. But an object (τὸ ἀντικείμενον) is merely that which is apprehended as opposed to the operation of apprehending it, and is not necessarily external to the apprehending subject. In sense, without being external, the object is still distinguishable from the operation; the hot from touch, the sweet from taste, the coloured from vision, the loud from hearing, the scented from smelling. Although, therefore, physical knowledge begins with sensation as an operation, it does not begin with sensation as a sensible object. Given, then, that physical knowledge begins with sense, we still have to ask, what is the object apprehended immediately by sensation; what is the sensibly hot, sweet, coloured, loud, scented? This is the question of the present chapter.

There are two main evidences of hypothesis—the direct and the indirect. Direct evidence is the best, if possible, but it is seldom attainable; for example, there is no direct evidence for the hypothesis of æther. But where direct proof fails, indirect should be all the stronger in compensation. It consists in using the facts to test the hypothesis, and that in two ways. First, the facts must be explained by the hypothesis; secondly, they must eliminate other explanations. Thus the hypothesis of an undulating æther, as the vehicle of light, though wanting in direct evidence, is proved by its power of explaining all the facts of light, and by the elimination of the hypothesis of emission, which explains some, but not all the facts.

I propose to apply these rules to the various hypotheses of sensible data, stated in the last chapter. Are the objects of sense, which form the data of science, psychical or physical; and, if physical, external or internal? On the one hand, how far is there direct evidence for any of these hypotheses? On the other hand, how do they stand the indirect test of the facts of science? That is, can the objects of science as facts of knowledge be explained by any hypothesis of the data of sense; and can the other hypotheses be eliminated? Being hypotheses, idealism and realism alike must be treated by the logical rules

of hypothesis. Sensible data must be made to explain
the scientific facts, as æthereal undulations have been
made to explain luminous facts. We must be on our
guard against synthetic hypothesis. What would be
thought of a natural philosopher, who dared to start
with the hypothesis of emission and denied all the facts
of light, which cannot be deduced from the emission
of corpuscles by a luminous body? What, then, shall
we think of mental philosophers, who start with the
hypothesis of sensations and deny all the insensible
world which cannot be deduced from the contemplation of sensations by sensation? I admit that there
may be direct evidence of an hypothesis. But even
so, unless that evidence be mathematical certainty, the
hypothesis must also be submitted to the indirect or
analytical evidence of explaining the facts. Now it
cannot be pretended that the direct evidence of the
hypothesis of perceiving sensations or any other hypothesis of sensible data is mathematically certain. Therefore all the hypotheses of idealism and realism must pass
through the alembic of analysis.

The first direct evidence is that of consciousness.
Consciousness is the immediate apprehension of oneself
performing some operation. Thus I am conscious
that I feel, that I perceive through my senses, that I
imagine, remember, reason, desire, will, act. Unfortunately, however, this operation of apprehending other
operations has come to be confused in psychology
with the operations themselves. Hamilton, seeing that
perception requires an object, and consciousness of
perception requires perception, falsely concluded that
the consciousness includes the perception of the object,
whereas it only requires it as a condition. He committed the common fallacy of confusing a thing with

its condition. Really, perception is the apprehension of the object, consciousness of perception the apprehension that I am apprehending the object. Mill, again, seeing that feeling pleasure and pain are the same as being conscious of feeling them, falsely concluded that every operation is the same as its consciousness. He committed the fallacy of over-generalisation. In feeling pleasure and pain there is no distinction between operation and object, and hence none between feeling and consciousness. But whenever there is a distinction between operation and object, the operation is concerned with the object and the consciousness with the operation. Hence to see white is different from being conscious of seeing white. So with other operations. Reasoning is a mediate operation from premises to conclusion. The consciousness of reasoning is an immediate apprehension that I am performing that mediate operation. Will is an active operation, the determination to act; its consciousness an intellectual operation, apprehending that I determine to act. To reason and to will, then, are not the same as being conscious that I reason and will.

It is not improbable that the lowest potency of sensitive life may have been mere feeling, and the beginning of consciousness mere conscious feeling; and that as, in the growth of the senses, the operation and the object became distinguished, consciousness became distinct from the operation, the operation being concerned with the object, and the consciousness with that relation of oneself to the object, in which an operation about an object consists. But whatever may have been the genesis of consciousness, its nature consists not in being the sense of objects but the sense of operations. When, as in feeling, there is no distinction between operation

and object, there is none between consciousness and
operation.   When, as in sensation, there is a distinction
between operation and object, the operation is concerned with the object, the consciousness with the operation.   Not that consciousness has no reference to the
object, but only that it is not the apprehension of it.
The operation, which is the apprehension of the object,
is a certain relation of subject to object : the consciousness, which apprehends the operation, is an apprehension
not of the object, but of the relation of the subject to the
object.   For example, I see white, I am conscious that
I am seeing white.

It was necessary to have thus defined consciousness
on account of the mass of confusion and inconsequence
imported into psychology by regarding consciousness
as identical with all the conscious operations.   Hamilton,
seeing that consciousness is intuitive, but falsely identifying it with the perception of an external world, falsely
concludes that perception of an external world is also
intuitive.   He ought by the same argument to have
made reasoning immediate, or else consciousness mediate,
either of which alternatives is absurd.   Mill, seeing that
consciousness is limited to the apprehension of mental
operations, and falsely identifying it with the mental
operations, falsely concludes that the mental operation
of sensation is also limited to the apprehension of
mental operations.   He might as well have said that
will, being identical with its consciousness, is an intellectual apprehension of a mental operation.   But as
will is an active determination to do something, while its
consciousness is an intellectual apprehension that one
has that active determination, so sensation is an apprehension of an object, while its consciousness is an
apprehension that one is performing that operation.

Sensation says, 'This is white or sweet'; consciousness says, 'I am seeing something white or tasting something sweet.'

This being consciousness, one operation of which I am conscious is that I know objects. What knowledge of objects am I conscious of possessing? In answering this question, it must be remembered that science is a kind of knowledge of which we are conscious. There is an ordinary consciousness and a scientific consciousness. The ordinary man thinks little or nothing about it, but the man of science is conscious that science passes beyond sense into the insensible, and beyond the objects represented by sense into what I have called the imperceptible world. We are conscious of knowing a sensible, an insensible, and an imperceptible world by natural philosophy.

Now, this knowledge does not appear to consciousness to apprehend a psychical object. When I reflect on my inferential knowledge of the number of corpuscles in a drop of water, or of the distance of the sun from the earth, or of the size of the earth; when, again, I reflect on my indirect perception of a fire, or the waves of the sea; when, finally, I reflect on my sensation of the white object I see or the hot object I feel; in all three instances, I appear to my consciousness to be apprehending not psychical, but physical facts. The conscious subject may be psychical, the conscious operations may be psychical; but I am not conscious that the vision of white, or the perception of a fire, or the inference of a corpuscle, apprehends a psychical object. So far as I am conscious of the sensations of my five senses, a white object in vision, a hot object in touch, a scent in my nostrils, a sound in my ears, a flavour in my mouth, cannot but seem to be apprehended as

physical objects.   Consciousness of the apprehension of
objects is in favour of realism.

But when I apprehend the white, the hot, a scent, a
sound, even a flavour, I further appear to be apprehending an object not only physical, but also external
to myself.   This seemingly conscious appearance is the
strong point of intuitive realism, which depends on it to
claim an intuition of an external world.   Nevertheless,
the appearance is a delusion, which we can trace to its
source.   From my earliest infancy, whenever a sensible
effect has been produced in my nervous system, I have
been accustomed to infer an external object.   By association, perhaps also facilitated by evolution, the inference has become so automatic as to be unnoticed.   The
consequence is, I think I am intuitively sensible of the
external object when I am really inferring it.   Nothing
can prevent the delusion.   I appear to see the paper
and its distance from me.   I cannot now consciously
disengage the sensation of the sensible object from the
inference of the perceptible original.

Hence the limits of consciousness as an evidence.
Consciousness does not become reflective, and therefore
a source of psychology, till many operations have
already become automatic in the conscious subject.
The process from the sense of the insensible object to
the inference of the perceptible original has been repeated an incalculable number of times before any man
is sufficiently adult to consciously reflect on what he
has been doing.   Accordingly, consciousness is the
source rather of the nature than of the origin of
knowledge; invaluable for what we know now, delusive
for how we came to know it.   I am conscious that
I somehow apprehend a sensible and an insensible
world; but I am not conscious of the exact point at

which it ceases to be sensible, and becomes insensible and inferred. Intuitive realists were right in appealing to consciousness for the nature of knowledge; only they should have appealed from the ordinary to the scientific consciousness. But they were quite wrong in appealing to consciousness for the ultimate origin of knowledge. They said truly, 'I apprehend an external world'; they said falsely, 'I apprehend it intuitively.'

Nevertheless, the antithesis between the nature and origin of knowledge must not be exaggerated. Consciousness tells us something of the origin of our knowledge. We are not conscious of the inferences of childhood: when we are old enough to take notice we become conscious of new inferences. We are not conscious of inferring an external world: we are conscious of inferring corpuscles. The exact limit is that we are not conscious of the primary data and the first inferences, but of adult inferences. But, again, consciousness has something to tell us concerning even the primary data of sense. It is not their direct but their indirect evidence. It tells us what is our knowledge of objects, and this conscious knowledge must be explained by the primary data. Thus consciousness, on the whole, is the apprehension of our knowledge of objects and the test of the primary data and origin; it is the direct evidence of the nature, the indirect evidence of the origin of knowledge. The facts of consciousness must be first described and then explained by all scientific psychology. The main fact to be explained is our consciousness that we somehow apprehend a sensible and an insensible physical world.

There is a superficiality of consciousness as there is of sensation. Yet each is the origin of a philosophy. Without sensation there would be no natural, without consciousness no mental philosophy. Sensation is necessary to the science of nature, consciousness to the science of mind. Sensation apprehends what is sensible, consciousness what is knowledge. Sensation carries us some little distance into physical causation, consciousness into the origin of knowledge. But sensation leaves us to infer *causæ essendi* in external nature, consciousness *causæ cognoscendi* in internal knowledge. Yet sensation is the indirect test of all hypotheses to explain the causes of sensible objects, consciousness of all hypotheses to explain the origin of conscious knowledge. Nevertheless, both in themselves are superficial ; for sensation has no immediate intuition of the external causes of nature, and consciousness none of the internal data of knowledge. As direct evidence, sensation tells us only the bare sensible effect and not its external causes, consciousness only what we know now, not how we came to know it. Sensation and consciousness are two senses, the outer and the inner. Neither is false ; both are limited. Truth is *in profundo* ; yet not in a bottomless abyss, but in depths to be plumbed only by reason, and that reason not *a priori*, but logical inference from the outer and inner senses. Not sensation, but reasoning from sensation, discovers external causes ; not consciousness, but reasoning from consciousness, discovers the primary data and origin of knowledge.

Consciousness, then, does not aid the idealist in his assertion that all the immediate objects of sense are psychical. It tells us that we somehow know physical objects. It is so far in favour of realism. Having, however, inferred long ago from sensible data that physical objects exist in the external world, we cannot now help seeming to be conscious of perceiving them intuitively. This confusion favours intuitive realism.

E

But consciousness cannot be used as direct evidence to tell us what we intuitively perceive, because our intuitions were overlaid with our inferences long before our consciousness became attentive. Moreover—and this is the main point—the confusion of what we intuitively perceive by our senses with what we mediately infer by our reason is cleared up by philosophy. What philosophy? This question brings us to the second kind of direct evidence for the data of sense. The philosophy which has distinguished the data of sense from their inferred causes is natural philosophy.

Natural philosophy has shown that the sensible object is not really identical with, but is an effect distinct from, its external original. When a person hears a cannon fired at a considerable distance, his first impression is that he hears the sound at the very moment the ball issues from the cannon's mouth, and that the cannon sounds as he hears it. But if he ascends a hill, and the cannon again fires, he finds that he sees the smoke of the cannon long before he hears the sound, and can count several seconds between the object seen and the object heard. There is only one possible explanation of this distinction. The object seen and the object heard are neither identical with one another, nor with the external object which produces them. The smoke ascends from the cannon and reflects the undulations of light, at the same moment as the ball leaves the cannon and communicates vibrations to the air. But the undulations of light travel faster than the vibrations of air, and produce a visible effect on the person before the audible effect is produced by the slower mode of motion. The visible effect produced by the undulations is not the smoke, and the audible effect produced by the vibrations is not the cannon's roar: else they would be apprehended at the same moment. Both are effects of, neither identical with, the external object.

Again, natural philosophy in the department of physics has shown that external things do not in all their attributes precisely correspond to their effects on our senses. They have duration, extension and motion corresponding to their attributes as sensibly perceived; but they have not heat or colour in the way in which we touch what is hot or see what is coloured. On the contrary, the causes of sensible heat and colour are insensible motions. The attributes which are in nature as they are in our senses, are called primary; while those which are not in nature as they are in our senses, are called secondary qualities.

Again, natural philosophy has proved that external things affect our senses by the causation of motion. To begin with motion before it affects the senses; either a given external thing may itself move from a distance, until it comes into contact with a sensitive subject, as a cannon-ball does when it hits a man; or it propagates a motion from particle to particle until the particles immediately in contact with the sensitive subject receive the motion, a process which takes place in the propagation of the undulations of light. In both cases the result is the same: the object immediately apprehended could not be the thing at a distance, but the thing immediately next to the sensitive organ. But we shall find that it is not even the nearest thing, as a matter of fact, but an effect within our senses.

Again, biology, from Galen onwards, has shown that the nervous system is the material cause susceptible of the effect produced by the efficiency of the external object. It has discovered much of the structure of the nervous system. The peripheral terminations of nervous

fibres are not actually exposed to external things.
Hence the motion has to be propagated through a non-
sensitive covering before it is actually brought to the
nerve. It is impossible, therefore, to be sensible of an
external object, from which the nervous substance is
divided by a medium in the body of the sentient being.
Moreover, when the peripheral termination of a nervous
fibre has been reached, the effect is still insensible till
the motion has been communicated to the brain. When
a nerve has been cut off from the brain, if the part
between the peripheral termination and the section be
irritated, no sensible effect takes place; but if the part
between the brain and the section be irritated by pressure, or electricity, or disease, the effect is sensible.
The brain, therefore, is an integral part of the nervous
material susceptible of a sensible effect. I say a part,
because there is no evidence that the brain alone would
be sensitive, if a whole nervous structure up to the
point at which it loses itself in the brain were removed.
But the whole evidence together clearly shows that no
sensible effect is produced by an external object until
the propagation of motion from the external object has
passed, not only the external medium, but what may be
called the internal medium of the periphery, has reached
the nervous fibres, and communicated itself to the brain.
The nervous system is the primary matter susceptible
of a sensible effect, and the sensible effect, therefore, is
internal.

It is further evident that, like other material causes,
the nervous system partly determines the effect. It is
susceptible of effects, like the primary qualities of external objects, but not like their secondary qualities.
Probably its structure is adequate to the former, but
not sufficiently subtle for the latter. Hence the dura-

tion, extension and motion of external bodies is able
to produce similar sensible duration, extension and
motion in the nervous system.   But when the delicate
vibrations of the air and the still more subtle undulations of æther strike upon the organs of hearing,
touch and vision, the nervous structure of these
organs is too coarse-grained to reproduce them, and
substitutes the heterogeneous effect of sensible sound
and the still more heterogeneous effects of sensible heat
and light.

Lastly, evolution has made it exceedingly probable
that, like other material causes, the nervous system has
itself been modified by the repeated action of the external efficient on its structure.   It is probable that, by
the frequent operation of appropriate stimuli on particular parts of the general sensitive system, the original
sense of touch has been differentiated into the five senses.
I would make two further suggestions.   First, it is
probable that as touch preceded the other senses, so the
feelings preceded touch.   In this case, the sentient being
at first simply felt mere pleasure and pain from external
objects; afterwards proceeded to the more complex
operation of touch, in which the sensation of touching
is distinct from the sensible object, hot or cold, in the
tactile nerves, and the consciousness of touching distinct
both from the sensation and the sensible object; and,
last of all, proceeded to infer external causes.   Secondly,
it is probable that, as the nervous system has become
more differentiated, it may also become more subtle, and
therefore more discriminative of secondary qualities.
Some approach to this ideal may be found in sensible
sound, in which there is some trace of vibrations, though
not adequate to the external vibrations.   Why, then,
may not the nervous system some day become more

attuned to represent æthereal undulations to some
extent in the wonderful sense of vision?

The discoveries of natural philosophy eliminate
intuitive realism, by proving that the external is not
identical with the sensible object, but is the cause
which produces it in the nervous system. Contenting
himself with crude consciousness and common sense,
forgetting how late consciousness becomes reflective,
and that common sense never becomes a science, the
intuitive realist takes the appearance that we have an
intuition of the external world for a fact, and sometimes even converts it into a first principle. But he
comes into contradiction with science. Natural philosophy shows that the external world affects us indirectly, and that we have no empirical intuition except
of ourselves. We might doubt between consciousness
and science, if we could not see that the supposed intuition of the external world is a delusion of association,
and that consciousness is put out of court by its inability to reflect at the time when the inference of the
external world was being made; made so often then as
to have become automatic, and now made so quickly
as to seem an intuition. On the strength of science,
then, we must reject the hypothesis that the data of
sense are to be found in the external world, in the
non-ego.

The same scientific discoveries raise a strong presumption in favour of physical realism, which simply
adopts the scientific account without further hypothesis. In the first place, I suppose that the effect
produced on the nervous system is the sensible physical
object, which we are conscious of apprehending, but by
a confusion believe to be an object external to ourselves:
for instance, when we see something white, it seems to

be the external paper, or what not, but it is really the
effect produced by the paper reflecting undulations on
the optic nerve.   Secondly, I suppose that as we know
the external physical cause to produce the sensible
physical effect, and as we must start from sense, we
must use the sensible physical object impressed on our
nerves to infer the external physical object, as cause.
The scientific account of the causation of the sensible
effect leads directly to physical realism, which simply
reads the process of causation backwards into a process
of knowledge.

Biology has brought the sensible effect within the
nervous system.   Has it carried it further?   The
attempt has often been made by biologists.   They suppose that the physical effect produced in the nervous
system is not yet sensible, even when it has reached the
brain; that it remains a mere impression, no more
sensible than the external object; and that when the
motion of the external object has produced the motion
of the medium, the motion of the medium the motion of
the nerves, the motion of the nerves the motion of the
brain, the process is not yet finished.   They suppose
that the cerebral motion, which is physical, produces a
sensation which is psychical; and they do not ordinarily distinguish the sensible object from the sensation.
From this hypothesis it would follow that the hot felt,
the white seen, the sweet tasted, the durable, extended,
and moving, apprehended by any sense are psychical
affections produced by cerebral motion.   The sensible
object will be neither the external object nor the internal effect in the nervous system, but the internal
psychical sensation.   If so, realism will have to succumb
to idealism.

The question we now have to ask ourselves is not

whether the external object causes our sensation in some way or other. The scientific evidence of the propagation of motion from external objects to our bodies and the conscious involuntariness of sensation are sufficient proofs that the external object does cause our sensation. It is, however, a different question how one causes the other. Secondly, the question we now have to ask ourselves is not whether there is any evidence at all that the sensation produced is purely psychical. What is to be said on this point will follow when we come to the Cartesian philosophy in detail. The present questions are, first, whether biology proves that within ourselves nervous and cerebral motion produces a psychical sensation; secondly, if so, whether it follows that the sensible object also becomes a psychical sensation. The answer is that biologists have gone beyond biology, and that no affirmative answer can be given to these questions from the observations, or direct inferences from sense, which are the evidences of their science.

In the first place, the nervous system is imperfectly known. It is quite clear that external objects propagate motions to the nerves, but it is not at all clear what happens when the effect has been produced. In optics, for example, so long as we are reading of the undulations of light, of the manner in which rays are communicated to the eye, of the structure of the lens by which the rays are made to converge on the retina, and of the general structure of the retina, and even of its nervous elements, everything is clear. But the further we penetrate from the retina along the optic nerve to the optic centres at the base of the brain, the darker the subject becomes, and fact seems to pass into hypothesis. It is the same with all our senses. Nay,

difficulties begin at the very terminations of the nerves.
What, for example, are the precise functions of the
tactile corpuscles, of the rods and cones of the retina,
of the rods of Corti in the ear?

We know more of nervous structure than of nervous
action. What is nervous action? This is an unsolved
problem. What is cerebral action? This is a more
unsolved problem. The structural connections of
afferent nerves with centres, of centres with efferent
nerves, of efferent nerves with muscles, and to some
extent the structural constituents of nerves and muscles
are fairly made out. It is also found that an appre-
ciable interval takes place between the stimulation of
an afferent nerve and the muscular motion which it
indirectly but ultimately produces. This interval proves
an important point about nervous action; it is a motion
because it takes time to go from place to place.

The genus of nervous action, then, is known to be motion. But what is its differentia? After the first crude
hypothesis of animal spirits moving in the nerves, nervous
motion was supposed to be the simplest form of mechanical motion by impact, as if the impression were
pushed along to the brain, as a series of bricks knock
one another over. Then it was supposed to be vibration. Later researches tend to show that it has relations
to the motions of electricity and of chemical action. It
is, no doubt, some molecular motion allied to other
motions of the same kind; but its peculiarity is its
slowness, compared, for instance, with electricity. Its
precise differentia is at present unknown. Cerebral
motion is still more unknown. It has been found,
by experimenting on various parts of the brain, that
different parts are to some extent connected with
different muscular motions, from which it is inferred

that they are also connected with different nervous motions. But how the brain moves between the stimulus of an afferent nerve and its effect on an efferent nerve is unknown. He would be a bold man who would come forward and say he knows the motion by which the effect impressed on the nerves is communicated to the brain and there made ready for sensation. How, then, can he say he knows that cerebral motion, of which in biology he is ignorant, produces a psychical sensation, which is beyond the venue of a physical science?

Secondly, the so-called transmutation of cerebral motion into psychical sensation is admitted to be performed in some mysterious way, unknown and inexplicable. This point may be made clear by the following quotation from Professor Huxley's Lay Sermon on Descartes' Discourse, in which the Professor is trying to prove that thought is existence, and, so far as we are concerned, existence is thought :—

' For example, I take up a marble, and I find it to be a red, round, hard, single body. We call the redness, the roundness, the hardness, and the singleness, " qualities" of the marble ; and it sounds, at first, the height of absurdity to say that all these qualities are modes of our own consciousness, which cannot even be conceived to exist in the marble. But consider the redness to begin with ; how does the sensation of redness arise ? The waves of a certain very attenuated matter, particles of which are vibrating with vast rapidity, but with very different velocities, strike upon the marble, and those which vibrate with a particular velocity are thrown off from its surface in all directions. The optical apparatus of the eye gathers some of these together, and gives them such a course that they impinge upon the surface of the retina, which is a singularly delicate apparatus, connected with the termination of the fibres of the optic nerve. The impulses of the attenuated matter, or æther, affect this apparatus and the fibres of the optic nerve in a certain way, and the change in the fibres of the optic nerve produces yet other changes in the brain ; and these, in some fashion unknown to us, give rise to the feeling, or consciousness, of redness. If the marble could remain unchanged, and either the rate of vibration of the æther, or the nature of the retina could be altered, the marble would seem not red, but some other colour. There are many people who are what are called colour-blind, being unable to distinguish one colour from another. Such an one might declare our marble to be green, and he would be quite as right in saying that it is green as we are in declaring it to be red. But, then, as the marble cannot, in itself, be both green and red at the same time, this shows that the quality " redness " must be in our consciousness, and not in the marble.'

Thirdly, the hypothesis of this unknown transmutation is inconsistent with one of the best established facts of the nervous system—its physical continuity. It supposes that physical motion of afferent nerves and brain causes psychical sensation, which causes psychical volition, which causes physical motion of efferent nerves, which causes physical motion of muscles. But wherever nervous structure is accessible to observation, the afferent nerves finally communicate with centres which communicate with efferent nerves, without any rupture of physical continuity. It might, indeed, be urged that the intermediate purely psychical processes nevertheless intervene insensibly in the centre between the afferent and efferent nervous processes. But this hypothesis is rendered most difficult by the phænomena of reflex action. In reflex action, the afferent and efferent nervous processes are certainly connected without any breach of physical continuity. It might again be objected that only the nerves of reflex processes are continuous. But we cannot divide the nerves of reflex action from those of conscious action, and say that the former nerves are physically continuous, whereas the latter are interrupted by purely psychical sensations and volitions, because the very same nerves, which are used in conscious, are used also in reflex actions. For example, we may wink either voluntarily or automatically. An object strikes the eye, transmits its motion to the afferent optic nerve, which communicates with the brain, which transmits the motion to the efferent facial nerve, governing the orbicular muscle of the eyelids, which makes them close. The whole of this process often takes place automatically, without any rupture of physical continuity. When it takes place consciously, are we to say that the physical motion, having arrived from the optic nerve to the brain, does not produce the motion of the efferent nerve, but produces a psychical sensation instead, which produces a psychical volition, which at length affects the efferent nerve? There is not a little of biological or any other evidence that the physical continuity is sometimes preserved sometimes broken in this manner in the very same series of nerves.

To escape this gratuitous hypothesis of psychical interruption, some of the mental physiologists resort to paradoxes, in order at once to preserve the physical continuity of the nervous system, together with purely psychical sensations. Allowing that in all cases the motion of the afferent nerves propagated through the centres produces the motion of the efferent nerves in a

continuous manner, some suppose that, standing quite
apart from these physical processes, the conscious subject is a sort of impartial spectator, performing purely
psychical operations that have no physical effects, while
others positively go the length of supposing that not
only in sentient beings, but in all nature, there are
always two independent but parallel streams, the well-
known physical motions and supposititious psychical
processes accompanying them. These hypotheses are
exceedingly like the Pre-established Harmony, and like
it in being made to get over a self-made difficulty.
They are hypotheses to cover an hypothesis. The
former alternative does not go beyond conscious beings,
but it fails to explain a fact of consciousness far more
certain than the hypothesis. We are certainly conscious that external objects somehow affect our feelings
and sensations, that our sensations, desires and inferences affect our volitions, that our volitions somehow
affect the motions of our bodies. It is absurd to suppose
that our conscious operations are inert and idle, when
they are consciously both passive and active, and that
the conscious subject is like a child, given his operations like a toy to make believe he is very busy, but
really to keep him quiet. The latter alternative which
carries this inert psychism into everything whatsoever,
without any evidence, except the original hypothesis
of two parallel streams in a sentient being, would have
us believe that the wind blows, the waves swell, the
earth moves, with some obscure sentience. Such a per-
sonification of nature was excusable in primitive religion,
but it is not worthy of modern science.

Lastly, to return to the usual hypothesis that nervous
motion produces psychical sensation, which again issues
in nervous motion, one cannot help asking what can be

the source of a biological hypothesis so foreign, nay, so contradictory to the evidence of biology? Biologists have become psychologists, and have fallen under the dominion of the idealists. Without any criticism, without any biological proof, simply because it is the fashion, and as if it were a first principle, they have accepted the idealistic hypothesis of purely psychical sensation, and thereon have reared an hypothesis of their own, that nervous motion produces this psychical sensation, which reproduces nervous motion.

Now, the present question, as I said before, is not whether there is a purely psychical sensation, but whether there is any evidence that motion propagated from the afferent nerves to the brain produces such a *tertium quid*, instead of producing motion from the brain to the efferent nerves. There is no evidence, either psychological or biological. As a psychologist, I am conscious that I perform the operation of sensation, which for argument's sake may be assumed as purely psychical; but I am not conscious of my nervous motion. I am not, therefore, conscious of sensation arising out of nervous motion. A biologist, not in himself but in another body, can observe a nervous system, its physical continuity, and the time of its action proving motion; but this dissector cannot either observe or be conscious of the sensation of another nervous system: he cannot, therefore, observe nervous motion issuing in sensation. That there is such a process from the physical into the psychical and back is sheer hypothesis, an arbitrary concordance of idealism and biology.

Nor is this all: they proceed to suppose that the effect produced by the external object on the internal nervous system is not yet sensible, but that, when the

psychical sensation is produced, the effect for the first
time becomes sensible, so that the sensible object is
either identical with the sensation, or at all events is
equally psychical. But, in the first place, even if a
purely psychical sensation is produced in this manner,
it does not follow that the sensible object becomes
psychical. There is no reason, except the old and ex-
ploded hypothesis *similia similibus cognoscuntur*, why
a psychical operation may not apprehend a physical
object. Secondly, whatever may be the nature of the
operation, it is most improbable in itself that the hot felt
through one's body, the white seen through one's eyes,
the loud heard through one's ears, is anything but a
physical condition of the tactile, optic and auditory
nerves in connection with the brain. The idealistic
hypothesis of psychical sensation, then, does not prove
the biological hypothesis of the transmutation of nervous
motion into psychical sensation, nor either hypothesis
the third hypothesis that the sensible object is psychical.

> Ter sunt conati imponere Pelio Ossam
> Scilicet atque Osse frondosum involvere Olympum.

The study of the mental physiology of the present
day suggests several reflections. In the first place, the
insensible and imperceptible motions of æther, their
reflections from other bodies, and their impact on the
senses are now well-established discoveries of science.
They are known qualities, which are not sensations, but
the insensible causes of sensations. Not all knowable
qualities, therefore, are sensations. Secondly, as we
recede from the external world behind the periphery
into the nervous system, science becomes more vague.
What are nervous and cerebral motions? Thirdly, we
are told that cerebral motion, which is physical, produces a heterogeneous sensation, which is psychical.

But we are given no evidence of this transmutation. We cannot observe it in a dissecting-room. If it be said we are conscious of it, we answer that we are conscious of sensation, but not of cerebral motion, and therefore not of cerebral motion producing psychical sensation as a separate and indeed heterogeneous fact. Fourthly, this transmutation of one unknown into another unknown is admitted to take place in an unknown manner. Fifthly, we are illogically asked to infer from this transmutation of cerebral motion into psychical sensation that the sensible object, e.g. the red seen in vision, is also a psychical sensation. Sixthly, we are not told how, if the object of sense thus becomes psychical, we infer the external causes, which, as we have seen, are much the clearest part of the whole business. Seventhly, we often find that, with more logic than consistency, the external objects which were previously made the scientific causes of sensation are nevertheless afterwards declared unknown and unknowable. Meanwhile, the fallacy of this so-called biology is its assumption of psychological idealism. All that is really proved by natural philosophy is that external redness, for example, is an insensible quality of insensible æther, consisting of a vibration of a certain velocity; and that, reflected by an external object, it produces in the optic nerves of a sentient being a sensible redness, which is not identical with the external vibrations nor itself a sensible vibration at all. The simple conclusion from these scientific facts would be that the nervous effect is the sensible redness, from which, together with sensible motion, the external motions of vibration are inferred. Nothing more is proved by mental physiology.

When we look back at the whole light thrown by natural philosophy on the sensible object, we shall find

that it is known that external physical objects produce
internal physical effects in the nervous system, but it is
not known that these internal physical effects in their
turn produce an internal psychical object of sense.
Meanwhile, we are conscious that, when we use our
senses, we somehow apprehend a physical object, which
seems by an illusion to be also external.   The simplest
hypothesis, which can be made in these circumstances,
is that the sensible object is neither external on the one
hand nor psychical on the other, but the internal
physical effect on the nervous system.   In other words,
there is a *via media* between intuitive realism and
idealism of all kinds, closer to the scientific facts than
either hypothesis; namely, physical realism.

At the same time, scientific observation is not a
positive proof of physical realism.   It brings the sensible
object within the man: it cannot decide whether it is
or is not within the soul.   Its ultimate result is that
the sensible object is not external but internal, not
without but within the sentient being, not identical with
the physical object in the outside world but produced
in the interior microcosm of the animal organism.   This
negative conclusion eliminates intuitive, but it does not
positively establish physical realism.   As a direct
evidence, natural philosophy, being founded on observation, is able to show that the sensible object is not
the physical object outside, but is within the nervous
system; not being founded on consciousness, it is not
able to decide whether this internal sensible object is
physical or psychical, whether it is the nervous effect,
or something even more internal.   It leaves this problem
unsolved.   Accordingly, there still remain two possible alternatives—physical realism and psychological
idealism.

F

Nevertheless, scientific observation makes physical realism the more probable alternative, because this hypothesis simply accepts the proved nervous effect as the sensible object, instead of hypothesising a further psychical object, which is unproved, and breaks the nervous continuity. When as a mental philosopher one adds consciousness to scientific observation, the probability of physical realism is increased. Consciousness tells us that we somehow apprehend physical objects, which appear also to be sensibly external. Scientific observation disabuses us of the appearance that the sensible object is external, but not of the consciousness that it is physical. Natural philosophy, as a direct evidence, may be said to remove the physical object of sense from the external to the internal world, but no further than the nervous system. The most probable mental philosophy would simply conclude that it there becomes sensible—though only the most probable.

We asked for direct evidence that the immediate object, hot, coloured, &c., perceived by our senses is a psychical phaenomenon, and we find there is none. Consciousness is so far from saying so, that it confuses the immediate and the mediate, and leads us to think that the immediate object is not only physical but external. Scientific analysis corrects this confusion, and teaches us that the immediate object is not external but internal, but does not go on to show that it is not only internal but psychical. I suspect that the idealists by a kind of confusion have changed the truth that the object of sense is not external but internal into the hypothesis that it is not physical but psychical.

The idealist may reply that direct evidence is not required for an hypothesis, and that the psychical object is like aether—something inaccessible to direct evidence,

but needed to explain the facts. I accept this issue.
I admit that, if the idealistic hypothesis of the sensible
object could explain the facts of the known world and
eliminate the hypothesis of physical realism, it would be
proved by this indirect evidence. There would still be
no direct evidence that a hot or coloured object is not a
physical but a psychical fact. But, contrary to all appearance, we should be obliged to conclude that, as
light is paradoxically but really an undulation of æther,
so is the seen, or felt, or heard, or tasted, or smelt, a
psychical, and not a physical, fact.

The gist of the idealistic hypothesis is that not some
but all the immediate objects are psychical, and that
no physical object whatever is apprehended by sense.
The consequence is that all our sensitive experience
will be limited to psychical objects; for, so far as it is
sensitive, experience is merely the sum of our sensations. Moreover, the supposition of *a priori* elements
of knowledge will not help us, for nobody pretends
that we have an *a priori* apprehension of the physical
to add to an *a posteriori* apprehension of the psychical:
such an hypothesis would be too great an inversion.
The consequence is that all the data of our knowledge
will be psychical. No doubt different idealists will provide more or less of such psychical data. Some will
have merely psychical sensations, others will add a
psychical subject, and others again psychical apprehensions *a priori*. But at the widest the data will all be
psychical facts of some kind or other.

Now the question arises, what can be known from
psychical data? If all the immediate objects I touch,
see, taste, smell, and hear are psychical, and I am psychical, and all my apprehensions are psychical, if all my
sensitive experience is of nothing but psychical phæno-

mena, if all the data which form the immediate premises of my mediate knowledge are psychical, what can I infer from such facts in the premises? To answer this question we must consult the logical rules of inference.

All inference is by similarity. Not to enter into the question whether there is one fundamental type, there are three apparent kinds of inference—induction, deduction, and analogical inference. All these are different modes of reasoning from similar to similar. In induction we apprehend that similar particulars have a similar characteristic, and infer that the class, including those and all other particulars similar to them, have that similar characteristic. In deduction we start with a proposition stating the similar characteristics of a class, either inferred by induction or otherwise known, as major premise; we combine it with a minor premise, asserting that something is one of the class of similar particulars; and from this combination we infer that this new but similar particular has the similar characteristic already known to belong to the class. In analogical inference, which is an imperfect substitute for induction followed by deduction, we apprehend that a particular has a characteristic, or several similar particulars have a similar characteristic; we apprehend by analogy that another particular is similar to the given particular or similar particulars; and from the analogy we infer that this new but similar particular may have the characteristic similar to that of the given particular or particulars. Various men are mortal, ∴ all men are mortal : all men are mortal, I am a man, ∴ I am mortal : the earth is inhabited, Mars is like the earth, ∴ Mars may be inhabited :—these inductions, deductions, and analogical inferences are nothing but inferences from similar to similar. They are founded also on the reality and knowledge of classes and laws. But what is a class except similar things, and what is a law except the fact that similar things possess similar characteristics?

From this limitation of inference to similarity it follows that whatever the character of the data, such will be that which is inferred. If all the data were psychical, then, by parity of reasoning, we could only infer the psychical. If we never had direct experience of anything physical whatever, then, there being nothing physical in the premises, nothing physical in the conclusion could possibly be inferred. From the similar the similar is inferred; from the psychical the psychical. But in order to infer the physical we must have some physical data.

The universal similarity between the data in the premises and the inferred in the conclusion requires to be guarded from misapprehension. I said above that the old hypothesis—like is known by like—is a fallacy. I now say that like is known from like. These positions are not inconsistent. The former refers to the relation of subject and object, the latter to the relation of object to object. There is no reason why the object apprehended should be like the subject apprehending; but there are reasons why objects inferred should be like the objects from which they are inferred—the rules of logic. If the subject has constantly had physical objects presented to it, it must apprehend them, or be useless. But when the subject has before it the immediate objects which can be presented to it, whether *a posteriori* or *a priori*, it has all the data from which reasoning can start; and if that reasoning is to maintain the consistency of truth, it can add nothing in the conclusion which is not justified by the presence of something similar in the premises. If reasoning contains, on the Kantian hypothesis, *a priori* apprehensions, these will be part of the data; but if it adds anything, not in the data but in the conclusion, which has no analogue in the premises, reasoning becomes paralogism. This fallacy is well known in deduction; but it is equally true of induction, which only generalises the subjects and predicates contained in the particular instances, and of analogical idference, which infers that one particular similar to another may be similar also in a characteristic already apprehended in that other. Therefore, although like objects are not necessarily immediately apprehended by a like subject, only like objects are inferred from like objects, not by any necessity in the relation of subject and object, but by the nature of reasoning. Hence a psychical subject may immediately perceive physical objects; but if it were a psychical subject and perceived psychical objects it could infer nothing but psychical things, similar either to the psychical subject perceiving or to the psychical objects perceived.

Again, the logical canon, like is known from like, must not be confused with the metaphysical hypothesis, like causes have like effects. Aristotle extended the principle of the propagation of the species from the organic to the inorganic world, and thought that every cause is homogeneous with its effect. Modern science has discountenanced this view, except in the far-off sense that all physical causation may be the propagation of motion in various forms. But when I say that we can only infer like objects, what I mean is not that we must infer causes like the effects, but causes like the causes which we have already known. For example, Newton, already knowing the effects requiring gravitation to cause them in terrestrial bodies, when he found similar effects in celestial bodies, inferred that their cause also is a celestial, similar to terrestrial, gravitation. Now, if all the data of sense were psychical, not only the effects but also the causes in sense would be psychical : conse- quently, when we came to a sensible effect, similar to other sensible effects, but not due to any sensible cause, we should have to infer a similar cause beyond sense ; and, as all the causes in sense would *ex hypothesi* be psychical, we should have to infer, by parity of rea- soning, a psychical cause, not because the effect was psychical, but because all previously known causes would be psychical. If, on the other hand, there were physical causes in the data of sense, we could then, and only then, infer a similar physical cause beyond sense.

Again, when I say that only like objects are inferred from like, I do not mean that nothing new can be inferred, but only nothing new which is not similar to the data. The conclusion is no mere restatement of the premises. What is inferred need not have been already experi- enced, nor is reasoning confined to merely reproducing the immediate data of the senses. But what is inferred must be similar to what has already been experienced. What is new, and has never been, nor ever will be, in experience, such as an æthereal undulation, can be in- ferred. But the æthereal undulation is a motion similar to the experienced motion of waves of water. Nothing new, which is not similar to the data, can be inferred. It is true of the Deity Himself, who, though not experi- enced, is inferred to be like man, but infinitely intensi- fied in the attributes which we already know in our- selves. Consequently, if all the data were psychical, we should be able to draw inferences to similarly psychical subjects and similarly psychical objects, new but similar to the data. But we should not be able to infer something wholly new, dissimilar and heterogeneous, for which there was no analogue either in the sentient subject or in the sensible objects. Hence, the physical, for which there would be *ex hypothesi* no analogue in the premises, could not be inferred. If, on the other hand, as I suppose, the sensible data are physical facts in my organism, I can then infer new but similar physical objects outside, although I have never immediately perceived them by sense.

Another misapprehension will immediately arise. It is said that one opposite implies another, and, therefore, though we experience only one opposite, we infer the other. Thus, it is supposed, from psychical data we infer their opposites, physical things. I am almost ashamed to write down Aristotle's distinction of contradictories and contraries; but it is necessary in an illogical age. Contradictory opposites are the positive and its negative, as relative and not relative, finite and not finite. Contrary opposites are the furthest removed positives, as white and black. Now contradictory opposites in a sense imply one another, but contrary opposites do not. White implies not white : it does not imply black. We might have apprehended white without having any conception of black, much less having proof of its existence. Secondly, great harm is done by such vague terms as 'imply' and 'implication,' which sometimes mean conceiving and sometimes inferring. The positive, when apprehended, makes us conceive the contradictory negative, but does not make us infer that it exists. Are we to fall into the old sophism of arguing that as something is contradicted by nothing, nothing exists?

It is a common argument that the relative which we experience implies the non-relative and absolute,

the finite implies the infinite. This is an utter confusion of contradictories and contraries. The relative implies the not relative; but the contradictory, not
relative, is not necessarily the positive contrary, absolute, for it also includes nothing; and the relative, in
implying the not relative, does not decide whether it is
absolute or nothing. As white implies not white, but
not necessarily black or any other particular colour, so
the relative implies not relative, but not necessarily the
particular species of not relative, absolute. The same
remark applies to the opposition of finite and infinite,
except that in this case the term 'infinite' is ambiguous,
being properly the not finite, but including both that
which is not finite, because it is nothing, and that
which is not finite, because it extends without limit.
The finite implies its contradictory, not its contrary : it
implies the negative not finite, but does not imply
the particular positive species, the infinite which
extends without limit. Secondly, the relative and
finite imply only in the sense of making us conceive
the mere contradictories, not relative and not finite.
The positive sides of the contradictions not only leave
the content of the negatives undetermined, but also
leave the question undecided whether we can infer
that there is anything corresponding to the ideas of
the negatives. Nor do they even give us the ideas
till we have not only apprehended the positives, but
also apprehended that they are relative and finite.
The relative and the finite, then, when apprehended to
be such, make us conceive the ideas of the not relative
and not finite, but give us no idea of a positive something absolute and extending without limits, much less
make us infer that this species of not relative and not
finite is something real as distinguished from nothing

at all. When we merely experience something which happens to be finite, we need not think of any opposite; if we think of it as finite, we must have an idea of the not finite; but we need not form an idea of the positive infinite, much less can we prove that there is something infinite, and say, 'I experience the finite and relative, therefore there is an infinite and absolute.' Men accept such arguments because they think it helps to prove the existence of a Deity. But the finite and relative do not make us conceive a positive infinite absolute, much less infer its existence; and theology has better arguments for a Deity than the confusion of negative and positive, of contradictory and contrary opposition, of conception and inference, of ideas and judgments.

Similarly, the psychical does not imply the physical. The physical and the psychical are contraries, not contradictories. The contradictory of the psychical is the not psychical, which may be anything else or nothing. Suppose that I had experienced nothing but psychical data. If I had never thought of them as psychical, but only as hot, red, and so on, I should have had no reason to conceive the not psychical. If I had thought of them as psychical, I must then have had the bare idea of not psychical as its contradictory. But I should neither have been able to have inferred that it existed nor what it was. The content of the idea would have been the bare negation or contradictory of the psychical. I should have had no idea of the physical as a positive contrary, much less have proved its existence. Just as the apprehension of white makes me conceive the idea of not white, but does not infer that there is any other colour, much less the contrary black, and just as the apprehension of the relative and finite makes me conceive the idea of not relative and not finite, but does not

infer that there is anything which is not relative and not
finite, much less the contrary absolute and extending
without limits, so the apprehension of the psychical
would make me conceive the idea of not psychical, but
would not tell me that there is anything positive which
is not psychical, much less that it is the contrary,
physical. To infer the existence of the positive contrary, the physical, I should have required other than
psychical data, which would, however, have been *ex
hypothesi* all the data possible.

In all cases the existence of a contrary is a matter not
of implication in the knowledge of the opposite contrary, but a matter of independent inference. Human
reasoning would indeed be easy, if without further
question the moment one had ascertained a thing, one
knew that its contrary existed; when one had experienced white, one knew black; when all experience had
been of the relative and finite, one knew the absolute
and infinite; when all the immediate data of all reasoning were psychical, one straightway knew that there
are physical things. Why, one contrary does not even
make us conceive the idea of another, much less infer its
existence. The white makes us conceive the idea, not
white: we want other evidence to infer the existence of
the black. The psychical makes us conceive the idea,
not psychical: we want other evidence to prove the
existence of the physical. A synthesis from psychical
data to physical things must be founded on some better
device than the fallacy of the implication of opposites.
But in reality the whole hypothesis of such a synthesis
is illogical. To infer physical things we require more
than psychical data, and their implications, and their
consequences: we require physical data in the premises
similar to the physical objects in the conclusion.

The canons of inference, then, teach us, first, that from similars similars are inferred; secondly, that what is inferred may be something new so long as it is similar to some of the data: and thirdly, that it cannot be the contrary of all the data. Therefore, on the idealistic hypothesis that all the data are psychical, in the first place, what is inferred would also be psychical; secondly, it would include other psychical subjects and other psychical objects similar to those which *ex hypothesi* form the data of inference; but, thirdly, it would not include physical things, for which there would be no analogy, and which are not implied in merely psychical data: for psychical data would not make us even conceive, much less infer their contraries, physical things. On the other hand, if some of the data are physical, what is inferred can be physical like the data, different yet similar objects, the data being in our own bodies, the inferred objects in the external world.

We constantly hear at the present day of two worlds and their correspondence—the psychical and the physical. It is not the purpose of this essay to deny this antithesis, nor to depend upon it. But it is also commonly supposed that all the data of our knowledge belong to the former world, from which the latter is inferred. Against this hypothesis I direct this essay. If all the data of sense were psychical, the parity of reasoning would have no data to infer the physical. But the physical world is the object of natural science, which is knowledge. Therefore, not all the data of sense are psychical. There must be similar physical data to infer similar physical objects.

Such, then, are the data required by the rules of reasoning to infer a physical world. We began by saying that, if the idealistic hypothesis led to the

only possible explanation of the facts, we must accept
it even on this indirect evidence. We now see to
what it logically leads. All that is inferred as well
as all that is perceived, all that is immediate and all that
is mediate, all that is apprehended in us and all that is
known beyond, will be psychical. That is, all known
realities will be psychical facts of some kind or another.
As Berkeley says, the whole known world will be mind
and ideas; with Hegel, thought will be being and
being will be thought. These are the logical idealisms.
Nothing physical, and not psychical, will be inferrible,
still less knowable.

This logical consequence of all psychological idealism
must be confronted with the discoveries of natural philosophy. A survey of these discoveries shows an enormous
mass of insensible and inconceivable realities, which
are scientifically known by inference from sensible data.
But they are physical realities, incapable of being resolved into any kind of psychical fact; being insensible they are not sensations, being inconceivable they
are not ideas. It follows, therefore, that some things
physical, and not psychical, are knowable, and not all
known objects are psychical.

The physical objects of scientific knowledge directly
eliminate pure idealism. Starting synthetically from
the common idealistic hypothesis that the sensible data
are psychical, the pure idealist draws the strictly logical
conclusion that all known objects, inferred from these
psychical data of sense, must also be psychical. According to him, then, there are no physical objects of knowledge. His logic is consistent, but his conclusion is
false. He has omitted the physical world which, being
beyond our sensations and ideas, cannot be resolved
into sensations or ideas, but which yet is an object of

science the most perfect form of knowledge. Not all
known objects, therefore, are psychical; some are physical. Pure idealism then is false, and some form of
realism true. As intuitive realism has already been
eliminated by natural philosophy, it only remains to
decide between the hypothetical realism of the cosmothetic idealist and the physical realism of this essay.

The physical objects of scientific knowledge indirectly eliminate cosmothetic idealism with its hypothetical realism. The cosmothetic idealist tries to
reconcile the idealistic theory, that the sensible data
are psychical, with the realistic theory that some objects
knowable by inference from these data are physical.
We have found that the realistic part of his theory is
correct. He has the merit of admitting that there are
physical objects of knowledge : this is his superiority to
the pure idealist. He has the merit of admitting that
they are not intuitively perceived by sense, but inferred :
this is his superiority to the intuitive realist. But he is
illogical. His defect is the inconsequence of supposing
that physical objects, though not intuitively perceived,
could be inferred from purely psychical data. But we
have seen that all inference is by similarity, and therefore physical objects could not be inferred from purely
psychical data. The physical would be the object
of a new term in the conclusion, absent and un-
justified in the premises. If all the data of sense
were psychical, then, by parity of reasoning, all objects
knowable from them would be psychical. But by the
discoveries of science, and by the admission of the
cosmothetic idealist, some objects knowable by inference
from the data of sense are physical. Therefore not all
the data of sense are psychical. *Sublata consequent
tollitur antecedens.*

Cosmothetic and pure idealism are mutually destructive of each other. The former admits that some objects are physical, which prove that the latter is wrong in supposing all objects to be psychical. The latter admits that only psychical objects can be inferred from psychical data, so that the former is wrong in supposing that physical objects are inferred from psychical data. Pure idealism fails to recognise, cosmothetic idealism fails to explain, the knowledge of an insensible and inconceivable physical world. If we combine both we destroy the common data of both. As the pure idealist says, if all the data were psychical all the objects would be psychical; but as the cosmothetic idealist admits, not all the objects are psychical. It follows that both are wrong in saying all the data are psychical. Their data fail to explain the physical objects of scientific knowledge. Science eliminates all psychological idealism.

Meanwhile the physical objects of scientific knowledge are not merely destructive of psychological idealism, but are also constructive of physical realism. They prove in themselves that some objects of knowledge are physical, and, in combination with the logical rules of inference, that some data of sense must be physical, to infer them. Similars are inferrible only from similars. Therefore the physical is inferrible only from the physical. But some objects of science are physical; therefore they are inferrible only from physical data. These data of sense, however, though physical, are proved by scientific analysis to be internal; therefore the data of sense are physical objects within our nervous system, from which we infer physical objects in the external world. This is the theory of physical realism, established by the logical rules of hypothesis.

I admit that the direct evidences are not a positive

proof of physical realism. Consciousness, alone, is even
in favour of intuitive realism. But scientific analysis
destroys this hypothesis by separating the sensible
effect from the external cause, and showing that the
sensible object must be internal. On the other hand, it
does not show that the sensible object is not only internal but psychical, and therefore does not favour
idealism. It makes the intermediate theory of physical
realism possible, even probable. I do not believe, however, that the data of sense are recoverable by any
direct method, because from our very birth, and with
inherited power, we overlay them with inferences.
Hence the shipwreck of modern philosophy, which supposes its hypotheses of sensible data to be first principles,
and has alternated between the opposite but equally
futile attempts to grasp physical things by sense, or to
leap from psychical data to physical things.

I admit, therefore, that the crucial evidence must
be indirect. That hypothesis of the data of sense must
be accepted, which explains the knowledge of the objects
of science. This insensible, this inconceivable, this
physical world of science is not an object of intuition,
is not a sum of psychical sensations and ideas, is not
inferrible from psychical sensations and ideas. Its
knowledge then must be accounted for otherwise. It
is inferrible from internal and physical data, the nervous
system sensibly affected by external objects. The data
of sense, then, are neither physical objects without,
which are the causes not the objects of sense ; nor
psychical objects within, from which nothing physica
could be inferred; but physical objects within, from
which physical objects without are inferred by all, and
known by science. Physical realism, therefore, or the
theory of internal physical data to infer external physi-

cal objects, is, in accordance with the logic of explanation and elimination, the only hypothesis of the data of
sense sufficient to explain the knowledge of the objects
of science.   It is a mental philosophy born of natural
philosophy, 'that great mother of sciences.' [1]

[1] Bacon, *Nov. Org.* i. 80.

CHAPTER IV.

ARISTOTLE remarks that we ought not only to criticise our opponents, but also to point out the causes of their errors. The origin of intuitive realism and its presentative theory of perception, is the inevitable tendency of ordinary man to confound sense with reason, and his sensations with his inferences. He has so long been accustomed to infer an external world, that at last he cannot but fancy his senses perceive it. He seems to himself even to be conscious that it is so, calls his confusion common sense, and at last defies philosophers to distinguish the sensible and the real. To have disabused philosophy of this confusion is one of the many services owed by mankind to Greek philosophers. The distinction of sense and reason soon dawned on the Greeks, and with it the discovery that the object of sense is not the external thing at a distance from ourselves, but some sort of result on our senses, from which the external thing is inferred by reason. In short, the Greek philosophers founded the representative theory of sensitive perception. But they did not agree about the nature of the sensible object, or representative of the external thing impressed on the senses. Without pretending to give a history of their views, we may distinguish two great epochs: the first, that in which the sensible object was regarded as a corporeal effect; the second, that in which it began to be regarded as an incorporeal essence in our senses.   In this second epoch the Greeks prepared the way for the theory that the sensible object is an incorporeal idea.   But they never actually reached the idealistic theory.

The first approach to a scientific theory of the objects of knowledge is to be found in the Atomists, Leucippus and Democritus of Abdera, the pioneers of a sound philosophy of nature.   To them we owe the dawn of the truth, afterwards developed into the distinction of primary and secondary qualities, that the real and original qualities of particles are figure, position and arrangement, whose different combinations, together with motion, give rise to qualities, such as heat and colour, which, though really derivative, appear equally original to our senses.

The manner, however, in which this important doctrine was presented to the world was not purely unexceptionable.   The Atomists, it is true, admitted that there is for every variety of sensible quality a distinct mode, or schema in their language, of the original qualities; for example, a sharp taste arises from angular, a sweet from round schemata.   But, to say nothing of their crude speculations on corpuscular structure and motion, they fell into the fallacy of confusing the derivative quality with its sensible effect in the famous dictum, ‘Conventionally there is sweet, conventionally bitter, conventionally hot, conventionally cold, conventionally colour; but really atoms and void.’[1]   From this Atomistic identification of secondary qualities with their sensible effects, assisted by the Heraclitean identity of contraries, it was but a short step to the sceptical theory of Protagoras, that all qualities are merely the

[1] Sext. Emp. Adv. Math. vii. 135.

appearances in our senses, without any correspondents in the fluent matter of nature.

The Atomists did not recognise sufficiently, the Sceptics not at all, the fact that derivative or secondary qualities are qualities of external things. There is also a common tendency in modern mental philosophy to identify secondary qualities with their sensible manifestations. But for every sensible quality, which is the product of an external object, there is a distinct quality in the external object. A primary quality is also like the sensible quality. A secondary quality, such as heat or colour, is not, indeed, like the sensible effect, being a mode of a primary quality, such as motion; but it is a distinct and specific variety of that primary quality; it is the motion of a different kind of matter, it goes on independently of the sensible effect, and it is a knowable object of science. Thus, it has been discovered in natural philosophy that heat and light are not molar but molecular motions, that they are motions of aether; that they are, *in rerum naturâ*, different motions of different lengths, the waves of mere heat being longer than those of light, and that they are so disseminated throughout the universe as to produce no sensible effect incalculably oftener than they excite touch or vision.

It was perceived by the genius of Bacon that heat is of two kinds, *in ordine ad universum* and *in ordine ad sensum*, the former being an insensible mode of corpuscular motion, the latter the same thing but with a relation such as is competent to sense.[1] The Atomists were too narrow in confining heat to the sensible effect of a distinct mode of matter in the external world, and Protagoras quite wrong in denying the distinctness of

[1] Bacon, *Nov. Org.* ii. 20.

the external quality ; Bacon was right in regarding heat
as a mode of motion in the external world, as well
as a sensible quality in our senses. So with all other
secondary qualities ; they are modes of primary qualities,
but distinct modes ; they have a generic resemblance to
other modes, but they have also specific differences.
Sound is a vibration of air, heat and light undulations
of æther.

The only plausible objection to this view would be
that the names 'heat,' 'light,' and so on, should be
confined to the sensible effects and not extended to
their external causes. It must be confessed, also,
that so long as distinctions of things are observed,
the use of names is comparatively unimportant. But
names are the vehicles of distinct ideas, and it is the
duty of every science to have some distinct name for
every real distinction of things. The specific modes
of primary qualities must receive some name or other.
It will not suffice to leave the external cause of sensible
sound to the periphrasis, vibratory motion among the
particles of an elastic aerial medium ; or that of light to the
periphrasis, undulations in an æthereal medium per-
vading interstellar spaces and bodies formed of ponder-
able matter. New names might be invented, but they are
not forthcoming, and it is doubtful whether they would
be superior to, and still more doubtful whether they
would be victorious over, the old names, 'sound' and
' light.'

Secondary qualities are real, though derivative,
qualities of external objects, as well as qualities of
sensible objects ; and their names should be equally
extensive. In support of this view, let us quote a
passage from Professor Stokes, ' On the Beneficial Effects
of Light,' all the more valuable because it was not

written to support any general philosophy of secondary qualities : —

' Beyond both ends of the visible spectrum there lie radiations which do not affect the eye, but are nevertheless, as we have every reason to believe, of the same physical nature as those which do, from which they do not differ by any inherent quality. As the agent which excites vision has been called from time immemorial " light," or whatever may be the corresponding term in other languages, it will be convenient to use the same word to designate the agent considered in itself, and irrespectively of its capacity for exciting vision, a capacity which would be regarded as a mere accident of light. in the technical logical sense of that word. Accordingly I shall now use the word "light" to designate what, for want of a better term, I have just been calling "radiation," a word which would more properly denote the process of radiation than the thing radiated, be it the material or immaterial, be it matter or undulations ' (p. 6).

Qualities, then, as distinguished by natural philosophy, are divided as follows :—

I. External, *in ordine ad universum.*

    1. Primary, original qualities; *e.g.* duration, extension, motion.

    2. Secondary, specific modes of primary qualities; *e.g.* sound, heat, light, as modes of motion.

II. Internal, *in ordine ad sensum.*

    1. Primary, and like external primary qualities, which cause them.

    2. Secondary, unlike external secondary qualities, which cause them.

It is to be noticed, in this division, that the derivative character of secondary qualities refers not to their sensible but to their external aspect. As sensible, we apprehend them in exactly the same way. Again, the ordinary man infers external qualities alike in both cases. The difference entirely arises when the scientific man begins to infer that external secondary are modes of primary qualities, because their sensible effects are so similar to those of primary qualities; for instance, that the effects of external sound, heat and light are the effects of motion by the laws of motion.

To the Atomists is due, not only the foundation of the theory of primary and secondary qualities, but also the discovery that the object of sense is not the external thing itself, but an effect produced by the external thing on the senses. They supposed that effluxes, continually thrown off from bodies, come into contact with our organs.[1] They thus anticipated modern physical inquiry on the senses, although their necessary ignorance of the laws of motion prevented them from realising the vibrations and undulations, which have taken the place of emissions, in the case of hearing, sight, and the perception of temperature by touch. The consequence of this supposition to the theory of knowledge in Greek philosophy was that its immediate object was henceforward generally agreed to be not the thing at a distance, but a result of the thing on the organs of sense.

In the Atomistic theory the immediate object of sense, though internal and representative, is neither immaterial nor psychical: it is a physical object. This point has never been disproved. Modern physiology, as we have seen, has brought the motions of matter as far

---

[1] Arist. *De Divin. per Somn.* 2 = 464 A 6 (Berlin ed.); cf. Plut. *De Plac. Phil.* iv. 8.

as the physical substances of the nerves; but it has never shown that this physical object is converted into a psychical sensation, either at the extremities of the nerves, or in the nervous fibres, or in the nerve centres, or in the brain itself, or beyond it. Why, then, should we not perceive the physical effect in our internal organs?

The physical character of the immediate object of sensible knowledge was not at first forgotten. It survived in the Epicurean philosophy. It even left a relic in the philosophy of Plato, who always represents sensation as a motion communicated from matter through body to soul.[1] Hence sense never appears in any Platonic dialogue as a part of the soul, nor the sensible object as something purely psychical. It is not in his theory of sense, but of reason, that Plato becomes idealistic. The objects of sense are, according to him, results of material motion communicated from body to soul; the objects of rational knowledge are results communicated from immaterial 'forms' to the pure soul.

Aristotle was the author of a new theory of the sensible object. He had an aversion to atomism, perhaps because he confused it with materialism. For atoms he substituted primary matter; instead of figure, position, and arrangement, he regarded heat and cold, dry and liquid, as its primary contrarieties.[2] The Atomists considered the external thing to be wholly corporeal; Aristotle divided it into two heterogeneous substances —corporeal matter and incorporeal form[3]—the former of which was different for each individual, the latter the same for all individuals of one kind. While the Atomists had held that the sensible object which results from the

---

[1] Plato. *Phil.* 34 A ; *Tim.* 42 A, 64. [2] Arist. *De Gen. et Corr.* ii. 1.
[3] Id. *Met.* Z 7 - 1032 B 14.

external thing is a corporeal efflux, Aristotle persuaded
himself and his followers that it is the identical incorporeal form transferred without the different corporeal
matter from the external thing into the sensitive faculty,
as an impression is transferred without the metal from
a metallic seal into wax.[1] For example, vision, according to him, receives the essence of white without the
matter of the external wax into the visual faculty.
Hence his distinction of nutrition and sensation : in
nutrition we receive the whole thing. in sense the form
without the matter of the thing. He agreed, indeed,
with his predecessors in the fundamental point that the
external thing is not presented, but that the sensible
object presented is a representative result of the external
thing. But this object in our senses, which, according
to the Atomists, was a corporeal efflux, was, according
to Aristotle, an incorporeal form, called by himself
αἰσθητὸν εἶδος, and by his scholastic followers, *species
sensibilis.* From his time onwards, the object of sense
began to be usually regarded as not only internal, but
also incorporeal, though not yet as a purely psychical
object.

Aristotle's new theory of the object and nature of
sensitive perception is charged with errors. He substituted for the explanation of the world by particles, the
abstractions of matter and form ; he inverted the real
order of primary and secondary by making heat and
cold original qualities ; he arbitrarily severed a single
corporeal thing into a corporeal and an incorporeal half,
and by this latter figment endeavoured to explain the
object of sense. We see here the beginning of the false
hypothesis that the object of sense is not a corporeal
fact. Aristotle was right in thinking that sense does

---

[1] Arist. *De An.* ii. 12.

not perceive the external thing, wrong in thinking that
what it perceives within is an incorporeal form.

Hamilton has misunderstood these Aristotelian errors.[1]
He says truly enough that Aristotle distinguishes proper
from common objects of sense,[2] and that the former
agree with the secondary, the latter with primary qualities. But he misses the real point by supposing that
Aristotle meant to derive the former from the latter.
Aristotle distinguished proper and common sensibles
solely in relation to the senses which perceive them.
Heat and cold, for example, are proper sensible objects
of touch: but so far from being regarded by Aristotle
as secondary qualities, they form one pair of his primary
contrarieties of matter. The classification into common
and proper is not intended by Aristotle for a classification into primary and secondary; so far from it, his
primary qualities are falsely taken from what are really
secondary qualities, heat and cold, dry and moist.

Secondly, Hamilton rightly says that Aristotle calls
such qualities as heat and cold affective qualities, because they produce affections in us.[3] But we must not
therefore infer that he meant either that they produce
this effect through insensible primary qualities, or that
they are themselves mere affections in us, or that, being
qualities outside, the affections are not like them. These
are opinions of people who hold an atomistic theory
of primary and secondary qualities, but they are not
Aristotelian. In fact, the most fundamental defect in
Aristotle's natural philosophy is the supposition that
heat and cold are primary contrarieties of matter incapable of further resolution. His opinion was that

---

[1] See Reid's Works, ed. by Hamilton, Note D, on Primary and
Secondary Qualities.

[2] Arist. De An. ii. 6.   [3] Id. Cat. 8 = 9 A 28 seq.

heat and cold are real and original qualities of matter, derived from no others, and that they produce in us affections of heat and cold similar to themselves. This, moreover, was his theory of the perception of all qualities.

Thirdly, Hamilton is right in saying that, according to Aristotle, there is an identity between the external object and the object perceived.[1] But he is wrong in inferring from this identification that, according to Aristotle, the external object is presentatively perceived without any intermediate object. The identity is not of existence but of essence, not numerical but specific, not *numero* but *specie*. Aristotle supposed that in all members of a kind there is one form, and that, when one member of a kind produces another member, it propagates the form, or, as we say to this day in organisms, the species, from its own matter to the matter of the new recipient of the form or species. Thus he supposed man to beget man.[2] Hence, in sensible knowledge, he supposed that the external object propagates the form of the sensible quality, such as heat, without its own matter into the matter of the sense, which thus receives the form or species of heat into its own matter without receiving the matter of the body which propagates the heat. Therefore the hot body and the hot affection of sense are the same only as the impression on the seal is the same as the impression on the wax, or as the father is the same as the son; that is, the same in form or essence, not in matter or existence, the same *specie* but different *numero*, like but not the same objects.

According to Aristotle, then, the sensible object is not numerically identical with the sensible object, but

---

[1] Arist. *De An.* iii. 2   425 B 25 7.
[2] Id. *Met.* Z 7 8, esp. 1033 B 29 1034 A 8.

only identical in essence. It is the form or species, without the matter of the external object, propagated into the senses. Aristotle was no intuitive realist. He held, indeed, that sense perceives the identical essence of the external thing, but not the external thing itself; and he held that it receives this essence into the sensitive faculty, and does not apprehend it in the external world. In short, his theory was a new form of representation, in which the object of sense was regarded no longer as a corporeal efflux, but as an incorporeal essence received without the corporeal matter from a corporeal object into the senses, and there perceived.

As the objects of sensible knowledge are sensible species, so the objects of rational knowledge are intelligible species, according to Aristotle. The difference is in the mode of production. The former are propagated by external objects into the sensitive faculty, the latter by active intelligence into passive intelligence. Aristotle has not explained this mysterious influence of intelligence on intelligence in the same soul; nor is it probable that he proceeded on any other fact than the consciousness that, while we depend on externals to perceive, we can command our own thoughts. It would be, however, useless to go into this question. The important point for our present purpose is that both sensible and intelligible species are, in the view of Aristotle, immaterial, not material, objects. In his philosophy, for the first time, we come to the view that all the immediate objects of knowledge are immaterial facts.

We must not therefore fly to the supposition that Aristotle thought them to be psychical because they were immaterial. We have not yet exhausted the mysteries of the Aristotelian form. A form is supposed by him to be not only one in connection with many

matters of different members of the same kind, but also
to be something different from matter, even when so
closely conjoined with matter in fact, and so inseparable
from it in definition, as concavity with nose in snubnose,
and soul with body in an animal. Every form, the form
of a triangle, the form of a stone, the form of a house,
is an immaterial substance, even when conjoined with
matter in a material substance.   The form of God Himself is pure, not in the sense of being less material than
other forms, but only in the sense of never being conjoined with matter.   Hence, sensible and intelligible
species or forms are immaterial, not because they are
in the soul, but simply because all forms are immaterial,
according to Aristotle, who thought that if I perceive a white paper, I receive from the paper into my
sensitive faculty an identical essence of white, which
was already incorporeal in the paper before it was communicated to the sensitive faculty of my soul.   The
object of sense, then, had, in his philosophy, ceased to
be material, but had not yet become a psychical fact :
it is an essence, which is not matter, whether it is
without or within a soul.

Descartes completed the separation of the sensible
object from the external world.   The Atomists had
taken the first step by discovering that the object of
sense is not the external thing, but an internal effect ;
but they admitted that it is, like its external cause,
purely physical, and no more has been proved to this
very day.   Aristotle, however, had proceeded to apply
the hypothesis of incorporeal forms to sense, and supposed that the object of sense is a sensible species,
similar to the physical cause in identical incorporeal
essence, but not in diverse corporeal matter.   It remained
for Descartes to take the final step and destroy the last

vestige of resemblance to the physical cause by identifying the object of sense with a psychical idea.

The history of philosophy had insensibly led, or
rather misled, Descartes into his ideal theory. In the
philosophy of Aristotle the incorporeal is wider than
the psychical, because all essences are incorporeal even
in physical things. But in the interval between ancient
and modern philosophy, the hypothesis of the incor-
porealism of essences was discredited, partly by the
attacks of Nominalism, but more successfully by the
revival of natural philosophy, and especially by the
return to Atomism, inaugurated by Bacon, from whom
it passed to Descartes. Bacon discovered that the
essence of anything physical is nothing but a uniform
mode of its matter.[1] Descartes thought that it is only
a psychical idea.[2] In these circumstances his hypothesis of the sensible object developed itself, as it
were, from the course of history. The sensible object
had been identified by Aristotle with the incorporeal
essence; the incorporeal had been recently expunged
by Bacon from the physical world; the essence was
limited by Descartes himself to the psychical idea.
What more natural than to regard the sensible object
also as a psychical idea?

Descartes, it is true, went back to the Atomists
for the analysis of nature into corpuscles. He might
also, especially since Galen's discoveries in the nervous
system, have restored the Atomistic theory that the
object of sense is a physical effect on our organs, and
have added that it is an effect on the nervous system.
His writings do, indeed, show that he was not always
certain whether the sensible effect is physical or psychical. Sometimes he even seems almost to express

----

[1] *Nov. Org.* i. 51; ii. 17, 20, 52.   [2] *Princ.* i. 58.

himself as if the idea itself were not distinct from the
nervous imprint. But he finally and deliberately separated it from the physical effect in the brain in his
Replies to the Objections raised against his . Meditations. The 'Responsio ad Secundas Objectiones' contains a synthetic statement of reasons for the existence of God, arranged in geometrical order, and the
second definition is a formal definition of the idea, as
follows :—

'By the name, Idea, I understand that form of any
thought, by whose immediate perception I am conscious
of that same thought; so that I can express nothing
in words in understanding that which I say, but that
from this very fact it is certain there is in me an idea
of that which is signified by those words.   And so
it is not only the images depicted in the fancy that I
call ideas: nay, these I here by no means call ideas,
so far as they are depicted in the corporeal fancy,
that is, in some part of the brain, but only so far as
they inform the mind itself turned towards that part
of the brain.'

The influence of Descartes did not at once make
itself felt in all parts of philosophy. English natural
philosophy in this as in other matters took an independent course, which accounts for one finding Aristotle's
theory of the sensible object surviving in Newton's
Optics. In Quæst. 20 Newton asks : 'Annon sensorium
animalium est locus cui substantia sentiens adest, et
in quem sensibiles rerum species per nervos et cerebrum
deferuntur. ut ibi praesentes a praesente sentiri possint ?'
Similarly English theology did not at first think it
necessary to salvation to consider sensible objects, or
sensation, or even consciousness itself, to be psychical, as we may see from the following passage in

'Tritheism charged upon Dr. Sherlock's new Notion of the Trinity,' by a Divine of the Church of England[1]:—

'I deny that there is any such thing as sensation, whether internal or external, belonging to spirits not vitally united to organised bodies. For sensation is properly the perception of a sensible object by a sensible species of it imprinted upon and received into the proper organ by which each sensitive faculty operates and exerts itself. This, I say, is sensation, and accordingly, as it is external or internal, so it has external or internal organs allotted to it; but still both of them corporeal. And therefore for this man to talk of spiritual sensation is nonsense and a contradiction in the terms, and consequently not to be allowed' (p. 15).

But mental philosophers, not only on the Continent but also in England, more quickly received the hypothesis of a psychical object of sense. At first, Locke simply accepted the Cartesian 'idea.' Then Hume distinguished the 'impression' from the idea. Kant made 'phænomenon' the fashionable term. Mill preferred 'sensation.' But all agree in some psychical object or other. Moreover, mental physiologists have passed over from Aristotle and Newton to Descartes, when they ought rather to have retraced their steps from Newton through Aristotle to the Atomists. The Cartesian hypothesis, that the object of sense is a purely psychical idea, is not so near the truth as Aristotle's hypothesis, that it is an incorporeal but not psychical species in the sensitive faculty; nor is the Aristotelian so near as the Atomistic hypothesis, that it is a purely physical effect on the bodily organs. All that is required to make this last, or rather this first, the truth is to substitute

[1] Dr. South.

for effluxes mechanical motions, and for the bodily organs the nervous system sensibly affected.

'Meanwhile,' says Bacon, 'let nobody expect great progress in the sciences (especially on their productive side) unless natural philosophy has been extended to the special sciences, and the special sciences reduced to natural philosophy. Hence it happens that astronomy, optics, music, most of the mechanical arts, and (what may seem more strange) moral and political philosophy, and the logical sciences, have little or no extent in depth, but only slide over the surface and variety of things: because, as soon as those special sciences have been divided and established, they are no longer nourished by natural philosophy; which, from the sources and true contemplations of the motions, rays, sounds, texture, and structure of bodies, affections, and intellectual apprehensions, had been able to impart to them new force and increase. It is not at all wonderful, if sciences do not grow, when they have been separated from their roots.'[1] The revival of Atomism by Bacon, together with the gradual establishment of the laws of motion in mechanics, from Galileo to Newton, produced an instauration of natural philosophy. Let us now, in the same spirit, return to natural philosophy, in order to restore mental philosophy. 'Interitus rei arcetur per reductionem ejus ad principia.'

[1] Bacon, Nov. Org. i. 80.

PART II.

PSYCHOLOGICAL IDEALISM.

'*Pessimum enim omnium est augurium quod ex Consensu capitur in rebus Intellectualibus.*'

BACON, *Nov. Org.* i. 77.

u 2

CHAPTER V.

DESCARTES.

PHILOSOPHY ought to begin in doubt. But I cannot doubt that I think. *Cogito, ergo sum.* As a thinking being, I am a soul, distinct from the body. Soul is thinking substance; body is extended substance; they are heterogeneous to each other. The soul immediately apprehends ideas, innate, adventitious, and fictitious. The clearness and distinctness of ideas are a criterion of truth, and by the veracity of God, enable me to know objects beyond ideas. Starting from ideas, I infer a physical world of bodies and insensible corpuscles, whose qualities are partly like and partly unlike those which I perceive as sensible ideas, and whose insensible modes produce sensible ideas. These are the cardinal points of Cartesian idealism.

Cogito, ergo sum.—I think, therefore I am. This is the indubitable fact, which Descartes had the undying merit of elevating into a principle in mental philosophy. The proposition was not new. Aristotle asserted our consciousness of our operations,[1] and even recognised this fact as a proof of our existence. But he did not convert the proposition into a psychological principle. He rightly founded the distinctions of operations on the distinctions of their objects: hence his discovery of nearly all that is known in mental philosophy. He

---

[1] *Eth. Nic.* ix. 9, 9.

wrongly neglected the consciousness of the operations about those objects : hence his tendency to dogmatism. Descartes supplied a defect in psychology when he discovered the necessity of using as a principle the consciousness which says to each of us : 'I think; that is, I feel, perceive, remember, imagine, judge, reason, desire, will : I therefore am.'

It is a principle. Is it the only principle of psychology ? How far will this conscious fact, that I am, carry me ? I am conscious that I am a thinking subject. But two further questions immediately present themselves : what am I, and what do I apprehend ? What is the thinking subject, and what the apprehended object ? Now the mere consciousness that I think will not of itself solve the nature of either subject or object. The new principle of thinking was no more fitted than the old principle of contradiction to be a universal source of all philosophy : it must be accepted, without pledging us to all the Cartesian deductions.

What is the thinking subject ? What am I ? This terrific question is answered by Descartes, as if it immediately followed from the principle, I think therefore I am, but really by another argument. He cannot say, I am conscious that I now think, as soul, without a body. He therefore substitutes the hypothesis, I can suppose that I had no body and was still thinking. He then concludes that I, as thinking subject, am not body but soul. Thus, by an easy transition, he leads his readers from thinking subject to soul, and makes, not the original principle, but an hypothesis and a problematic conclusion the real premises of his philosophy.

In order that we may feel the weakness of this *non sequitur*, let us quote from the 'Discussion on Method,' Part IV., the passage which immediately follows the

enunciation of the principle, I think therefore I
am :—

'In the next place, I attentively examined what I
was, and as I observed that I could suppose that I had
no body, and that there was no world nor any place in
which I might be ; but that I could not therefore suppose that I was not; and that, on the contrary, from
the very circumstance that I thought to doubt of the
truth of other things, it most clearly and certainly followed that I was ; while, on the other hand, if I had
only ceased to think, although all the other objects
which I had ever imagined had been in reality existent,
I would have had no reason to believe that I existed ; I
thence concluded that I was a substance whose whole
essence or nature consists only in thinking, and which,
that it may exist, has need of no place, nor is dependent
on any material thing ; so that " I," that is to say, the
mind by which I am what I am, is plainly distinct from
the body, and is even more easily known than the
latter, and is such, that although the latter were not, it
would still continue to be all that it is.'

'I could suppose I had no body.' What is the
nature of this proposition ? It is an hypothesis of what
might be but is not. I am not conscious that I have no
body ; I am at best only conscious of the supposition,
which does not become any less a supposition through
my being conscious of making it. Nor is it deduced
from the consciousness that I think, but is a separate
hypothesis. Again, how do we get to the proposition,
I am a thinking substance wholly distinct from the
body ? It is a conclusion not from the original principle
alone, but also from the subsequent hypothesis, requiring
also a second hypothesis, that without a body I should
still be thinking.

We must, therefore, most carefully distinguish the original principle, *cogito, ergo sum*, from the subsequent conclusion, I am a soul. In the first place, I am conscious of the former, not of the latter. I am conscious that I am a thinking subject: I am not conscious that this thinking subject is not body but soul. Secondly, in order to deduce the conclusion, the principle requires the intervention of two hypotheses—that I could have no body and that I should still be thinking; and in both cases I am conscious of making the suppositions, but not conscious of the facts that I have no body and am still thinking. But *sectetur partem conclusio deteriorem.* An hypothetical premise produces an hypothetical conclusion. The conclusion, then, that the thinking subject is not body but soul, has not the certainty of the principle, *cogito, ergo sum*, but is vitiated by the hypotheses combined with it. Thus does Descartes lead his reader to confuse the thinker and the soul, and transfer the conscious certainty of being *res cogitans* to the hypothesis of being *res a corpore plane distincta.*

That I am a thinking subject is a fact of consciousness; but what I am, as thinking subject, is a matter of argument. There are three possible alternatives: the body, the soul, the man. Nor can we decide between these three alternatives by consciousness alone. Consciousness, without hypothesis, never made a philosopher either a materialist or a spiritualist. We must not make a fetish of consciousness, but interrogate it carefully, remember its superficiality, add to it observation, and combine both with reasoning.

In discussions of this kind a false issue is generally raised at once by speaking of the consciousness of thoughts. This is an abstraction, useful indeed for some purposes, but still an abstraction, or rather a double abstraction. There is no such a thing as consciousness, and no such a thing as a thought; I am conscious, and I am conscious that I think. Consciousness and thought are not there, waiting for a subject; they already have a subject, or rather subjects—myself, yourself, every other thinker. Descartes, in a great measure at all events, avoided this fallacy of hypostasising abstractions. He was aware that there is no consciousness of thoughts, but I am conscious that I think. He surreptitiously changed the thinker into soul, but not into abstract thoughts. Those modern philosophers who suppose consciousness of thoughts are not votaries of consciousness, but victims of abstraction.

I am, then, not thoughts, but a thinker or thinking subject. But what is this subject which thinks? What part of me is the factor, or what parts are the factors of thinking? In this mortal state, in which I cannot apprehend myself without my body, I am not conscious that I think without my body. Nay, I am conscious that I think with my body. Whatever operation I take, I invariably find that I am conscious, not of the operation, which I may afterwards abstract, but of myself performing it; I am not conscious that I perform it by my soul without my body, because, though I am conscious that I am a thinking subject, I am not conscious that this is a soul; nor am I conscious that I do it by my body without my soul, for reasons to follow presently. I am conscious that I perform every operation by my body, partly, somehow, and somewhere. I consciously feel pleased and pained in various parts of my body. I cannot disengage my consciousness of toothache from my mouth, or of headache from my head. I am conscious of using my bodily senses in touch, taste, vision, hearing, and smell. I do not consciously first feel the sensation and then refer it to the bodily member; I am not conscious of these two steps. Reasoning is the highest kind of thinking; I am conscious of doing it in my head, and by no force of abstraction can I get it out of my head. Similarly I am conscious that I will in my head, and I am conscious that my head may ache with reasoning, and deliberating, and resolving. My body is not a mere companion but a conscious partner of all my thoughts.

But consciousness is a superficial power. In speaking of the data of sense I remarked that by an illusion, arising from the confusion of sense and inference, we cannot help seeming to be conscious that sense perceives an external object, though we can make ourselves independent of the illusion by science, which distinguishes the external from the sensible. There is a similar illusion about our consciousness of the thinking subject, and fortunately we can explain it and conquer it by science. The illusion is that we perform some of our operations on the surfaces by the superficial members of our bodies. The causes of the illusion are that we often observe the outer surfaces of our bodies when we are performing an internal operation, and we are at the same time unconscious of the inner structures and motions of our nerves and brain. The way to make ourselves conquer the illusion is by the study of science, which shows that what performs the operation is not the outer surface but the inner nervous system. For example, we are conscious that we see something red somehow by our bodily organs of sight. Now, though we are sensible of the optic nerve so far as it is sensibly affected with red, we are neither sensible nor conscious of it as nervously constituted. But from very early infancy we observe, i.e. directly infer from sensation,

the surfaces of our bodies. By putting our hands on
our eyes we find that they no longer see red, and we
infer that it was our eyes that saw red. It is so with
all our external senses, as they are called from this
illusion of observation. Not consciousness, but observation from very early infancy, made us believe that it
was the periphery that is sensitive. But the inference
became automatic before we were attentively conscious,
and we cannot help seeming to be conscious that our
eyes see. Really, however, as science discovers at last,
the eyes are but avenues to vision, and what sees is not
our eyes but the optic nerve in connection with the
brain. A more complicated instance is when a person
who has lost a limb believes that the pain, which he
really feels in the nerves, is still in the limb. His consciousness told him but vaguely where he feels the pain,
his observations connected it with the surface of the
limb; hence the illusion. Science alone can conquer
such illusions of observation.

The rough-and-ready way of dealing with this evidence is to draw the further inference that we do not
localise any operation except by observation and anatomy, and that consciousness has nothing to do with the
body. But this inference goes far beyond the facts.
Observation is limited to the surface of the body, but
the operations, of which we are conscious, are not.
Now, even when they are purely internal, we are still
conscious that they are somehow performed by the
body, without observation and before science. For
example, we are conscious of the pangs of hunger in
the region of the stomach, to descend to the depths of
consciousness: to rise to its summit, we are conscious
of the process of reasoning in the region of the head.
But in neither case does observation of the surface of

the body reveal the whereabouts of the operation: yet we are conscious of the body performing it, without waiting for science.

But there is another defect, for which the conscious-ness of the body as a factor in thinking is responsible. It tells me very indefinitely what part is engaged in a particular operation. The cause of this indefiniteness is the unconsciousness of nervous structure and motion. The correction of it is the science of nervous structure and motion. Thus, confining ourselves entirely to in-ternal operations, the locality of which is not accessible to external observation, I am conscious of the pain of hunger somewhere in the region of the stomach; science reduces this indefinite verdict to definiteness by proving the connection of the nerves of that region with the brain. Consciousness again says indefinitely, 'I think in my head'; science tells me, 'Yes, in your brain.'

Here science only corrects consciousness: it does not contradict it. Consciousness apprehends the indefinite region at work, science discovers the definite nervous structure in the direction of that region. Secondly, unless consciousness apprehended the region, science could not assign the nervous structure; if we were not already conscious of reasoning in the head, anatomy would not convince us that we reason in the brain. Thirdly, sometimes consciousness apprehends the region without science having yet discovered the nervous structure; for example, we are conscious, in what is inadequately called muscular sense, not indeed of mus-cular motion but of the action of our limbs, though but vaguely and indefinitely; but on this occasion science is still more vague and indefinite, having dis-covered the nervous mechanism of muscular motion, but not of muscular sense. Finally, however wrong

consciousness may be in the definite locality of a particular operation, science never disproves that we are
conscious of its being performed somewhere in the
body. I am conscious that I perform all my operations
somehow or another, partly by the body, with more or
less definiteness ; science discovers the definite locality,
still within the body.

There are two points, which sometimes appear in
biological treatises, but are not proved. In the first
place, as we have already seen, there is no biological
proof that cerebral motion is transmuted into a psychical sensation. Secondly, biologists often distinguish
a sensation from its localisation ; at the same time they
sometimes confuse its localisation in the body with the
inference of its external cause. There is a great difference between a sensation of an internal sensible object
and the inference of its external cause, as we have
already seen in this essay. But there is no difference
between the sensation and its internal localisation in
the sentient subject ; there is no proof of these two
steps. I am conscious of the sensation in a locality of
my body. Neither consciousness nor science proves
that I first have a sensation, then localise it in my
body, and, thirdly, infer its external cause. They prove
together that I first have a sensation located in some
part of my body, and then infer the external cause
which produces it.

There is another point, which is proved in biology,
but does not disprove the consciousness of the body as
a factor in thinking. I refer to subjective sensations.
We have sensations similar to our ordinary sensations,
but not produced by the ordinary external cause. Thus,
a prize-fighter may be made by a blow to see stars ; a
drunkard under the influence of delirium tremens may

have a vision of the devil. Such sensations are excellent instances to show that the sensible object is different from the external original, and is not always caused by it; that there are internal causes of sensations in the nerves; and that the superficial structure of the eye is a cause, not a subject, of vision. But they do not show that the soul is the sole subject of vision. A prize-fighter seeing stars, a drunkard's vision of the devil, are odd proofs of psychical sensations. The term 'subjective' sensations is misleading, because, in the recent sense of the word, it suggests 'psychical,' without proving it.

There is no evidence that sensation, or any other operation, is purely psychical. There is evidence that the body is a factor in all thinking. It is the evidence of consciousness, interpreted by science. I am not conscious first of a sensation, and then of its localisation. I am conscious that I feel, perceive, reason, will, partly by my body. External observation connects some of these operations with the surface of the body. Science shows that I do all of them by my nervous system. Science dispels the illusion of observation, and corrects the indefiniteness of consciousness. Science further traces the continuity of the nervous system, and leaves no gap for purely psychical operations. Now, ordinary and scientific observation being limited to the body, if I were only conscious of mere thinking, I should know my body only as an unthinking cause. But when I cannot be conscious that I perform any operation without being conscious that I perform it somehow in my body, that I feel headache, that I use my bodily senses to see, touch, hear, and so on, and that I reason in my head, scientific observation becomes an interpreter of my consciousness that I use my body to think,

and shows that the part which I use is the brain in connection with the nervous system. The body is a patent
factor of the thinking subject. The neglect of it is the
fallacy of spiritualism.

It does not follow that the body is the sole factor of
thinking. Man does not know the whole of himself,
either by consciousness or by scientific observation ; the
former is superficial, the latter limited. I am conscious
that I perform my operations partly by my body : science
observes the nervous system, and in combination with
consciousness, infers that the nervous system is that by
which the body in part performs these operations. But
I am not conscious that my body, nor does science
observe that the nervous system, is the whole thinking
subject. There is no operation which can be traced
throughout its whole course. I am conscious that I
use my bodily senses in sensation and my head in
reasoning. Science observes the nervous system and
brain. But it has not solved the problem of nervous
and cerebral motion. If it solved that problem, it would
still remain to prove that nervous motion is completely
identical with the operation of which I am conscious.
It is partly so, because I am conscious of partly performing the operation by the body, in which science observes the nervous system and the motion it performs
during the operation. But it is another thing to prove
that the conscious operation and the nervous motion
are completely identical, because I am conscious of the
operation without observing it, and science observes
the motion without being conscious of it. This difference of evidence does not, indeed, prove a complete
difference, because nervous motion and conscious operation may be the same fact approached from different
sides, but the very difference of evidence makes it diffi-

cult to prove a complete identity of fact. Another
evidence might be evoked—the method of explanation.
If all the facts of conscious operations were known, and
nervous motions were known, it might be urged that
the former are explicable by the latter, as the facts of
light are explicable by undulating motion. But there
is a great difference in the two cases. In the case of
light, we can say that its facts are such as the known
effects of undulation by the laws of motion. But the
operations, of which we are conscious, do not seem to
consciousness to be the kind of effects produced by any
known motion according to any known laws of motion.
There is a latent factor in all thinking, the soul. The
neglect of it is the defect of materialism.

Two opposite errors must be avoided, spiritualism
and materialism. The former neglects the patent, the
latter the latent, factor of the thinking subject. The
former despises the consciousness of the body as a factor,
and the science of the nervous system as the part of
that factor, engaged in every conscious operation : the
latter transgresses the limits of science. Hence the
former falsely supposes the subject to be all soul, the
latter all body. Both neglect the man ; yet as men we
think. There is room for an intermediate theory of the
thinking subject ; for a theory which is founded on the
combined evidence of consciousness, of observation,
ordinary and scientific, and of reasoning about oneself ;
for a theory which avoids the opposite difficulties of
disturbing the physical continuity of the nervous system,
and of inventing a mere parallelism of neurosis and
psychosis. I suppose that brain and soul are co-opera-
tive factors in all conscious operations, in passive operations together affected by external causes, in active
operations together producing external effects. The

thinking subject is man, thinking partly by his body, that is, his nervous cerebral system, and partly by a latent factor, his soul, co-operating, as by the composition of forces, in every operation.

But what are the objects which I apprehend in thinking? This is the second question, suggested by the consciousness that I think, but not answerable without further argument. Descartes assumed that all the immediate objects are psychical ideas, while physical things are only mediate objects known through the medium of ideas. So far as this theory recognises the distinction between the internal objects of sense and external objects of inference, it is correct, and in accordance with the scientific evidences already given in the First Part of this essay. But it contains a further supposition, namely, that objects of sense and all other immediate objects are not only internal but psychical, are ideas. Descartes never proved this ideal theory.

In the Third Meditation we find the following passage :—

‘ Nevertheless I before received and admitted many things as wholly certain and manifest, which yet I afterwards found to be doubtful. What, then, were those? They were the earth, the sky, the stars, and all the other objects which I was in the habit of perceiving by the senses. But what was it that I clearly (and distinctly) perceived in them? Nothing more than that the ideas and the thoughts of those objects were presented to my mind. And even now I do not deny that these ideas are found in my mind. But there was yet another thing which I affirmed, and which, from having been accustomed to believe it, I thought I clearly perceived, although, in truth, I did not perceive it at all; I mean the existence of objects external to me, from which

I

those ideas proceeded, and to which they had a perfect resemblance ; and it was here I was mistaken, or if I judged correctly, this assuredly was not to be traced to any knowledge I possessed.' [1]

Now Descartes does not state precisely how he arrived at this conclusion that what he perceived were ideas. No doubt he was unconsciously influenced by the previous course of philosophy, detailed in my last chapter, and thought himself entitled to accept the conclusion much more rapidly than he ought. But he probably also thought that it followed in some way from the principle, *cogito*—from the consciousness, I think. Now it is true that I think includes the consciousness, I sensitively perceive. But I am not conscious that my senses apprehend ideas. As I walk in the fields, I am conscious of perceiving something green, which, so far from being an idea or any psychical fact, appears to be not only physical but also external. Science disabuses me of the externality, but not of the materiality of the sensible object. What further evidence, then, had Descartes to disprove its physical and prove its psychical character?

Descartes derived his ideal theory of the sensible object apparently from his principle, *cogito, ergo sum*, but really from his secondary hypothesis, ' I am a soul.' Having convinced himself that the whole subject is soul, he defined soul as a purely thinking substance, and body as a purely extended substance. From these definitions he deduced the heterogeneity of mind and matter, of soul and body. Hence he thought it would follow that the soul by its very essence thinking cannot apprehend body by its very essence extended, but is limited to its ideas. The real Cartesian evidence is this :

[1] ' Ex vi meæ perceptionis,' in the Latin edition.

the subject is soul, the soul is such as to apprehend only ideas; therefore all immediate objects are ideas. But neither premise is proved.

It is not true that the whole subject is the soul. Descartes, as we have seen, exaggerated the soul from a part to the whole thinking subject. The man is the whole subject : the body is part of that by which he thinks; and, being a factor in thinking as well as extended, it is not a purely extended substance. The assumption at the bottom of the Cartesian definition of body is that thinking and extension are different. So they are in the abstract; but the same thing may possess both attributes in the concrete. Number is not extension, but the same thing is numerable and extended; extension is not thinking, but the same body may be both extended and think. When we appeal from abstractions to consciousness, we find it does think. The body, therefore, is not purely extended substance, but also thinking. Again, the soul is a factor in thinking, and is in other respects latent : it does not follow that it is nothing else. Rather such a supposition is impossible; for, as Locke wittily remarked, men think not always, and if the soul were purely thinking substance, either it must always think in order to be, or it must have an intermittent existence, both of which alternatives are impossible and absurd. Descartes resolved body and soul into the two opposite abstractions of extension and thinking. But he did not thereby prove that body is purely extended, nor that soul is purely thinking, nor their heterogeneity, nor that the body is no factor in thinking, nor that the whole thinking subject is the soul.

But if we concede that the soul is the whole thinking subject, and that thinking is accordingly a purely psychical operation, whether it be feeling, perceiving, reasoning, willing, or what not, what do we know about its nature? On this point we have a dictum of Sir W. Hamilton, so admirable that we cannot pass it by. 'We know,' he says, 'and can know, nothing *a priori* of what is possible or impossible to mind, and it is only by observation and generalisation *a posteriori* that we can ever hope to attain any insight into the question.'[1] The most we know of the soul is that it thinks, whatever else it is; we cannot enter further into its secret nature to determine what it thinks. We must, therefore, judge of it by its fruits. Now, when I appeal to consciousness, I am not conscious of perceiving only ideas, but physical things apparently external; and when I correct the illusion of externality by science, I find that sense perceives internal things, but not ideas; and further, that it must perceive physical things within in order to infer physical things without. I conclude, therefore, that, as we apprehend the physical as a fact, the soul must have a power of apprehending it; for we only know what the soul must by what it does apprehend. It is not true, then, that the soul is such as only to perceive ideas.

Even, therefore, if the first premise of Descartes be true, his second is false, so that his conclusion does not follow. If the soul is the whole thinking subject, it is not true that its nature is such as only to immediately perceive ideas; for all we know of its thinking is that, as a matter of fact, it immediately perceives physical, though internal, effects on the nervous system. Thinking we know is not extension, but know nothing about thinking to prevent it perceiving the extended, nor anything about the psychical to prevent it perceiving the physical. Let vision be purely psychical, white seen can

[1] Hamilton's *Metaphysics*, Lect. xxv. p. 122.

still be physical. Granted, then, that the subject is the
soul, it is a *non sequitur* that it perceives only psychical
ideas.

A fortiori, if the subject is the man, he can perceive
the physical in himself. A certain conditional plausibility is given to the idealistic theory of the sensible
object by the spiritualistic theory of the sentient subject.
Although we cannot say that if the subject is purely
psychical the object is psychical, we can say that the
object is not psychical unless the subject is purely psychical. But if the body is a factor of the thinking subject,
there no longer remains any plausibility in the ideal
theory of the sensible object. The physical can apprehend the physical, the extended the extended, within
the nervous system. The thinking subject, body and
soul, does apprehend the physical: it therefore can.
What we apprehend as a fact is better known than what
we are to apprehend it. Knowable objects must be
explained, not denied, by knowing subjects.

Descartes was a clear and distinct writer; he was
not so clear and distinct a thinker. His works are
full of confusion. He was the first to confuse the
object with the operation of sense. Hence, when he
speaks of an idea of white, we never feel quite sure
whether he means the white perceived or the sensation of white. Now, if the subject is soul, the operation
is purely psychical; and, if the object be undistinguishable from the operation, it also becomes psychical: if
the white perceived is the same as the vision of white,
and this be psychical, that becomes psychical. But we
found in the First Part that the white seen is not the vision
of white, the sensible object is not the operation of sensation. Hence, it does not follow, even if the operation
of vision be psychical, that the white seen is psychical.

A further confusion was necessary before Descartes could call a sensible object an idea. Confusing it with a sensation would only have enabled him to call it a sensation. But why an idea? Because he merged sensation in conception. There are two kinds of simple apprehension : sensation, the apprehension we have of an object when the original is present ; and conception, when the original is absent or non-existent. Aristotle had clearly distinguished them as αἴσθησις and φαντασία, and their objects as αἴσθημα and φάντασμα. But the poverty and abstractness of modern languages and the growth of conceptualism obliterated these distinctions, and enabled Descartes first to confuse the sensible with its sensation, and then the sensation with the conception or idea. Nothing can be more misleading than the word ' idea,' because it may signify either the conception or the concept, to use later phraseology. But Descartes arrived at his theory that the sensible object is an idea by a fusion of sensible object, sensation, conception, and concept.

A final confusion followed the rest. Wherever there is no distinction between object and operation, as in feeling, there is none between the operation and its consciousness. Accordingly, Descartes, having first confused the sensible object with the sensation and then the sensation with the idea, having no object left, confused the operation of sensation with its consciousness.[1] The white, its vision, its idea, its conception, its consciousness became all merged : there was no distinction left between sensible object, sensation, idea, conception, and consciousness. Thus the sensible object historically became a state of consciousness by a series of confusions,

---

[1] Cf. *Princ.* i. 9.

from which mental philosophy has never quite recovered itself.

So much for the evidence of the Cartesian theory that all immediate objects are ideas. He derived it not from the principle, *Cogito, ergo sum*, but from at least four hypotheses :—

(1) The subject is the soul.

(2) The soul is such as to perceive ideas.

(3) The sensible object is undistinguishable from the sensation.

(4) The sensation is undistinguishable from the idea.

Not one of these hypotheses is true ; at any rate, all are uncertain. But if any one of the hypotheses is false, it vitiates the reasoning ; and if any one is uncertain, it renders the reasoning uncertain. The Cartesian method is apparently synthetic demonstration, but really synthetic hypothesis. There is a lesson of psychological method to be derived from it. We cannot logically start with the subject, and from its supposed nature deduce the immediate and mediate objects of knowledge ; but we must first find what objects the subject knows, as a fact, in the sciences, then the immediate objects of sense, and finally conclude that the nature of the subject is such that it can know what it does know. The method must be not synthetical but analytical, because it must proceed from the more certain to the less certain, not from hypotheses to facts, but from facts to hypotheses.

We have not yet, however, exhausted the Cartesian theory of ideas as the immediate objects of knowledge. Although he thought that all sensible objects are ideas, Descartes was well aware that there are ideas which are not sensible. There are, according to him, three sorts of ideas—innate, adventitious, and fictitious. This celebrated theory of the origin of ideas has at all events two very great merits : first, it called attention to the important problem of the origin of ideas ; secondly, under the head of innate ideas, it recognises ideas which are not sensible. He remarks that ' the philosophers of the schools accept as a maxim that there is nothing in the understanding which was not previously in the senses, in which, however, it is certain that the ideas of God and of the soul have never been.' [1]

It is well known that Descartes repudiated the theory that some ideas are innate in the sense of being always present. In his replies to the objections raised against his Meditations, the ' Responsiones Tertiæ ' contain the following passage :—' Denique quum dicimus ideam aliquam nobis innatam, non intelligimus illam nobis semper observari, sic enim nulla prorsus esset innata ; sed tantum nos habere in nobis ipsis facultatem illam eliciendi.' [2] This doctrine of ideas, innate in the sense of elicited from one's own faculty of thinking, is developed at length in the 'Notes on the Programme of Regius,' [3] and was the foundation of the celebrated maxim of Leibnitz : ' Nihil est in intellectu quod non prius in sensu nisi ipse intellectus.' By innate ideas Descartes meant ideas, not acquired, like adventitious ideas, by sense from external objects, nor yet inborn, but capable of being elicited from the faculty of thinking, which is supposed to be endued with a capacity of conceiving them.

This Cartesian mystery of eliciting ideas from the faculty of thinking is nothing really but the ordinary

----

[1] *Discourse on Method*, Part IV.   [2] Page 102 (ed. 1685).
[3] Id. pp. 184-6.

operations of consciousness and reasoning, hidden under
a fine-sounding phrase. It is quite true that we find
certain ideas in ourselves which have never been in
sense. We arrive at some of them, such as that of
thought and that of truth, not from sensation but from
consciousness. But consciousness is a kind of sense,
and ideas derived from consciousness of oneself are not
elicited from oneself, but apprehended as belonging to
oneself. They are, as Locke afterwards showed, ideas
of reflection, not innate, but acquired by apprehending
ourselves performing conscious operations. There are,
indeed, other ideas of the insensible, which are not
acquired either by sensation or by consciousness. We
neither see God nor are conscious of God in us. Such
ideas also are, according to Descartes, elicited not from
sense, but from our faculty of thinking. In his 'Notes
on the Programme of Regius,' after disposing of tradi-
tion and observation, he thinks himself entitled to conclude that the idea of God is innate in the sense of
elicited from the faculty of thinking. But there is
another alternative—reasoning from sensation and
consciousness. Logical reasoning is an indirect origin
of insensible ideas.

When Descartes said that ideas were elicited from
the faculty of thinking, perhaps he had some obscure
unanalysed hint of ideas generated by reasoning. But,
then, such ideas are not innate, but acquired, and are
the most deviously acquired of all ideas. In the first
place, we reason from sensation, and infer that there are
objects, like the sensible, but insensible. We then conceive an idea of the insensible. This is plainly the
origin of the idea of a corpuscle, which is an idea
neither sensible, nor conscious, nor innate, but acquired
by reasoning from sense. Secondly, we reason from

sensation and consciousness, and infer other thinking
beings. For example, we are conscious of being able by
reason and will to produce good effects. By reasoning
from sense we infer the goodness of nature. By combining these evidences we infer a being who reasons
and wills to produce the goodness of nature. We then
conceive an idea of this being similar to ourselves, but
infinitely more perfect in reason and will. This is at least
one origin of the idea of God, which is neither an idea
of sensation, nor of consciousness, nor innate, but acquired by reasoning from sensation and consciousness.

Before a theory of the origin of ideas can be admitted two conditions of hypothesis must be satisfied.
Other hypotheses must have been eliminated ; and
any hypothesis, which without going beyond known
operations explains the facts, must be preferred to an
hypothesis which supposes an unverified power. But
the theory of innate ideas is imperfect in elimination
and in verification. It shows that not all ideas arise
immediately from sensation, but it fails to show that
the rest are not due to consciousness and reasoning,
and accordingly the unverified power of eliciting ideas
must yield to the verified powers of sensation, consciousness, and reasoning, which are together a sufficient explanation of the origin of ideas.

We have now all the immediate data of knowledge,
and their origin, according to Descartes. They are the
soul known as subject, and its ideas, innate, adventitious
and fictitious, known as objects. What knowledge, then,
even if we have innate ideas, should we get ? What
apprehension of reality, immediate and mediate ? We
should know that we really are souls. We should also
know that we really apprehend ideas. But what else
should we know mediately beyond the soul and its

ideas? Descartes replies: from our ideas we should know that there are real objects beyond them.

Aristotle had distinguished simple and complex apprehension, conception and judgment, and had pointed out that truth and falsity arise with judgment. As long as we merely apprehend an idea, *e.g.* of a man or a centaur, we express no belief about the existence of an object. But when we judge about objects we apprehend a relation of combination or separation, which, in its simplest but not its only form, is a relation of existence or non-existence; *e.g.* a man exists, a centaur does not exist. Hence our judgment may be either true or false: true, if it agrees with a real relation of combination or separation; false, if it does not. The question is, how are we to know that our judgments about objects are true? How are we to know that there is a real relation?

Descartes, though he confused two kinds of simple apprehension, sensation and conception, was aware of the distinction between conception and judgment. He also saw that the possibility of falsity begins with judgments.[1] But he thought that true judgments can be derived from ideas themselves, by their own inherent characteristics. He proposed a new criterion of truth, and a new method of forming true judgments from ideas themselves.

In the first place, he thought that the mere idea of God proves God's existence. This theory he applied in two arguments, one of which proceeded from the idea of necessary existence. The mind, he says, from perceiving necessary and eternal existence to be comprised in the idea which it has of an all-perfect Being, ought

---

[1] *Meditation* III.

manifestly to conclude that this all-perfect Being exists.[1]
This ontological argument, as it is called, which has
become famous from the criticisms upon it, especially
that of Kant,[2] and from its revival by Hegel,[3] is a most
transparent fallacy. Descartes surreptitiously omitted
the word 'idea.' An idea only comprises ideas, and
our idea of God comprises, not necessary and eternal
existence, but only the idea of necessary and eternal
existence, which only proves that the idea of this all-
perfect Being exists.

The other argument proceeded from the objective
reality of an idea; that is, according to the proper
meaning of 'objective,' the reality of an idea *quatenus
objicitur intellectui*. This argument follows the former
argument in the Principles,[4] but is stated at greater
length in the Third Meditation. Shortly, it comes to
this : more reality cannot be produced by less ; the idea
of God has more objective reality than the actual, or
formal, reality, of a finite substance ; therefore it cannot
be produced by a finite substance, but must be received
from God Himself. The major is true ; the minor is
false, because the objective reality of an idea is always less
real than the actual reality of the thinker, and therefore
can be produced by him. God has more reality than
man ; the idea of God has more reality than the idea
of man ; but man has more reality than his own
idea of God. We can therefore retort on Descartes
the following syllogism : the less real can be produced
by the more real ; the idea of God is less real than the
thinker ; therefore the idea of God can be produced by
the man who thinks it. As for the way in which a
man produces, not God, but his idea of God, we have

---

[1] *Princ.* i. 14.   [2] *Critique*, pp. 364-70 (Bohn).
[3] *Logic of Hegel* (Wallace), pp. 91-2.   [4] i. 17-19.

already described it. He produces it, not by the bare
idea of his own finite substance, but by reasoning from
nature to nature's God, and then forming an idea of
a Being, reasoning and willing like himself, but infinitely more perfect. Man has no power to produce
God; but, by reasoning to God's perfect existence, he
can produce his very imperfect idea of God. The origin
of natural theology is reasoning: the origin of the idea
of God is rational idealisation.

Secondly, conceding the reality of God, though not
proved by these two arguments from ideas, but rather
by a third argument which he adds from our not having
made ourselves, let us proceed to the further use of
ideas as a criterion of truth by Descartes. He accepted
the Christian doctrine that God is not the cause of our
errors.[1] He pointed out that some of our ideas are
clear and distinct,[2] others obscure and confused. He
concluded that those ideas, which are clear and distinct, must be true, otherwise God would be a deceiver.[3]
In short, he made the clearness and distinctness of ideas,
backed by the veracity of God, a criterion of truth, by
which we may argue from ideas to objects beyond
them.

By this internal criterion of ideas, he supposed
that from our psychical ideas we may infer a physical
world[1]:—

'Although we are all sufficiently persuaded of the
existence of material things, yet since this was before
called in question by us, and since we reckoned the
persuasion of their existence as among the prejudices
of our childhood, it is now necessary for us to investigate
the grounds on which this truth may be known with
certainty. In the first place, then, it cannot be doubted

---

[1] *Princ.* i. 29.　　[2] *Id.* i. 45.　　[3] *Id.* i. 30.　　[4] *Id.* ii. 1.

that every perception we have comes to us from some object different from our mind; for it is not in our power to cause ourselves to experience one perception rather than another, the perception being entirely dependent on the object which affects our senses. It may, indeed, be matter of enquiry whether that object be God, or something different from God; but because we perceive, or rather, stimulated by sense, clearly and distinctly apprehend, certain matter extended in length, breadth, and thickness, the various parts of which have different figures and motions, and give rise to the sensations we have of colours, smells, pain, &c., God would, without question, deserve to be regarded as a deceiver, if He directly and of Himself presented to our mind the idea of this extended matter, or merely caused it to be presented to us by some object which possessed neither extension, figure, nor motion. For we clearly conceive this matter as entirely distinct from God, and from ourselves or our mind; and appear even clearly to discern that the idea of it is formed in us on occasion of objects existing out of our minds, to which it is in every respect similar. But since God cannot deceive us, for this is repugnant to His nature, as has been already remarked, we must unhesitatingly conclude that there exists a certain object extended in length, breadth, and thickness, and possessing all those properties which we clearly apprehend to belong to what is extended. And this extended substance is what we call body or matter.'

By the same internal criterion of ideas he thought that he could infer that distinction in nature which Locke called ' the distinction of primary and secondary qualities ' [1] :—

' As belonging to the class of things clearly appre-

_____
[1] *Meditation* III.

hended, I recognise the following, namely, magnitude,
or extension in length, breadth, and depth ; figure,
which results from the termination of extension ; situation, which bodies of diverse figures preserve with
reference to each other ; and motion or change of situation ; to which may be added substance, duration, and
number. But with regard to lights, colours, sounds,
odours, tastes, heat, cold, and the other tactile qualities,
they are thought with so much obscurity and confusion,
that I cannot determine even whether they are true or
false ; in other words, whether or not the ideas I have
of these qualities are in truth the ideas of real objects.'

The clearness and distinctness of our ideas are facts
of our consciousness ; but we are also conscious that
they do not always correspond to our knowledge.
Many ideas are clear and distinct where the objects
are known to be unreal. Nothing can be clearer or
more distinct than the ideas I have of Achilles and
Agamemnon, of Ulysses and Nestor. Am I, then, to
infer that these Homeric heroes lived in the flesh?
Many ideas are obscure and confused where the objects
are known to be real. The idea of the earth as a vast
globe revolving round the vaster sun is neither clear
nor distinct. Yet the earth revolves round the sun.
Nor do the degrees of truth correspond with the
degrees of clearness and distinctness. My ideas of
Hamlet and Macbeth are clearer and more distinct than
my ideas of the Prime Minister and the Leader of the
Opposition Am I to infer that the persons are also
more real? I have proofs to prevent such an inference,
you will say. But that is to introduce another criterion,
over and above the clearness and distinctness of ideas.

Ideas are clear and distinct by proximity to sense,
as well as by accuracy of science : hence, as science

recedes from sense, it often proves insensible objects
to exist, of which it forms but obscure and confused
ideas. Science assures me that matter consists of incon-
ceivably small particles moving with inconceivable
rapidity on the one hand, and on the other hand that it
extends over an inconceivable immensity of space. These
things are known to exist. Yet the ideas of them are
so far from being clear and distinct that I cannot be
said to have any direct ideas of them at all. If I try to
form an idea of a particle in a drop of water, I divide it
and divide it, but the division baffles my conception.
If I try to conceive the immensity of space, I enlarge
my idea of a limited space, as the frog tried to swell
himself out to the size of the ox, and with much the
same success. Are we to say that these scientific facts
are not real, because we have but obscure and indistinct
ideas—or rather have no direct ideas of them at
all ?

Again, science is based on the distinction of the
apparent and the real, in time and space, in bulk and
motion. The real in all cases is regarded as more truly
real than the apparent ; but the apparent is more
clearly and distinctly conceived. My idea of the apparent sun moving apparently over the apparent earth
is clear and distinct : my idea of the real earth moving
really round the real sun is obscure and indistinct.
Am I then to infer that the sun moves over the earth,
and not the earth round the sun ? Again, the ideas of
secondary qualities in sense are as clear as, if not clearer
than, the ideas of primary qualities. For example, the
idea of sensible heat is as clear and distinct as that of
sensible extension. The difference is not in the ideas,
but in the inferences of the qualities ; and there must
be some other ground than ideas, which are equally

clear and distinct, to justify the differences between our inferences of insensible heat and insensible extension.

To say that God does not deceive us is to raise a false issue. He does not deceive those who use sense and reasoning by the laws of logic. But we should deceive ourselves if we were to follow Descartes and substitute mere ideas for the logical organs of truth. We are often deceived when we have clear and distinct ideas. We are deceived about the bodily locality of our sensations and the externality of the object of sense, about the reality of secondary qualities, about the beautiful and about the good. A man often has a clear and distinct idea of a duty which is no duty. I might justify any wickedness, if I allowed myself to argue, I have a clear and distinct idea of the rightness of this action, and God will not deceive me, therefore it is right. The Inquisition, no doubt, had a clear and distinct idea of the justice of punishing heretics, and a belief that God never deceived them: on the logic of Descartes, they would have been justified in punishing Galileo as a heretic, for saying that the earth goes round the sun. This lazy logic of ideas would justify any arbitrary conclusion, and defy all rational criticism. For, who is to know whether or not one has clear and distinct ideas? But Descartes lived in a reaction against logic.

An idea is an apprehension in the absence of an external object. It contains no opinion whether the object is only absent or also non-existent. Its clearness and distinctness depend on other causes besides the belief of existence, and especially on the proximity of the idea to sense. Hence conception does not in itself guarantee the existence of an external object. Moreover, we are conscious of its limits : everybody knows that however

K

well he conceives, he is not justified in judging without further evidence. If we were not conscious of the frequent disagreement of ideas with facts, God might have been a deceiver; but, as it is, He does not deceive us into thinking that our clear and distinct ideas conform to facts, but, on the contrary, makes us conscious that they often do not, and gives us an opportunity of going beyond them by reasoning. We are conscious that our ideas do not justify judgments of existence without rational proof.

But the words, conception and idea, are so vague that they often get confused with belief, just as the inconceivable is often confounded with the incredible. Descartes shows traces of this confusion, in the very act of drawing a valuable distinction between imagination and pure intellection, in the Sixth Meditation:—

'To render this plain, I first examine the difference which there is between imagination and pure intellection. For example, when I imagine a triangle, not only do I understand that it is a figure comprehended by three lines, but at the same time I intuite those three lines as formed by the glance of my mind; and this is what I call imagining. But if I wish to think of a chiliagon, I equally well understand that it is a figure consisting of a thousand sides, as I understand that a triangle is a figure consisting of three, but I do not in the same way imagine those thousand sides, or intuite them as present.'

Everybody would at once suppose that by intellection he simply meant the belief that there is such a figure as a chiliagon; but, if we look a few lines further down, we find the very reverse. He says that 'the mind, which understands, turns itself in a way towards itself and considers one of the ideas which are in it;' and he

repeats the same view in the 'Responsiones Quintæ.'
According to Descartes, then, the pure intellection that
a chiliagon is a figure consisting of a thousand sides is
a consideration of ideas. When he thus merged the
conception of ideas and the understanding of objects,
no wonder he thought that clear and distinct ideas
enable us to know objects beyond ideas. But, really,
we judge very clearly that a chiliagon is a figure with
a thousand sides, but we conceive a very obscure idea
of so many sides, if we can be said to have any direct
idea of them at all. Conception is not co-extensive
with understanding. The criterion of truth is not inherent in ideas.

As it requires something more than clearness and
distinctness of ideas to know objects, how do we know
them? How do we know when our judgments agree
with them? What is the criterion of truth? Objects
are twofold, internal and external. About the internal
we judge immediately by sensation and consciousness,
the objects of sensation being effects of external objects
on the nervous system, the object of consciousness
oneself as subject thinking in the widest sense: about
external but similar objects beyond ourselves we judge
from sensation and consciousness mediately by inference. Truth is the agreement of a judgment with the
sensible, the conscious, or the inferred from the sensible
and the conscious, on the logical rule that, if the
premises are true, the conclusion is true. The criterion
of truth is double; being first the immediate apprehension of the sensible and the conscious within, and
thereupon the mediate apprehension of the similar
but insensible and unconscious without, by parity of
reasoning. Reasoning without the immediate data is
mere consistency, upon them it is the consistency of

K 2

truth. Knowledge is the apprehension of reality, immediately by sensation and consciousness, mediately by logical reasoning therefrom. To know by reasoning requires at least two conditions ; sensible data and logical consistency. Whether it requires more, we will decide, when we come to Hume and Kant.

As, then, we know objects beyond ideas, not by the clearness and distinctness of these ideas, but by rational inference, what are the data required for this inference ? This question is the crucial test of the Cartesian philosophy, which aspires to a knowledge of things through ideas. Descartes did not supply adequate data to infer the knowledge he admitted. Hence his philosophy ends in inconsequence. We have already seen, in the First Part, that it requires like data to prove like conclusions, and, therefore, physical data to prove physical conclusions. If all the data were psychical, physical objects would not be inferrible. If all the data of a man's knowledge were his soul and ideas, he could know nothing but other souls and ideas. But Descartes admitted that physical objects beyond souls and ideas are knowable. The data of knowledge, then, cannot all be, as he supposed, a soul and its ideas.

Descartes was a man of subtle genius, retiring, as it were, within the chamber of his own soul to survey his own ideas, and trying to think what they could reflect of a world without. Let us follow him into this retirement, and imagine ourselves each to be a pure soul contemplating pure ideas. A man must have a difficulty in performing this feat, because he neither is the one nor does the other. He cannot rid himself of his body, nor fail to contemplate the effects on his nerves. Philosophers take advantage of this superhuman difficulty ; feigning a psychical man, but knowing all the time that each of us will add the physical factor and complete his human being. Hence a man fails to realise the extraordinary consequences that follow, if he really has to suppose himself to be a disembodied soul, perceiving nothing immediately but incorporeal ideas. However, let me try.

I should not be able, in the first place, to infer that the body is a material cause of my ideas, nor that my ideas are an efficient cause of moving the body. As all the causes and effects immediately perceived by me would be my psychical soul and its ideas, all those that I could mediately infer would be psychical souls and ideas. Now, Descartes asserted the heterogeneity of soul and body, but not exactly their incommunicability, still less the non-existence of the body. His view was that soul and body are in contact in the pineal gland, that the motions of the body cause ideas and ideas volitions, while this interaction requires the concourse or assistance of God. This hypothesis, or series of hypotheses, is anatomically false, because it disturbs nervous continuity without proving any connection between the pineal gland and thinking. Logically, it is false on Cartesian principles, not merely because soul and body are supposed heterogeneous, but because all the causes and effects immediately perceived being supposed psychical, a physical body either as cause or effect of ideas could not be inferred. There is no proof that Descartes himself ever drew this conclusion, though involved in the Cartesian theory. He knew that the body is scientifically inferred to be cause and effect. Consequently, his theory that soul and ideas are all the data of inference must be false, because they cannot be the data of that scientific inference.

It was left for his successors to draw the logical

conclusion and contradict science. The Cartesian School
denied that the body is either cause or effect of ideas.
Instead, Geulinx invented occasionalism, or the hypothesis that on the occasion of bodily changes God calls
forth an idea of perception in our soul, while on the
occasion of an idea of volition in our soul He moves
our body for us. Malebranche developed this doctrine
into the vision of all things in the Deity. Leibnitz,
rightly characterising occasionalism as a perpetual
miracle, had recourse to a pre-established harmony
between body and soul, established by God before our
creation. But the pure idealists have a more logical way
out of the difficulty than any of the Cartesians. It is
that no body is known to exist at all. If all immediately
known causes and effects were my soul and its ideas, I
should have no data to infer a physical body, much less
that it is wound up like a clock to go with my soul.
Nevertheless, Descartes was right in saying that I have
a body, whose motions science proves to be causes
and effects of thinking. Therefore, immediately known
causes and effects are not all my soul and its ideas, from
which no body could have been inferred.

Secondly, if all the data were my soul and its ideas,
and I could somehow or other infer the body, at any
rate I could not infer that my body was a part of
myself. How should I know that I have a body?
Precisely as I should be supposed to know any other
external object, mediately through ideas. I should
have an idea of warmth, and refer it to a fire; an idea
of toothache, and refer it to the body. But if I knew
my body in this indirect manner, I should not regard it
any more than the fire as part of myself. It may be
objected that I should find it always with me. But so I
do the earth and the atmosphere. It would seem with

them part of my environment; not a part of me, but only my nearest and dearest companion. Descartes vacillated on this point. When he is deducing the consequences of his hypothesis, he says, 'I am the mind by which I am what I am, as distinct from the body.'[1] When he is saving facts, he contradicts his hypothetical deductions. 'Nature,' he says, 'teaches me by those senses of pain, hunger, thirst, &c., that I am not only present in my body as a sailor in a ship, but so closely conjoined with it, and, as it were, intermixed, that I compose something one with it;'[2] and, again, 'it is plainly certain that my body, or rather myself as a whole, so far as I am composed of body and mind, can be affected by various advantages and disadvantages from surrounding bodies.' Quite so; but he has given us two inconsistent theories of personal identity, of which the first is false, the second true, but quite inconsequent. if I am a soul perceiving my own ideas.

If, then, I steadily suppose myself a soul perceiving its ideas, I find that I cannot infer my own body to be a part of myself. This is a conclusion so impossible, so absurd, so ludicrous, yet so common to idealists, that it is no credit to modern thought to have tolerated for so long a time hypotheses from which it logically follows. Really, Descartes was right in inconsequently and inconsistently admitting that he is body and soul. But the admission is fatal to the hypothesis that he is a soul, and to the hypothesis that the objects of all immediate perceptions are ideas. If I perceived nothing but ideas, I could not know my body. Since I do know my body, I must perceive something else but ideas. The truth is, I know my body in four ways: first, I am conscious of it as a factor of myself as

---

[1] *Discourse on Method*, Part IV.   [2] *Meditation* VI.

thinking subject; secondly, my senses perceive my own
nervous system as sensibly affected, although I have
long confused this sensible object with the external
cause I infer; thirdly, from one part of my body
sensibly affected I infer another part; e.g. I see a reflection on my optic nerve, and infer that it represents
my hand; fourthly, by science, founded on all these
evidences, I know that I am a single organism. By
combining all these ways of knowing my body, I know
it better than anything else, and to be a part of myself.

Having feigned myself to be a pure soul contemplating pure ideas, I could not infer my own body, or
at any rate not as part of myself. But could I infer
any external body? Descartes, in a passage already
quoted,[1] dwells on the involuntariness of sensible effects,
and many of the idealists have relied on this argument
for an external cause. I freely admit the force of the
argument. But what sort of external cause? I could
infer only causes similar to those in the data. Either
by sensation or by consciousness, or by both, I should
apprehend an interaction of my soul and ideas, and
of my ideas among themselves; and also that some
of my ideas are involuntary; from which the parity of
reasoning would then allow me only three logical alternatives: another soul; this would be Berkeley's Divine
Spirit: a cause unknown; this would be Hume's inexplicable something: another idea; this would be Hegel's
absolute idea.

A logical idealism would further conclude that, so
far from being known to be a physical part of myself,
interacting with my soul and ideas, my body, if known,
is something psychical, and, not being my soul, is a
system of my ideas, while any other soul, if there is

[1] *Princ.* ii. 1.

such a thing, must follow from another similar system of my ideas. Such a logical deduction escaped Descartes, but it has not escaped Mill, who only substitutes sensations for ideas : [1]—

'Whatever sensation I have, I at once refer it to one of the permanent groups of possibilities of sensation which I call natural objects. But among these groups there is one (my own body) which is not only composed, like the rest, of a mixed multitude of sensations and possibilities of sensation, but is also connected, in a peculiar manner, with all my sensations. Not only is this especial group always present as an antecedent condition of every sensation I have, but the other groups are only enabled to convert their respective possibilities of sensation into actual sensations by means of some previous change in that particular one. I look about me, and though there is only one group (or body) which is connected with all my sensations in this peculiar manner, I observe that there is a great multitude of other bodies, closely resembling in their sensible properties (in the sensations composing them as groups) this particular one, but whose modifications do not call up, as those of my own body do, a world of sensations in my consciousness. Since they do not do so in my consciousness, I infer that they do it out of my consciousness, and that to each of them belongs a world of consciousness of its own, to which it stands in the same relation in which what I call my own body stands to me.'

Now, the scientific Descartes knew well that bodies are neither non-existent nor unknown, neither sensations nor ideas. He admitted that involuntary sensible data

---

[1] *Examination of Sir William Hamilton's Philosophy*, pp. 244-5 cf. Lotze, *Metaphysics*, Book III. chap. iv.

enable us to infer physical bodies as causes beyond
sense and conception in the external world, that these
bodies consist of insensible particles, that the external
world is like the sensible in some qualities, unlike in
others, and that the modes of insensible particles produce sensible effects on our bodies, which are physical
parts of ourselves; after the first step, proceeding
logically enough from inference to inference. Let us
add to our previous quotations one passage as a sample
of this profound scientific spirit :—

'But to the insensible particles of bodies, I assign
determinate figures and magnitudes and motions, as if I
had seen them, and yet I confess them to be insensible ;
and therefore some will perhaps ask, whence then I
recognise them such as they are. I answer that I first,
from the simplest and most known principles, whose
knowledge has been implanted by nature in our minds,
considered generally, what could be the principal differences among the magnitudes and figures and positions
of bodies, insensible only on account of their smallness,
and what sensible effects would follow from those various
concourses. And then when I noticed some similar
effects in things sensible, I considered that they arose
from a similar concourse of such bodies ; especially since
no other mode of explaining them seemed capable of
being excogitated.'[1]

But the psychological Descartes could not logically
take the first step. He had supposed, as 'the simplest
and most known principles,' hypotheses about the
subject and its data, which never could have been the
premises of such a science of bodies and their insensible
particles. If all immediately perceived effects and
causes had been soul and ideas, there would have been

[1] *Princ.* iv. 203

no primary data to infer bodies—not even one's own body, much less other bodies, and their corpuscles, whose structures and motions cause sensible effects in one's own body. But, as Descartes admitted, bodies are known and inferred from sensible data. Therefore the data cannot be soul and ideas. From similars dissimilars cannot be inferred. From soul and ideas, nothing else follows. But something else is known to science; therefore, not from soul and ideas. Physical bodies and corpuscles, structures and motions, require physical data of sense.

After the dogmatism of mediæval philosophy, Descartes was right to doubt. He was right also in beginning with the certain fact of consciousness; I think, therefore am. But, at the same time, he forgot that there are other facts of consciousness. There is a universal consciousness of the thinking subject, but there is also a scientific consciousness that the thinking subject knows physical objects. Instead of this, Descartes substituted the hypothesis that the thinking subject is a soul which perceives ideas, and then, in defiance of logic, attempted a synthetical deduction from this idealistic hypothesis of psychical data of sense to a realistic knowledge of physical objects of science. The deduction may be attacked both by *enstasis* and *elenchus*; in its premises and in its conclusion. On the one hand, the subject is not purely psychical, and, if it was, would not be limited to psychical data: on the other hand, if the data were psychical, we could not infer physical objects of science, which are admitted by Descartes, and are more certain than any hypothesis of the nature of the subject and its data. Hence the hypothesis of soul and ideas must be surrendered, because the thinking subject is not the soul but the man, because sensible

objects are not ideas but physical effects on the nervous
system, and because soul and ideas would not enable
man to infer physical objects of science.   Descartes, the
original genius of modern idealism, was too introspective.
Of himself he says, 'Totos dies solus in hypocausto
morabar, ibique variis meditationibus placidissime vaca
bam.'[1]   This seclusion in a hot room is an admirable
way of distilling thoughts, provided only these vapours
of the heated brain can be condensed into a knowledge
of the outside world.

[1] *Diss. de Methodo,* ii.

CHAPTER VI.

LOCKE.

LOCKE, at the outset of the 'Essay concerning Human Understanding,' states that it is his purpose to enquire into the original, certainty and extent of human knowledge and opinion, without troubling himself about the essence of mind.[1] That is, he rejects the Cartesian method of using the nature of the thinking subject to deduce our knowledge; and rightly, because it was a method from the less to the more certain. But he leaves the Cartesian deduction, that the data of the understanding are ideas, simply removes the hypothesis from the premises to the conclusion, and nowhere throughout gives any new evidence that ideas are the data of knowledge. The hypothesis of the soul is thus replaced by the hypothesis of ideas, as a principle. Now, there had been some plausibility in the argument the subject is the soul, therefore its immediate objects are ideas. There was nothing but *petitio principii* in the hypothesis the immediate objects of understanding are ideas. Yet this hypothesis in one form or other has remained ever since Locke's time as the putative principle of all idealism. Many a philosopher, who has with Locke recovered from the Cartesian hypothesis that the subject is soul, and has followed Hume in correcting Locke's confusion of sensations and ideas, nevertheless clings to the hypo-

[1] *Essay,* I. 1, 2.

thesis that all immediate objects are some psychical state or other, without any evidence, whether of Cartesian deductions, or of psychological consciousness, or of natural science.

Locke, having begun at a new beginning, proceeds to his method, which is as synthetical as that of Descartes : —

'I shall pursue this following method.

'*First*, I shall inquire into the *original* of those *ideas*, notions, or whatever else you please to call them, which a man observes, and is conscious to himself he has in his mind; and the ways whereby the understanding comes to be furnished with them.

'*Secondly*, I shall endeavour to show what *knowledge* the understanding hath by those *ideas*, and the certainty, evidence, and extent of it.

'*Thirdly*, I shall make some inquiry into the nature and grounds of *faith* or *opinion*, whereby I mean that assent which we give to any proposition as true, of whose truth yet we have no certain knowledge. And here we shall have occasion to examine the reasons and degrees of *assent*.'[1]

From this passage we can see how vain is psychological synthesis. The smallest mistake at the beginning vitiates the whole procedure and every consequence. A man is here said to be conscious of having ideas in his mind. It is true that he is conscious of having ideas. But even the followers of Locke himself would deny that this is all he is conscious of. Hume would say that he is also conscious of impressions, and Mill would add judgments. Yet to a philosophical use of the synthetic method by Locke it was necessary that ideas should be all the materials of knowledge ; for the next question

---

[1] *Essay*, I. 1, 3.

is—what knowledge can be gained by ideas; which is
a false issue, if ideas are not the whole material of
knowledge. But as they are not the whole, it is not to
be wondered at that, in the sequel, Locke oscillates
between two contrary tendencies, a logical but false
reduction of knowledge to ideas, and an illogical but
true extension of it to things beyond. Moreover, to
inconsequence he adds inconsistency. He tries to begin
with an understanding of ideas and end with a knowledge of things.

The firstfruits of idealistic hypothesis are at once
manifest. Having assumed that ideas are all the materials,
he consistently assumes that they are all the objects of
understanding :—

'Thus much I thought necessary to say concerning
the occasion of this inquiry into *human understanding*.
But before I proceed on to what I have thought on this
subject, I must here, in the *entrance*, beg pardon of my
reader for the frequent use of the word *idea*, which he
will find in the following treatise. It being that term
which, I think, serves best to stand for whatsoever is
the object of the understanding when a man thinks, I
have used it to express whatever is meant by *phantasm,
notion, species*, or whatever it is which the mind can be
employed about in thinking; and I could not avoid
frequently using it.'[1]

These words, which, if anywhere, ought to have
come as a proved conclusion at the end, occur as an
undoubted principle at the entrance of the Essay. They
contain a double hypothesis; first, that ideas are the
immediate, secondly, that they are all, the objects of
understanding, and therefore of knowledge. The first
part is the ideal hypothesis of Descartes, the second is

[1] *Essay,* I. 1, 8.

Locke's corollary.   It is a logical corollary, not however scientific, but hypothetical from an hypothesis.   Three hypotheses started modern idealism ; the subject is psychical, the data are psychical, the objects are psychical.   Never was such a gigantic system of *petitio principii.*

The aftermath of idealistic hypothesis appears at the very end of the Essay.   After adopting the Stoic division of the sciences into physics, ethics and logic, he concludes in the spirit of science, but in utter contradiction of his original hypothesis, with the following peroration :—

' This seems to me the first and most general, as well as natural division of the objects of our understanding. For a man can employ his thoughts about nothing, but either the contemplation of things themselves, for the discovery of truth, or about the things in his own power, which are his own actions, for the attainment of his own ends ; or the signs the mind makes use of, both in the one and the other, and the right ordering of them for its clearer information.   All which three, viz. things as they are in themselves knowable ; actions as they depend on us, in order to happiness ; and the right use of signs in order to knowledge, being *toto cælo* different, they seemed to be the three great provinces of the intellectual world, wholly separate and distinct one from another.' [1]

In the same chapter he has already told us what he includes under things and signs.   On the one hand, by signs he means ideas and words.[2]   On the other hand, under things, he includes, as objects of understanding, ' the nature of things, their relations and their manner of operation ;' while physics is, as he says, ' the knowledge of things, as they are in their own proper beings,

[1] *Essay.* IV. 21, 5.   [2] Ib. IV. 21, 4; cf. IV. 5.

their constitutions, properties, and operations, whereby
I mean not only matter and body, but spirits also.'[1]
He finally admits, then, that things and ideas are *toto
cælo* different, that not ideas but things and their relations are the objects of physics and natural philosophy,
and that not only ideas, but also things, are objects of
understanding, knowledge, and science.   Which was
right, the original hypothesis of ideas, or the final admission of things?   The latter, because things inconceivable but not incredible are objects of science. Locke, like
Balaam, came to curse, but went away blessing.

To return to the original hypotheses : the consequence is that the whole emphasis of the Essay falls on
the origin of ideas, as Locke himself admits at the very
beginning of the Second Book.[2]   'Every man being
conscious to himself, that he thinks, and that which his
mind is applied about, whilst thinking, being the ideas
that are there :' this is his assumption : 'it is in the
first place to be inquired, how he comes by them :' this
is his hypothetical conclusion. Meanwhile, the origin
of knowledge is postponed till the Fourth Book, and the
Second and Fourth Books are never welded together.
This is the beginning of a serious evil in modern philosophy, the emphasis laid on the origin of ideas in pre-
ference to the far more important problem of the origin
of knowledge, and the tendency to let the limits of ideas
determine the extent of knowledge.   But ideas do not
dictate knowledge so much as knowledge dictates ideas.

Locke begins the problem of the origin of ideas well by
rejecting innate ideas.   No doubt most of his objections
touch the broader form of inborn ideas rather than the
elicited ideas of Descartes.   But they have the merit of
pointing out that many ideas, supposed universal, are not

---

[1] *Essay*, IV. 21, 2.   [2] Cf. also I. 1, 8.

possessed by savages, and Locke in this respect has been confirmed by modern travellers.[1] Moreover, he touches Descartes himself, when he shows that experience has not really been eliminated,[2] and that consciousness, or, as he usually says, reflection, is not a mystical revelation, but an inner sense. As sensation apprehends sensible objects only when present, so consciousness apprehends one's own operations only when one performs them. There is no greater source of error in philosophy than the confusion of the intuitive with the *a priori*, and of the conscious with the innate. Consciousness is an intuitive, not innate nor *a priori*, experience of oneself performing operations.

Locke did a signal service in showing that there are two kinds of sense, sensation and reflection :—

'Let us then suppose the mind to be as we say, white paper, void of all characters, without any *ideas*; how comes it to be furnished? Whence comes it by that vast store, which the busy and boundless fancy of man has painted on it, with an almost endless variety? Whence has it all the materials of reason and knowledge? To this I answer in one word, from *experience*: in that, all our knowledge is founded; and from that it ultimately derives itself. Our observations employed either about *external sensible objects, or about the internal operations of our minds, perceived and reflected on by ourselves, is that which supplies our understandings with all the materials of thinking.* These two are the fountains of knowledge, from whence all the *ideas* we have, or can naturally have, do spring.'[3]

Modern criticisms of this theory often turn on the comparison of the mind to white paper, which is said to

---

[1] Cf. Moffat, *Missionary Labours in South Africa*, chap. ix.
[2] Cf. *Essay*, I. 2, 1; II. 1, 1.   [3] II. 1, 2.

be inconsistent with evolution. But Locke rather overlooks evolution than contradicts it. The theory of
evolution is often exaggerated. It shows that our senses
become more and more readily adapted to apprehend
their objects when presented. It does not show that
they ever come to evolve ideas or apprehend anything *a
priori*. Its evidence is in favour not of *a priori* ideas, but
only of intuitive perception. For example, the more the
senses have been exposed to light the quicker and clearer
they have apprehended its sensible effects when presented;
by its action a special sense of vision has been gradually
evolved to perceive them; but there is no evidence that
at last vision will, of itself, without light being presented,
apprehend sensible light *a priori*. Such a jump from
light presented in sense to light constructed by sense is
not proved by evolution, but arises from confusing the
intuitive with the *a priori*. Evolution has shown that
we hereditarily tend to use our organs better, and that
by use the organs become more differentiated; but it
has not shown that they ever evolve an *a priori* idea.
Now Locke, it is true, overlooked hereditary adaptation; but he was quite right, and would be right to-day,
in resisting *a priori* ideas, in saying that we begin
' without any ideas,' and in recognising two kinds of
sensitive intuition, sensation and reflection, both presentative.

The really vital question for the critic of the Essay
is a question seldom asked. All knowledge begins
with sense; but what are the objects of sense? Locke's
answer is, ideas; ideas presented to both senses; ideas
of sensation and ideas of reflection. His doctrine of ideas
was modelled on that of Descartes. Perhaps he distinguished sensation from conception better than his predecessor, but he left the consequences of the Cartesian

confusion of these operations in his doctrine that ideas
are the objects alike of sensation and conception. Again,
he followed Descartes in confusing object and operation,
the idea and its perception.[1] The object of sensation,
then, being regarded as an idea, the idea as nothing
but its perception, and the perception as psychical, it
follows that the object of sensation, with Locke as with
Descartes, becomes a psychical result in our minds, distinguished not only, as it should be, from the external
object, but also from the nervous impression, as it should
not. 'If then,' says he, in speaking of the ideas of
primary qualities, 'external objects be not united to
our minds when they produce ideas in it, and yet we
perceive *their original qualities* in such of them as singly
fall under our senses, 'tis evident that some motion
must be therein continued by our nerves, or animal
spirits, by some parts of our bodies, to the brain, or the
seat of sensation, there to *produce in our minds the
particular* ideas *we have of them.*'[2] Thus the ideal
hypothesis of Descartes was accepted by Locke, and
without further evidence. Moreover, it remains to this
day the current hypothesis, with the sole alteration of
idea into sensation. But, as we have already found, the
sensible object, though internal, is not the sensitive operation. Even, then, if the sensation were a purely psychical
operation, it would not follow that the sensible object
is either a psychical sensation or a psychical idea.

Locke also added to the doctrine of ideas; and his
first addition was the sensible idea of resistance.[3] Descartes, with his mathematical genius, had emphasised
the mathematical qualities of body, and especially extension, by which he defined it.[4] Locke accepted extension

---

[1] *Essay*, II. 8, 8; II. 10, 2; II. 19, 1.
[2] II. 8, 12.   [3] II. 4.   [4] Descartes, *Princ.* ii. 4.

and the sense of extension, but went on to show that
resistance is also necessary to body, and therefore added
a sense of resistance. But he spoilt this great contribution to the philosophy of matter and sense by his
theory of ideas. If I perceived nothing but sensations
or ideas, I should perceive only a sensation or an idea of
resistance. I should not perceive one part of my body,
or nervous system, resisting another; I should have to
infer it. But there would be no data for the inference,
for from psychical sensations or ideas physical resistance between parts of a body would not follow. The
sense of resistance, therefore, supplies a new argument
to prove that the real object of sense is the nervous
system, and its various parts resisting one another.

Again, Descartes had confined the ideal theory to
sensation; he had allowed a direct consciousness of
thinking. Locke, with more consistency though with
less truth, interposed an idea not only between outer
sense and the nervous impression, but also between
inner sense and its operations; so that the direct objects
are ideas of sensation and ideas of reflection. But
Descartes rightly regarded consciousness as a direct
apprehension of thinking; and Locke, instead of trans-
ferring the ideal theory to consciousness, should have
retracted its application to sensation, and regarded sensation as a direct apprehension of the nervous impression.

Thirdly, Descartes had begun by saying, 'I am
conscious that I think, not of thinking.' The object of
consciousness is not the quality, thinking, but a thinking
subject. Inconsistently with this truth, when he came to
substance, he had fancied that we do not directly perceive it, but 'from perceiving that some attribute is
present, we conclude that some existing thing, or substance to which it can be attributed, is also necessarily

present;'[1] and he had applied this theory both to soul and body. Locke developed this hint into a formal theory that we perceive the simple ideas of qualities, while 'we accustom ourselves to suppose some *substratum*, wherein they do subsist and from which they do result, which, therefore, we call *substance*.'[2] This theory he applied to body and spirit; and from him has descended the ordinary hypothesis that the objects of sense and consciousness are qualities, while substance is inferred—without data to infer it.

This error will meet us again in this chapter. At present it will be sufficient to quote a passage from another part of Locke's Essay: '*Our simple ideas have all abstract as well as concrete names*: the one whereof is (to speak the language of grammarians) a substantive, the other an adjective; as whiteness, white; sweetness, sweet.'[3] This is the well-known logical distinction of abstract and concrete, but its consequences are often overlooked. Locke, for instance, forgot to ask in which meaning he should call a simple idea an object of sense. The abstract whiteness is a quality; the concrete white is the qualified. Now, nobody ever saw whiteness; the object of vision is the white, the red, &c. Similarly, the object of taste is not sweetness, but the sweet; and so on with all sensible objects. Universally, then, an object of sense is never a quality, but always the qualified; and a quality is an abstraction; and, though we may sometimes speak of perceiving it, we do so only for convenience. But the qualified is a substance; whiteness and sweetness are qualities, but the white and the sweet are substances. The object of sense, therefore, is always a substance. I do not mean that sense perceives a whole substance at once, but only

---

[1] *Princ.* i. 52.   [2] *Essay*, II. 23, 1.   [3] III. 8, 2.

so far as it is sensible to a given sense; sight perceives
a substance so far as it is white; taste perceives a substance so far as it is sweet, and so on.   Nor do I mean
an external substance, for I am a substance, consisting,
too, of an immense plurality of substances, which I perceive so far as they are sensibly affected.

These conclusions apply both to outer and inner
sense.   In sensation, I perceive not a mere quality, nor
a whole substance at once, nor an external substance;
I perceive my nervous system, not so far as it is nervous structure moving, but so far as it is sensibly
affected in different parts, the optic nerve so far as it is
visibly white, the gustatory nerve so far as it is sweet
to taste, and so on. Similarly in consciousness, I perceive,
not mere thinking, nor the whole of myself, but myself
thinking, in the manner described in the last chapter.
The object of my sensation is myself as a physical substance sensibly affected; the object of my consciousness
is myself as a thinking substance. Descartes rightly said,
'I think.'   He ought not to have deserted this principle.   Locke ought to have returned to it, and have
applied it from consciousness to sensation.   Modern
philosophy ought now to give up the sensation of
qualities and inference of substance, because there is a
direct sensation of my nervous system sensibly affected,
and a direct consciousness of myself thinking, both of
which are senses not of qualities, but of the qualified.
We have a sense of substances, in order to infer them.

Locke's complete theory is that all sense perceives
a simple idea.   Really, sense always perceives a substance qualified.   It is doubtful whether the substance,
as perceived, is ever simply qualified; for instance,
even when I feel simply pained, I doubt whether I do
not feel pained for a time.   But, in any case, I do not

perceive anything simple in the sense of a simple
quality, which is only simple in the sense of abstract;
but I perceive at least the simply qualified. Secondly,
I do not perceive anything simple in the sense of a simple
idea, which is really conceived, not perceived; but I
perceive, in sensation, my nervous system sensibly
affected, and in reflection, myself thinking. The object
of sensation, and the object of consciousness, so far
from being simple ideas, are not ideas at all. They
are two sets of materials of knowledge, of which
neither is a quality, and neither is an idea, but each
a substance. Locke's attempt to make the origin of
ideas determine the origin of knowledge breaks down
at the very outset by substituting abstractions for concrete data of sense.

At the end of what he has to say on simple ideas,[1]
Locke comes to the operations which he supposes to
make other ideas out of them, and to the ideas thus
made.[2] 'The acts of the mind,' says he, 'wherein it exerts
its power over its simple *ideas*, are chiefly these three:
First, combining several simple *ideas* into one compound
one, and thus all complex *ideas* are made. The second, is
bringing two *ideas*, whether simple or complex, together,
and setting them by one another, so as to take a view of
them at once, without uniting them into one, by which
way it gets all its *ideas* of relations. The third, is separating them from all other *ideas* that accompany them in
their real existence. This is called *abstraction*, and
thus all its general *ideas* are made.'[3] He then remarks that ideas, made up of several simple ones put
together, he calls complex; such as are beauty, grati-
tude, a man, an army, the universe. Next he divides
complex ideas under three heads: modes, substances,

---

[1] *Essay*, II. 2 11.   [2] II. 11 *seq.* to the end of the Third Book.   [3] II. 12, 1.

relations. Complex ideas of modes are ideas of affections of substances, subdivided by him into simple,
or combinations of the same simple idea, *e.g.* a
dozen, formed of units, and mixed, or combinations
of simple ideas of several kinds, *e.g.* beauty, theft.
Complex ideas of substances are ' such combinations of
simple ideas as are taken to represent distinct particular
things subsisting by themselves, in which the supposed,
or confused *idea* of substance, such as it is, is always
the first and chief;'[1] they are subdivided into ideas of
single substances, *e.g.* a man, and collective ideas of
several substances, *e.g.* an army. ' The last sort of
complex *ideas*,' he says, ' is that we call *relative*, which
consists in the consideration, and comparing one *idea*
with another,'[2] *e.g.* father and son, bigger and less,
cause and effect.[3] The consideration of all these complex ideas in their order occupies the remainder of the
Second Book ; while that of abstract ideas follows, along
with general words, in a general treatment of language
in the Third Book.[4]

The whole discussion is full of variety. But it is
vitiated by two incurable errors. In the first place,
the objects of knowledge are complicated with their
mere ideas. But many scientific objects are known to
exist, without being conceivable. Secondly, no thorough
analysis is attempted of the three acts of mind, which
are supposed to be the sole causes capable of producing
out of simple ideas all other ideas. Locke calls them
composition, comparison and abstraction ;[5] making the
first to be the origin of all complex ideas of modes and
substances, the second the origin of all complex ideas
of relations, the third the origin of all general ideas.

[1] *Essay*, II. 12, 6.   [2] II. 12, 7.   [3] II. 25, 2.
[4] Cf. II. 33, 19.   [5] II. 11.

He saw the foundation of these operations on sense; but he forgot to ask their relation to reason.

After sense, we conceive particular ideas in the reproductive imagination, and general ideas by abstraction from sense.   It does not follow that all general ideas are thus formed; on the contrary, it is impossible that the idea of an insensible object should be either reproduced or abstracted from sense, in which it has never been. Again, we may compare and compound ideas.   But at the same time we also judge about sensible objects and apprehend their relations.   In judgment we use ideas, particular and general.   But, as Mill has pointed out,[1] we also judge about sensible objects in order to apprehend their relations.   I am in pain; this is a judgment that I, who am real, am in pain, which is real.   Now, reasoning starts from such judgments about the relations of sensible objects, and sometimes by analogy, sometimes and better by induction and deduction, infers rational judgments, no longer about simple objects, nor about ideas, but about the relations of real objects; on the principle, if the premises are true, the conclusion is also true.   That is, starting from judgments of sense, we infer rational judgments on evidence about relations, as real as the sensible relations. Nor is this all; as I showed in the last chapter, reason, having from sensitive concluded rational judgments, forms indirect ideas, roughly corresponding to the objects inferred, like to the ideas of sensible objects but not the same, and only capable of being made by reason. For instance, reason, having inferred that there are particles in bodies, causes the idea of a corpuscle; a general idea of corpuscles, which is not a result of mere abstraction, and particular ideas of this or that cor-

[1] Mill, *Logic*, i. 5, 1.

puscle, which are not results of composition and comparison of ideas, but of inference from judgment to judgment. Beyond sense and imagination, besides composition, comparison and abstraction of ideas, there are also judgments of sense about the relations of sensible objects, and reasoning from these judgments to the relations of insensible objects, producing rational conceptions of ideas, due to no other source but reasoning. The narrow problem of the origin of ideas cannot be separated from the whole problem of judgment, reasoning, and the origin of knowledge.

Locke, in the Second and Third Books, saw only one side of thinking, and that its weakest side : imagination and abstraction, comparison and composition, of ideas from sense. Rational inference of realities, beyond sense and ideas, he allowed to fade into the distance of the Fourth Book. Consequently, he found only the direct sources of ideas, and missed their indirect source in reason. No doubt he was influenced by the Cartesian logic of his day, which knew only the order—idea, judgment, reason. But there is a second order—reason, judgment, idea. As soon as judgment begins to act on the senses, reason begins with it, and, never stopping except to sleep and rise again refreshed, constantly forms new judgments issuing in new ideas. But Locke postponed reasoning, ignored rational conception, and therefore always fell short even of the origin of ideas.

Even in the ideas of simple modes, the very simplest department of complex ideas, this defect is noticeable. After sensations of motion, we may form ideas of motion by imagination; and the ideas of simple modes of sensible motion by composition.[1] But reason also

---

[1] *Essay*, II. 18, 1 2.

infers simple modes of insensible motion in nature, such as electricity and magnetism, cohesion and chemical attraction, which were never in sense, and frames indirect ideas of these motions. Similarly, we may imagine ideas of sensible duration and extension, and compound ideas of these simple modes; but when Locke goes on to suppose that the mind extends itself to infinity simply by repeating these ideas, he neglects the rational evidences of the unbounded nature of time and space. Unless men had thought they had reason to infer infinity, no mere repetition of ideas of the finite would ever have given the idea of the infinite, which is always accompanied by a rational inference that the infinite itself is beyond any idea we can possibly form of it.

The mischievous consequences of omitting reason in the formation of ideas are best seen in Locke's doctrine of mixed modes and relations. Without reasoning, mere composition and comparison, as soon as they go beyond sense, would produce at most artificial ideas, the vagaries of imagination. Consequently, it is not surprising that Locke treats the ideas of mixed modes and relations, which he supposes to be formed by pure composition and comparison from and beyond sense, as artificial, and even goes so far as to contend that not merely the ideas, but mixed modes and relations themselves, have no other reality but what they have in the minds of men, and are real only in the sense of being consistent, not in the sense of representing real things. This paradox is a serious matter, for it affects the reality not only of a mixed mode, such as beauty, or a relation, such as father and son, but all moral modes and relations. It reduces morality itself to an idea.[1]

[1] Cf. *Essay*, II. 22, 2; II. 25; II. 30, 4 5; II. 32, 10; III. 4, 2; III. 5.

But obligation is a mixed mode, which is real; theft, drunkenness, lying, are mixed modes which are only too real, and the conformity of morality to law is a relation, which is also real, though perhaps less common; and the complex ideas of these mixed modes and relations are not artificial, but really, though inadequately, correspond to real morality and immorality. We may admit that morality is not altogether immutable; it is not therefore unreal. We may admit that the ideas of the beautiful, of the good, and of law, are differently compounded in ancient and modern morals; they are not therefore artificial. We may admit that actions of virtue are uncommon; but virtue is not an idea. By reasoning, man finds out the moral relations suited partly to humanity in general, and partly to the circumstances of his time. By rational conception, he apprehends ideas of moral relations, immutable and mutable. Happy he who can also realise these ideas, and be

> Virtutis veræ custos rigidusque satelles.

There is even a certain fashion of ideas, which Locke illustrates by the Greek idea of ostracism and the Roman idea of proscription. But these ideas were not on that account artificial: they represented real mixed modes at Greece and Rome: to be ostracised or proscribed was anything but a mere idea. The Greeks and Romans inferred that these institutions would serve certain purposes, and thus both established the real mixed modes and represented them by corresponding ideas. The modern historian from his evidence infers that these mixed modes existed in the past, and conceives the ideas in the present. Similarly, the relation of paternity is not the idea of that relation, nor a mere product of comparison. It is a real relation of generation, which from sensible data we infer really to take place, and of which we afterwards form an idea, rational and by no means artificial, though but superficially representing the actual physical process of propagation. Mixed modes and relations, and their ideas beyond sense, are not always artificial constructions of composition and comparison of sensible ideas; but reasoning from judgments of sense discovers real mixed modes and relations, and then forms indirect ideas, really, though inadequately, corresponding to these realities, in science, in art, and in morals.

The fallacy of omitting reason again appears in Locke's treatment of universals in the Third Book. He thinks that the sole source of general ideas is direct abstraction from sense. The consequences he draws are that all classes are abstract ideas, that no real essence is knowable beyond ideas, that simple ideas are undefinable, and that universal truths are merely the agreements and disagreements of our abstract ideas.[1] All these consequences would follow if we had no higher power than abstracting general ideas from particular sensible objects. All classification would be artificial. But there is a second source of general ideas. Reason, by discovering the numerous similarities of particulars, infers real kinds or natural classes, which are not indeed eternal but as constant as the similarities, and thereby causes new, general, often very indirect ideas representing these real classes, but not identical with them; e.g. the rational general idea of a corpuscle. Again, a simple idea of sensible light is undefinable; but light in the universe is not, as Locke thinks, undefinable. On the contrary, optical reasoning proves that the real essence or fundamental similarity on which its pro-

[1] *Essay*. IV. 3, 31; IV. 12, 7.

perties depend is an æthereal undulation, and defines
it accordingly. Lastly, whatever we may think of
essences and definitions, if Locke's theory that direct
abstraction is the sole source of general ideas, and that
classes are abstract ideas, were true, it would follow
that all uniformities would be universal relations of
abstract ideas; and he accepted the consequence; even
the variety of Locke's mind refusing to entertain a conceptualism of classes along with a realism of natural
laws. If ships and liquids were abstract ideas, the laws of
flotation would be universal relations of abstract ideas.
These laws, however, are universal relations of real ships
and real liquids, inferred by reason. Therefore the
classes so related are realities beyond abstract ideas.
Abstraction of ideas from sense is not the sole source of
generality, as Locke thought: reason infers natural
classes and laws, and indirectly produces general ideas,
not identical with them, but representing them, not arti-
ficially but really, though inadequately.

Curiously enough, Locke himself saw, through a glass
darkly, the interference of reason in the origin of one
complex idea, that of substance. If sense perceived
simple ideas of qualities, and composition united simple
into complex ideas, the only complex ideas we could
have would be complex ideas of qualities. We might
have, for example, a complex idea of a combination of extension, solidity, motion, thinking, and nothing more. But Locke saw that we have something
more. He, therefore, suddenly introduced, beyond
sense and over and above composition, a supposition;
and says that 'not imagining how these simple *ideas*
can exist by themselves we accustom ourselves to
suppose some *substratum*, wherein they do subsist
and from which they do result; which, therefore,

we call *substance*.'[1] Secondly, he allowed that this
supposition causes an obscure and confused idea of the
supposed but unknown support of qualities. He recognised two such supposed and conceived substances :
body, the substratum to those simple ideas we have
from without ; and spirit, the substratum to those we
have from within.[2] Finally, he regarded both these
substances as unknown, and neither of their ideas as
clear and distinct. Nevertheless, he thought that the
ideas of substance were real in a different way from those
of other complex ideas. The complex ideas of mixed
modes and relations were, according to him, real if consistent ; those of substances real only if agreeing with
things without us.[3] It is the supposition of existence,
over and above the composition of ideas, which made
him allow this agreement with existence to ideas of
substances. Inconsistent as this supposition is with
his general theory of the composition of complex
ideas, it is nevertheless the truth, though in a very
imperfect shape. Let us then proceed to correct it,
by showing what is the real nature of this inference,
which Locke calls a supposition.

It is true that external substances are inferred. But
there are three views of what a substance is inferred to
be. Some say that it is only a combination of qualities.
But qualities are abstractions ; and a body is not extension, solidity, motion, or any number of further
abstractions, combined, but the extended, solid, moving,
&c Locke went to the opposite extreme of supposing
a substance to be a substratum or kind of support on
which the qualities rest, and this is the ordinary view,
descended indeed from the compound, or 'concrete,'
substance of Aristotle, composed of matter and form.

---

[1] *Essay*, II. 23, 1.   [2] See II. 23, 1 5.   [3] II. 30, 4-5.

But here are two abstractions, the subject abstracted
from the qualities and the qualities from the subject.
If a body ceased to be extended, solid and moving, it
would cease to be; there would be no substratum or
support left. Hence the third view, that a substance is
a qualified subject, the extended, solid, moving, &c. ; in
which the qualities are nothing except as characterising
the subject, and the subject nothing except as characterised by the qualities; from which subject or substratum, qualities or attributes are opposite abstractions.

Secondly, external substances must be inferred from
similar data. To infer qualified subjects beyond sense,
there must be qualified subjects in sense. If the data
were ideas, we could only infer other ideas. If the
data were qualities, we could only infer qualities. *A
fortiori*, if the data were ideas of qualities we could
never infer a real qualified subject, for which there
would be no analogue. Therefore, again we find that
Locke's sensible data were false. He thought that by
sense we perceive simple ideas of extension, resistance
or solidity, motion, &c., and then without rhyme or
reason suppose something totally different, a real support in the external world. Really, sense perceives
qualified subjects, the extended, resisting, moving, &c.
within; hence reason infers similar extended, resisting,
moving, qualified subjects without. It must not be
forgotten that muscular sense was not noticed in Locke's
day; but the logic of reason had been known since
Aristotle's day, and he ought not to have neglected it.

Thirdly, substances are not unknown : they are the
only things that are known. Everything else is real,
and is known, only so far as it belongs to substance ;
and although qualities are abstracted and spoken of as
real and known for mere convenience, what is really

M

known in mathematics is not the quality of extension, but the extended; in physics, not the quality of gravity, but the gravitating; in morals, not the quality of goodness, but the good. Substances would be unknown, and uninferred, on Locke's data. But substances are known, because sense perceives them within, and reason infers them without, by parity of reasoning. They are the data and conclusions of all our knowledge. Sensation perceives the nervous system in different parts as sensibly white, sweet, extended, moving, &c. Reason infers similar physical substances or bodies. Science goes on to infer similar corpuscles. Nor does it stop till it infers the body of the universe. Consciousness perceives myself as thinking subject, partly body, partly soul. Reason, from the signs of bodily organs, language, actions, and productions of others, infers similar thinking subjects. Natural theology, not from bodily organs, but from physical creations, infers God, not as a body, but as a Creator. All this is knowledge of substance, logically inferred from sensation and consciousness; and only because the objects of outer and inner sense are substances, can reason logically infer substances, physical and psychical. It does not follow, however, that reason is infallible: it is fallible so far as not logical from sense. Nor does it follow that we know substance completely. We begin with sense, and perceive subjects only as sensibly qualified. Reason reveals subjects insensibly qualified. But we never know the whole of any substance whatever, not even ourselves, not even a crystal which we seem to see through and through. This imperfection of human knowledge misleads philosophers into agnosticism. But the truth is, sense and reason enable us to know substances not wholly but partially.

Finally, the knowledge of substance creates the idea

of it. The original ideas are derived from my own substance. From myself as sensible I derive my idea of a physical subject ; from myself as conscious, my idea of a thinking subject, partly physical, partly psychical; from both, my idea of a qualified subject. But my ideas of all other known subjects are results of reasoning, which first infers similar subjects, and then forms ideas of them. Ideas of substance are right, so far as they correspond to really known substances sensible and inferred, and their correctness varies in accordance with sense and reason. They are clear, distinct, and adequate, in proportion partly to their proximity to sense, and partly to the extent of reasoning about any given substance ; but they are seldom or never adequate to what is known of a substance.

Locke, though inconsistent, was justified in allowing that the complex ideas of substances are not due to mere composition of simple ideas ; and he ought to have made the same admission in the case of other ideas, because not all ideas of mixed modes are due to composition, nor all ideas of relations to comparison, nor all general ideas to abstraction. He was justified in allowing that we infer substance, in order to conceive the idea of it, beyond ourselves. He was justified in allowing that ideas of substances are right, so far as they represent real objects. But he was unable to found a philosophy of substance, because, in the first place, he failed to apprehend that sensation and reflection both perceive substances within ; secondly, he was accordingly, but falsely, constrained to reduce the inference of substances without to a mere supposition—a supposition without any data, illogical, and impossible to reason ; thirdly, he had to call all substances, all qualified subjects, the only things in the world we

know, unknown; and all ideas of substances obscure
and confused, when really the clearest and distinctest
ideas we have are those of stones, waters, houses, plants,
animals, cats, dogs, men and other substances.

There are many sources of ideas. Sensation and
reflection are not directly concerned with ideas, as
Locke thought, but with sensible objects. But after
sense, reproductive imagination without reasoning conceives particular ideas of the objects of sense, memory
refers the ideas to their objects, and abstraction conceives general ideas of the objects of sense. Reasoning
infers insensible objects and forms their ideas. There is
a rational imagination of ideas. Rational ideas of known
objects are not artificial. Locke partly saw this in the
case of substance. But the ideas of modes and relations
are also rational and correct, so far as they agree with
modes and relations properly inferred as belonging to
external substances. While, however, rational ideas of
the insensible are not artificial, they are often inadequate; *e.g.* of a corpuscle, of infinite space and time,
of gravitation, of the universe, of God. Lastly, the
inventive imagination makes artificial ideas, such as
those of a centaur, a fairy, 'The Iliad,' 'A Midsummer
Night's Dream.' But it has never yet been successfully
analysed. Perhaps even the comparison and composition of artistic imagination are founded on reasoning, not
to the actual and real, but to the possible and ideal.

Let us now suppose that Locke's general account of
the origin of ideas is immaculate and superior to our
objections, that sensation and reflection perceive simple
ideas; that comparison, composition and abstraction
are the three acts which form compound ideas; and
that the introduction of a supposition of substance was
a momentary lapse of a philosopher from the consis-

tency of philosophy. What will be the consequence?
As he says himself, ideas will be the instruments and
materials of our knowledge.[1] Then, by parity of reasoning, all that we can know from such materials will be
other ideas, and, as he has said himself, ideas will be
also all the objects of our understanding.[2] Locke you
would imagine to be the founder of pure idealism. We
should have expected him to go on to show that everything in the world of science is an idea. At the end
we should have been inclined to say—

> There are more things in heaven and earth, Horatio,
> Than are dreamt of in your philosophy.

But Locke had a various, though not a logical mind.
He was a student of Descartes; he was also imbued
with the English devotion to nature. From the former
source he derived the theory of ideas, from the latter
the reality of things. Locke, after assuming that all
objects of understanding are ideas, admitted that external realities exist. The Essay contains an undercurrent of ontology, which comes up first in the famous
distinction of primary and secondary qualities,[3] recognising external qualities as real, as external causes of
our ideas of sensation, and even as externally related
as cause and effect to each other :—

‘The qualities then that are in bodies, rightly considered, are of three sorts.

‘*First*, the bulk, figure, number, situation, and
motion or rest of their solid parts; those are in them,
whether we perceive them or no; and when they are
of that size, that we can discover them, we have by
these an *idea* of the thing, as it is in itself; as is plain
in artificial things : these I call *primary qualities*.

---

[1] *Essay*, II. 33, 19.   [2] I. 1, 8.   [3] II. 8.

'*Secondly*, the *power* that is in any body, by reason of its insensible *primary qualities*, to operate after a peculiar manner on any of our senses, and thereby *produce in us* the *different ideas* of several colours, sounds, smells, tastes, &c. These are usually called sensible qualities.

'*Thirdly*, the *power* that is in any body, by reason of the particular constitution of *its primary qualities*, to make such a *change* in the *bulk, figure, texture, and motion of another body*, as to make it operate on our senses differently from what it did before. Thus the sun has a power to make wax white, and fire to make lead fluid. These are usually called powers.'[1]

The same undercurrent of ontology reappears in the admission of substances, and real essences, though unknown. It becomes most marked in the Fourth Book, where Locke adds to all his other entities, one's own existence, the existence of God, and the existence of other things, such as the clippings of our beards and the parings of our nails. Finally it springs up into an elaborate picture of the insensible universe beyond the reach of our ideas.[2] It is a dangerous thing to be an unconscious metaphysician. Locke's metaphysical theory of existence is quite outside his psychological theory of ideas. How does it agree with his logical theory of knowledge? If it be true to say, that beyond ideas there is an external world of qualities, real and causal, real substances and real essences, my own existence, God's existence, the existence of bodies, and of insensible corpuscles, what is truly said by a philosopher, who is after all but human, must be known to a man. What then does Locke, the philosopher who says all this, say about the knowledge of man?

---

[1] *Essay*, II. 8, 23.   [2] IV. 3, 24.

The Fourth Book, which is on knowledge and opinion, starts with a theory quite consistent with the previous Books, on the origin of ideas :—

'Since *the mind*, in all its thoughts and reasonings, hath no other immediate object than its own *ideas* which it alone does or can contemplate, it is evident that our knowledge is only conversant about 'em.

' *Knowledge* then seems to me to be nothing but the *perception of the connection and agreement, or disagreement and repugnancy of any of our ideas*. In this alone it consists.' [1]

Locke proceeds to divide knowledge into intuition and reasoning. He says that 'sometimes the mind perceives the agreement or disagreement of *two ideas* immediately by themselves without the intervention of any others: and this, I think, we may call *intuitive knowledge*.' [2] He adds that 'when the mind cannot so bring its *ideas* together, as by their immediate comparison, and as it were juxtaposition, or application one to another, to perceive their agreement or disagreement, it is fain, by the intervention of other *ideas* (one or more, as it happens), to discover the agreement or disagreement, which it searches : and this is what we call *Reasoning*.' [3] Afterwards, he writes a whole chapter [4] on Reason, in which he again defines it as the perception of the agreement or disagreement of ideas by intermediate ideas. At the same time he rejects the syllogism, although the process which combines two extremes by the intervention of a middle is clearly the same process as his own. But the main point to be observed is that, according to him, reasoning begins with an intuitive perception of the relation of ideas

[1] IV. 1, 1 2.	[2] IV. 2, 1.
[3] IV. 2, 2.	[4] IV. 17.

and ends with a mediate perception of the relations of ideas.

A theory of reasoning such as this must confine all reasoned knowledge, and therefore all science, to relations of ideas. This actually is his view of mathematics and morals. 'I doubt not,' he says, 'but it will be easily granted, that the *knowledge* we have of *mathematical truths* is not only certain, but *real knowledge*; and not the bare empty vision of vain insignificant *chimeras* of the brain: and yet, if we will consider, we shall find that it is only of our own *ideas*.'[1] He says the same of moral knowledge, which he also holds to be as certain as mathematics.[2] I admit that if all objects of reasoning are ideas, mathematical knowledge is only of our ideas. But, in this case, it is not of the bulk, figure, number, structure and motion of bodies and particles, which Locke himself recognises beyond our ideas. Sir Isaac Newton, then, must have been wrong in saying that all the particles of matter gravitate to one another with a force varying inversely to the square of the distance; for he was pretending to a mathematical knowledge of the motions of particles beyond ideas. What a curious *contretemps*, that in 1687 Newton should discover to mankind the Mathematical Principles of Natural Philosophy in every particle of matter, and in 1690 Locke should publish an Essay concerning Human Understanding to prove that the knowledge of mathematical truths is only of our own ideas!

We are relieved from further criticism of this pure idealism, however logical, because Locke himself deserts it for realism, however hypothetical. At first he deliberately confines all knowledge to the perception of the re-

---

[1] *Essay*, IV. 4, 6.   [2] IV. 4, 7.

lations of ideas, and throughout applies these limits strictly to mathematics and morals. But all of a sudden he introduces us to a knowledge of real things in other departments of knowledge, and, as it were, writes a second essay on another human understanding. The manner in which he makes this abrupt transition is highly instructive. Having defined knowledge to be only conversant about ideas, and to be nothing but the perception of the agreement and disagreement of ideas,[1] he reduces these agreements and disagreements of ideas to four sorts—identity or diversity, relation, coexistence, and real existence.[2] The knowledge of the first three sorts proceeds consistently enough, when suddenly. without any previous preparation, much less argument, he lays down the following dogma :—

‘*Fourthly*. The fourth and last sort is that of *actual real existence* agreeing to any *idea*.’[3]

On his original hypothesis that ideas are all the objects of understanding, on his theory of the origin of ideas in the Second Book, on his definition of knowledge in the very same chapter of the Fourth Book, he ought to have said, the knowledge of the *idea* of actual real existence agreeing to any *idea*. But just as Descartes passed from the idea of God's existence to His existence, so Locke passed from the knowledge of the idea of existence to the knowledge of existence agreeing to any idea. But while Descartes had been inconsequent, Locke to inconsequence added inconsistency ; he had begun by saying that all objects of understanding are ideas ; he afterwards admitted a knowledge of ‘existence agreeing to any idea.’

He afterwards divides this knowledge of existence into three departments—an intuitive knowledge of our

---

[1] IV. 1, 1-2.   [2] IV. 1, 3.   [3] IV. 1, 7.

own existence, a demonstrative knowledge of the existence of a God, a sensitive knowledge of objects present to the senses,[1]—and devotes a chapter to each.[2] In Locke's philosophy, all three ought to have been knowledges of ideas; they are knowledges of the real and actual existence of things. Again, the Fourth Book presents us with two theories of a proposition to support this inconsistency. First, he divides propositions into two kinds; mental, wherein ideas, and verbal, wherein words, the signs of our ideas, are put together.[3] Afterwards, he says that there are two sorts of propositions; one, concerning the existence of anything answerable to an idea, and the other, concerning the agreement or disagreement of our abstract ideas.[4] I am not referring to all these places to criticise Locke for inconsistency, which is a weakness of human nature, a weakness even of philosophers, who are but men, and an amiable weakness, because one of two contradictories must be true. My object is rather to show that Locke at last came to the truth, that not all objects of knowledge, of propositions, of understanding are ideas. But there is a further question, How do we know these actual existences? or, to use Locke's own phrase, 'How shall the mind, when it perceives nothing but its own *ideas*, know that they agree with things themselves?'[5]

The intuitive knowledge of our own existence is settled in a single section, short but significant, in which he gives up his original theory that we perceive nothing but ideas :—

'As for *our own* existence, we perceive it so plainly, and so certainly, that it neither needs, nor is capable of any proof. For nothing can be more evident to us than

---

[1] *Essay*, IV. 3, 21; IV. 9, 2.   [2] IV. 9-11.   [3] IV. 5, 5.
[4] IV. 11, 13.   [5] IV. 4, 3.

our own existence.   I *think*, I *reason*, I *feel pleasure or
pain* : can any of these be more evident to me than my
own existence ?   If I doubt of all other things, that
very doubt makes me perceive my own *existence*, and
will not suffer me to doubt of that.   For if I know I
feel pain, it is evident I have as certain perception of
my own existence as of the existence of the pain I feel :
or if I know I *doubt*, I have as certain perception of the
existence of the thing doubting as of that thought which
I call *doubt*.   Experience then convinces us that *we
have an intuitive knowledge of our own existence*, and an
internal infallible perception that we are.   In every act
of sensation, reasoning or thinking, we are conscious to
ourselves of our own being ; and, in this matter, come
not short of the highest degree of *certainty*.' [1]

This passage breathes the very spirit of Descartes.
Cogito, ergo sum.   I am conscious that I am a thinking
subject.   This is the fact that never ought to have been
deserted.   Descartes deserted it for an inference of
substance, and Locke followed him out of the right path,
but he had to come back to it after all.   Consciousness
reveals to me not thoughts but a thinker.   This consciousness is indeed inconsistent with the previous statements of Locke ; first, that reflection perceives the ideas
of operations, whch is two removes from consciousness ;
secondly, that there is a supposition of a substance as
unknown substratum to those operations, which would
be a baseless inference from data containing nothing but
ideas of operations.   Nevertheless, the direct consciousness of our existence is the fact.   How then is it that it
is constantly disappearing out of philosophy, not only
in the seventeenth, but also in the succeeding centuries ?
Because philosophers are perpetually confusing abstract

and concrete, forgetting that thoughts are abstract qualities but the thinker the real being, and thus concluding that consciousness and reflection reveal thoughts, leaving the subject to inference and supposition, when really consciousness and reflection tell me that I am a thinking subject, from which I infer other thinking subjects.

Unfortunately, in another part of the Essay, Locke had exaggerated the truth, I am conscious that I am a person, a thinking intelligent being, into the falsity, I am that very consciousness.[1] But in the first place, I am conscious that I perform numerous operations besides the operation of being conscious, that I am a sensible, remembering, reasoning, desiring, willing subject; consciousness therefore itself tells me that I am more than itself. Secondly, it is not my only source of information about myself. I am conscious that I am partly body thinking, but I also indirectly observe my body. I reason from my consciousness and observations, and infer that I am a permanent substance, when I am asleep as well as when I am awake, when I am conscious and when I am unconscious. Thirdly, consciousness is interrupted; if I were consciousness I should have an intermittent existence. Finally, Locke has confused the *causa cognoscendi* with the *causa essendi*. Consciousness is necessary to *tell* me, I am a person; but it does not *make* me a person; this am I made by being a permanent substance, partly body and partly soul, capable, when awake, of reasoning, and therefore of the status of a rational being.

At the end of Butler's ' Analogy,' the Dissertation on Personal Identity contains an excellent statement of its relation to consciousness, as follows :—

---

[1] *Essay*, II. 27, 9 *seq.*

'But though consciousness of what is past does thus ascertain our personal identity to ourselves, yet to say that it makes personal identity, or is necessary to our being the same persons, is to say that a person has not existed a single moment, nor done one action, but what he can remember, indeed none but what he reflects upon. And one should really think it self-evident that consciousness of personal identity presupposes, and therefore cannot constitute, personal identity ; any more than knowledge, in any other case, can constitute truth, which it presupposes.'

Locke, then, is right in saying that consciousness is an intuitive knowledge of oneself, wrong in saying that it is oneself. Not from the false identification of self and consciousness, but from the consciousness of self, that is, from the intuitive knowledge we have of our own existence, as cogitative beings, Locke deduces our knowledge of the existence of a God by an argument, which is an extension of the third argument in the 'Principia Philosophiæ' of Descartes.[1] A finite thinking subject requires an infinite thinking subject to create it. Yes, but this argument holds only if we are conscious of ourselves as thinking subjects. God is not an idea, and consequently cannot be inferred from mere ideas. Thus, if Locke had clung to his ideas of reflection, he could not have proved a God: the consciousness, not of mere thoughts, but of a thinking subject, is necessary to natural theology. Similarly, it is necessary to infer any other thinking subject but myself. If, then, I were conscious only of ideas of operations, and even if I were conscious directly of operations, I could not infer thinking subjects, and I could not infer God. The object of consciousness, there-

[1] IV. 10 ; cf. Descartes, *Princ.* i. 20.

fore, is not operations, still less their ideas, but thinking subjects. Here again, too, we find that not all objects, and not all data, of understanding are ideas. Locke was obliged to surrender his theory of ideas in order to prove his own existence, the existence of others, the existence of God.

Next, we come to what Locke calls our sensitive knowledge of objects presented to our senses. Here, with Cartesian inconsequence, he tried to maintain his theory of ideas, and yet show how we know external realities, or originals, by inference. In the Fourth Book he returns to this point again and again. He begins by proposing this problem. 'There can be nothing more certain,' he says, ' than that the idea we receive from an external object is in our minds. But whether there be any thing more than barely that *idea* in our minds, whether we can thence infer the existence of any thing without us, which corresponds to that *idea*, is that, whereof some men think there may be a question made ; because men may have such *ideas* in their minds, when no such thing exists, no such objects affect their senses.' [1] He answers the question by saying that a man is conscious of a different perception when he looks on the sun by day and thinks on it by night, and concludes that this is a knowledge not intuitive nor demonstrative, but sensitive. Again, he divides the problem by simple ideas and complex ideas of substance ; and argues that, in the first place, simple ideas, which the mind can by no means make to itself, must necessarily be the product of things operating on the mind in a natural way, and that the idea of whiteness in the mind answers that power which is in any body to produce it there ; [2] and, in the second place, the reality of our

[1] *Essay.* IV. 2, 14.   [2] IV. 4, 4.

knowledge of substances is founded on our complex
ideas of them being such as are made up of such simple
ones as have been discovered to coexist in nature.[1]
Finally, he devotes to the knowledge of objects without
us a chapter,[2] in which he contends that its certainty is
as great as we are capable of concerning the existence
of anything but oneself and God, and that it deserves
the name of knowledge. He adds four arguments to
the preceding : first, that those who want the organs of
sense want the ideas of that sense ; secondly, that sometimes I cannot avoid the having those ideas produced
in my mind ; thirdly, that many of these ideas are produced with pain, which afterwards we remember without offence ; fourthly, that our senses in many cases
bear witness to the truth of each other's report. Finally,
he falls back on the practical argument that we have at
all events a knowledge of the external world by the
happiness and misery we receive from it. The whole of
these arguments are summed up in this one : I have
ideas of sensation, which I do not produce myself ; I
infer that they are produced by external bodies. It is
the Cartesian argument from the passivity or involuntariness of sensations and ideas.

Locke's admission of the reality and knowledge of
external bodies is right and honest. but completely
destructive of his original hypothesis of the objects
and data of understanding. It is true, as he admits,
that we know external bodies. But this admission destroys his original doctrine that knowledge is always
concerned with ideas. Again, it is true, as he admits,
that we know bodies by inference. But this destroys
his doctrine that reasoning begins and ends with ideas.
Both admissions also destroy his original doctrine that

---

[1] IV. 4, 12.   [2] IV. 11.

ideas are all the objects of understanding. It is also true, as he says, that we infer external bodies from the passivity of sensation. But is it true that we could have drawn this inference from sensible data, if sensation had been a perception of nothing but ideas? This is what Locke makes no attempt to prove. It is contradictory to his own logic. Like Descartes, he recognised that real truth is the agreement of our propositions with external reality.[1] But unlike Descartes, he has given up any special criteria of truth. The veracity of God he uses only for revelation;[2] and regards the inherent clearness and distinctness of ideas not as positive criteria, but only as conditions of truth.[3] The consequence is that he has no organon except the rules of reasoning; and he is aware that, as the data of reasoning are, according to him, ideas with their agreement and disagreement, so the conclusions are logically confined to the agreement and disagreement of ideas.[4] Yet he expects us also to believe that reasoning starting with ideas of sensation can be logically extended to external bodies.

All logic demands that, as are the data, so are the conclusions. I find that some of the sensible objects I perceive are passive. I have a right to infer some other cause. But I must by parity of reasoning infer a cause similar to those already known. Now, what data does Locke supply me? Granting him every advantage and all his inconsistencies, I should have ideas of sensation and reflection, and compound ideas from the Second Book: from the Fourth Book, I should have consciousness of myself, and a demonstration of other thinking subjects, and of God. These, *ex hypothesi*, are all the data,

---

[1] *Essay*, IV. 5.   [2] IV. 16, 14.

[3] IV. 2, 15.   [4] IV. 17.

direct and indirect, at the very best. What would be
the logical inference? I could infer, from the passivity
of sense, that it resulted either from other ideas, or from
other thinking subjects, or from God. I could not, being
without bodily data, infer that it resulted from external
bodies. Locke saw the importance of the passivity of
sense, but forgot the rules of logic.

Newton and Locke were contemporaries. What,
then, was Locke's attitude to natural philosophy? He
recognised its discoveries, and especially the corpuscular philosophy revived by Bacon, developed by Descartes, and brought to its perfection by Newton. We
have followed him in his 'little excursion into natural
philosophy'[1] to distinguish primary and secondary
qualities. He there admits the existence of corpuscles,
real qualities, primary and secondary, though insensible,
and real powers between qualities, e.g. the power of fire
to make lead fluid. There is no fault to find here
except with his definition of a quality as 'a power to
produce any idea in our mind.'[2] A quality is really a
characteristic of a subject or substance. It has various
powers, and among them the occasional power of affecting our senses. For instance, motion is a characteristic
of every corpuscle, and has a power of affecting every
other corpuscle, and sometimes of affecting human senses
in the way of sensible motion, light, heat, sound, and so
forth. But to define it by its sensible power, would be
to convert a very occasional accident into the essence of
motion, forgetting that there are myriads and millions
of motions which come nowhere near the earth, much
less man, and are not powers of producing any ideas in
his mind.

Locke defined quality by a separable accident.

[1] II. 8, 22.   [2] II. 8, 8.

N

Hence also a mistake in his definition of a secondary quality as a power of an insensible primary quality to produce in our senses a sensible idea. This is only an occasional and accidental power; and a secondary quality is a specific modification of a primary quality, which exists whether it produces a sensible effect or not. Thus heat is a mode of motion transferred from star to star, and before the origin of animals much of it was exhausted without having the power of producing sensible heat With these corrections, Locke expresses the scientific distinction of primary and secondary qualities in the universe. He fully recognises the existence of that part of insensible nature, which I have called the imperceptible, to distinguish it from the insensible but inferentially perceptible originals of sensible objects. He recognises corpuscles as well as masses, the particles of this paper as well as the paper.

But when he came to give these imperceptible corpuscles a place in the human understanding, he began to vacillate. In the Fourth Book, he distinguishes knowledge and opinion, as respectively the perception and the presumption of agreements and disagreements of ideas, as certain and probable. Strictly, he could put natural philosophy in neither, because he admitted that it was not about ideas, but things. But the alternative to which he leaned was to draw the line between knowledge and opinion, exactly between the paper and its particles, between the mass and the corpuscle, between the perceptible and the imperceptible; and, therefore, to call the first inferences from sense knowledge, and the subsequent inferences of science opinion. On the whole, according to him, knowledge[1] includes mathematics and morals because they are about ideas, knowledge of self

¹ *Essay*, IV. 3, 5; IV. 10, 6; IV. 11, 9; IV. 11, 13.

because it is intuition, knowledge of God because it is demonstration from this intuition, and knowledge of external originals directly inferred from sense : here ends knowledge. In opinion falls natural philosophy. Why? Because the further from sense the less, he thought, our knowledge. Because we are not capable of the ideas of things so remote and minute, and this defect, as he thought, keeps us in ignorance of the things. Because we merely make experiments which are not science Because we can only guess and probably conjecture, use hypothesis and analogy. 'Analogy,' says he, 'in these matters, is the only help we have, and 'tis from that alone we draw all our grounds of probability. Thus observing that the bare rubbing of two bodies violently one upon another, produces heat and very often fire itself, we have reason to think that what we call heat and fire consists in a violent agitation of the imperceptible minute parts of the burning matter : observing likewise that the different refractions of pellucid bodies produce in our eyes the different appearances of several colours ; and also that the different ranging and laying the superficial parts of several bodies, as of velvet, watered silk, &c., does the like, we think it probable that the colour and shining of bodies, is in them nothing but the different arrangement and refraction of their minute and sensible parts.'[1] But knowledge of these insensible qualities he denies. He doubts 'that how far soever human industry may advance useful and *experimental* philosophy in physical things, *scientifical* will still be out of our reach ;'[2] and he suspects that 'natural philosophy is not capable of being made a science.'[3] Yet this very Locke winds up his Essay by

[1] IV. 16, 12 ; cf. IV. 3, 16 ; IV. 3, 24 end ; IV. 6 ; IV. 12, 9 13.
[2] IV. 3, 26.   [3] IV. 12. 10.

a triple division of science, one of which is Physics or Natural Philosophy, the knowledge of things.[1]

It is a matter of deep regret that Locke should have written thus of natural philosophy in the very time of Newton. There is some truth in what he says, but marred by exaggeration. There is a huge abyss of ignorance, but it is not altogether an incurable ignorance. Much of what is called science is opinion, but fresh evidences convert opinion into science. Because there are probabilities in natural philosophy, it does not follow that there is nothing certain. We cannot have a perfect knowledge of nature, but we can know something without knowing everything. We cannot always discover real essence, but there is a knowledge of co-existences and causes, of the conservation and correlation of physical forces, as in electricity and magnetism, without always knowing their essences. Locke rightly saw that there is more of the universe unknown than known, and much which is only opined; but he lost sight of the main fabric of science. By the mere elimination of chance such a concatenation of laws cannot but be true.

Locke was ignorant of the logic of science. The two greatest men of science in his own country were Bacon and Newton, of whom the former had shown that there is an experimental science of nature, the latter that natural science is capable of physical deductions from mathematical principles. But Locke, like Hobbes, was silent about Baconian induction, and oblivious to everything except the old method of intuition and demonstration, which suits mathematics, but not the whole of natural philosophy. Everything outside demonstration, he calls hypothesis and analogy. He did not recognise the variety of method, the *ana-*

[1] *Essay*, IV. 21.

logia demonstrationum pro natura subjecti, desiderated
by Bacon. He did not see that the corpuscular
philosophy is made independent of this hypothesis and
that analogy, by many different evidences in many
different departments—gravity, light, heat, sound, electricity, magnetism, chemical attraction, nervous and
muscular motion—all of which point to corpuscles, their
motions, according to Newton's laws, their modifications
constituting secondary qualities, their convertibility
and indestructibility as motion. He did not recognise
that there is a circumstantial evidence, which in law is
sufficient to hang a man, in nature sufficient to prove a
fact; and an approximate certainty, by accumulation
of evidence, ever indefinitely approaching absolute
necessity.

But his greatest, though characteristic, blunder was
his attempt to carry inference beyond sense to the external original inferentially perceptible and then stop
short; to allow us to know the paper and not the particle, the mass and not the molecule. Such a logic
is arbitrary. If insensible modes of primary qualities
are truly said to be, as Locke allows, then they are
knowable. The same laws of reasoning which enable
us to infer from sensible effects an external cause, enable us from that cause to infer another cause, and so on
till we have completely explained facts of sense by laws
of science. If it were not so, how could science correct
ordinary knowledge? Ordinary knowledge infers an
external object, like in secondary as well as primary
qualities. Science declares that the external world is
like in primary but not in secondary qualities to the
sensible effect. But if the former is knowledge and the
latter opinion, by the first principle of method ordinary
knowledge, as more certain, is to be preferred to the less

certain science; so that the ordinary man is right in his theory of external light and heat, and the natural philosopher wrong! Locke's line between knowledge and science gives the ordinary man, with his inference of bodies, knowledge, but the scientific man, with his inference of corpuscles, opinion. He elevates ordinary above scientific knowledge, which is absurd.

There is a standing difference between natural and mental philosophy, and Locke has done much to produce it. He would make theology and morals not only sciences, which they are, but more scientific than natural philosophy, and tells man, whose real function is to know all and do all, that his proper business is his moral duties and his future state.[1] Newton had just written the 'Optics' and the 'Principia,' but Locke's theory of science would reduce these works to mere opinions. The whole history of science is against him. On the foundation of Newton's mechanics of motion has been gradually reared a system of science which has eventually revealed to us the insensible and imperceptible causes of our sensations in the external world. On the other side stand the mental philosophers, *philosophantes secundum sensum*, considering primarily their sensations and ideas, and with difficulty extending their thoughts even to the external originals, then gazing stupidly at the perceptible world, and never dreaming that they have to explain the knowledge of imperceptible nature. Locke's hypothesis that we have a sensitive knowledge from ideas of objects presented to sense, a mathematical and moral science of ideas, and an uncertain opinion of the physical universe, undervalues natural philosophy. It immediately produced the false attitude of Berkeley and Hume towards nature, but it has affected the whole

[1] *Essay*, IV. 12, 11.

course of mental philosophy, which has unduly neglected the problem of knowledge, presented to it by natural philosophers. Hence, while natural philosophy has shown that the insensible is the *causa essendi* of the sensible, mental philosophy has never yet shown how the sensible is the *causa cognoscendi* of the insensible.

But let us suppose that the whole fabric of science is opinion, the whole imperceptible world unknown. Yet it is at least an object of understanding and reasoning, because, as Locke himself says, 'not but that it is the nature of the understanding constantly to close with the more probable side,'[1] and, as he admits, reason may end either in certainty or in probability, either by demonstration or an *argumentum ad judicium*.[2] This being so, imperceptible probabilities are objects of understanding and reason, but are not all ideas ; therefore not all objects of understanding and reason are ideas.

Nor could they be reasoned from ideas as their data. This want of consequence brings us to another defect in Locke's theory of primary and secondary qualities ; his false view of their sensible aspect. In his opinion, as external they are powers, as sensible they are ideas. But they are neither mere powers nor mere ideas. If, as sensible, they were ideas, we could not logically infer insensible primary qualities, which are admitted not to be ideas, yet inferrible. Therefore, even as sensible, primary and secondary qualities are not ideas, but physical qualities in sense, from which to infer physical qualities beyond. So universally, the inference of imperceptible corpuscles with real qualities and powers beyond sense, even if only probable, could not be drawn from mere ideas of sensation. The natural

[1] IV. 20, 12. [2] IV. 17.

philosophy of the physical world, whether it be knowledge or opinion, demands physical data of sense.

How came Locke, having said that ' whatsoever the
mind perceives in itself or is the immediate object
of perception, thought, or understanding, that I call
idea,'[1] immediately to conclude real primary qualities of
matter? Through the Cartesian habit of surreptitiously
passing from the idea to the thing, and his own supposition of a bastard sensation of the thing. His one argument for the reality of primary qualities is that they are
' such as sense constantly finds in every particle of matter,
which has bulk enough to be perceived.'[2] But according
to him sense is of ideas. All then he could consistently
say would have been that primary qualities are such as
sense constantly finds in the *idea* of every particle of
the *idea* of matter, which has the *idea* of bulk enough
to be perceived. But this consistency with his hypothesis
would not have proved the fact of the material reality
of primary qualities beyond ideas. At the same time,
his lapse into a direct sense of matter is of interest,
because it is a distinct anticipation of intuitive realism.
It exhibits the constant tendency of the philosopher to
relapse into the ordinary man, and to fancy he directly
perceives the external thing, or, using the inaccurate terminology of modern psychology, after contending that
what we are conscious of is subjective affections, to suppose a consciousness of objective existence. As Locke
tried to bridge over the gulf from ideas of sensation to
qualities by a kind of bastard sensation of qualities,
so his modern followers try to bridge the gulf from
subjective affections of consciousness to objective existence by an undefinable consciousness of objective existence. But it is certain that sensation perceives not the

[1] *Essay*, II. 8, 8.   [2] II. 8, 9.

external thing, but its internal effect ; and the only way
in which we can reach external qualities of things is not
by sense but by inference from adequate internal data,
which cannot be mere ideas, nor any psychical states of
subjective consciousness.

The 'Essay' concerning Human Understanding'
begins by assuming that all objects of understanding,
as well as all data of sense, are ideas : it ends by admitting that things beyond ideas are objects of understanding, reasoning, science. The end is better than
the beginning, though the conclusion does not follow
from the premises. External bodies are properly inferred by ordinary men, as Locke admitted; and
imperceptible corpuscles and their qualities are known,
with more certainty than he admitted, by men of science.
Therefore, in the first place, not all objects of understanding, reasoning, science, are ideas. Secondly, the
data of sense are neither ideas of sensation nor external
qualities of matter, but internal effects on the nervous
system, sensibly qualified as extended, moving, hot,
coloured, and by other primary and secondary qualities.
From internal, ordinary knowledge infers external, substances. From these again science, correcting ordinary
knowledge, infers imperceptible corpuscles, qualities
primary and secondary as the modifications of primary
powers exerted between those corpuscles, and powers
of affecting our senses. Locke's 'Essay' throughout, to
make it thoroughly correct, consistent, and consequent,
would need two fundamental alterations :—

1. Some objects of understanding are physical things.
2. Some data of sensation are physical effects on
   the nervous system.

CHAPTER VII.

BERKELEY.

THE two philosophers hitherto discussed assumed hypotheses, but admitted facts, and tried to explain them. Descartes assumed that ideas are the data of sense, but admitted the knowledge of physical objects, and broke down on the inconsequence of reasoning from psychical data in the premises to physical objects in the conclusion. Locke made the same assumption, the same admission, and the same failure. But he went further into hypothesis, and to inconsequence added inconsistency. He assumed that ideas are not only all the data but also all the objects of understanding, and then admitted that physical objects are also objects of understanding. The admission is true, and therefore, while it contradicted, also destroyed the double hypothesis. We now come to a philosopher who, accepting the whole ideal hypothesis, consistently denied facts   Berkeley assumed, with Descartes, that ideas are the data, and with Locke, that they are the objects, of human knowledge, and consistently, but falsely, deduced man's ignorance of a physical world.

The 'Principles of Human Knowledge,' after an Introduction on Abstract Ideas, begin in the following manner :—

'It is evident to any one who takes a survey of the objects of human knowledge, that they are either ideas

actually imprinted on the senses, or else such as are
perceived by attending to the passions and operations
of the mind, or lastly, ideas formed by help of memory
and imagination, either compounding, dividing, or
barely representing those originally perceived in the
aforesaid ways. By sight I have the ideas of light and
colours with their several degrees and variations. By
touch I perceive, for example, hard and soft, heat and
cold, motion and resistance, and of all these more or
less either as to quantity or degree. Smelling furnishes
me with odours, the palate with tastes, and hearing
conveys sounds to the mind in all their variety of tone
and composition. And as several of these are observed
to accompany each other, they come to be marked by
one name, and so to be reputed as one thing. Thus,
for example, a certain colour, taste, smell, figure and
consistence having been observed to go together, are
accounted one distinct thing, signified by the name
"apple." Other collections of ideas constitute a stone, a
tree, a book, and the like sensible things ; which, as
they are pleasing or disagreeable, excite the passions of
love, hatred, joy, grief, and so forth.'[1]

Here are most of the errors in the Second and Third
Books of Locke's Essay accepted as principles. Without proof, ideas alone are supposed to be perceived ;
ideas of qualities without a qualified subject, and
ideas of operations without a thinking subject. Reasoning from the data of sense to their causes is entirely
postponed in favour of representing, compounding and
dividing ideas. Ideas, simple or complex, are consistently declared to be all the objects of human knowledge.
But these so-called principles are mere hypotheses.
There is not one word of proof that either the data or

[1] *Princ.* i.

the objects of human knowledge are ideas.   Locke, not human nature—and not even the whole of Locke—was the oracle of Berkeley.

Berkeley, however, being a less various but a more logical thinker than Locke, was truer to the data of his predecessor.   Locke, as we found, having assigned comparison, composition and abstraction as the three acts, which form new ideas from sense, suddenly, and without any justification, introduced a fourth act of supposition, which is a kind of reasoning, to account for our idea of substance.   Berkeley avoided the after-thought, and, at the same time, the truth, that reason does intervene in the formation of ideas from sense. Adhering to Locke's first thoughts, he perceived that what his predecessor had allowed about other complex ideas equally applied to complex ideas of substances. If we start from ideas of sensation, such as those of colour, taste, smell, figure and consistence, and merely compound these ideas, we can construct a collection of ideas and account it one distinct thing, called an apple ; but we cannot, without introducing a qualified physical substance into sense, and restoring its privileges to reason, either perceive or infer an external physical substance.   Berkeley thus reduces Locke to logic ; nor has mental philosophy ever recovered this purely hypo-thetical theory of substance.

Berkeley also made an important correction in one of Locke's three acts, abstraction.   Locke had supposed that we can form a perfectly abstract idea of a triangle, which is ' neither equilateral, equicrural, nor scalenon, but all and none of these at once.' [1]   Berkeley devoted the Introduction of the ' Principles ' to a criticism of this modern conceptualism, and founded modern nominalism.

[1] *Essay*, IV. 7, 9.

He denied that he could abstract or conceive separately
qualities which cannot exist separately, or form a
general notion in Locke's sense.[1] He admitted that
he could consider a figure merely as triangular, without
attending to its particular qualities, but not form an
abstract general inconsistent idea of a triangle.[2] Similarly, Hume afterwards said, that all general ideas are
nothing but particular ones annexed to general terms.[3]

The essential truth at the bottom of this theory is
that abstraction is only a kind of attention. But, as
often happens, one extreme view begets another. We
cannot rise to a purely abstract idea, nor need we fall
to a purely particular idea; we cannot form an idea of
triangle in general, nor need we think of a single
triangle. We can frame a general idea of a miscellaneous assemblage of similar individuals.[4] Secondly,
the point about classes is, not what we conceive, but
what we infer and know. But, while correcting
Locke's exaggeration of abstraction, Berkeley left its
independence of reasoning. The consequence is that,
according to him, the limit of generalisation would be
some single simple idea or some single collection of
simple ideas of sense viewed generally. This narrow-
ness pervades his whole philosophy. There is, indeed,
such a simple abstraction of ideas from sense, as we admitted in the last chapter. But reason, at the same
time, starts from sense and first infers classes of insensible objects, and then constructs general ideas of
them in the rational imagination. Finally, this rational
imagination of general ideas accompanies a rational
abstraction; like direct abstraction, attention, but attention to objects of reason. We can abstract, in the sense

---

[1] *Princ.* Introduction, x.   [2] Id. xvi.
[3] *Treatise*, ii. § 7.   [4] Cf. Mill, *Logic*, iv. 2, 1.

of attending to, an insensible object, not apart from the qualities which belong to it, but apart from the quality of being sensible, which does not belong to it. The idea of an object will indeed contain some sensible qualities, and usually some visible colour. But having inferred that the invisible object is coloured only in the sense of reflecting æthereal undulations, by abstraction I consider the object as so qualified, without attending to it as visibly coloured. In short, I know by scientific reasoning that objects exist apart from merely sensible qualities, and I can attend separately to their existing apart. Berkeley fell into the error of postponing inference about classes, and therefore of limiting abstraction to direct formation of ideas from sense. Really, there are objects known by sense, and objects known from sense by reason; and there is an abstraction from sense, and an abstraction from reason, though in both cases the abstraction is but attention to sensible and rational objects of knowledge.

According to Berkeley, then, starting from the Second and Third Books of Locke's Essay, all the objects of human knowledge are ideas of sensation and reflection, and the collections of ideas made out of them by memory and imagination, to which he reduced abstraction of ideas, and without reasoning about causes. But it is impossible for errors to remain perfectly logical. Though he had just said that all objects known to us are ideas, he proceeds, like Locke, dogmatically to assert that a thinking subject exists:—

'But besides all the endless variety of ideas or objects of knowledge, there is likewise something which knows or perceives them, and exercises divers operations, as willing, imagining, remembering about them. This perceiving active being is what I call *mind*, *spirit*, *soul*,

or *myself*. By which words I do not denote any one of
my ideas, but a thing entirely distinct from them,
wherein they exist, or which is the same thing, whereby
they are perceived; for the existence of an idea consists in being perceived.'[1]

Berkeley was dogmatic, but right, in asserting the
existence of himself; but he was wrong in calling this
thinking subject a thing entirely distinct from his ideas,
and in supplying no data for his knowledge of it.
I am a thinker, from whom the subject and the
thoughts are opposite abstractions. But, in spite of his
criticism of abstract ideas, Berkeley had already followed Locke's Second Book in supposing all the objects
of reflection to be mere ideas of operations. The question then arises, how he could possibly know that he
was also a thinking subject. Locke had said that the
thinking subject is a matter of mere supposition.
Berkeley went a stage further: he said that 'it cannot
be of itself perceived, but only by the effects which it
produceth.'[2] But there are several difficulties in allowing him to take this view on his hypotheses.
In the first place, if it is true, there is something which
is known, though indirectly, without being an idea;
therefore, not all objects of understanding, but only all
objects of sense, will be ideas. Secondly, if all the objects
of sensation and reflection were ideas of sensible qualities
and ideas of operations, as he supposes, the whole of
these data would contain no subject, not of course a
physical nor even a psychical subject, and nothing like
a subject, for a subject is, as Berkeley admits, not an
idea; therefore, no subject, even no psychical subject,
could be logically inferred. We must choose, therefore,
between the original data and the illogical conclusion.

[1] *Princ.* ii.   [2] Id. xxvii.

But Berkeley was right in admitting the existence and knowledge of a thinking subject. Therefore, the data of sensation and reflection cannot be mere ideas. Even if not sensation, at least reflection must be perception of myself as a thinking subject, from which I infer other thinking subjects, and God Himself.

Berkeley ought to have returned to Descartes, and begun with the consciousness, 'I think.' But, although he saw that we cannot abstract what cannot exist separately, he was so enthralled by Locke that he began by supposing that we perceive ideas of qualities and ideas of operations, when we cannot even abstract these objects except in the sense of attending to them in their subjects. The idea of colour and the idea of willing are as much abstractions as the idea of a triangle. We really perceive, by sensation, at least, the coloured, and by consciousness, at least, the willing. But Berkeley, like Locke, began all sense with abstract ideas of qualities and operations. Though, unlike Locke, he saw that he could derive no physical subject from the former, he illogically thought he could derive a thinking subject from the latter ideas, although, like Locke, he had no data for a logical sequence from the conscious ideas of operations to the thinking subject.

Curiously enough, he ended, like Locke, in after all returning to Descartes, and in admitting, 'I know or am conscious of my own being.'[1] This admission that I am conscious of myself is quite inconsistent with the original hypothesis that I perceive ideas of operations directly, and the subsequent corollary that I perceive myself only indirectly by my effects. Nevertheless, the admission is true, and the hypothesis and its corollary false. I cannot infer a thinking sub-

---

[1] *Hylas and Philonous*, Third Dialogue.

ject from mere operations. I am not conscious of operations, still less of ideas of operations—an abstraction, two removes from the truth. I am conscious of myself, as thinking subject.

But Berkeley involved his admission of a thinking subject with another hypothesis. He accepted the Cartesian transition from self to soul without a word of proof.[1] As I have already shown, I am not conscious of this identification, I am conscious of the very reverse. The combined evidence of consciousness, observation, and reasoning teaches me that I am a man thinking partly by my body and partly by my soul. But, you will say, Berkeley was a theologian, who, knowing that God is a spirit, rightly inferred that man is a spirit. The answer is that man is not God. It is true that there is a resemblance, but there is also a difference. When I infer that there are other men, I observe, by direct inference from sense, two sorts of signs, bodily organs and physical works, from both of which I infer a man like myself, body and soul. But God only offers me one of these signs, His works of nature, but no signs of a body. Hence I have a right to infer that He is similar to myself, so far as He by intelligence and will produces works of order, beauty, and goodness, similar to those of man, but I have no right to infer either that He, like man, is also a body, or that man, like Him, is a pure spirit. Nor have I a right to infer that—

> All are but parts of one stupendous whole,
> Whose body nature is, and God the soul.

Nature is to God as works are to man; and as a man's body is not his works, so neither is nature the body of God. 'Hic omnia regit,' says Newton[2] about the Deity,

---

[1] *Princ.* ii.

[2] Newton, *Principia*, Lib. III. Scholium Generale (*sub fin.*).

'non ut anima mundi, sed ut universorum dominus.'
God has no body ; for how could He have a body proportionate to His infinite intelligence and will, and show
it not ? God, then, is a spirit ; man is not.

Now, it is true that God, for a time, gave a bodily
sign, when He took upon Himself a body and made
Himself man. But the incarnation of Christ is a very
proof of the difference between God and man. Christ
ceased to be a pure Spirit, became flesh, and dwelt
among us. Berkeley cannot explain this union of the
Divine and the human in Christ. God is a spirit ; but
if man is also a spirit, what is the incarnation ?
Berkeley's only logical answer would be the gratuitous
hypothesis that Christ took upon Himself certain ideas,
called the human body. But Christ had the ideas already
from eternity. What He wanted was the very body, represented by those ideas, for a time. There is nothing
for it, but that God is a spirit, and Christ took upon
himself a body and became man, and man is both body
and spirit in one. The idealistic hypothesis that I am
a spirit is inconsistent both with philosophy and with
Christianity. Yet in our own time a false philosophy
of man as a purely spiritual subject is supposed to be
a justification of Christian theology.

Berkeley, in the Introduction and the first two sections of his ' Principles,' furnished himself with his premises. They are anticipations of human nature, mainly
derived from Descartes and Locke, with an occasional
assumption of his own. Let it be granted, from Descartes, that the thinking subject, myself, is a mind,
spirit, soul. Let it be granted, from Locke's Second
Book, that not only all data, but all objects of knowledge, are simple ideas of sensation and reflection,
and ideas compounded by memory and imagination,

without taking any notice of reasoning; and let us avoid Locke's inconsistency of supposing an external physical substance beyond a collection of ideas, and his error of purely abstract ideas. Let the premises, which he owes to Descartes and Locke, be granted to Berkeley, without his proving them. What follows? Why, the purely hypothetical, fairly logical, wholly synthetic deduction from false and unproved hypotheses, known as the Berkeleian philosophy. He who is foolish enough on the mere authority of this doctor to swallow the hypotheses, like pills, will find that the deductions will purge him of all knowledge beyond spirit and ideas.

Berkeley begins his deductions by explaining the existence of what he calls sensible things, and denying that what he calls unthinking things exist except as perceived :—'The table I write on, I say, exists, that is, I see and feel it ; and if I were out of my study I should say it existed, meaning thereby that if I was in my study I might perceive it, or that some other spirit actually does perceive it. There was an odour, that is, it was smelled ; there was a sound, that is to say, it was heard ; a colour or figure, and it was perceived by sight or touch. This is all that I can understand by these and the like expressions. For as to what is said of the absolute existence of unthinking things without any relation to their being perceived, that seems perfectly unintelligible. Their *esse* is *percipi*, nor is it possible that they should have any existence out of the minds of thinking beings which perceive them.' [1]

So far as this argument follows from its premises it is hypothetically unanswerable. The *esse* of ideas is *percipi*; if, then, all objects of human knowledge are ideas, their *esse* will be *percipi* ; and again, an unthink-

[1] *Princ.* iii.

ing thing, which is not an idea, will not be humanly known to exist. Berkeley was entitled to these hypothetical conclusions. But his argument conceals a further false hypothesis, namely, that what is unknown by man to exist, being unintelligible to him, is non-existent; from which he concluded that a purely unthinking thing is not only unknown by man, but also non-existent. Thus to hypotheses and hypothetical deduction Berkeley added dogmatism. He dogmatically asserted the existence of mind and the non-existence of matter.

The importance of the deductions which immediately follow consists in their entire omission of reasoning from the data of sense to their causes, and its consequences, when combined with Locke's premises. Houses, mountains, rivers, and, in a word, all sensible objects, are supposed to have a separate existence. Now, says Berkeley, they are what we perceive by sense, and what we perceive are ideas or sensations; therefore they are ideas or sensations.[1] He adds that it is only the doctrine of *abstract ideas* which makes us distinguish the existence of sensible objects from their being perceived.[2] But it is not true that a house is a sensible object which we perceive by sense; sense perceives only a sensible effect of an external house, which is inferred by reasoning, and can be distinguished from the sensible effect by the attention of abstraction. But it is true that if we choose to omit reasoning about causes, and suppose that sense perceives ideas or sensations, the only house we should know would be, not the house now inferred, but only what we should then perceive, a mere collection of ideas or sensations, incapable of being abstracted from being perceived.

[1] *Princ.* iv.   [2] Id. v.

This strict though hypothetical logic from Locke's Second Book removed Berkeley into another arena of philosophy. Descartes and Locke had admitted the existence and knowledge of an external world, not merely psychical but also physical; that a house is an external object causing our ideas; and, in accordance with the representative theory, that perception presents ideas but represents external objects. Berkeley, agreeing both with Descartes and Locke in the perception of ideas, but aware that neither philosopher supplied data from which to infer an external object, and following Locke in postponing reasoning about it, logically concludes that the external object and the sensible object are one, and that in perceiving an idea or sensation, we are perceiving not a sensible effect of an external house, but the house itself. His pure idealism produced the metaphysical theory that objects, supposed to be external, are nothing but ideas or sensations in the mind, and the psychological theory of a presentative perception of ideas or sensations, representing nothing.

Having hypothetically deduced that the *esse* of all objects known to man is *percipi*, and that what are called external objects are really ideas or sensations, Berkeley proceeds to the conclusion that 'all the choir of heaven and furniture of the earth; in a word, all those bodies which compose the mighty frame of the world,' exist in my mind, or in that of some created spirit; or else subsist in the mind of some eternal spirit.[1] This conclusion also follows from the premises. If all objects of knowledge are ideas, and ideas subsist in the mind of some spirit, it follows necessarily that the whole known world subsists in the mind of some spirit. So far, indeed, as the human spirit goes, we could only speak

[1] *Princ.* vi.

of the whole *known* world. We saw above that Berkeley, while speaking even of man,[1] denied the existence
of what was not an object of human knowledge. He
now corrects this defect by the addition of the eternal
spirit,[2] to whom whatever exists is known, while what is
not known does not exist. Of the Divine spirit at least
Berkeley could say, whatever exists is an object of His
knowledge; if, then, all objects of knowledge are ideas,
and ideas subsist in the mind of a spirit, whatever exists
subsists in the mind of the eternal spirit of God. Even
so, however, it might be objected that, if ideas are the
objects of human, it does not follow that they are the
only objects of Divine knowledge. But in Berkeley's
'Principles' there is a perpetual *équivoque* between the
sensible ideas of man and the intellectual ideas of God.

'From what has been said it follows that there is
not any other substance than spirit;' this is the next
hypothetical consequence.[3] It is an immediate corollary. If there were only man, the only *known* substance
would be spirit, but add God and it would follow that
the only *existing* substance is spirit, so that there remains
no unthinking substance.[4] Berkeley further proceeds to
deduce this denial of matter from the hypothesis of
ideas. He is perfectly logical. Ideas cannot exist in
an unthinking substance; if then sensible qualities were
ideas, there would be no unthinking substance or *substratum* of those ideas or qualities.[5] Again, he warns us
against those who maintained that, though unthinking
substance is not the substratum of sensible ideas, ideas
are nevertheless the copies or resemblances of unthinking
substance. 'I answer,' he says, 'an idea can be like nothing but an idea.'[6] This memorable sentence marks

---

[1] *Princ.* iii.   [2] Id. vi.   [3] Id. vii.   [4] Id.
[5] Id.   [6] Id. viii.

the return of the logic of reasoning into mental philosophy. Berkeley at this point begins to think about
reasoning, though too late ; for he had already fixed the
objects of knowledge without it. But he thinks about
it as a logician, and gives the answer to the illogical
attempt of Descartes and Locke to first enclose man
within psychical ideas, and then, without any clue in the
data, expect him to discover physical objects. In the
case of physical substances, if the data of inference were
sensible qualities as ideas, we could infer a similar collection of qualities as ideas ; if they were qualities without being ideas, we could infer a similar combination of
qualities ; but in neither case could we infer a physical
substance, for which we should have no analogue in
sense.[1]

This rigorous logic from Locke's hypotheses of ideas
enabled Berkeley to destroy Locke's theories of material
substance and its primary qualities at a blow :—

'Some there are who make a distinction betwixt
primary and *secondary* qualities : by the former, they
mean extension, figure, motion, rest, solidity or impenetrability, and number ; by the latter they denote all
other sensible qualities, as colours, sounds, tastes, and so
forth. The ideas we have of these they acknowledge not
to be the resemblances of anything existing without the
mind or unperceived ; but they will have our ideas of
the primary qualities to be patterns or images of things
which exist without the mind, in an unthinking substance which they call *matter.* By matter, therefore, we
are to understand an inert, senseless substance, in which
extension, figure, and motion do actually subsist. But
it is evident, from what we have already shown, that
extension, figure and motion are only ideas existing in

[1] Cf. *Princ.* xxxvii.

the mind, and that an idea can be like nothing but another idea, and that consequently neither they nor their archetypes can exist in an unperceiving substance. Hence it is plain, that the very notion of what is called *matter* or *corporeal substance* involves a contradiction in it.'[1]

Yes ; if, and only if, qualities as sensible are ideas, an idea is like nothing but another idea, and therefore we could infer no external qualities of matter ; neither insensible primary qualities like primary qualities as sensible, nor insensible secondary qualities as modifications of primary qualities and causes of secondary qualities as sensible. Now, matter is nothing without qualities : therefore, we could not infer matter at all. The argument is quite logical, if we once admit with Locke, that, as sensible, all qualities are ideas. If with modern idealists we should substitute sensations, it would equally follow that we could infer no insensible qualities of matter, and therefore no matter at all.

Berkeley added a second argument to prove that all qualities exist only as ideas in the mind and not in matter and its particles :—

'They who assert that figure, motion and the rest of the primary original qualities do exist without the mind in unthinking substances, do at the same time acknowledge that colours, sounds, heat, cold, and suchlike secondary qualities, do not, which they tell us are sensations existing in the mind alone, that depend on and are occasioned by the different size, texture, and motion of the minute particles of matter. This they take for an undoubted truth which they can demonstrate beyond all exception. Now if it be certain that those original qualities are inseparably united with the other

[1] *Princ.* ix.

sensible qualities, and not, even in thought, capable of being abstracted from them, it plainly follows that they exist only in the mind. But I desire any one to reflect and try whether he can, by any abstraction of thought, conceive the extension and motion of a body without all other sensible qualities. For my own part, I see evidently that it is not in my power to frame an idea of a body extended and moved, but I may withal give it some colour or other sensible quality which is acknowledged to exist only in the mind. In short, extension, figure, and motion, abstracted from all other qualities, are inconceivable. Where, therefore, the other sensible qualities are there must these be also, to wit, in the mind, and nowhere else.'[1]

This argument does not touch Locke, so far as it depends on the admission that secondary qualities are mere sensations; for Locke said that, as sensible, they are ideas, and, as external, powers. But it touches later theories of secondary qualities, realistic and idealistic. It is true that if secondary qualities are sensations, primary qualities, as sensible, will also be sensations, from which no external quality, and therefore no matter, could be inferred. Moreover, the argument is interesting as another instance of Berkeley's reduction of the external to the sensible. He saw that on the conjoint hypothesis that sense perceives qualities as sensations, with abstraction of ideas, but without reasoning to causes, we should only be able to infer and attend to qualities, primary and secondary, as they are fused in sensation. Hence his followers invariably regard primary and secondary qualities merely as various kinds of sensations, and not as external qualities.

By this series of hypothetical arguments Berkeley

[1] *Princ.* x.

arrived at the following conclusions : all subjects are
spirits and all objects ideas of spirits. This absolute
universality logically applies only to the eternal spirit.
As far as the human spirit goes, Berkeley's conclusions,
so far as they are logical, must be put in a more
moderate form. If there are spirits, and all objects of
knowledge are ideas, then all known subjects are spirits
and all known objects are ideas ; a physical subject of
qualities is not known to exist, and qualities, primary
and secondary, are known as ideas or sensations in our
minds, but are not known to be external qualities of
physical subjects, bodies and corpuscles, in an external
world. What, then, is to become of the minute particles
of matter, their latent sizes, textures, and motions; to
say nothing of their priority, and their production of
our sensations? What, again, are the causes of the ideas
or sensations in the mind of a human spirit? Berkeley,
like Locke, at last found himself face to face with the
problem of reasoning to causes. Given ideas of spirits
as all the data and objects of knowledge, what causes
can reason infer?

We might feel tempted now to say that Berkeley,
having the universe of Divine ideas, as it were, in his
grasp, would at once say that the external world of
bodies, their corpuscles, and their qualities, which the
natural philosopher has discovered to be the insensible
causes of sensible qualities, even æther and its motions,
are Divine ideas, by which the Deity produces the sensations of man. But Berkeley no more than the modern
Berkeleian resorts to this Hegelian alternative. He
precluded himself from taking it, both by his identification of the external with the sensible object, and by
his doctrine of the inactivity of ideas. As the former
deprived him of the external world as a distinct object,

so the latter prevented him from regarding insensible causes as ideas. 'All our ideas,' says he, 'sensations, or the things which we perceive, by whatsoever names they may be distinguished, are visibly inactive; there is nothing of power or agency included in them, so that one idea or object of thought cannot produce or make any alteration in another.'[1] So far from resolving insensible scientific causes into Divine ideas acting on us, he uses the theory of the inactivity of ideas to deny insensible scientific causes. 'Whence, it plainly follows,' he concludes, 'that extension, figure, and motion cannot be the cause of our sensations. To say, therefore, that these are the effects of powers, resulting from the configuration, number, motion, and size of corpuscles, must certainly be false.'[2]

Berkeley, having decided that the cause is not the qualities of corpuscles, proceeded to infer that it is the spirit of God :—

'We perceive a continual succession of ideas, some are anew excited, others are changed, or totally disappear. There is, therefore, some cause of these ideas whereon they depend, and which produces and changes them. That this cause cannot be any quality or idea, or combination of ideas, is clear from the preceding section. It must, therefore, be a substance; but it has been shown that there is no corporeal or material substance. It remains, therefore, that the cause of ideas is an incorporeal active substance or spirit.'[3]

Berkeley, like Descartes and Locke, saw that there is an involuntariness in our sensations which requires some cause. They might have all stopped there, and said that the nature of the cause is unknown; but they were too philosophical to be agnostics. Descartes

---

[1] *Princ.* xxv.   [2] Id.   [3] Id. xxvi.

and Locke, however, were not logical enough to see what cause could be inferred from their data; but guided by real facts rather than by their theories illogically supposed that, without anything physical in the data, we could infer a physical cause. Berkeley, on the other hand, was the first of the psychological idealists to see that the data and objects of knowledge must determine the inference; so that, if the data and objects are mind and ideas, when we find ideas in sensation, which are due neither to one's own ideas nor to one's own mind, we cannot infer a corporeal or material substance, but must infer that the cause is either other ideas or another mind. He had eliminated other ideas by his doctrine of the inactivity of ideas. There remained another mind. Now, proceeds he, though we are conscious of being able to produce some ideas by will, yet the ideas of sense have not a like dependence on our will; there is therefore some other will or spirit that produces them, and in an order which proves that this cause is the spirit of God.[1] Thus, the solution, which was suggested by Descartes, as a possible alternative in his 'Principia Philosophiæ,'[2] and which ought to have been taken by Locke in the Fourth Book of his Essay, when he had deserted mere ideas in favour of an intuition of oneself and a demonstration of God, was at length adopted by Berkeley in his 'Principles.' If all the data are ideas and minds, created and eternal, and if ideas are inactive, the only logical conclusion is that the sensible ideas of created minds are direct imprints of the eternal Spirit of God.

This logical conclusion of psychological idealism, evaded by Descartes and Locke, was accepted by Berkeley, with all its hypothetical consequences. As

---

[1] *Princ.* xxviii.-xxx.   [2] Descartes, *Princ.* ii. 1.

usual, he felt the double edge of his weapon, and was
prepared not only with what is, but with what is not.
On the one hand, he concluded that God is, and on the
other hand, that matter is not, the cause of our sensations.[1] Secondly, he concluded that ' the set rules or
established methods, wherein the mind we depend on
excites in us the ideas of sense, are called the *laws of
nature*.'[2] Thirdly, he concluded that God is not merely
the prime cause, but the immediate and sole cause of
sensible effects, setting aside second causes, such as the
sun and the motion of bodies :—

' And yet this consistent uniform working, which
so evidently displays the goodness and wisdom of that
governing spirit, whose will constitutes the laws of
nature, is so far from leading our thoughts to him, that
it rather sends them a-wandering after second causes.
For when we perceive certain ideas of sense constantly
followed by other ideas, and we know that it is not
of our own doing, we forthwith attribute power and
agency to the ideas themselves, and make one the cause
of another, than which nothing can be more absurd and
unintelligible. Thus, for example, having observed
that when we perceive by sight a certain round luminous
figure. we at the same time perceive by touch the idea
or sensation called *heat*; we do from thence conclude
the sun to be the cause of heat. And in like manner
perceiving the motion and collision of bodies to be
attended with sound, we are inclined to think the latter
an effect of the former.'[3]

Finally, he presents us with his complete theory of
real things, when second causes have been expunged :[4]—

' The ideas imprinted on the senses by the author of
nature are called *real things*; and those excited in the

[1] Berkeley, *Princ.* xxvi.   [2] Id. xxx.   [3] Id. xxxii.   [4] Id. xxxiii.

imagination, being less regular, vivid and constant, are more properly termed *ideas* or *images of things*, which they copy and represent. But then our sensations, be they never so vivid and distinct, are nevertheless *ideas*, that is, they exist in the mind, or are perceived by it, as truly as the ideas of its own framing. The ideas of sense are allowed to have more reality in them, that is, to be more strong, orderly and coherent than the creatures of the mind; but this is no argument that they exist without the mind. They are also less dependent on the spirit, or thinking substance which perceives them, in that they are excited by the will of another and more powerful spirit; yet still they are *ideas*, and certainly no *idea*, whether faint or strong, can exist otherwise than in a mind perceiving it.'

This passage marks a turning-point in the history of idealism. Hitherto, the line between ideas of sensation and ideas of conception had not been so carefully drawn as that between all ideas and the physical realities which cause them. Now, Berkeley, having deduced the destruction of physical realities, while still preserving the hypothesis that ideas are the objects of sensation, was puzzled to find some boundary between the real and the ideal. He drew it between the ideas of sensation and the ideas of imagination, partly by their vividness and faintness, but mainly because the former are directly produced by God. Hence, he identified sensible ideas with real things, at the same time explaining that they are after all only ideas.

Sensible ideas he declared to be his *rerum natura*.[1] He even admitted corporeal substances, 'taken in the vulgar sense for a combination of sensible qualities,' not 'in the philosophic sense for a support of accidents or

---

[1] *Princ.* xxxiv.

qualities without the mind.'[1] So sure was he that sensible
ideas are the real things, that he even said that 'we are fed
and clothed with these things which we perceive immediately by our senses;' that is, by sensible ideas.[2]
Thus did he reduce reality to ideas imprinted on our
senses by God without the intervention of physical
causes, sense to the presentation of sensible ideas representing no external bodies, and knowledge to collections
of ideas inferring no external cause except God. He
took the show of sense for the nature of things, and
thought that, if the veil were uplifted, we should see
nothing but God.

This doctrine of reality, much more logical, but
also far narrower than that of Descartes and Locke, is
the transition to Hume's distinction of impressions and
ideas, and has ended in the ordinary sensationalism of
modern Berkeleians, such as Mill, who do not indeed say
that God is the direct cause of our sensations, but give up
the problem and leave sensations in mid-air, nor dogma-
tise about all reality but confine themselves to known
reality, in other respects differing in nothing but terminology from Berkeley. The fundamental character of
Berkeleianism is the theory that everything real is either
my sensations and combinations of sensations, or those
of other minds. 'I do not believe,' says Mill, 'that the
real externality to us of anything, except other minds,
is capable of proof.'[3]

It is often said that Berkeley is unanswerable, in his
final position that the real world consists of ideas imprinted on our senses, not by nature, but by the spirit
of God. He cannot be answered by the hypothetical

---

[1] *Princ.* xxxvii.　　　　　　　　　　[2] Id. xxxviii.
[3] *Examination of Sir W. Hamilton's Philosophy*, chap. xi, note,
sub fin.

realism of cosmothetical idealists, such as Descartes and Locke and their modern successors, because they start knowledge, like Berkeley, with nothing but psychical data, from which nothing but the psychical could be inferred, and only suppose it to infer physical causes, by bad logic. Berkeley was the first logician of idealism. Cosmothetic idealism is an inconsequence, which must end in pure idealism at last.

Again, he cannot be answered by intuitive realism, because it rests on the false identification of the sensible and external world by common sense, instead of appealing to the distinction of the sensible effect from the external cause by science. It is no use to knock the stick on the ground, when Berkeley resolves the ground and the stick into ideas, and the agent into a spirit. It is no answer to assert that the things immediately perceived are real things; for Berkeley admits it, but says that they are also sensible ideas or sensations.[1] It is no answer to oppose a presentative perception of apples and houses to a philosopher, who agrees but rejoins that the things presented are only collections of ideas. If Berkeley is equal to the intuitive realist on the ground of common sense, he is superior on the ground of science and philosophy. The intuitive realist supposes that the real world directly perceived is external; science shows that it is within; Berkeley adds that it is within the mind. The intuitive realist supposes that a secondary quality is directly perceived as a mere sensation in the mind, a primary quality as a real quality in the external world; Berkeley, in a far more philosophic spirit, shows that they are directly perceived in the same manner, for, as sensible it is impossible to separate extension, figure and motion from other sensible qualities. Both confuse two

[1] *Princ.* xxxiii. *seq.*; *Hylas and Philonous*, Third Dialogue, *sub fin.*

realities, distinguished by science, the sensible and the external; but, if this common confusion could be overlooked, it would be more scientific to make the real object of immediate perception, with Berkeley, entirely internal, than, with intuitive realism, partly internal and partly external—as if I could perceive the light of a candle within me, and its extension in the outside world.

The truth is that idealists and realists have had too many errors in common with Berkeley to answer him. Idealists share his error that the data are ideas, realists that the real world is the object of immediate perception. All of them, also, confine themselves too much to perceptible bodies, to the neglect of imperceptible corpuscles. Within that narrow circle Berkeley has no difficulty in resolving apples and houses, and even mountains and rivers, into sensible ideas. But we must turn the corner of pure idealism. The question is not what it makes of the sensible and the perceptible, but what it does with the imperceptible. The true contradictory instance against Berkeley's position is the natural philosophy of the imperceptible world of corpuscles, which cause, but are not, and cannot be inferred from, sensations or sensible ideas. This is the answer of physical realism. Let us proceed to its details.

In one way God, in another way nature, causes our sensations. There are two opposite extremes to be avoided—the substitution of nature for God, and that of God for nature: the former the temptation of the natural philosopher, the latter that of the natural theologian. The natural philosopher prolongs the chain of physical causes, until at last he feels tempted to believe that he has expelled intelligence from nature, and say, 'I have swept the universe with my telescope and cannot find God.' The natural theologian, dazzled

P

by the universal cause, is apt to neglect the subordinate agency of physical causes, and forget nature in the love of God.

Natural philosophy is limited by the nature of its evidence. God is inferred by combining the evidence of outer and inner sense; but natural philosophy reasons only from sensation and observation, without consciousness and reflection. Of itself, nature can neither prove nor disprove a deity. Even within its own limits natural philosophy is limited. Evolutionists, for example, have been more successful in dealing with organisms than in the far larger problem of the inorganic world. Evolution consists in the differentiation of homogeneous matter. Now differentiation invariably requires one of two conditions: either one efficient cause must act on different materials, as when the same kind of motion produces molar motion in one body and molecular in another; or different efficient causes must act on one kind of material, as when different lengths of undulation produce sensible heat or sensible light in the nervous system. Both alternatives presuppose difference; the former difference in the patient, the latter difference in the agent. There is no known instance of one kind of cause acting on one kind of material and producing different kinds of effects. Hence, if we suppose matter, absolutely homogeneous, universally diffused, and reciprocally acting in its various parts, it would contain no difference either of agent or patient to produce the different effects of actual nature; but all its particles, at equal distances, would exert all forces equally in all directions, and produce an exact balance, with no differences whatever. The theory of evolution, therefore, is no explanation of the beginnings of difference. But given a pre-existing difference, even of two groups of particles with dif-

ferent arrangements of their primary qualities, however slight, evolution is the further differentiation,
not of the absolutely, but of the relatively homogeneous into the more heterogeneous, arising from
different structures acted on by one kind of agent, or
different agents acting on one kind of structure, or
different agents acting on different structures, and so on
ad infinitum, not *a parte ante*, but *a parte post*. There
must, however, be something else to cause an original
difference in things. But limited as natural philosophy
is within, it is still more limited from without. Having
only reasoning from outer sense and observation, it discovers physical causes; but it cannot tell what else they
may be.

Natural theology now steps in, to supplement sensation by consciousness, observation by reflection, and to
reason from both outer and inner sense. To observation, a workman and a product have the mere appearance of cause and effect; but when we add conscious
reflection, we infer that he is an artist using means to an
end; and, when we observe again a similar work, we still
infer an artist. So from His work, natural theology
infers a Divine Architect of nature, establishing the
original difference of things, and developing further
differences, by using physical causes of effects as means
to ends. 'Omnia quae agunt in virtute primi agentis
agunt.' When science shows that evolution develops
living organs, this is no reason why this very evolution
should not be a Divine means of producing fresh life.
The growth of a tree has not been regarded as inconsistent with Divine agency; why, then, should not Divine
power be exercised in the whole growth of the world?
On the other hand, the natural theologian must not
forget that, after all, the existence of nature must be

more certain than that of God, and that, indeed, without the order of nature the main part of the evidence for a God disappears. If God is the intelligent cause, most certainly the means used are physical causes. All attempts to argue that because God is the cause of all effects, insensible motions are not causes, or that there can be no evolution, must fail, because nothing is more surely established than the powers and laws of motion. To convert God from an Intelligent Will using physical means into the direct and sole cause of every effect, even to the threshold of our senses, is the greatest danger that can befall natural theology, which must then yield to the laws of the communication and conservation of motions.

No reconciliation of theology and science will be found superior to that of Bacon,[1] which admits too of being perpetually enlarged with every physical discovery: God having made nature uses it as a means; the more physical causes, the more means at His command; the more elaborate and indirect the physical process, the more subtle the Divine Architect; who, having established a difference in corpuscular structure, uses the evolution of one particle acting on another as His further process of differentiation and His most ingenious plan; and natural philosophy is always, however unconsciously, prolonging the chain of physical causes to the throne of God. 'Sic Dei sapientia effulget mirabilius,' says Bacon, 'cum Natura aliud agit, Providentia aliud elicit, quam si singulis schematibus et motibus naturalibus Providentiæ characteres essent impressi.'

Berkeley for nature substituted God. By his hypotheses and logical deductions he was compelled to say

---

[1] *De Augmentis Scientiarum*, iii. 4, *sub fin.* (Ed. Ellis and Spedding, vol. i. p. 570.)

that ideas are imprinted on our senses, not by the insensible motions of physical substances, but by the
direct agency of God Himself. Instead of an Intelligent
Agent, using nature as the means to produce effects on
our senses, God, without the intervention of insensible
nature, thus becomes the direct and sole cause of every
sensible effect. There is God, then, and no nature, but
the nature of man. The good bishop flattered himself
that he was thus serving the cause of his religion. But
how different is the doctrine of the Bible! In the
beginning God created the heavens and the earth; and,
only after nature, man. This is the meeting-point of
religion and science.

In substituting God for nature, and denying second
causes, Berkeley not only falsified religion but also
contradicted science. He said that God is, but nature
is not, the cause of our sensations. His followers have
deserted his theory of religion, but they have supplied
no adequate theory of science. Any mental philosopher, who says that real things are our sensible ideas or
sensations, whether he says that they are produced by
God, with Berkeley, or, with the modern Berkeleian,
gives up the knowledge of the causes of our sensations, in either case he is following Berkeley in rejecting
the positions of natural philosophy that the external
sun is the cause of sensible heat, that the motion and
collision of particles of air insensibly proceed till at last
they produce sensible sounds, and that imperceptible
corpuscles, with their configuration, number, motion,
and size, cause our sensations.[1]

Psychological idealism had gradually brought mental
philosophy into this state of paradox by the very poverty
of its data. Descartes was a scientific genius, labouring to

_____
[1] Cf. *Princ.* xxv., xxxii.

bring a narrow mental into harmony with a wider natural philosophy. Locke, beginning to feel the difficulty, depreciated natural philosophy, because he could not explain it. Berkeley, logically deducing the vanity of the attempt at explanation, boldly wrote a polemic against the natural philosophy of corpuscles and their motions.[1] This sad, but inevitable, defect is generally omitted or extenuated by historians of philosophy. But Berkeley himself was well aware what were the logical consequences of idealism. One passage from his polemic will be sufficient :—

'Some have pretended to account for appearances by occult qualities, but of late they are mostly resolved into mechanical causes ; to wit, the figure, motion, weight, and such-like qualities of insensible particles : whereas, in truth, there is no agent or efficient cause than *spirit*, it being evident that motion, as well as all other *ideas*, is perfectly inert. (See sect. xxv.) Hence to endeavour to explain the production of colours or sounds by figure, motion, magnitude, and the like, must needs be labour in vain. Accordingly, we see the attempts of that kind are not at all satisfactory.'[2]

But we have seen, since Berkeley's time, a sure progress in the natural philosophy of mechanical causes. A striking contrast to the passage just quoted may be found in the following quotation from Professor Tyndall's 'Fragments of Science'[3] :—

'The domain in which this motion of light is carried on lies entirely beyond the reach of our senses. The waves of light require a medium for their formation and propagation ; but we cannot see, or feel, or taste, or smell this medium. How, then, has its existence been established? By showing that, by the

---

[1] *Princ.* ci. *seq.*   [2] *Id.* cii.   [3] Pp. 72-8.

assumption of this wonderful intangible *æther*, all the
phænomena of optics are accounted for, with a fulness,
and clearness, and conclusiveness which leave no desire
of the intellect unsatisfied.   When the law of gravitation first suggested itself to the mind of Newton,
what did he do ?   He set himself to examine whether it
accounted for all the facts.   He determined the courses
of the planets ; he calculated the rapidity of the moon's
fall towards the earth ; he considered the precession of
the equinoxes, the ebb and flow of the tides, and found
all explained by the law of gravitation.   He therefore
regarded this law as established, and the verdict of
science subsequently confirmed his conclusion.   On
similar, and, if possible, on stronger grounds, we found
our belief in the existence of the universal æther.   It
explains facts far more various and complicated than
those on which Newton based his law.   If a single phænomenon could be pointed out which the æther is
proved incompetent to explain, we should have to give
it up ; but no such phænomenon has ever been pointed
out.   It is, therefore, at least as certain that space is
filled with a medium, by means of which suns and
stars diffuse their radiant power, as that it is traversed
by that force which holds in its grasp, not only our
planetary system, but the immeasurable heavens themselves.'

Berkeley's idealism is unscientific.   From this point
we must retrace our steps by the method of analysis.
By the falsity of the consequences we must destroy the
original hypotheses and find the real data of reasoning
from sense to science.   By a chain of logic, he had hypothetically deduced that, if all objects of human knowledge are ideas, derived from outer and inner sense, and
by the help of memory and imagination variously com-

pounded into collections of ideas, in the minds of created spirits, then such a spirit will be able to infer nothing but ideas and spirits, and to conclude that, if all ideas are inactive, our sensible ideas, which are passive and not caused by our own will, must be imprinted on our senses by the will of the eternal spirit of God ; so that real things, as distinguished from mere ideas of imagination, will be the sensible ideas directly imprinted on our senses by Divine, without the intervention of physical causes. Now, the flaw in this chain is in its last link, in the logical but false rejection, with which it ends, of the bodies, corpuscles, and mechanical causes, discovered by natural philosophy.

What is corpuscular science ? In brief, there are bodies insensible and imperceptible, or corpuscles. They possess primary qualities, various species of which are secondary qualities ; especially, they possess motion, a primary quality, whose secondary species are undulations of æther, vibrations of air, &c., and which also exists in various forms, such as cohesion, gravitation, chemical attraction, electricity, magnetism, &c. Corpuscles have innumerable similarities and uniform relations or laws of nature, and especially the laws of motion and of the causation of motion by motion. They are also the particles of masses, or larger bodies, which are partly inorganic and partly organic. Among organisms are bodies containing nervous systems, which consist, like other masses, of corpuscles having the various motions of bodies in general and a peculiar nervous motion, combined with muscular motion. Lastly, some of the other bodies, among their innumerable processes of cause and effect, produce in nervous systems sensible effects, such as sensible motion, sensible heat, &c. Such are the objects of corpuscular science.

Corpuscular science destroys Berkeley's idealism in his logical conclusion from his original hypotheses. He denied second causes; but motions producing motions are second causes. He said that God's will is the sole cause of sensible effects; but corpuscular motions, acting on the corpuscles of the nervous system, also produce sensible heat, colour, sound, &c. If God is the prime cause, nature is the second cause, by means of which He acts on man. He said that the rules wherein God excites in us the ideas of sense are the laws of nature. But the uniform relations of corpuscular motions among themselves are an immense system of laws, compared with which the laws of their action on the nervous system and the senses are but a diminutive fraction. What account would it be of the universal law of gravitation, of every particle to every particle in the universe, to say that it is merely a rule to excite in us the sensible idea or sensation of weight? God, then, is not the only cause, but under Him nature is also the cause and law of sensible effects. Again, Berkeley said that sensible ideas imprinted on sense by God are the real things, and external bodies are not: the Berkeleian says the same thing of sensations, only without dogmatism about the sole causation of God and about the absolute non-existence of external bodies. But the natural philosopher knows that external bodies are not sensations, but the causes of sensations and sensible ideas. For example, the gravitations of particles are not sensations, but are the known causes of sensible weight being felt by us. Therefore, so far from being non-existent, or so far from not being known to exist, external bodies and their motions are known to exist as causes of sensible effects. To the Berkeleian, then, we must answer, not all known realities are sensations; to Berkeley himself, not all realities are sensible ideas imprinted on our senses by the Author of our being; but some known realities are external bodies and their qualities producing sensible effects in us. There is a known world of real bodies, intervening between God and man, and used by God as a means to cause effects in our senses.

Corpuscular science destroys Berkeleian idealism not only in its hypothetical conclusions but also in its original hypotheses of the objects and data of human knowledge. Insensible corpuscles and their qualities are not our ideas, but the causes of our ideas. They are objects of natural philosophy, which, in the hands of Newton and his successors, is a kind of knowledge. Therefore, not all objects of knowledge are ideas, and some of the objects are corpuscular causes of our ideas. Again, if the original data were ideas, these corpuscular causes could not be inferred, as Berkeley logically showed. But they are scientifically inferred by natural philosophy. Therefore, neither the original objects nor the original data are mere ideas. Corpuscular science deals double death to logical idealism.

Berkeley had logically deduced from his hypothesis that all qualities are only sensible ideas. But natural philosophy has shown that insensible corpuscles have the primary quality of insensible motion, obeying various laws, and that insensible modes of corpuscular motion are the secondary qualities of light, heat, and sound in the universe. Sir Isaac Newton showed that, beyond the sensible resistance or weight which we feel, there is an insensible gravitation of particles which pervades the universe, which connects parts of bodies inaccessible to our senses, and which, in one of its myriad applications, causes bodies to feel heavy in our hands.

Qualities, then, primary and secondary, are known in natural philosophy to belong to external bodies, as well as cause sensible effects in us. Moreover, their range in the insensible world of science is infinitely more extensive than their perception by sense. Qualities, therefore, are not mere sensible ideas or sensations, but are mainly the external characteristics of masses and corpuscles in nature. But, again, external qualities of bodies could not be inferred from sensible ideas of minds. Therefore, qualities, even as sensible, are not sensible ideas. Berkeley was compelled by the logic of his idealism to reduce all qualities to sensible ideas, but he was doubly wrong in point of fact. Primary and secondary qualities, as known to corpuscular science, are neither reducible to, nor inferrible from, sensations or sensible ideas.

Again, from Locke's hypothesis that sense always perceives ideas of qualities, Berkeley consistently deduced that we cannot suppose an unthinking substance,[1] that Locke's substratum is an abstraction, like *materia prima*,[2] and that the only known substance is a combination of sensible qualities, or ideas, with which we are fed and clothed.[3] But are these conclusions true and scientific? The matter, known to natural science, is durable, extended, moving, causing and receiving motion; it is not, indeed, also something else distinct from being these things; nor, however, is it mere duration, extension, motion, causation, and reception of motion, distinct but combined. In other words, matter or body is not the abstract substrate supposed by Locke, nor the equally abstract combination of qualities substituted by Berkeley, but a qualified subject, characterised by a number of qualities. Now, besides all this, it is

---

[1] *Princ.* vii.   [2] Id. xi., xvi.
[3] Id. xxxvii. xxxviii.

not, though it sometimes causes, a collection of sensible ideas. A drop of water contains the particles enumerated in the first page of this essay; but the sensible effect of it on any of my senses, and the ideas I afterwards form of it, do not contain anything of the kind, and are totally incapable of containing such a number of units of any kind, which are only inferred by reason. If there are so many particles in a drop of water, how many in a river, and how many in the ocean? The truth is, that an analysis of a substance into particles is not a division of the sensible object, sensation, or sensible idea, but of the external object inferred. Corpuscles, then, are a proof of external bodies. Hence it follows that known substances are not abstract substrates of qualities, nor abstract collections of qualities, nor still more abstract ideas of collections of ideas of qualities, but qualified subjects, some of which are thinking and partly psychical, others unthinking and entirely physical. Again, as physical substances are not qualities nor ideas, so neither could they be inferred from such data. If sense never perceived anything but spiritual sensations or sensible ideas or qualities, science could not infer durable, extended, moving bodies containing corpuscles. But these substances are the very subjects of the laws of motion and gravitation. It follows, then, that the data of sense from which they are inferred are not mere qualities, still less sensations, least of all ideas, but the nervous substance sensibly qualified.

To return at last to Berkeley's first principle. He said that all the objects of human knowledge are ideas imprinted on the senses, or else such as are perceived by attending to the operations of the mind or collections of these ideas. This supposed principle is a false hypothesis containing two fundamental errors; an error about objects known, and an error about objects perceived. The insensible and imperceptible corpuscles discovered by natural philosophers are not ideas of any of these kinds, though they are causes of them. Not all the objects of human knowledge, then, are ideas. Secondly, if the objects imprinted on the senses were ideas, the insensible corpuscles could not have been inferred. Not all the objects of human perception, then, are ideas. Insensible imperceptible corpuscles are physical objects of knowledge inferred from physical data of sense. Similarly their *esse* is not *percipi*, as it would be if they were ideas. The *esse* of ideas of sensation is *percipi*. The *esse* of a sensible object is *percipi* by sense. An accident of the *esse* of an external body, *e.g.* water, is *percipi* by inference. But the *esse* of an imperceptible corpuscle, *e.g.* in a drop of water, is not *percipi* at all.

Berkeley, by a confusion of *esse* and *percipi*, adopted a presentative theory of perception, like the intuitive realists; by a confusion of the sensible object with a sensible idea, his presentative theory is not realistic but idealistic; by a confusion of the sensible and the real, it is a theory that we present sensible ideas as the real things.[1] He recurs again to this theory, as the very kernel of his philosophy, at the end of the Third Dialogue between Hylas and Philonous :—

'*Phil.* I do not pretend to be a setter-up of *new notions*. My endeavours tend only to unite and place in a clearer light that truth, which was before shared between the vulgar and the philosophers; the former being of opinion, that *those things they immediately perceive are the real things*; and the latter, that *the things immediately perceived are ideas which exist only in the*

[1] Cf. *Princ.* iv.

mind. Which two notions put together do, in effect, constitute the substance of what I advance.'

Each one of the propositions in this theory is false. First, the things we immediately perceive are real things, but not *the* real things. There is an immense multitude of real things known to science, but not immediately perceived. The apple, the table, the house, the river, the mountain, cause sensible effects, which are real enough; but they are external bodies whose corpuscles are known to have a like but different structure from that of the sensible effects; the particles of a table are not the particles of my hand lying on it, nor of my tactile nerves, still less of the operation of sensation. Secondly, the things immediately perceived are not ideas which exist only in the mind. It is true that they are within me, and here is Berkeley's superiority over the intuitive realist. But, apart from the absence of direct evidence that the hard, or hot, or heavy felt is an idea within my mind ; if it were so, I could never infer the bodies and corpuscles, which, as we have found, are too well established in natural philosophy to be any longer denied. Therefore, things immediately perceived are, not ideas which exist only in the mind, but bodily effects of bodies on the nervous system. Lastly, Berkeley wishes us to draw the conclusion that ideas which exist in the mind are *the* real things, and that physical objects are not real things. His premises to prove it, however, are both false ; for, as we have seen, the things immediately perceived are neither *the* real things, nor ideas. Hence his syllogism only proves that ideas are real things, and some real things are ideas ; which is true enough, but also consistent with other real things. Now, corpuscular science proves bodies which are real things in the external world ; and, to infer them, logic requires bodily data, which are real things in the nervous system. Other real things, then, are known and perceived, besides ideas.

Berkeley's idealism—and we may add all Berkeleianism—is false, metaphysically, psychologically, and logically :—

1. His metaphysical theory of existence is false, because not all real things are sensible ideas whose sole cause is God ; but some realities are known to be physical causes.

2. His psychological theory of immediate perception is false, because we immediately perceive neither sensible ideas, nor sensations, nor *the* real things, but real physical effects, representing real physical causes.

3. His logical theory of reasoning is false, because from the first he prefers imagination and memory of ideas to reasoning about causes, and reasoning synthetically from hypotheses to reasoning analytically from facts.

Berkeley omitted nature, between sense and God. Starting from Locke's hypothesis of the objects of knowledge, he rejected discoveries of natural philosophy, when he ought to have preferred the latter to the former. He ought to have gone still further, and surrendered not only Locke's hypothesis of the objects, but also the hypothesis of Descartes that the data of knowledge are psychical ideas. When Newton had shown what could be done in natural philosophy, mental philosophy should have reformed its data to explain his discoveries. But how seldom philosophers realise that their theories of man ought to explain a Shakespeare, a Bacon, a Newton ! To infer the Newtonian philosophy, the senses of man must perceive, not ideas of qualities, but various parts of the physical substance of the nervous system sensibly

qualified as durable, extended, moving, as well as sounding, heated, coloured ; from which even an ordinary man
infers insensible bodies, a scientific man their imperceptible corpuscles and motions and laws. If all objects
of human knowledge were ideas of spirit, man could
infer nothing but spirit and ideas. But the antecedent
is an hypothesis, for which Berkeley had no authority
except Descartes and Locke : the consequent is false,
being contradictory to corpuscular science : therefore,
the antecedent hypothesis is also false, because from
true premises it is not possible to draw a false conclusion. The real world includes, between the sensible
and the supernatural, the natural world of insensible
bodies and imperceptible corpuscles, which are physical
objects of scientific knowledge inferrible only from
physical data of human sense. Such is the answer of
physical realism.

CHAPTER VIII.

BERKELEY'S THEORY OF VISION.

In answering the objections which might be made against his 'Principles,' Berkeley refers to his 'Essay towards a New Theory of Vision' as follows :—

'Thirdly, it will be objected, that we see things actually without or at a distance from us, and which consequently do not exist in the mind, it being absurd that those things which are seen at the distance of several miles should be as near to us as our own thoughts. In answer to this, I desire it may be considered, that in a dream we do oft perceive things as existing at a great distance off, and yet for all that, those things are acknowledged to have their existence only in the mind.

'But for the fuller clearing of this point, it may be worth while to consider, how it is that we perceive distance and things placed at a distance by sight. For that we should in truth see external space, and bodies actually existing in it, some nearer, others farther off, seems to carry with it some opposition to what hath been said, of their existing nowhere without the mind. The consideration of this difficulty it was, that gave birth to my " Essay towards a New Theory of Vision," which was published not long since. Wherein it is shown that *distance* or outness is neither immediately of itself perceived by sight, nor yet apprehended or judged of by lines and angles, or anything that hath a necessary connexion with it : but that it is only suggested to our thoughts by certain visible ideas and sensations attending vision, which in their own nature have no manner or similitude or relation, either with distance, or things placed at a distance. But by a connexion taught us by experience, they come to signify and suggest them to us, after the same manner that words of any language suggest the ideas they are made to stand for. Insomuch that a man born blind, and afterwards made to see, would not, at first sight, think the things he saw, to be without his mind, or at any distance from him. See sect. xli. of the forementioned treatise.

'The ideas of sight and touch make two species, entirely distinct and heterogeneous. The former are marks and prognostics of the latter. That the proper objects of sight neither exist without the mind, nor are the images of external things, was shown even in that treatise. Though throughout the same, the contrary be supposed true of tangible objects : not that to suppose that vulgar error, was necessary for establishing the notions therein laid down ; but because it was beside my purpose to examine and refute it in a discourse concerning *vision*. So that in strict truth the ideas of sight, when we apprehend by them distance, and things placed at a distance, do not suggest or mark out to us things actually existing at a distance, but only admonish us what ideas of touch will be imprinted in our minds at such and such distances of time, and in consequence of such and such actions. It is, I say, evident from what has been said in the foregoing parts of this treatise, and in section cxlvii. and elsewhere of the Essay concerning Vision, that visible ideas are the language whereby the governing spirit, on whom we depend, informs us what tangible ideas he is about to imprint upon us, in case we excite this or that motion in our own bodies. But for a fuller information on this point, I refer to the Essay itself.' [1]

Here we find from Berkeley's own words that he had more than one object in writing the 'Theory of Vision.' It is an essay half physical, half psychological, and this doubleness of purpose has ever since clung to the subject. On the one hand, he wanted to destroy the exaggerations introduced by mathematicians into optics, by showing that the eye is not fitted to see any-thing, and therefore not any lines and angles, beyond itself; on the other hand, he wanted to support the idealistic theory, which he had already conceived, and shortly intended to publish in the 'Principles,' by show-ing that, whereas we do not see things without, we do see visible ideas and sensations. In its first purpose, the main thesis of the 'Theory of Vision' is a great optical discovery, though exaggerated; in its second purpose, it is an excellent disproof of intuitive realism, but no proof at all of psychological idealism. Perhaps no treatise has ever evinced such a singular compound of genius and confusion. The effect both of its truth and its falsity persists to this very day, especially in the hypothesis of 'local signs.'

What does Berkeley prove about the sense of vision? He divides the subject into four parts—distance, magni-tude, situation, and the difference between sight and touch.[2] On the first point, he says that 'distance being a line directed endwise to the eye, it projects only one

[1] *Princ.* xlii. xliv.

[2] *Theory,* i. Distance is discussed in i. li.; Magnitude, lii.-lxxxvii.; Situation, lxxxviii. cxx.; The difference between sight and touch, cxxi. to end.

point in the fund of the eye, which point remains invariably the same, whether the distance be longer or shorter.'[1] This proves, according to him, that we do not see distance at all, but really that we do not see remote distance, in depth or the third dimension, vertically from the eye. As he says elsewhere, we see no solidity or profundity.[2] On the second point, he shows that we do not see the real magnitude, greater and smaller, of an external object. 'Thus, for instance,' he very properly remarks, 'the very same quantity or visible extension, which in the figure of a tower doth suggest the idea of a great magnitude, shall in the figure of a man suggest the idea of much smaller magnitude.'[3] On the third point, he relies on the inverted image in vision to show that we do not see the real situation, as high and low, of external objects. On the fourth point, he makes the instructive remark that there is no vision of resistance,[4] and he has brought out more clearly than any of his predecessors that 'there is no one self-same numerical extension perceived both by sight and touch,[5] and that 'we never see and feel one and the same object.'[6]

This conclusion is the great stumbling-block to the ordinary man, who has so overlaid sense with inference, and, we may add, had so many visible pictures of his hand and other members visibly touching visible objects, all within his sense of vision, that he finds himself almost incapable, even when he becomes a philosopher, of realising to himself that he is really seeing one set of objects within the retina and feeling another within the tactile nerves, while he infers an external object in re-

[1] *Theory*, ii.   [2] Ib. cxxxv., cliv.
[3] Ib. lvii.   [4] Ib. cxxxv.
[6] Ib. cxxi.   [5] Ib. xlix.

lation to both. Nevertheless, Berkeley verified the previous scientific discovery of the distinction between external and sensible objects by his new discovery of the invisibility of remote distance. Since we do not see distance in the third dimension from the eye, we cannot see, but only infer, a remote object. The visible object might, indeed, still be an object touching the eye; but even this hypothesis is negatived by the further study of the nervous system.

What did Berkeley not prove about the sense of vision? On the very first point, while he proved that we do not see remote distance he did not prove that we do not see distance at all. He did not prove that we do not see a surface painted on the retina, with its distances. There are three dimensions of extension or space; in each there is distance—distance from point to point of a line, from line to line of a surface, from surface to surface of a solid: in each dimension the parts or places, which are distant, are out of one another. Now what he proved was that there is no vision of the third dimension, not that there is none of the other two; that there is none of distance in depth, not that there is none of distance in length and width; that there is none of outness in the external world, not that there is none of outness of parts on the surface painted on the retina; that there is none of solid, not that there is none of superficial extension; that there is none of distance endwise to the eye, not that there is none of space and its distances within the eye. In short, he concluded more than he proved. ' It is,' he says, ' I think, agreed by all, that distance, of itself and immediately, cannot be seen.'[1] It is still agreed by present psychologists; but we want something more than agreement to prove

[1] *Theory*, ii.

that, because remote distance is not seen, therefore no distance can be seen. 'From what we have shown,' he says, 'it is a manifest consequence that the ideas of a space, outness, and things placed at a distance, are not, strictly speaking, the object of sight; they are not otherwise perceived by the eye than by the ear.'[1] But he had proved only that we do not see external things placed at a distance and their outness in space. It still remained, and remains even now, to be proved that the space, the outnesses, and the distances, within the surface of the picture painted on the retina, are not objects of sight.

Therefore, he did not prove that we have no vision of space. He vacillated; sometimes allowing, sometimes denying that the extended is visible,[2] and finally deciding that 'what we strictly see are not solids, nor yet plains variously coloured; they are only diversity of colours.'[3] But the same evidence, which proves that we do not see solid distance, proves that we do see a plain, with its superficial extension and the distances on its surface. 'There is, at this day,' as he says himself, 'no one ignorant that the pictures of external objects are painted on the *retina*, or fund of the eye.'[4] He began then with the external object and the retina. Very well; but what is the external object, and what the retina? Both of them have surfaces. Undoubtedly the former reflects what the mathematician abstracts as rays, but what the physicist knows to be undulations, which ultimately impress the terminations of nervous fibres in the retina of the eye. We do not see the sides of these rays or undulations : hence we do not see distance in the third dimension. But we do see the imprints of

[1] *Theory*, xlvi.   [2] Cf. ib. xliii., xlv.–xlvi., xlviii., civ.

[3] Ib. clviii.   [4] Ib. lxxxviii.

their ends. Now, in the first place, the end of any wave of æther, however small, is a surface; in the second place, the end of every single optic fibre is a surface; thirdly, as a fact, no one undulation of æther ever reaches the eye alone; and, fourthly, no one nervous fibre is excited alone, but the whole retinal surface by a whole undulatory surface of æther. Though, therefore, the visible picture painted on the retina by the external world is not itself solid, it is painted by the surface of one solid on the surface of another. Not remote distance, but superficial extension is visible.

It is unscientific in the extreme to arbitrarily select one part of the optical evidence and reject the rest, or to see through the mathematical abstractions of the line and the angle, and then to confuse mathematical points with the extended ends of physical objects. This is the mistake of Berkeley. He knows that the rays of light are not mathematical lines, yet he says at the opening and often repeats, what has been repeated after him again and again *ad nauseam* to the present day, that a point is presented to the retina. Nothing of the kind; it is not a point, but, to say the very least, a physical ray's extended end, which is a surface, presented to the extended end of another physical object which is a surface, the end of a nervous fibre. There is, no doubt, a *minimum visibile*, which may be coextensive with the end of a nervous fibre; but it is not a point, it is a surface. The whole point-to-point theory of vision is nothing but a mathematical abstraction converted into a physical reality.

It is true that the retina itself may not be sensible; but whatever part of the optic nerve or of the brain itself is first sensible, that part is a surface. It is true,

again, that we have admitted a psychical element in
sensation, but we can only interpret its object by consciousness, observation, and reasoning. We have seen
the verdict of the two latter evidences : every physical
part without and within us has a surface. Now, what
does consciousness of vision say ? Why, I cannot help
being conscious that I am at this moment seeing an
extended surface. I confuse this picture within, I
admit, with what I infer without ; but the scientific
distinction between the external and the sensible only
shows that I was wrong in the supposition of the externality or remote distance of the sensible, not that I was
wrong in being conscious that I see an extended surface, a plain variously coloured. The whole evidence,
scientific and conscious, is in favour of the visible
object being like a painting, or still more like a picture
in a *camera obscura*, flat to sense, inferred by a complex
process of reasoning to represent an external solid,
but confused, by a long-standing association, with the
external solid itself.

Again, on the second point, Berkeley proved that we
do not see the real magnitude of an external object.
That is no reason why we should not see the magnitude
of the visible object impressed on the retina, nor why it
also should not be a real magnitude, though distinct
from external magnitude. On this point, again, he
vacillated. First he admits a size of things seen, that
they grow greater and smaller, and that there is not
only a tangible but a visible magnitude ; then he says
that visible extension, though immediately perceived, is
nevertheless little taken notice of ; and finally contends
that the ideas of visible magnitude are equally fitted to
bring into our minds ' the idea of small or great, or of
no size at all of outward objects,' like the words of a

language.[1]   The truth is, that we see an extended
coloured plain, as we have already said.   We are not
able to alter its whole size on a single retina, because
the whole retina is used at once ; and this is a great
point of difference from touch, wherein we use a finger,
a hand, or our whole body to touch at pleasure.   The
only variation we can get in the size of the whole
picture is the difference of magnitude between the area
of a single retina, and the whole field of vision covered
by both eyes.   Usually, however, both eyes are used at
once, when the visible picture has a single fixed magnitude.   But the parts of it have very varying degrees
of magnitude ; for example, the black spot made by a
blot of ink covers a trifling amount of the retinal magnitude, compared with that impressed by the white
paper before me.   Hence within a single visible magnitude, fixed on the retina, we see all sorts of sizes of the
parts not behind but beside one another, some greater,
others smaller, and therefore having various relations of
size to the whole retinal picture.   It is on this sensation
of varying degrees of magnitude of the parts relatively
to the fixed magnitude of the whole of the superficial
picture on the retina, that the wonderful subtlety of the
sense of sight is founded.   In itself, this vision of magnitude within a magnitude carries us no further ; but
when allied with data of other senses, it becomes the
basis of countless inferences about external size.   For
example, the sight of Snowdon, when I am in the open
air, is smaller than the sight of my own room, when I
am indoors ; but knowing in other ways the real size of
Snowdon and of my room, I can from sight measure the
relative sizes of parts of each in a way possible to no
other sense.   There is another element in the vision of

---

[1] *Theory,* xxviii., l., liv., lxi., lxiv.

size about which we must be careful. We see the magnitude of the parts relatively to the whole retinal magnitude. There are *minima*, beyond which this deduction of visible parts cannot go, supposed to be connected with the distinction of nervous fibres. But, as I said before, a *minimum visibile* is not a point but an extended end, like the end of a pencil. Secondly, it is tempting, with Berkeley, to conclude that the *minimum* is always the same size in vision.[1] But it is not at all impossible that the parts impressed on adjacent nervous fibres may not be always visibly distinct. In looking at an object of a single colour, as a white leaf of a book, we do not so carefully distinguish small parts as when the object is very varied, as in reading the printed matter. The *minimum*, impressed on each fibre, may be always the same, and yet the *minima*, distinctly visible, greater or smaller according to the intensity and variety of the excitations. On the whole, then, there is a visible magnitude of the picture, always of the same size, determined by the retina ; visible parts, greater and smaller, in reference to the whole size ; *minima visibilia*, beyond which vision cannot go, but to which, perhaps, it does not in every act of vision reach.

On his third point, Berkeley proved that we do not see the real situations of external objects and, in especial, that we do not see which is up and which down, but an inverted image. He did not prove that sight sees no places in its inverted picture ; nor has any of the many philosophers, who have strangely attacked visible places, ever disproved them. Berkeley, as before, vacillated : he first denied them and then admitted them. He first says that a blind man returned to sight ' would not at first think that anything he saw was

high or low, erect or inverted.'[1] Afterwards, he says
that ' we denominate any object of sight, high or low, in
proportion as it is more or less distant from the visible
earth.'[2] The latter is the truth. In the visible flat
extended picture, of a constant retinal magnitude, we
not only see some parts greater and some smaller, but also
some in one place, some in another, though all inverted.
Nor is there any occasion to suppose that the image is
ever re-inverted. It includes images of our own body
and of the earth. From the data of touch, we infer
that our feet are down towards the earth's centre, and our
heads erect as away from it ; next, we find, over and
over again, that these inferred objects, in this order,
have in the visible picture various parts corresponding
to them, in a corresponding order—one part for the
earth, another for our feet, another for our heads : consequently, from this combined evidence of touch and
sight, we do not see but infer that the part of the retinal
image answering to the head represents up, and the part
corresponding to the feet represents down, and so on
with all other visible places.

On the fourth point, Berkeley proved that we do
not see and feel the same object, and that the visible
picture is numerically distinct from the tactile impression produced by the same external object; e.g. my
retinal picture of the paper before me is in my optic
nerve, my tactile impression in my nerves of touch.
But he asked the further question whether they are also
specifically distinct, or whether there is anything in
common, or similar, in the visible object and the tangible
object. After having, though in the vacillating manner
already stated, admitted in the visible picture a visible
extension, visible magnitude greater and smaller, and

<hr />

[1] *Theory,* xcv.   [2] Ib. cxi.

visible situations high or low in relation to visible earth,
he answered the question by denying that there is anything common to sight and touch. The true answer is
that his previous admissions were better than his final
theory. Vision sees a picture visibly extended in the
above-mentioned ways : touch feels a tangible imprint
extended in the same ways. The visible and tangible
objects, so far as the former is coloured and the latter
heated, are dissimilar; so far as the former is in the
optic and the latter in the tactile nerves they are not
numerically the same; but, so far as they are both extended, they are similar. Aristotle was right in distinguishing special and common sensibles, and in assign-
ing the extended both to sight and to touch.[1] Locke
was right in repeating the distinction.[2] Berkeley was
wrong as well as inconsistent in rejecting it. But his
rejection has infected the whole subsequent course of
the science of vision, the metaphysics of space, and the
psychology of sense.

Berkeley's theory contains a double paradox. In
the first place, he supposed that we see no visibly extended object, when all he had proved is that we see
no visibly remote object. He used the action of the
external object on the retina, to prove that we do not
see a line endwise, but a point ; and then discarded it
when it would also prove that we do not see a point
but a surface broadwise presented to the retina.[3] He
had no definite idea of what is meant by distance. He
evidently confused it at first with the third dimension
of space.[4] Afterwards, he saw that there is a visible
distance between interjacent visible points.[5] But he
never fairly faced the fact that distance is the interval

---

[1] *De Anima*, ii. 6.   [2] Locke, *Essay*, ii. 5.
[3] *Theory*, clvii.   [4] Ib. ii.   [5] Ib. cxii.

between any places, that there is a distance in length
and width, as well as in depth, and that, though distance
in depth is invisible, distance in both the other dimensions is visible. He coolly rejected the constant appeal
of the geometer to visible figures.[1] He supposed a
person without touch but with sight, and asked what
kind of geometry he would produce ; a useless question,
because man is an animal, and an animal without touch
impossible. This supposititious seeing geometer would
have certain limits, as Berkeley says : first, he would
have no sense of a solid,[2] which requires distance in
the third dimension ; secondly, he would have no sense
of resistance, which requires touch.[3] He would, therefore, infer no external world. But he would have a
sense of an extended plain with its distances, the magnitudes of its parts, and the situations of its places. He
would, therefore, see a plain, and on that plain the
outnesses of the parts to one another, and their distances
from one another in length and width. He would have
a sense, not a science, of space. Yet Berkeley denied all
these consequences of his previous admissions, assuming
that an object presents a point endwise to the eye. In
short, throughout the 'Essay,' the same merit is constantly vitiated by the same defect, the discovery of
the invisibility of remote distance confused with the
assumption of the invisibility of extended space.

In the second place, he constantly asserts that what
we strictly see are not solids, nor yet plains variously
coloured ; they are only diversity of colours.[1] He then
defies us to assign any similitude between the visible
and the tangible, and concludes that the objects of
vision are not similar to external objects, but mere

<hr>

[1] *Theory*, cl. *seq.*   [2] Ib. cliv.   [3] Ib. cxxxv.
[1] Ib. xliii., lxv., ciii., cxxix. cxxx., cliii. clviii.

signs, like words; so that ' the proper objects of vision
constitute an universal language of the Author of
nature.' [1] Meanwhile, all he has proved is, that we
do not see remote distance in the third dimension.
Secondly, he has forgotten his constant admission that
we see visible extension, visible magnitude, visible
situations. Thirdly, he is plainly under the dominion
of the abstraction of qualities. He says very truly that
we can neither abstract the idea of visible extension
from colour, nor that of colour from visible extension.
But the extraordinary thing is, that he thinks this
argument proves, not that we see something coloured
and extended, but that we see colour, not extension.[2]
He is evidently under the dominion of this simple
fallacy : colour is not extension ; what we see is colour ;
therefore it is not extension. But in reality, though
colour is not extension, what is coloured can be also
extended ; what we see is a picture at once coloured and
extended, and that is the reason why we cannot separate
colour and visible extension, but only attend the more
to colour, or the more to visible extension in the self-
same picture. Hence, the visible object is not an
arbitrary sign, but similar to the tangible object felt,
and, we may add, to the external object inferred, in
extension. The visible figure in geometry is not, indeed, the object of the science, but it is the best illustration of the object to the sense and imagination of the
geometer. The visible object is not like a word, and
vision not like a language, which may or may not be
like what is signified, but the former is the sensible
object, and the latter the sense, most correspondent to
the extended external world, though not the most
direct way of inferring it. In short, vision sees the

[1] *Theory*, cxlvii.; cf. li., lxiv.–lxv., cxliii.　　　[2] *Ib.* cxxx.

visibly extended, touch feels the tangibly extended, reason infers the externally extended; and all three objects are similar, though not the same, in extension.

So far, we have seen how brilliant, and how delusive, was Berkeley's discovery of the invisibility of remote distance, in its physical aspect. But, as we said above, he wrote the 'Theory of Vision' also in a psychological interest. He certainly proved in it that we do not see an object at a distance; and it is a curious problem that, after this discovery, the intuitive realists should have advanced their hypothesis that we immediately perceive the external world. The reason is that Berkeley buried his discovery under such a heap of errors, that we can hardly be surprised if the truth for a time lay hid. He found out that we do not see depth, and confirmed the theory that we do not see anything without. But he also proceeded to infer that we do not see visible space, but only various colours. Not content with this double paradox, he proceeded to another, which was indeed a main object of the 'Essay;' namely, that we see only visible ideas, visible ideas of colours. There is no better instance of the extraordinary way in which the assumption of idealism is made in books of philosophy, than its sudden appearance in the 'Theory of Vision.' After he has concerned himself with the external objects, and the rays of light, and the retina of the eye, we suddenly find ourselves transplanted into quite a new world with the words: 'It is evident that when the mind perceives any idea, not immediately and of itself, it must be by the means of some other idea.'[1]

The invisibility of distance in the third dimension proves that we do not see external objects at a distance from the eye. The propagation of undulations to the

---

[1] *Theory,* ix.

retina and the consequent nervous motion prove that
we do not see external objects at all.   But neither
evidence proves that we see something not merely
within ourselves, but also within our minds, or that the
visible object is a visible idea.   Berkeley, however, falls
into this ordinary idealistic *non sequitur*, without any
evidence, either physical or psychological, throughout
the ‘Theory of Vision.’   For instance, he says that ‘a
man born blind, being made to see, would, at first, have
no idea of distance by sight; the sun and stars, the
remotest objects as well as the nearer, would all seem
to be in his eye, or rather in his mind.’[1]   Similarly,
he assumes it as agreed on all hands that colours are
not without the mind, from which, of course, it
would follow that neither is visible extension.[2]   He
even uses the mere assumption that what is in the eye
is in the mind to argue that, as the objects of sight
do not exist without the mind, the pictures painted on
the bottom of the eye are not the pictures of external
objects![3]   Meanwhile, the evidences, which are all
drawn from the way in which external objects affect
the retina, prove that there is a variously coloured
picture produced in the *camera obscura* of the eye upon
the retina, but prove absolutely nothing at all about
visible ideas within the mind.

Let us now shortly resume what Berkeley proved
and did not prove about vision as a sense.   We see no
remote distance, no real magnitude, and no real situations of external objects; no solidity, no resistance, no
protrusion; no outness of the world in external space:
this is what he proved.   He vacillated about visible
extension, and finally concluded, but did not prove, that
‘what we strictly see are not solids, nor yet plains

[1] *Theory*, xli.; cf. xcv.   [2] Ib. xliii.   [3] Ib. cxvii.

variously coloured; they are only diversity of colours.'
Nor did he prove that the visible object is not on the
retina, nor in the optic nerve, but is a visible idea in
the mind; this is a *petitio principii* committed very early
in the 'Essay.'[1] Consequently, he did not prove that
vision is a universal language, and that visible objects are,
like words, mere signs of extended objects without being
extended. The same optical evidence, which proves
that we do not see remote distance endwise, proves
that we do see the extended imprinted broadwise on the
retina of our eyes. The visible picture, with distances
not endwise but broadwise, magnitudes of parts, and
situations of places, though numerically different, is
specifically similar to the tangible imprint, and to the
inferred original of both, in physical extension.

But while Berkeley's psychological interest was en-
ticing him to resolve optical effects into visible ideas,
his physical discovery was at the same time forcing
him to recognise external objects to cause them. At
the very outset he admits the existence of a distance
projecting an effect on the eye.[2] In the sequel, he
allows that 'the object which exists without the mind
and is at a distance' is different from the visible object,[3]
the former remaining the same while the latter alters
according to the remoteness of the eye from the external
object. He talks of our advancing forward to it so
many paces or miles.[4] He considers that it affects not
only our bodies but even our minds. 'We regard,' he
says, 'the objects that environ us in proportion as they
are adapted to benefit or injure our own bodies, and
thereby produce in our minds the sensations of pleasure
and pain.'[5] No realist requires more admissions. Given
only the eye, and all the universe follows, bathed through-

---

[1] *Theory,* ix.   [2] Ib. ii.   [3] Ib. lv.   [4] Ib. xlv.   [5] Ib. lix.

out its mass and its molecules in that light which is reflected from external bodies on the retina of the eye.
Optics requires external bodies to reflect and a sentient
body to receive light.   As soon as Berkeley becomes a
natural philosopher, he deserts the pure idealism of
his ' Principles,' and admits between God and the ideas
within our minds the intervention of 'unthinking' objects
projecting effects on the retina and causing visible ideas.

Nevertheless, he proceeded to misinterpret the external object.   In the ' Principles,' with much consistency though with no truth, he emphatically denies that
any sensible object, any primary or secondary quality,
is anything but an idea within the mind.   But in the
' Essay,' while he thought that visible objects are
ideas within the mind, he identified the external and
the tangible, and supposed that tangible objects exist
without the mind.   ' For,' says he, ' all visible things
are equally in the mind, and take up no part of the
external space ; and consequently are equidistant from
any tangible thing, which exists without the mind.' [1]
This view, which is entirely inconsistent with the
idealism of the ' Principles,' is curiously like intuitive
realism.   But even if it were possible that colour and
extension could be wholly separated in this manner, at
any rate the identification of tangible and external extension is a confusion of effect and cause.   Really, the
externally extended object is the common original of
the visible and the tangible objects, both of which are
within ourselves.

Berkeley's identification of the external and the
tangible led him into two false consequences.   In the
first place, it led him to deny any common cause of
sight and touch.   ' It is a mistake,' he says, ' to think

---

[1] *Theory*, cxi. ; cf. lv.

the same thing affects both sight and touch. If the
same angle or square which is the object of touch be
also the object of vision, what should hinder the blind
man, at first sight, from knowing it?'[1] It is true that
the square felt and the square seen are not the same:
one is in the tactile, the other in the optic nerves. It
is true, also, that a blind man, when first restored to
sight, would have a difficulty in comparing them. But
this is no proof, and it is not true, that the external
square object which causes the tangible square is
different from the square which causes the visible square.
Trafalgar Square is one object, though it is one thing to
look at it and another to walk round it. It is the same
crystal which presses the hand and dazzles the eye of
the natural philosopher, though the modes of motion,
by which it gravitates towards the hand, and by
which it reflects undulations towards the eye, are
different. Otherwise, science would be impossible, for
it would never be concerned with one and the same
object. Secondly, the identification of the external
and the tangible led Berkeley into a paradoxical theory
of the object of geometry. He proved, in the end of
the 'Theory of Vision,' that 'neither abstract nor
visible extension makes the object of geometry.'[2] But,
by a false disjunctive judgment, he thought himself
entitled to conclude that the object of geometry is therefore tangible extension. This conclusion entailed the
corollary that a geometrical square is really a tangible
square, and is not even represented by a visible square,
which, according to him, has four parts rather than four
sides.[3] But who ever heard of a geometer feeling a square
rather than looking at one? Through his confusion of
the external and the tangible, Berkeley has entirely

[1] *Theory,* cxxxvi.   [2] Ib. clix.   [3] Cf. ib. cxli. cxlii.

R 2

overlooked the real square of the geometer, which is neither an abstract idea nor visible nor tangible, but an object of reasoning, capable of being partially represented by a tangible square, much better by a visible square, but perfectly by neither. In elementary geometry, a geometrical figure is better represented by sight than by touch; even sight fails adequately to represent more complicated figures, such as a chiliagon, while in the geometry of infinites a polygon with infinite sides is a pure object of reasoning.

But Berkeley's confusion of external and tangible objects needs no further criticism, for having published it in 1709, he retracted it in 1710. In his 'Essay towards a New Theory of Vision,' it was put forward as the explanation of the external object, considered by geometry, and required by optics. In his 'Principles,'[1] he calls it himself a 'vulgar error.' But he at once flew to the opposite error, and confused the tangible object with a tangible idea; falsely identifying the physical with the psychical, and logically but falsely resigning the external object altogether. At the same time, he insinuated that this oscillation between intuitive realism and psychological idealism made no difference. In reality, it spoilt his theory of external objects in both books. In the 'Essay,' his confusion of the external and tangible concealed from him that the external object is the common original of touch and of vision, distinct from the objects of both. In the 'Principles,' his confusion of the tangible, as well as the visible, with ideas made him omit the external object altogether. Although the object at a distance directing a line endwise to the eye had been the foundation of his discovery of the invisibility of remote distance, he now proceeded,

---

[1] *Princ.* xliv., quoted at the beginning of this chapter.

in defiance of the science of optics, to make visible as well as tangible ideas effects of 'the governing spirit,' with not a single word about external objects without our minds. At the price of the physical truth of the 'Essay' he saved the psychological idealism of the 'Principles.'

Berkeley, in the 'Principles,' is a logical idealist; but Berkeley, in his works, is, like Locke, two philosophers in one. On the one hand, take the 'Theory of Vision.' Here he is Locke, with his admissions. In the same somewhat half-hearted way he recognises the external objects of science : he has an undercurrent of ontology : he is a cosmothetic idealist in visible ideas which he supposes to be projected by external objects, and an intuitive realist in tangible objects which he supposes to be externally felt, as Locke, after limiting sensation to ideas, had supposed primary qualities without to be objects of a kind of bastard sensation. On the other hand, take the 'Principles of Human Knowledge.' Here he is Locke, reduced to logic. He sees that mind and ideas end in mind and ideas, and that if, as Locke himself had at first said, ideas are all the objects of knowledge, then, as Locke ought to have concluded, not unthinking body but the Divine Mind is the only external cause.

But Berkeley's optics were superior to his psychology. We must appeal from the 'Principles' to the 'Theory of Vision.' 'There is,' says he in the latter treatise, 'no one ignorant that the pictures of external objects are painted on the *retina* or fund of the eye.'[1] Then, these external objects are not tangible, nor visible, nor sensible at all, but are causes of sensible objects, or, as Berkeley would say, of ideas. Not all objects

[1] *Theory*, lxxxviii.

of knowledge, then, are sensible ideas. Again, these external objects, whose pictures are painted on the retina, are not God, and yet are causes of sensible effects. God, then, is not the sole cause. In short, optics require, between God and our ideas, an intervening nature. The scientific admissions of the 'Theory of Vision' are sufficient to destroy the pure idealism of the 'Principles of Human Knowledge.'

Besides the optical discovery of the invisibility of remote distance, the psychological hypothesis that we see visible ideas, and the ontological recognition of the existence of an extended world without the mind falsely confused with the tangible object, the 'Theory of Vision' finally contains a logical speculation on the origin from vision of our knowledge of the extended beyond vision. Like the main thesis, this speculation contains much that is true, and especially that we do not see but infer an external world. It is also most suggestive, and in fact was the first hint of the hypothesis that association may be an account of, or rather a substitute for, the origin of knowledge. But it does not in the least explain the knowledge of extended objects in the external world, required by optics and admitted by Berkeley. We must not be led away by the appearance of simplicity, but keep steadily before us the known facts to be explained, and by them test the hypothesis.

We do not see remote distance: we do judge and infer it from sight: this is the essential truth in Berkeley's theory.[1] The question is, how this judgment and inference are made. He answers that when the mind perceives any idea not immediately and of itself, it must be by the means of some other idea:[2] distance, then,

---

[1] *Theory.* iii.   [2] Ib. ix.

is suggested to the mind by the mediation of some
other idea, which is itself perceived in the act of seeing.[1]
He finds three ideas, which arise according to the
different distances of objects : the first, the lessening or
widening the intervals between the pupils of our eyes,
attended with a sensation ;[2] the second, the more or
less confused appearance ; the third, the prevention of
this confusion by straining the eye, with its sensation.[3]
These are the ideas which he thinks will suggest the
idea of the distance of the external object : not that
there is any natural or necessary connection of those
ideas with distance, but that there is an habitual or customary connection between these ideas and the idea of
distance.[4]

This process implies that the idea of distance itself
has been acquired in some other way. This way,
according to Berkeley, is touch combined with motion.
He gives the whole process in the following passage :—

'Having of a long time experienced certain ideas
perceivable by touch, as distance, tangible figure, and
solidity, to have been connected with certain ideas of
sight, I do upon perceiving those ideas of sight, forthwith conclude what tangible ideas are, by the wonted
ordinary course of nature, like to follow. Looking at
an object I perceive a certain visible figure and colour,[5]
with some degree of faintness and other circumstances,
which from what I have formerly observed, determine
me to think, that if I advance forward so many paces
or miles, I shall be affected with such and such ideas of
touch.'[6]

This process, by which visible ideas suggest tangible

---

[1] *Theory*, xvi.   [2] Ib. xvi.   [3] Ib. xxvii.
[4] Cf. ib. xxviii. with the above sections.
[5] Note this admission of visible figure as well as colour.   [6] Ib. xlv.

ideas of distance, is what is ordinarily called association. Berkeley describes this operation with great clearness. 'That one idea,' he says, ' may suggest another to the mind, it will suffice that they have been observed to go together, without any demonstration of the ne cessity of their co-existence, or without so much as knowing what it is that makes them so co-exist.' [1] There is such an operation, and its recognition was not new in philosophy. Plato and Aristotle, Hobbes and Locke were aware of it. Aristotle, for instance, says that we recollect from what is similar or contrary or contiguous.[2] But what was new in Berkeley's 'Theory of Vision' was the hypothesis, afterwards developed by Hume, that this process of recovering ideas is sometimes the analysis of what we call knowing objects. The ordinary man, when he uses his eyes, supposes that he knows, nay sees, that there is an external object at a distance from him. Berkeley tells him that he is really letting visible ideas suggest to him tangible ideas of distance ; that is all.

There is a negative value in Berkeley's analysis. It is greatly superior to the ordinary supposition that we see a distant object. Berkeley, though he exaggerated when he said that we do not see any distances at all, showed conclusively that we do not see but infer a distant object in the external world. It is also superior to the supposition of 'Descartes and others' [3] that we infer the distance of objects from the angles they make with our eyes. Berkeley disposed of this ' humour of making one see by geometry,' when he showed that the lines and angles between the external objects and the eyes are as invisible as the external

---

[1] *Theory*, xxv.   [2] *De Mem.* 2 = 451 B, 18-20.

[3] *Theory*, iv. not

objects themselves.[1] Mathematical opticians had fallen
into the blunder of supposing that lines and angles,
known only to themselves by science, are sensible data
which ordinary men use in vision to infer an external
world.

There is also positive information in Berkeley's
analysis. It contributed some new truths on the senses.
In the first place, about sight ; he did not indeed show
that there is no vision of space, but he did show that
it is in a way unnecessary. He called attention to the
scientific observation of the misfortune of the blind,
who have no eyes, yet feel and infer space. Again, his
remark, that no resistance is perceived by sight, contains the true reason why from sight alone we could
not infer an external world, and therefore must appeal
to touch and motion. Lastly, though it is not the case,
it is possible that sight might, like hearing, or, at any
rate, like language, contain no apprehension of extension,
and yet enable us, when combined with a sense of extension, to infer an extended object. On the whole, he has
not shown that the visible object is not an extended
picture ; but he has shown that, whatever the visible
object is, we can know an extended object in the
external world without it, and not by it alone.

Secondly, he has the great merit of having hinted,
however imperfectly, at what is now called the muscular
sense. When he speaks of 'the motion of his body
which is perceivable by touch,'[2] though he may be exaggerating its connection with touch, he is recognising a
sense of motion. He also saw that in vision there is
something more than seeing. What he calls 'lessening
or widening the intervals between the pupils,' which is
'attended with a sensation,' is the convergence or diver-

[1] *Theory*, iv., xii., lii.-liii.   [2] Ib. xlv.

gence of the optic axes by the internal and external *recti* muscles, with their muscular sense. When he speaks of the confused appearance caused by objects brought too close to the eye, and of preventing the appearances growing more confused 'by straining the eye,' and of its sensation,[1] he is pointing towards the increase of the convexity of the crystalline lens, for the more rapid convergence of rays from near objects to the retina, by the action of the ciliary muscle, with its muscular sense. He also refers to the movements of the eyes up and down, to the right and left, which are performed by the four *recti* muscles.[2] In none of these cases did he analyse the muscular movements or assign them a distinct muscular sense. Nevertheless, he called attention to movement, to the sense of movement in touch, and to the sense of some kind of action in sight, connected with the knowledge of extension.

At the same time, these great achievements are quite consistent with equally great blunders about our senses, of which there are two, at opposite extremes. On the one hand, he underrates the efficacy of vision when he tends to confine it to visible ideas of colour; on the other hand, he exaggerates the efficacy of touch when he tends to extend it to external objects. Really, the former is the vision of the extended in the optic nerves, the latter is the feeling of the extended in the tactile nerves. However, these errors do not touch the exact question before us. Whatever else it may be, the object of vision is certainly not the external object at a remote distance. Now, the question is whether, when we say that there is such an external object, corresponding to what we see, we are only letting visible ideas suggest tangible ideas of remote distance.

[1] *Theory*, xxi. xxvii.   [2] Ib. xcvii. xcviii.

In solving this problem, two concessions must be at once made. In the first place, from vision, being no sense of resistance, we do not infer the external world directly, but only indirectly through touch and motion. Secondly, visible ideas do suggest tangible ideas, and other ideas also for that matter, by the customary tie of association, which is a real fact of human nature. But we must also ask ourselves whether this suggestion is all that happens. If so, we should only have the ideas; we should not infer that, over and above the ideas, the object seen corresponds to an extended object in the external world. For example, at this moment, my vision of the white would suggest my tangible idea of the extended ; but I should not infer, as I really do, that over and above the tangible idea there is an extended paper in an external world, corresponding both to the object of touch and the object of sight. Berkeley substituted the suggestion of ideas for the inference of external objects.

Even in the 'Theory of Vision,' in spite of having admitted the existence of the external object, and its action on the retina, Berkeley partly accepted the consequence. 'Sitting in my study,' he says, 'I hear a coach drive along the street; I look through the casement and see it ; I walk out and enter into it ; thus common speech wou'd incline one to think, I heard, saw, and touch'd the same thing, to wit, the coach. It is nevertheless certain, the ideas intermitted by each sense are widely different, and distinct from each other ; but having been observed constantly to go together, they are spoken of as one and the same thing.'[1] Similarly, he afterwards says that, though the objects are different, as they are called by the same name, he will, to avoid

[1] *Theory*, xlvi.

tediousness and singularity of speech, speak of them as belonging to one and the same thing.[1]

Now, it is quite true that the audible, visible, and tangible are different objects, and also that, if nothing happened except that ideas of the audible and visible suggested ideas of the tangible, no real identification could take place. But something further does take place. In the first place, when I hear something sounding in my auditory, see something coloured in my optic, and feel something hard in my tactile nerves, and have often experienced these sensible objects in a similar order, I infer that there is one external object, which is the common original of these sensible objects on any given occasion. Secondly, I call this common original by one and the same name, 'coach,' because I infer it to be one thing. It is true that I have an habitual tendency to confuse the one external object with the several and different auditory, visible and tangible objects within me. But it is not true that there is no identity but an identity of name. There is an identical external object, the coach, which I infer, and which I can disengage from the confusion with its different sensible results, by means of science. Now, if the auditory, visible and tangible objects had been mere ideas in my mind, and if these ideas merely suggested one another, I could never have inferred the one external object, and it is most improbable that I should have even called the different ideas by one name. But I do infer one external object, and am justified by optics and other sciences connected with the senses. Therefore, in the first place, the process of this inference of one external object cannot be a mere suggestion of different ideas; and secondly, the data of this inference of an external object cannot be

[1] *Theory,* lv.

auditory, visible and tangible ideas. In reality, from physical data in the several nerves, I infer one physical coach, and give it, not them, one name.

In the 'Theory of Vision,' however, Berkeley did not fully realise the consequence of reducing the inference of external objects to the suggestion of tangible ideas, because he combined this association of ideas with an intuitive touch of external objects. Hence, later on, he says of a man, that 'when he has by experience learned the connexion there is between the several ideas of sight and touch, he will be able, by the perception he has of the situation of visible things in respect of one another, to make a sudden and true estimate of the situation of outward tangible things, corresponding to them. And thus it is, he shall perceive by sight the situation of external objects, which do not properly fall under that sense.'[1] Such an estimate would require the impossible identification of tangible ideas, tangible objects, and outward things. But, in the first place, touch does not feel the outward thing. Secondly, a visible idea suggests a tangible idea, but not a tangible object. Thirdly, what we really do is to estimate the situation not of a tangible idea, nor of a tangible object, but of an outward thing corresponding on the one hand to the tangible, on the other hand to the visible, object within ourselves. We cannot bolster up the association of ideas by an intuitive touch of outward things.

In the 'Principles,' when he had retracted the confusion of the external and the tangible, and the intuitive touch of the external, the consequence of supposing that the inference from vision is nothing but an association of ideas came out in its simple nakedness. He

[1] Ib. xcix.

then saw that, in this case, ideas of sight only admonish us what ideas of touch will be imprinted on our minds, and do not mark out to us things actually existing at a distance.[1] I freely admit that Berkeley was right in retracting the tangible intuition of the external world, and that if we start with visible ideas, and by the suggestion of ideas let these visible suggest tangible ideas, and have no tangible intuition of extended objects in the external world, we shall begin and end in ideas. But we do not end in ideas. His own optics require that we know external objects, and that no one is ignorant of their painting pictures on the retina of the eye. His hypothesis of the suggestion of ideas does not account for the knowledge of their causes. It is, therefore, false.

The cause of Berkeley's error was that neglect of logical inference which made its appearance in the Second Book of Locke's 'Essay,' and led to the postponement of reasoning to all kinds of lesser powers. Like Locke, Berkeley was aware of the difference between association and reasoning.[2] But, like Locke, he kept in the background, and to the last, reasoning, the one power which will be heard and will not wait. Hence, in the 'Principles,' he supposes that ideas suggest ideas, until reason at last infers a God. Hence, in the 'Theory of Vision,' he substitutes for inference a false touch of outward things and an imperfect suggestion by visible of tangible ideas. He overlooks in both the human, though complex, inference of an external extended object which causes both sight and touch.

The 'Theory of Vision' contains the discoveries of

---

[1] *Princ.* xliv., quoted at the beginning of this chapter.
[2] Cf. Locke, *Essay*, ii. 33, 18; Berkeley, *The Theory of Visual Language Vindicated.* § 42.

the invisibility of remote distance, and of the combination of sight and touch with a sense of motion. It is a very good answer to those who say that we see the external world; though even they could retort on Berkeley that he says himself that we feel it. It is no answer to those who say that we know the external world. It is a good answer to those who say that we infer it directly from sight by lines and angles, or by any other direct inference, from sight, which feels no resistance. But it is no answer to those who say that we infer an external extended world first from the resistance felt in the senses of touch and motion, and then from the correspondence in extension between inferred, tangible, and visible objects. Finally, Berkeley's 'Theory of Vision' contains two fundamental errors of omission: the first, that there is no vision of an extended object within; the second, no inference of an extended object without, common to our senses of sight and touch.

CHAPTER IX.

HUME.

THE academical or sceptical philosophy of Hume admits of being summarised as follows. All the perceptions of the mind are impressions and thoughts or ideas.[1] All our ideas or more feeble perceptions are copies of our impressions or more lively ones.[2] Association is a principle of connection which, by resemblance, contiguity or causation, on the appearance of a perception suggests thoughts or ideas.[3] All the objects of human reason or inquiry may naturally be divided into two kinds, to wit, *Relations of Ideas* and *Matters of Fact.* Of the former kind are the sciences of geometry, algebra, and arithmetic, and, in short, every affirmation which is either intuitively or demonstratively certain.[4] The origin of our beliefs, *i.e.* vivid ideas, of matters of fact, is experience of a constant conjunction of impressions, and association which, from this constant conjunction, begets such a connection in the imagination that, on the appearance of the antecedent, we have the idea, *i.e.* belief, of the consequent and of their connection as cause and effect.[5] The mind has never anything present to it but the perceptions, and cannot possibly reach any experience of their connection with objects. The supposition of such a connection is, therefore, with-

---

[1] *Inquiry,* § 2. [2] Ib. [3] Ib. § 3.
[4] Ib. § 4. [5] Ib. §§ 4 7, esp. § 7, Part II.

out any foundation in reasoning.[1] The great subverter
of *Pyrrhonism*, or the excessive principles of scepticism,
is action.[2] There is, indeed, a more *mitigated* scepticism,
or *academical* philosophy, which may be both durable
and useful, and which may, in part, be the result of this
Pyrrhonism or *excessive* scepticism, when its undistin-
guished doubts are, in some measure, corrected by
common sense and reflection.[3]

The point of this academical philosophy is that man
has the faculties to receive impressions and conceive
ideas or thoughts; and by association to make vivid
ideas of causation, which are his only beliefs on
matters of fact; but not by reasoning to infer external objects. Hume published it twice over, first in the
'Treatise of Human Nature,' afterwards in the 'Inquiry
concerning Human Understanding.' The earlier work is
more elaborate, containing in the First Part a fuller
discussion of the origin of ideas, modelled on the Second
Book of Locke's 'Essay,' but with the stress laid on association; in the Second Part, a theory of the apprehensions of time and space, which hardly appears at all in
the later work; in the Third Part, a longer but less
elegant exposition of his theory of association as the
origin of the belief in causation; and in the Fourth
Part, a long discussion of the apprehension of objects,
answering to the last section of the 'Inquiry,' but comprising a sceptical theory of substances, both material
and thinking, which he afterwards omitted but by no
means retracted in his later work. Since the 'Treatise'
was published when the author was a young man of
twenty-seven, the 'Inquiry' ten years later in the prime
of life, the impartial critic must dwell mainly on the more

---

[1] *Inquiry*, § 12, Part I.   [2] Ib. § 12, Part II.
[3] Ib. § 12, Part III.

mature work; especially as in his account of 'My own Life' Hume says himself, 'I had been guilty of a very usual indiscretion in going to the press too early'—a useful warning to youthful philosophers. Nevertheless, the essence of both 'Treatise' and 'Inquiry' is the same: it is a reduction of man to mere perceptions. Berkeley had attacked natural science: it remained for Hume to attack the human intellect. But we must take care not to be argued out of our wits.

Hume's philosophy is founded on the following distinction of perceptions into impressions and ideas, which he identifies with thoughts :—

'Here, therefore, we may divide all the perceptions of the mind into two classes or species, which are distinguished by their different degrees of force and vivacity. The less forcible and lively are commonly denominated *thoughts or ideas*. The other species want a name in our language, and in most others; I suppose, because it was not requisite for any, but philosophical purposes, to rank them under a general term or appellation. Let us, therefore, use a little freedom and call them *impressions*; employing that word in a sense somewhat different from the usual. By the term *impressions*, then, I mean all our more lively perceptions, where we hear, or see, or feel, or love, or hate, or desire, or will. And impressions are distinguished from ideas, which are the less lively perceptions, of which we are conscious, when we reflect on any of those sensations or movements above mentioned.'[1]

The distinction between impressions and ideas is an important discovery, or rather re-discovery. Aristotle had, in the 'De Animâ,' carefully distinguished between *æsthemata*, or the objects in sense when an external object is present, and *phantasmata*, or their relics in the

[1] *Inquiry*, § 2.

imagination when the external object is absent. But,
as we have already seen. Descartes afterwards confused
the object of sensation and conception under the name
' idea,' and Locke and Berkeley had followed him. So
long as it was admitted that some external object is
also known, this confusion had no very serious consequences; for the reduction of sense to a purely psychical object at all was a far more fundamental error
than the reduction of this psychical object to an idea.
But when it began to be doubted whether any external
object could be known, it then became a serious question, how we can distinguish an adventitious idea imprinted on the senses from a fictitious idea generated by
the imagination.

Berkeley felt this difficulty,[1] and got over it partly
by supposing that adventitious are more vivid than
factitious ideas, but mainly by his theory that the
former are directly inspired by God. Now, Hume
doubted our knowledge of any cause of our perceptions, natural or spiritual. Moreover, he saw that
' the word *idea* seems to be commonly taken in a very
loose sense by Locke and others, as standing for any of
our perceptions, our sensations and passions, as well as
thoughts.'[2] In these circumstances, he revived the
ancient distinction of *æsthema* and *phantasma* under
the new names ' impression ' and ' idea,' yet without
resorting either to matter or to God. As he says in the
' Treatise,' ' By the term of " impression," I would not be
understood to express the manner in which our lively
ideas are produced in the soul, but merely the perceptions themselves.'[3] Consequently he had to look out for
some fresh criterion to distinguish the thing as well as
the term, and found it in the liveliness of an impres-

---

[1] *Princ.* xxxiii.   [2] *Inquiry*, § 2, note.   [3] *Treatise*, i. § 1, note.

sion as contrasted with an idea. In the 'Rhetoric,' Aristotle had described, without meaning to define, imagination as a kind of weak sense.[1] Hobbes had exalted this description into a definition—'*Imagination being* (to define it) *conception remaining, and by little and little decaying from and after the Act of Sense.*'[2] Berkeley had made faintness a partial test of an idea of imagination : Hume exalted it into the sole criterion, and committed himself to the consequences. 'The most lively thought,' says he, 'is still inferior to the dullest sensation.'

The hypothesis that there is no more distinction between sense and imagination than between vivid and faint perceptions, or states of consciousness, as they now call them, has become a favourite with modern idealists, simply because they have destroyed the real criterion afforded by the presence and absence of external objects. But there is a difference in kind between sense and imagination, of which 'different degrees of force and vivacity' furnish no adequate criterion. The faintest impressions would be undistinguishable from the most vivid ideas. This objection Hume had noticed himself in the 'Treatise,' and tried to evade it :—

'The common degrees of these are easily distinguished : though it is not impossible but, in particular instances, they may very nearly approach to each other. Thus, in sleep, in a fever, in madness, or in any very violent emotions of soul, our ideas may approach to our impressions : as, on the other hand, it sometimes happens that our impressions are so faint and low, that we cannot distinguish them from our ideas. But, notwithstanding this near resemblance in a few instances, they

[1] Ar. *Rhet.* i. 11   1370 A, 28.
[2] Hobbes, *Human Nature*, chap. iii. § 1.

are in general so very different, that no one can make a
scruple to rank them under distinct heads, and assign
to each a peculiar name to mark the difference.' [1]

The conclusion of this passage exhibits a common
practice of trying to get round a contradictory instance.
It is true that, on the whole, the livelier would be distinct from the fainter perceptions, but there would still
be a margin between the lively and the faint, which, in
the absence of any other criterion, it would be arbitrary
to place among either impressions or ideas. But there
is a still more fatal objection: some ideas are livelier
than impressions, and would have, by the bare criterion
of lively and faint, to change places with them. Yet
Hume, to save his theory, has to say that ' all ideas,
especially abstract ones, are naturally faint and obscure,' while ' all sensations, either outward or inward,
are strong and vivid.' [2] But abstract ideas of mathematicians are often brighter than their concrete impressions, as in the case of the mathematician who in a fit
of abstraction held the egg in his hand while he boiled
his watch. Ideas of men in disease are often so vivid
as to be mistaken for impressions. The artistic imagination is sometimes stronger than ordinary sensation, as
Handel, on being asked how he wrote the ' Hallelujah
Chorus,' said, ' I did see all heaven before me, and the
great God Himself.'

This superior vividness of imagination is finely described by Addison :—

' Words, when well chosen, have so great a force in
them, that a description often gives us more lively ideas
than the sight of things themselves. The reader finds a
scene drawn in stronger colours, and painted more to
the life in his imagination, by the help of words, than

---

[1] *Treatise*, i. § 1.　　　　[2] *Inquiry*, § 2.

by an actual survey of the scene which they describe.
In this case the poet seems to get the better of nature;
he takes, indeed, the landskip after her, but gives it
more vigorous touches, heightens its beauty, and so en-
livens the whole piece, that the images which flow from
the objects themselves appear weak and faint, in comparison of those that come from the expressions.'[1]

Hume, in distinguishing impressions and ideas,
rightly restored the word 'idea' to its original sense,
from which Descartes had perverted it in making it
stand for all our perceptions. But he tried to put new
wine into old bottles. The Aristotelian distinction of
impressions and ideas does not accord with Hume's
distinctions of vivid and faint perceptions, and can only
be explained by the Aristotelian criterion of the presence and absence of an external object, which was
repugnant to Hume's philosophy. Sensation is the apprehension of an object presented to the senses representing an external object; while hallucination, or
'subjective sensation,' is a similar apprehension produced by pressure on a sensory nerve: imagination is
the apprehension of an idea representing a sensible
object or something similar to it and inferred from it.
But the presentations of sense are often less vivid than
the afterthoughts of fancy.

Hume's second point is the empirical doctrine that
impressions are the originals of all our ideas, which, as
before, he identifies with our thoughts:—

'But though our thought seems to possess this
unbounded liberty, we shall 'find, upon a nearer examination, that it is really confined within very narrow
limits, and that all this creative power of the mind
amounts to no more than the faculty of compounding,

[1] *Spectator*, No. 416.

transposing, augmenting, or diminishing the materials afforded us by the senses and experience. When we think of a golden mountain, we only join two consistent ideas, *gold* and *mountain*, with which we were formerly acquainted. A virtuous horse we can conceive; because, from our own feeling, we can conceive virtue; and this we may unite to the figure and shape of a horse, which is an animal familiar to us. In short, all the materials of thinking are derived either from our outward or inward sentiments: the mixture and composition of these belongs alone to the mind and will: or, to express myself in philosophical language, all our ideas or more feeble perceptions are copies of our impressions or more lively ones.'[1]

The conclusion of this passage is a neat summary of the argument in the Second Book of Locke's 'Essay.' Sense is the source of ideas, however indirect the process of their formation. Locke had disposed of innate ideas.[2] As Hume puts it, 'all our impressions are innate, and our ideas not innate,'[3] meaning that the former are intuitive and the latter derivative. But when we are told that all our ideas are copies, direct or indirect, of our impressions, several questions present themselves. First, what are those impressions which have to be the originals of all ideas? Secondly, what are the processes which enable us to copy the original impressions? Thirdly, what are the ideas and thoughts which we are able to reach? We shall have to ask ourselves about our impressions, our processes, our ideas, and our thoughts.

What are impressions? It is surprising how little Hume condescends to tell us on this subject, incomparably the most important in his philosophy. In the 'Treatise' he says that ' the examination of our sensations

[1] *Inquiry*, § 2.   [2] Cf. *Treatise*. iii. § 14.   [3] *Inquiry*, § 2. note.

belongs more to anatomists and natural philosophers than to moral : and, therefore, shall not at present be entered upon.'[1] It never is entered upon in the 'Treatise'; and in the 'Inquiry' all that is said on the subject is that impressions are more vivid than ideas, that they are the origin of ideas, that there are impressions of sensation and impressions of reflection, and that in all cases the mind has never anything present to it but perceptions, which are either impressions or ideas. We are left to gather that the sensible object of the impression, being a mere quality not distinct from the operation, is, in short, the impression itself. Bare abstract impressions are the data of Hume's empiricism. But it is one thing to admit that knowledge begins with sense, another to assume that it begins with a sense of impressions.

When we reflect that these impressions are deliberately stated to be the premises of all our conclusions by a philosopher who truly says that 'one mistake is the necessary parent of another,' the omission of an examination of sensation strikes us with the greatest surprise. But when we consider that all the idealists have taken their data of sense with the same coolness, the wonder ceases. As, to begin with, Descartes had attempted no formal proof that a soul must perceive ideas, while Locke and Berkeley simply accepted the hypothesis that it does perceive ideas, so Hume assumed that the mind has never anything present to it but perceptions, and so, after him, Kant begged that the matter of sense, and Mill begged that the information which the senses give us concerning objects, is our sensations.[2]

[1] *Treatise*, i. § 2.

[2] Cf. Hume, *Inquiry*, § 12 ; Kant, *Critique* (ed. Hartenstein, pp. 33, 55 6 ; Meiklejohn's translation, Bohn), pp. 1, 21 ; Mill, *Examination of Hamilton's Philosophy*, chap. ii.

In order to correct Hume's theory of impressions, and his followers' theory of sensation, it is necessary to repeat, what we have already proved, that sense apprehends neither itself nor abstractions. It is, in the first place, always an operation of a subject apprehending an object, internal, but not identical with the operation. Secondly, its object is always a qualified substance, internal but not resolvable into abstract qualities. Thirdly, when it is outer sense, sensation, and sensitive observation, the substance apprehended is the nervous substance sensibly qualified in different parts as coloured, heated, &c. Fourthly, when it is inner sense, consciousness and conscious reflection, the substance apprehended is the thinking subject, body and soul. An impression without a substantial subject and object is an abstraction, never perceived, never known, with difficulty made an object of attention. A man is a substantial subject impressed with a substantial object, and can be conscious of himself being so impressed, as well as conceiving, reasoning, and performing other operations.

Hume's theory of impressions, when corrected by being converted from the abstract into the concrete, contains the valuable point, too often neglected, that, even without judgment, a man's simple sensation of the white, or the hot, is a beginning of knowledge, and no mere abstraction. Nay, as we saw in the first part of this essay, we can even trace knowledge to a still simpler origin. I begin to know when I feel pained or pleased; not, be it remembered, when there is pain or pleasure, which are afterthoughts. My first act of knowledge is having a simple feeling in the concrete: my second act of knowledge is having a simple sensation of a sensible object in the concrete.

There are two ways of criticising Hume's theory of impressions. The wrong criticism is to accept it as a complete account of sensation, conclude that pure sensation is an abstraction which never occurs in consciousness, and yet assume these very abstractions to be the elements of a psychological synthesis.[1] Those who take this view are too much tarred with the brush of Hume. A pure sensation, or impression in Hume's terminology, is an abstraction; but so far from being an element of knowledge, it is a subsequent result of concentration on the mere operation of knowing, to the neglect of subject and object, and is only put for the real elements of knowledge by a convenient form of speech. The right criticism is to point out that Hume substituted the after-abstraction of sensation for the data of sense and the elements of knowledge, which are always a substantial subject sensibly perceiving substantial objects within the nervous system and consciously perceiving himself. There is no such a thing *in rerum naturâ* as an impression and a consciousness, which are merely abstracted *post rem*, but there is such a thing as man impressed with an object and man conscious of himself. Sensation and consciousness, in this concrete shape, are, moreover, not only the real elements of knowledge, but are themselves knowledge; for, as Aristotle saw, though sense is not science (ἐπιστήμη), on the other hand it is knowledge (γνῶσις).

Next, we come to the association of ideas, thus described by Hume :—

' It is evident that there is a principle of connection between the different thoughts or ideas of the mind, and that, in their appearance to the memory or imagination,

---

[1] Cf. Wundt, *Physiologische Psychologie*, ii. 196.

they introduce each other with a certain degree of method and regularity.'[1]

He also assigned three principles of connection among ideas, namely, resemblance, contiguity in time or place, and cause or effect; for example, a picture leads our thoughts to the original; the mention of one apartment in a building suggests a discourse concerning the others; and if we think of a wound, we can scarcely forbear reflecting on the pain which follows it.[2] Such is the association of ideas on these three principles; a process, which Hume did not exactly substitute for all reasoning, for he regarded mathematics as intuitive and demonstrative, and founded morals on sympathy and reason; but which he did make the substitute for reason in all matters of causation, the organ of natural philosophy, and, after sense, the main origin of our ideas, which in the passage just quoted are, for the third time, identified with our thoughts.

Association of ideas is a *vera causa*; this is the great advantage of Hume over Kant. We are conscious that when we have been sensible of two objects together, and have a sensation or idea of one, we, in consequence, have the idea of the other: we are not conscious that we have an *a priori* idea, or any other apprehension of an object which we have not apprehended beforehand, either immediately or mediately. The simplest way, in which this conscious suggestion of ideas acts, is when simple feelings or sensations and their ideas introduce the ideas of one another. That is not a bad instance given by Hume; the idea of a wound suggests the idea of pain. The conditions of such a simple sensitive association, as we may name it, are, first, simple feelings or sensations occurring together; secondly, their being

[1] *Inquiry*, § 3.   [2] Ib.

repeated together; thirdly, imagination, or the power of conceiving ideas; fourthly, the appearance of one of the feelings or sensations, or of one of their ideas; and finally, the association itself, which consists in the consequent introduction of the idea of the other feeling or sensible object.

A question may, indeed, be raised, which is evaded by Hume and by many of his disciples. Need we only have had the original impressions together, or must we have also perceived their relation, or the relation of their objects? For example, must we have been sensible not only of the wound and of the pain, but also that the wound was cause of the pain, before it would suggest the idea of the pain? Hume, starting as he did from simple impressions, would no doubt have answered this question in the negative. He would probably have been right; and, moreover, he was aware of the reason, which is the anatomical connection of the parts of the nervous system,[1] though how, if everything we know is perceptions, he could know about the nervous system, which is the material cause of these perceptions, he did not vouchsafe to explain. The unconscious connection of nervous centres, e.g. between those which control the contraction of the iris and those which act on the ciliary muscle to increase the convexity of the crystalline lens in the eye, the facts of automatic action in general, and those of unconscious cerebration in particular, make it exceedingly probable, notwithstanding the difficulty of isolating such a fact in consciousness, that when a connection has been set up between nervous centres, through two simple sensations repeatedly occurring together, then the occurrence of one will, by an association founded on the nervous connection, in-

---

[1] *Treatise*, ii. § 5; cf. Locke, *Essay*, ii. 33, 6.

troduce the idea of the other, without our having ever
perceived that the two sensations or their sensible
objects were connected. In accordance also with that
gradation of animal faculties first noticed by Aristotle,
it is not at all improbable that some animals, which
have got beyond feeling and simple sensation to the
phantasy of imagination, may possess this simple sensitive association of ideas, which also, through the power
of ideas over passions and passions over movements,
may be the guide of their lives.

It is a very different question how far simple sensation, ideation, and association would carry a man on the
path of rational life. All association of ideas is an act
of reproductive imagination. It merely reproduces the
idea of something already known somehow or other.
We shall find, in the sequel, that as knowledge widens
association widens with it. But at present we are dealing with the simplest kind of association from simple
sensations, which is also the only kind which Hume
formally recognises. Now, his doctrine is that when we
have had simple impressions together, ideas are their
copies, and association introduces these ideas by the
laws of connection among the impressions. This can
only mean that association reproduces the idea of an
object already sensible; for example, if having been
hurt I felt pain, being hurt again will reproduce the
idea of the previously felt pain.

An idea of a previously felt pain is quite a different
thing from the idea of a similar pain not yet felt; the
former represents a previous impression, the latter a
future impression; the former is an object of simple
reproductive, the latter of simple productive imagination. Now, simple sensitive association reproduces in
the present the idea of a particular pain already actually

felt in the past ; but neither Hume nor any of his disciples has shown that it will perform the very different operation of producing the similar but new idea of a similar but new pain to be possibly felt in the future. Here is the limit of association : it always reproduces the idea of something already apprehended : never produces the idea of something not yet apprehended. I have been hurt and felt pain: I am now hurt; I imagine the ideas of previous pain when I was hurt; I also imagine the idea of a pain now to follow the hurt, but not yet felt. Association reproduces the former ideas ; and why ? Because the particular impressions, of which the particular ideas are copies, have occurred together. But this reproductive act will not of itself produce the latter idea, the impression of which has never occurred at all. Association from simple impression reproduces particular ideas of particular objects previously sensible : it does not produce a particular idea even of a single particular object, not yet sensible ; *a fortiori*, it is powerless to generate a general idea.

Hume's critic must constantly keep before him the question—Is all the reasoning of the natural philosopher nothing but a reproduction of sensible ideas by simple association ? This question brings us to Hume's main point, that while all mathematical reasoning is a process from intuition through demonstration to relations of ideas, all reasoning about facts is a process from experience of constant conjunction of impressions through association to ideas, *i.e.* beliefs, of cause and effect. The discussion of this complicated theory compels the consideration of many points : belief or judgment and reasoning or inference, intuition and demonstration, causation and our knowledge of cause and effect. Judgment and

reasoning alone almost require a logic. I propose to
confine myself to these, leaving the remaining points
for subsequent discussion. We must not leave the most
precious of all man's gifts to be stolen from him without
striking a blow. What was wanted, and is still a de-
sideratum, is, not a Critique of Pure Reason, but a
Vindication of Logical Reasoning.

'Nature,' says Hume, ' by an absolute and uncon-
trollable necessity, has determined us to judge, as well
as breathe and feel.' [1] He saw the importance of judgment or belief. He also set himself, both in the 'Treatise'
and in the 'Inquiry,' [2] to 'examine more accurately the
nature of this belief.'   But in both cases he adopted the
same extraordinary paradox, that, as impression is only a
more vivid perception than an idea, so a belief is only a
more vivid idea than a fiction.   'I say that belief is nothing but a more vivid, lively, forcible, firm, steady conception of an object than what the imagination alone is
ever able to attain ': such is Hume's definition of belief. [3]

Why did he fall into this extraordinary confusion of
simple and complex apprehension, of conception and
judgment, of an idea and a belief?   Because, wanting
to derive all beliefs from association, and being aware
that association terminates in ideas, there was nothing
for it but to reduce beliefs to vivid ideas. He cut his
coat according to his cloth—in a thoroughly idealistic
style of tailoring. 'Whenever,' he says, 'any object
is presented to the memory or senses, it immediately,
by the force of custom, carries the imagination to conceive that object which is usually conjoined to it ; and
this conception is attended with a feeling or sentiment
different from the loose reveries of the fancy. In this

---

[1] *Treatise*, iv. § 1.   [2] Ib. iii. § 7; *Inquiry*, § 5.
[3] *Inquiry*, § 5. Part II.

consists the whole nature of belief.'[1] All he really
shows is that, if association is the origin of beliefs, they
would be mere ideas; but he does not prove that they
are so. It was to prepare for this confusion of conception and belief, that he had said first that all perceptions are impressions and ideas or thoughts, that all
ideas or thoughts are copies of impressions, and that
association is a principle of connection of ideas or
thoughts; as if all thought were ideas and ideas our
only thoughts!

Judgment, or belief, is, like conception, an apprehension, but not like it in being the apprehension of an
idea; nor can any accumulation of epithets added to a
conception make it a judgment. Judgment is the
apprehension of a relation. Hume entirely missed this
point, by which judgment is differentiated from all conception whatever. He was, no doubt, much deceived
by the conceptualistic theory of relation in Locke's
'Essay.' But Locke, though he had confused relations
with their ideas in the Second Book, changed his key
when he came to the Fourth Book, and regarded judgments as perceptions of the agreement and disagreement
of ideas, without resolving these relations into ideas, as
strict consistency would have demanded. It should be
noticed that this differentia of judgment holds even
when the things related are ideas; when I judge that a
dragon is a serpent breathing flame, I have only ideas of
a dragon and of such a fiery serpent, but I judge that
the ideas actually have the relation of identity, which I
can express in a proposition by the copula, *is*. Locke,
then, might at least have taught Hume that a judgment
perceives, not mere ideas, but the agreement and disagreement of ideas. But, as usual, the Second Book

[1] *Inquiry,* § 5, Part II.

attracted philosophers to the neglect of the Fourth
Book of Locke's · Essay.'

But though Locke's theory of judgment is wider
than Hume's, it is not adequate; not all judgments
apprehend relations of ideas ; for some judgments apprehend relations of sensible objects. This point has been
excellently made by Mill, the logician of the school of
Locke and Hume, in his 'Logic,' when he says that
' believing is an act which has for its subject the facts
themselves, though a previous mental conception of the
facts is an indispensable condition. When I say that
fire causes heat, do I mean that my idea of fire causes
my idea of heat? No; I mean that the natural phænomenon, fire, causes the natural phænomenon, heat.
When I mean to assert anything respecting ideas, I give
them their proper name ; I call them ideas ; as when I
say that a child's idea of a battle is unlike the reality.' [1]
Hence, Mill's · Logic' recognises judgments of relations
between phænomena as well as between ideas, from
which the founder of the modern distinction of impressions and ideas could hardly have escaped. Not
that even Mill's analysis is adequate. In the first place,
Mill's list of judgments is incomplete ; there are judgments of relations between sensible objects, between
ideas, between insensible, and between imperceptible
objects, judgments of sense, of conception, of inferential
perception, and of transcendental inference ; secondly,
even if, so far as judgments are premises, conceptions
may be their conditions, so far as they are conclusions,
the judgment is often the condition of the conception,
as when we infer a corpuscle, and then conceive it.
But for our present purpose it is sufficient that, as Mill
says, there are judgments of relations between phæno-

[1] Mill, *Logic*, i. 5, 1; cf. also *Exam. of Hamilton's Phil.* chap. xviii.

T

mena, sensible objects, the objects of simple impressions. Such a judgment is not an apprehension of a relation of ideas, much less an idea of a relation.

It would not be difficult to distinguish judgments from ideas by Hume's admissions. In the first place, he recognises relations, reducing them in the 'Treatise'[1] to seven general heads: resemblance, identity, those of space and time, quantity or number, degrees of quality, contrariety, and cause or effect; and, in both 'Treatise' and 'Inquiry,' admitting the relations of resemblance, contiguity, and sequence of impressions, on which association is founded. There are, then, relations to be judged. Secondly, he held that mathematics are concerned with relations of ideas, and unwarily admits Locke's doctrine that a mathematical proposition expresses a relation.[2] Thirdly, and most curiously, in the very chapter in which he had defined belief as an idea made vivid by association, he goes on to allow that, when a picture introduces the idea of a friend, the association presupposes a belief in the friend's existence. ' We may observe,' says he, ' that in these phænomena the belief of the correlative object is always presupposed; without which the relation would have no effect. The influence of the picture supposes that we *believe* our friend to have once existed.' What can this belief in a friend's existence be, according to Hume, except Mill's apprehension of a relation of phænomena or impressions? And are not there such beliefs, not only of existence, but also of the other relations of phænomena, mentioned by Mill—coexistence, sequence, resemblance, even if not of causation?

Hume would, perhaps, reply that we have a vivid idea of the relation between our friend and his exist-

---

[1] *Treatise*, i. § 5.   [2] *Inquiry*, § 4.

ence, in which the belief consists. It is true that we
have such an idea. But, in truth and in Hume's philosophy, this idea must be copied from an impression;
there must, therefore, be a prior impression of the relation between our friend and his existence, in which
the belief consists. We first judge of a relation and
then conceive the idea of it, in consequence of the
judgment—an important source, by the way, of complex
ideas of relation.

If the judgment were merged in the mere idea of
the relation, it could not be distinguished from fictitious
ideas of relation. Hume, indeed, tries to distinguish
'ideas of the judgment' from fictions of the imagination
by his usual criterion of vivacity, contending, for instance, that 'these ideas take faster hold of my mind
than ideas of an enchanted castle.'[1] This may be true
of Walpole's 'Castle of Otranto.' But Hume wrote before
the appearance of Scott's historical romances, after
which he could not have failed to see that the mere
idea of a relation in belief is often very inferior in
vivacity to the idea of a relation in fiction. There are
few scenes in history so vividly painted in my imagination as my idea of Quentin Durward conducting the
Countess Isabelle out of France to Liège, and from
Liège into Burgundy. But, in spite of the force of the
idea, I do not believe in the relation, and why not?
Because I do not judge or apprehend that the relation
ever occurred, and only conceive the idea of it in
imagination, stimulated by the genius of Sir Walter
Scott.

Belief, then, is not conception: a judgment is not
an idea, but the apprehension of a relation. Now, what
is the relation of judgments to association? According

----

[1] *Inquiry*, § 5; cf. *Treatise*, iii. § 7.

to Hume, all of them are its results; only, however, if they are nothing but ideas, because the association of ideas terminates in ideas. Well, as no judgment is an idea, not one judgment, not even one which apprehends a relation of ideas, is a result of association, which never can give an apprehension of a relation. Secondly, a judgment which apprehends a relation of sensible objects, such as, I am hurt and feel pained, cannot be an effect of association, because the judgment signifies, in Hume's language, a relation of two impressions, while in association, even when that which suggests is an impression, that which is suggested is an idea, and because the judgment is prior to any association in which one of the two impressions suggests the idea of the other. Thirdly, those judgments which apprehend relations of objects not now in sense are not results of association, because they are not ideas, and are not concerned with ideas.

Hence association is not an adequate origin of memory and expectation, which are judgments of the past and of the future. Memory, according to Hume, is a more vivid idea. But ideas of fancy are often more vivid than those of memory. Memory contains an idea, but it is a judgment that the idea represents a previously apprehended object. Now association can reproduce the idea, but not produce the judgment of memory. Still less is expectation a result of association. It contains an idea, but is a judgment that the object will or may be apprehended. When the idea represents an object already apprehended, as in the case of memory, association reproduces the idea, but does not produce the judgment of the object expected. When, as in expectation, the idea represents an object similar to previously apprehended objects, but not itself

yet apprehended, association does not even produce the
idea of the expected object; for, as we found before,
association only reproduces ideas. History and prediction are not results of association, because they consist
of judgments, because their objects have never been in
sense, because their ideas are ideas of insensible objects.
A fortiori, science, an apprehension of laws, or similar
relations between an indefinite number of insensible
objects, cannot be a result of association. The association of ideas could not make us conceive the idea,
much less judge that the cities of the plain once existed,
which we never saw; nor that the earth will one day
be too cold for habitation, when we shall not be alive
to see that day; nor that all fluids propagate their
motions equally in all directions, which we judge to
be universal, but cannot perceive, nor conceive universally. The association of ideas does not produce the
judgments of history, prediction, and science. In short,
judgments are apprehensions of present relations in
objects of sense, of past relations in memory and history, of future relations in expectation and prediction,
of universal relations in science, which, not being ideas,
are not results of association, but of sense and reasoning.

Association of ideas reproduces an idea : it does not
produce an idea : it neither produces nor reproduces a
belief. How, then, do we get these beliefs or judgments? That is the whole question. How does judgment apprehend present relations of objects in sense?
That is the first and fundamental question, never faced
by Hume. I have admitted that, when his abstractions
have been interpreted, he was right in saying that we
have simple impressions in the sense of simply feeling
pleased and pained, simply perceiving sensible objects,
the white, the hot, &c., and simply being conscious of .

ourselves operating, feeling. seeing, touching, &c. These
are simple acts of knowledge. A simple sensation requires, indeed, a subject apprehending an object, and
must not be resolved into a mere abstraction. It does
not follow that it contains a conscious judgment of the
relation of subject and object, as some philosophers
suppose. It requires also to be different from other
sensations, in accordance with the principle of Hobbes—
' Idem sentire et non sentire ad idem recidunt.' It does
not follow that it contains a sense of discrimination.
When light is presented to my retina, by simple sensation, I see a visible object in my optic nerve, without
judging its relation to myself, or to other sensible objects,
and so far as I see it, know it. But though I have
simple sensations or, as Hume calls them, impressions,
without judgment, yet I also judge of the relations of
sensible objects. Hume rightly recognised simple sensation. wrongly ignored sensitive judgment.

The source of sensitive judgment is synthetic sense.
Unless I actually had a sense of the succession of being
hurt and being pained I could not judge that the
succession occurred. Moreover, there is a synthetic
sense of other relations, on which sensitive judgment
is founded, of the relations enumerated in Hume's
' Treatise,' of the relations regarded in his ' Inquiry ' as
necessary to association, of the relations truly regarded
by Mill in his ' Logic ' as part of the very import of a
judgment and a proposition. Hume should have distinguished two kinds of impressions, simple and synthetic ; impressions of sensible objects and impressions
of relations of objects. ' Like simple tastes and smells,
or feelings of pleasure and pain,' as Professor Huxley
says, ' they are ultimate irresolvable facts of conscious
experience ; and, if we follow the principle of Hume's

nomenclature, they must be called *impressions of relation.* But it must be remembered that they differ from
the other impressions, as requiring the pre-existence of
at least two of the latter.'[1] In this way, when two sensible objects are presented to us, we are sensible of their
succession, their coexistence, their similarity, and so
forth.

The first point to notice about this sense of a relation is, that as the sensible objects, so the sensible relations, are not external but internal, yet not psychical.
When I feel a tangible effect in my tactile nerves, produced by laying my arms on a table containing paper,
cloth, pens, &c., I feel several tangible objects coexisting
with one another within my tactile nerves. Secondly,
this sense of a relation is as presentative as any simple
sense, and does not construct relations but apprehends
them, when they are present, between the sensible objects. In a word, the immediate apprehension of a relation is not a psychological synthesis of abstract sensations, but a synthetic sense of sensible objects. In the
books of idealists, sensation is an abstraction from a
substantial subject perceiving a substantial object of
sense; and synthesis is a second abstraction, founded on
the first, from the receptivity of a sensible relation. But
in reality there are two apprehensions by a subject of
sensible objects, both equally sensitive; first, simple
sensations of particular objects, and secondly, synthetic
sensations of particular relations of particular objects.
There are also two kinds of experience: the first, a sum
of simple sensations, *e.g.* of being pained; the second,
a sum of synthetic sensations, *e.g.* of being pained at
repeated blows in a fight.

Curiously enough, Hume over and over again men-

---

[1] Professor Huxley, *Hume*, chap. ii.

tions instances of synthetic sense and synthetic experience intervening between impression and association, yet without formal acknowledgment. In the
'Treatise,' he says that 'when both the objects are
present to the senses along with the relation, we call
this perception rather than reasoning; nor is there in
this case any exercise of the thought, or any action,
properly speaking, but a mere passive admission of the
impressions through the organs of sensation.'[1]   Again,
in speaking of the data of the idea of causation, he
says: 'The nature of experience is this: We remember to have had frequent instances of the existence of
one species of objects; and also remember, that the
individuals of another species of objects have always
attended them, and have existed in a regular order of
contiguity and succession with regard to them.   Thus
we remember to have seen that species of object we call
flame, and to have felt that species of sensation we call
heat.   We likewise call to mind their constant conjunction in all instances.'[2]   In the 'Inquiry' we find passages close together, one implying synthetic sense
followed by another implying synthetic experience:—
'Suppose a person, though endowed with the strongest
faculties of reason and reflection, to be brought on a
sudden into this world; he would, indeed, immediately
observe a continual succession of objects and one event
following another. . . . Suppose again that he has
acquired more experience, and has lived so long in the
world as to have observed similar objects or events to be
constantly conjoined together; what is the consequence
of this experience?   He immediately infers the existence of one object from the appearance of the other.'[3]

---

[1] *Treatise*, iii. § 2.   [2] Ib, iii. § 6; cf. § 8.
[3] *Inquiry*, § 5, Part I.

Similarly, in a well-known passage, he says : 'All events seem entirely loose and separate. One event follows another, but we never can observe any tie between them. They seem *conjoined*, but never *connected.*' [1] Whatever Hume may say about impressions, he constantly admits an immediate observation and experience of any relations, short of connection; when he says that events seem loose and separate, he does not mean that they seem quite isolated; and he allows a power of apprehending constant conjunction, though without causation, prior to association. How then could he refuse to call this sensitive apprehension of a relation belief, or contend that such a sensitive belief is a result of association?

Thus we find that belief or judgment is not an idea, but an apprehension of a relation; and not a result of association, but originally derived from a synthetic sense of relations. What are the consequences? In the first place, synthetic sense and judgment are not associations, because the objects related are both sensible; neither is an idea; and one does not suggest the other, but their relation is presented. Secondly, synthetic sense, experience, and judgment having apprehended a relation in particular instances, cause a complex idea of the relation; thus forming a source of ideas unnoticed by Locke and his followers. Thirdly, although simple sensations and experiences sometimes, by the anatomical connection of their nervous centres, without any judgment of their relation, produce an association of ideas; nevertheless, in an animal capable of judgment, it more frequently happens that synthetic sense, experience, and judgment apprehend the relation of the sensible objects, and cause an association of the ideas of the objects and

[1] *Inquiry,* § 7, Part II.

of their relation, which I propose to call synthetic sensitive association. In these cases, so far from association producing belief, belief produces association. For example, I judge that one object follows another in my senses, and when one appears again, I consequently have not only the idea of the other, but also the idea of their sequence, which I could not get from simple sensitive association. Here, perhaps, is another stopping place in animal intelligence. Fourthly, synthetic sense and experience of relations, being the sources of sensitive and empirical judgments without association, supply the original evidences of reasoning without association. The want of a formal recognition of synthetic sense, at the very time he was accumulating instances of its action, concealed from Hume the true sources of reasoning, and its independence of association.

The problem of inference or reasoning hinges on two questions; the origin of new judgments, and the origin of new ideas. We have achieved some of the data for solving this problem; by showing that we have judgments of synthetic sense to start with, that no judgment is an idea, and that association, in reproducing ideas of objects already sensible, does not produce an idea of an object not yet sensible, and does not produce a judgment at all. These data of themselves indicate a difference between the association of ideas and the inference of judgments, and also point to an origin of ideas other than association. Reason starts directly from judgments of synthetic sense, and, without passing through association, infers judgments, issuing in rational ideas.

'Man,' says Hume, 'is a reasonable being; and, as such, receives from science his proper food and nourishment.' [1] Hume did not deny reasoning, nor resolve it

[1] *Inquiry,* § 1.

all into association. He had no general theory on the subject; and this is one of the weaknesses of his philosophy. But he admitted, in mathematics, a species of reasoning, not only distinct from association, but even consisting of demonstration from intuition. However, in spite of his distinction of impressions and ideas, in the spirit of Locke, he thought that this mathematical reasoning is limited to the relation of ideas. The point of his polemic against reason was that it never reaches matters of fact. He wanted to prove that judgments of fact, being mere ideas, are mere products of association. He failed, because judgments are not ideas, because association does not produce ideas much less judgments, and because reasoning from sensitive judgments produces rational judgments of fact, and rational ideas. In this part of his philosophy he shows a remarkable spirit of inquiry, and as remarkable a power of missing the point of difference between one operation and another.

All conclusions about facts, he thought, are about cause and effect, all conclusions about cause and effect are from experience. '*What*,' he asks, '*is the foundation of all conclusions from experience?*' 'I want,' he says, 'to learn the foundation of this inference.'[1] 'All inferences from experience, therefore, are effects of custom, not of reasoning:'[2] this is the starting-point of his answer. 'All our reasonings concerning matters of fact are founded on a species of *analogy*, which leads us to expect from any cause the same events which we have observed to result from similar causes:'[3] this is his interpretation of customary inference. This interpretation was required for his main point, that customary infer-

---

[1] *Inquiry*, § 4, Part II.   [2] Ib. § 5, Part I.
[3] Ib. § 9; cf. § 5, Part I.

ence is the same as the association of ideas; for analogy
supplies the inference most like the association of ideas.
'When a sword,' he says, 'is levelled at my breast, does
not the idea of wound and pain strike me more strongly
than when a glass of wine is presented to me, even
though by accident this idea should occur after the
appearance of the latter object? But what is there in
this whole matter to cause such a strong conception,
except only a present object and a customary transition
to the idea of another object, which we have been
accustomed to conjoin with the former? This is the
whole operation of the mind in all our conclusions
concerning matter of fact and existence.'[1]   That is,
judgments are strong conceptions, and inferences are
analogies, which are associations of ideas.

Analogous inference is like synthetic association in
data. Both start with the same synthetic experience,
which, in Hume's example, is—

Swords levelled at me have already pained me;
This sword is like previous swords.

This synthetic experience sets up three processes: (1)
this sword, being like previous swords, reproduces the
idea of having been already pained; (2) the combination of the two sensitive judgments produces the new
judgment that this sword may possibly pain me; and
(3) this new judgment produces the idea of being
possibly pained. Of these processes, the first is association of ideas, the second is analogous inference, the
third is analogous conception. Now, analogous inference is further like synthetic association in process.
Both are customary processes in obedience to certain
laws; the laws of association, and the law of analogy.

[1] *Inquiry,* § 4, Part II.

The law of analogy is expressed in logic as a general
axiom thus: what is related in experience to particulars in experience is possibly related to other particulars
like them in experience. This axiom, however, does not
appear in the premises of the inference, but as the laws
of association are laws we spontaneously obey in reproducing ideas, so the law of analogy is the spontaneous
law which, without knowing it, we obey in inferring
from particular to particular judgment. It is afterwards discovered by logicians, and then is expressed as
the law of the form of analogous inference; but it would
be a sad confusion to suppose that because logicians know
it everybody who uses analogy knows it. The axiom
of analogy is a mechanical law of analogous inference;
and the man who has not studied logic infers from the
above-stated premises that a sword may pain him, not
by reasoning from the axiom as a major premise, but
by the habit of using it as a mechanical law. The
nearest animals to man probably infer by the very same
habit of analogy, as Hume and Mill after him have remarked. We have already suggested that some animals,
after the lowest stage of mere feeling and the stage of
mere sense, may stop at simple sensitive association,
while others may rise to synthetic sensitive association.
Perhaps the analogous inference, which we are now
describing, is the highest limit of brute reasoning.
Finally, analogous inference is like synthetic association,
not only in data and process, but also in result. Both
end in particulars.

Where, then, is the difference? One ends in an
idea of the past, the other in a judgment of the
possible. The association of ideas terminates in an
idea of having been previously pained; the analogous
inference concludes with a judgment that this sword

may now possibly pain me. As a judgment is not an
idea, so there must be something different in the processes
which produce the one and the other. The difference
consists in the laws which the processes habitually
use: association, acting by the laws of the reproduction
of ideas from resemblance, contiguity and sequence,
&c., analogous inference by the law of the analogous
production of a particular judgment : what is related in
experience to particulars in experience is possibly related to other particulars like those in experience.
Finally, besides terminating in a judgment, analogous
inference produces another effect, to which association
is incompetent; the conception of an idea of being
possibly pained, which is not to be confused, as Associationists confuse it, with the idea of having been formerly
pained. This further operation I propose to call *analogous conception*. It is an important operation. Thus,
having by analogy inferred that Mars, being like the
earth, may be inhabited, my analogous conception
pictures an idea of Martial men. If I mistake not,
analogous conception comes much nearer than association to the productive imagination of art. Analogous
inference, then, is custom, but not association. Association is customary reproduction of ideas; analogous
inference is customary inference from particular to particular judgment; and analogous conception is the
conception in the productive imagination of an idea of
a new particular inferred by analogy.

Hume's reduction of inference from experience to
association breaks down at the very first touch of logic.
It would not be worth while to pursue the subject, had
he not made an audacious attack on induction, reducing
it to analogy, in order to identify it with association.
Moreover, a similar attempt appears in Mill's reduction

of induction to inference from particular to particular,[1]
though in a much more half-hearted fashion, partly because he does not in his 'Logic' further identify analogy
with association, and partly because, immediately and in
the sequel, he proceeds to treat induction in quite a different manner. We shall find that induction is not analogous inference, much less association of ideas. We must
retrace our steps from Mill, through Hume, to Bacon,
who says :—'Aut enim defertur judicium *ab experimentis
ad experimenta*; aut *ab experimentis ad axiomata*, quæ
et ipsa *nova experimenta* designent;'[2] and to Aristotle,
who, as if foreseeing logical scepticism, warns us that
'inference by example is neither as particular to general,
nor as general to particular, but as particular to
particular.'[3]

Induction is not analogy, because the aim of induction is to arrive at a general judgment. By analogy
we infer, not a general but a particular conclusion : by
induction we infer not a particular but a general conclusion. Hence induction does not contain the very
point of analogical inference, the analogy itself. To
judge that a particular sword is like previous swords is
necessary, if we want to reason about that one in particular, but not if we want to conclude generally that
all swords whatever are painful, when levelled at one's
breast. It is true that there is a point in common between the two processes the judgment that swords
levelled at me have already pained me, which is also
present in synthetic association. But the difference is
that, when a similar sword is levelled at me, by association I reproduce the idea of having been formerly

---

[1] Mill, *Logic*. ii. 3, 7.

[2] Bacon, *De Aug. Scient*. v. 2 (p. 622; ed. Ellis & Spedding); cf. *Nov.
Org*. i. 103.

[3] Ar. *Prior. An*. ii. 24 = 69, A 13 15.

pained, and by analogical inference I infer that this sword may pain me again ; while, without a similar sword being present, by induction I conclude generally that all swords, levelled at me, would be painful. Association ends in a particular idea, and analogy in a particular judgment. Induction ends, not in particulars, but in a general judgment, beyond the reach both of association and of analogy.

There is, however, a difficulty in the superior claims of induction, which did not escape Hume's inquiring mind. How do we go from the particulars of experience to the general conclusion of inference, from many to all; for in the vast majority of cases we cannot experience all? In the first place, particulars, which at once prompt us to association and analogy, do not justify logical induction. In order to draw a general conclusion, we must not rest content with this or that particular, but accumulate instances of three kinds, as Bacon showed : instances of presence or agreement, of absence or difference in similar circumstances, of comparative degrees or concomitant variations.[1] Secondly, even then, we have only experience, albeit scientific, of many, not of all. There may, in the remaining instances not experienced, be an exception. 'Mox enim prodibit,' says Leibnitz, 'qui negabit ob peculiarem quandam rationem in aliis nondum tentatis veram esse.'[2] There is a leap in induction from various members to the whole class, from the particulars to the general, from many swords to all. How do we effect this leap? By the axiom of generality : things so related as to be always present, absent, and varying together in experience are, with a probability proportionate to the extent of the experience in time, place, and circumstance, so

[1] Nov. Org. ii. 11 seq.   [2] Leibnitz, De Stilo Philosophico Nizolii, xxxii.

related in all similar cases. This is the law of the form of induction, distinguishing it from association and analogy by the power of inferring a general judgment, leaving it indeed a probable inference, yet with an approximate certainty continually tending to absolute certainty.

Three mistakes are often made about this axiom of generality: first, it is stated most carelessly, as if it were simply that what is true of many things of a class belongs to the rest, omitting both the scientific character of the experience and the problematic character of the conclusion; secondly, it is frequently confined to laws of causation, omitting inductions of coexistence, &c.; thirdly, it is often regarded as if it were known to all men who induce, as an assumption involved in every case of induction, and even as a major premise converting induction into deduction. The first and second mistakes I have just corrected by attempting a more precise and general statement of the axiom. The third mistake is really too absurd; overlooking, as it does, that men, from time immemorial, however primitive, have made, and at the present day, however savage, do make inductions without dreaming of the axiom; while Aristotle, the founder himself of the logic of induction, even contradicted the law of uniformity by holding that nature has only a uniform tendency, and that there are exceptions to universality caused by accident inherent in matter.[1]

This false view of the axiom of generality, by which it is made a supposition involved in induction, gave Hume his opportunity: he saw that it would involve us in a circle. 'To endeavour, therefore,' says he, 'the proof of this last supposition by pro-

[1] Cf. Ar. *Met.* E. 2 1027 A, 5–15.

U

bable arguments, or arguments regarding existence, must be evidently going in a circle, and taking that for granted which is the very point in question.'[1] This difficulty has been often felt : we require an induction to found the axiom, which is nevertheless supposed to be the assumption involved in all induction. To surmount it, some resort to the theory that the axiom is *a priori*, though many, including Aristotle, have not even believed it. This was not the alternative of Hume, whose plan was to surrender universality, and renounce the inductive inference from particular to general judgments, in favour of the analogical inference from particular to particular judgment, which he falsely, as we have seen, reduced to association from particular impressions to particular ideas :—

'What, then, is the conclusion of the whole matter ? A simple one ; though, it must be confessed, pretty remote from the common theories of philosophy. All belief of matter of fact or real existence is derived merely from some present object to the memory or senses, and a customary conjunction between that and some other object ; or, in other words, having found, in many instances, that any two kinds of objects, flame and heat, snow and cold, have always been conjoined together : if flame or snow be presented anew to the senses, the mind is carried by custom to expect heat or cold, and to *believe* that such a quality does exist, and will discover itself upon a nearer approach.'[2]

Hume was right in rejecting a quasi-inductive deduction from the supposition of generality. It does not follow that induction becomes mere analogy, still less association. Such an alternative is inadequate to the extent of general reasoning. Moreover, if induction

---

[1] *Inquiry*, § 4.   [2] Ib. § 5, Part I.

were analogous inference and association, the analogy must always be present, as Hume was well aware. Wherever he mentions his analysis, he admits that the analogous object is present, about which the inference is made. In the instance above, flame analogous to previous flames has to be ' presented anew to the senses,' in order that we may expect its heat, and snow, analogous to previous snows, in order that we may expect its cold. In the instance of the sword, having experienced that swords levelled at us have been painful, I again experience that another sword is present, in order to infer that this particular sword is painful. If a new particular, similar to previous particulars, were not present in the premises, how could analogy infer an attribute of that particular in the conclusion, or association use it to introduce an idea? Now, this condition, though essential to association and analogy, is unnecessary, or rather completely extraneous, to induction. Having experienced the relations of former particulars, without any new particular being present, it infers that all flame is hot, all snow is cold, all swords levelled at one's breast are painful.

We must find some other alternative, then, which neither surrenders the inference of generality nor makes the axiom of generality a supposition antecedent to induction, whether by an inductive circle or by *a priori* mysticism. We have already chosen such an alternative in explaining analogous inference: it is also applicable to induction. As the axiom of analogy is the law of the form, without being a premise, of analogical inference, so the axiom of generality is the law of the form, without being a premise, of induction; a law not known, but mechanically and spontaneously obeyed by the ordinary man, and only afterwards discovered by logicians. The

reason why we induce from some flame is hot, some
snow is cold, some sword-thrusts are painful, is because
we have accumulated so many instances, in which the
related objects have been present, absent and varying
together in our synthetic experience, that, by the law of
generality acting on us without our knowing it, we
cannot but infer general judgments that all flame is hot,
all snow is cold, all sword-thrusts are painful.

Induction, then, like analogy, is the inference of a
judgment; but is distinguished from analogy, because
it proceeds from such an experience as will enable it
by the law of generality to infer a general judgment.
Induction, like association, is not a deduction from the
law of its form, but a customary process by that law.
But its custom is not association. First, association is
a reproduction of past ideas, induction an inference of
general judgments; secondly, in order to suggest an
idea, synthetic association contents itself with experience
of any relation of objects; but in order to produce a
general judgment, induction logically requires experience of a relation of objects, present, absent and varying together; thirdly, the form of association is governed
by the spontaneous laws of the reproduction of ideas,
the form of induction by the equally spontaneous but
different law of generality. Finally, association and induction differ not only in themselves, their experience,
and their laws, but also in their result on conception:
association produces no new idea of a particular, much
less a general idea; induction, having inferred a uniformity, produces what we may call an inductive idea
of the uniformity, e.g. of the heat of flame in general,
of the cold of snow in general, of the painfulness of
sword-thrusts in general.

Deduction from induction must be discarded by

every philosopher such as Hume, who resolves induction into analogy, because, in that case, the inference from particular to particular usurps the double function at once of the inference from particular to general, and of the inference from general to particular. Suppose, as Mill would say in imitation of Hume, this universal type of all inference : swords have been painful ; this sword is like previous swords ; therefore it is or may be painful. Then there is nothing left for the double process up to the general judgment about swords as a whole class, and down to a particular judgment about a sword not previously known. Accordingly, Hume banished reasoning, by which he meant deduction, entirely from empirical conclusions ; and Mill declared syllogism to be no inference, regarding the double inference from particulars through a generality to a new particular as an unnecessary circuit.[1]

But induction and deduction are integral and complementary parts of a double process of inference, from particular to general, from general to particular. As we have seen, induction is not analogy ; it begins with particulars, but ends, not with a new particular, but with a general judgment about a class. Deduction from induction, or empirical deduction, as we may call it, completes the double process : it combines the general judgment with a particular judgment, that a new particular belongs to this class, and infers that what belongs to the class belongs to the new particular. Empirical deduction differs from analogy in starting, not directly from particulars, but from a general judgment, given by induction ; it differs from induction, not only in using this general judgment as major premise, but in adding a minor, and drawing a particular or less general con-

[1] Mill. Logic, ii. 3.

clusion. It may be called the complement of induction, needed to convert generalities into particulars, and bring the double process of general reasoning to a particular conclusion, like that of analogy, but reached through a generality.

Deduction, as discovered by Aristotle, and disengaged from the mere schematism of Galen and later logicians, consists of three orders or figures. They are three different ways of thinking. Sometimes I want to prove or disprove by means of a class; for example, belonging to the class of magnitudes whose angles are equal to those of a perpendicular falling on a straight line, proves that a triangle has its angles equal to two right angles : this is the first figure or order of deductive thinking. Sometimes I want to disprove by means of a difference ; for example, as a demagogue differs from a statesman in being a truckler, he is not a statesman : this is the second order of deductive thinking, the figure of difference. Sometimes I want to prove by an instance or disprove by an exception ; for example, the genius of Nelson is sufficient to prove what Englishmen were capable of at the beginning of this century : this is the third order of deductive thinking, the figure of instance. Each of these figures has its own axiom ; that of the first being the *dictum de omni et nullo*, discovered by Aristotle ; those of the second and third being respectively the *dictum de diverso*, and the *dictum de exemplo et excepto*, discovered by Lambert.[1]

I have a purpose in calling attention to these three axioms of the three orders of deductive reasoning. They are necessary laws of deduction ; yet they are not in the premises. Moreover, as men, in deducing conclusions, know nothing about them, they have not already been

[1] Lambert, *Neues Organon*, i. 4, § 232.

acquired by a previous induction, still less are apprehended *a priori*. They are not presupposed, but used.
What is the explanation? Precisely the explanation
already given for the law of analogy and the law of
generality. They are spontaneous laws used by every
deducer, but discovered afterwards by the logician.
Hence they never appear in a syllogism, being not its
premises, but the laws of its form, each of the three
dicta being the law of its own order of deductive thinking. As Aristotle said, 'the nature of a syllogism is
not premised in a syllogism.'[1]

Deduction would not be an inference, if it were not
an advance in knowledge; but it is an advance in
knowledge. If induction were founded on a complete
examination of all members of the class, there would be
no occasion for deduction. But usually we only examine
some members, from which induction leaps, by the
axiom of generality, to the class; and this very fact is
what, according to Mill, makes induction an inference:
we need only know some, not all particular men, to say
that all men are mortal. Hence there is, so to speak, a
generality about induction which only says that everybody who may be a man is mortal: it does not, and
cannot, enumerate every particular man. The consequence is that the subsequent process of deduction,
which, by combining the generality in the major premise
with a new particular in the minor, enables us to discover that a particular object, which we never apprehended before to be a man, is mortal, must be an
advance in knowledge, and therefore a process of
inference.

Mill would reply that, in this case, we are committing
a *petitio principii* by adducing in proof of a particular

[1] Ar. *Post. An.* ii. 6 = 92 A, 11.

a general judgment which presupposes it. This objection can only mean that the general judgment, all men are mortal, ought to have been inductively proved by examining all men: otherwise it does not presuppose every particular man. But, according to his own showing, the general judgment is not to be proved by every particular: therefore it does not presuppose every particular, but only the original particulars of induction; and therefore the process, which adds to the general judgment a new particular, is not using a general judgment which presupposes that new particular, and is not a *petitio principii*. Mill made the beauty of induction the vice of syllogism: he first says that only some particulars are presupposed to induce a universal, and then that the universal presupposes every particular to deduce a particular. Really, the justification of induction is the justification of deduction from induction. Induction from many of the particulars concludes all in general: deduction adds the rest of the particulars.

Mill was deceived by another mistake: he thought the inference was over when we get to the general judgment, and the remainder is deciphering our notes. But the major premise is as powerless without the minor premise as the minor without the major. 'It is evident,' as Aristotle says, 'that a syllogism consists of two premises, and no more; for three terms make two premises.' [1] We therefore require two sets of notes in order to decipher a conclusion, and their combination in the two premises is the essence of syllogism. Mill was further deceived by writing down two simple premises, and thinking that, as the syllogism consists in drawing the conclusion, which is contained in the premises, it does not advance our knowledge. But a

[1] Ar. *Pr. An.* i. 25 = 42 A, 32 3.

syllogism does not consist in merely drawing a conclusion; and, when you have written down the two
premises, the essence of syllogism is over : the difficulty
is in combining the premises, and although the syllogism
does not discover each premise, it does combine the
two.   So important an act is this, that, as Aristotle
says, 'a man may know that all B is A and all C is B,
and yet think that C is not A ; e.g. that every mule is
barren, and this is a mule, and yet think it is going
to foal, through not considering each of the two premises
in combination.' [1]

Syllogism, then, from induction is an inference,
because it is an advance in knowledge by adding particulars not contemplated in induction ; a legitimate
inference, because it presupposes only the particulars
contemplated in experience, and the indefinite generality
inferred by induction, but not the new particular it is
about to prove ; a complex inference, which consists
neither in merely interpreting a major premise, nor in
merely drawing a conclusion, but in a new combination
of premises, or a direct comparison of two things with a
third thing, so as to draw an indirect conclusion about
their relation.   In order to express the essence of syllogism as a process of inference, I propose to define it : a
combination of two premises so as to produce a conclusion, not presupposed in either separately, though contained in their combination.   Hume's theory of inference
is inadequate, because it ignores this process of reasoning from experience and induction ; and Mill's is false,
because it ignores the combination of premises, which
produces a new conclusion, advancing our knowledge.

There are two ways of inferring from particular to
particular ; directly by analogy, and indirectly through

----

[1] μὴ συνθεωρῶν τὸ καθ' ἑκάτερον. Ar. Pr. ii. 21   67 A, 33 7.

a generality by induction and deduction.   Mill, following Hume, confuses them.   'The mortality of John,
Thomas, and others,' he says, ' is, after all, the whole
evidence we have for the mortality of the Duke of Wellington.   Not one iota is added to the proof by inter-
polating a general proposition.' [1]   Why, he asks, should
we not take the shortest cut?   We often do: we go,
like brutes, from particular to particular.   But Mill
himself gives a very good reason why we should not ;
that to pass through a general proposition is ' a security
for good reasoning.' [2]   Now, surely the aim of every
honest man is, not reasoning, but good reasoning ; and
logic is the art of reasoning well.   We must avoid the
shortest cut and go round the circuit of induction and
deduction to rational truth, as we must avoid the broad
and choose the narrow path to eternal life.   We may be
sure also that there is something more than usual in
a security for good reasoning.   That something more is
the evidence of induction.   We saw that we want less
evidence for association and for analogy, which begin
directly after experience, than for induction, which
requires experience to be accumulated and sifted, by
finding things present, absent, and varying together, so as
to bring into operation the law of generality, by which
we spontaneously induce a general judgment.   In order
to deduce a new particular we must have apprehended
not only the original particulars, but also that they are
sufficient to authorise a general judgment, which is the
same thing as inferring it.   The beauty of induction is
the virtue of the syllogism.   It is because analogy has
not, induction has, sufficient evidence to infer a general
judgment, that syllogism from induction is a security
for good reasoning.   I do not say that this security is

---

[1] Mill, *Logic*, ii. 3, 3.   [2] Ib. ii. 3, 8.

more than general probability. But analogy has not this general probability: it varies, indeed, in probability, but directly its evidence guarantees general probability, analogy becomes induction followed by deduction. Induction is the inference of general probability and empirical deduction the inference from general probability; and the probability of the double process, induction and deduction, varies, according to the original synthetic experience, from uncertainty to approximate certainty.

Few modern logicians seem to have a sense of the enormous importance of syllogism or deduction. They do not feel the indefiniteness of the subject of a general judgment, which signifies all whatever they may be I do not know, the consequent imperfection of induction without deduction, and the necessity of syllogism to give definiteness to our inferences from experience beyond experience. It is but little use knowing that when the earth intervenes between the sun and the moon there will be an eclipse, unless we are prepared to combine this mere generality with minor premises stating when the earth will be in this position. It is by deduction that we go back to the distant past: for example, nations which have words in common, expressing a degree of civilisation, too many to be explained by nature, chance, or communication, lived together up to that degree of civilisation; the Greeks and Romans had a multitude of words in common up to the stage of settled agriculture; therefore they lived together to that point. It is by deduction we dive into the imperceptible present: for example, perceptible bodies elastic and compressible have parts and pores; solid bodies are elastic and compressible; therefore they consist of parts and pores, though imperceptible. It is by deduction that .

we predict the future : for example, a planet deflected
from the path prescribed by its gravitation to the sun
gravitates to another planet in the direction of deflection ; Uranus was found so to deflect ; therefore, a new
planet was predicted in the direction of deflection, and
the new planet, Neptune, was afterwards discovered in
that direction.　Inferences of this kind are sometimes
analogical, but they are often deductive, and they are
so whenever induction has established a general judgment.　They are sometimes confused with induction,
as when Mill calls the discoverer of a murderer by
circumstantial evidence induction.[1]　But when such an
inference is not analogy it is deductive, because it contains, besides the circumstances in the minor premises,
a number of major premises judging such circumstances
to be signs of murder, and a particular conclusion inferring a murderer.

Empirical deduction, like analogical and inductive
inferences, is not association, and for the same reason ;
it ends, not in conception, but in judgment.　Even
syllogism is a customary inference ; but its custom is
not an association of ideas, but a habit of inferring
judgments by the three laws of the three figures.　Association, even of the more developed kind which starts
from synthetic experience, gets as far as reproducing
the ideas of the objects in that synthetic experience,
and there stops.　At that point we have not even got at
the beginning of deduction : induction intervenes to
infer the general judgment, which, as we have seen, is
no result of association.　Empirical deduction, then,
begins with this general judgment, which at once distinguishes it from all sensitive synthetic association.
It proceeds frequently to ask synthetic experience for a

[1] Mill, *Logic*, iii. 14, 7.

minor premise, *e.g.* this is a sword; and thus returns to the arena of association. But association deals with this new particular merely to reproduce ideas of former pains already apprehended by experience, analogy, and induction. Syllogism goes on to infer a new particular judgment that this sword will also prove painful.

Nor is this all the difference: we must not deceive ourselves by taking too simple an instance. Through the power of general judgments we at last deduce particulars not only beyond sense, but insensible and imperceptible to us, *e.g.* the existence of insensible particles or corpuscles of solid bodies. Association, from the premises of this deduction and before deduction has drawn the conclusion, will reproduce only the ideas of the parts of bodies previously known : without deduction it will not enable me either to judge that the particular bodies in the minor premise consist of parts, or to conceive ideas of their particular parts. Deduction, on the other hand, proceeds to draw the conclusion and then conceive the idea. Not association of ideas, but deduction, produces the judgment of the existence, and through this judgment the deductive conception of the idea, of a corpuscle.

Hume, in the 'Treatise,' said : 'I form an idea of Rome, which I neither see nor remember, but which is connected with such impressions as I remember to have received from the conversation and books of travellers and historians. . . . All this, and everything else which I believe, are nothing but ideas.'[1] This inadequate account of my knowledge of Rome goes further than could be justified by Hume, but not so far as is justified by history. Association of itself would not even give me an idea of Rome, which I have never seen ; history

---

[1] Hume, *Treatise,* iii. § 9.

infers the judgment that Rome has existed, perhaps from the time of Romulus, certainly since the transition from the monarchy to the republic. If association of ideas were substituted for deduction, on being told that there is a city like London and other cities I have experienced, I could only reproduce my particular idea of London, my particular ideas of other cities in my experience, and, with induction, my general idea of cities : I could not produce a new particular idea of Rome beyond my experience. But deduction from the conversation and books of travellers and historians enables me to produce a belief that Rome exists, and has existed for centuries, which is not an idea, and, moreover, besides the belief, an inferential idea of the eternal city in my productive imagination. Deduction is not association of ideas, because it directly produces deductive judgments about the existence, and indirectly deductive ideas ; of objects beyond sense, such as the danger of a sword which has not yet hurt me ; of insensible objects, such as historic Rome ; of imperceptible objects, such as a physical corpuscle.

Hume, having falsely identified ideas with thoughts, and resolved beliefs into ideas, could allow only one succession of thoughts, the succession of ideas. But judgments are not ideas but apprehensions of relations, inferences are not successions of ideas, but successions of judgments, and rational judgments are thoughts which are not ideas. From synthetic sense, which produces our first judgments of relations, there arise two streams of thought, synthetic association, which is a succession of ideas, and reasoning or a succession of judgments. These two streams flow together, yet distinctly ; but the stream of reasoning is the main river of human thinking, compared with which the stream of

association is a mere rivulet. Hume and his followers
are like those explorers of the sources of the Nile who
have taken a mere tributary for the main river.

Inference and association are alike, not only so far
as both start from synthetic sense and experience, but
also in both being involuntary, spontaneous, customary. Impressions involuntarily suggest ideas, though
we also recall them by voluntary reminiscence; nor can
we help inferring judgments, though we also reason
voluntarily. Association and inference both spontaneously use laws, neither inductively nor *a priori*, but
mechanically and without knowing it: as the laws of
association, by resemblance, contiguity, succession, &c.,
are spontaneously used to introduce ideas, so is the
law of analogy spontaneously used to infer from particular to particular judgment, the law of generality to
infer a general judgment, the laws of the three figures
to infer from general to particular judgments. The explanation is probably the same in all cases, namely, the
evolution of an habitual tendency by the action of nature
on our organs without our knowing it. Again, analogy
and induction are not deductions from the laws of their
forms, but independent inferences from experience; nay,
deduction itself is not a deduction from the laws of its
forms or figures, but from major and minor premises:
all three processes of inference use their laws to produce judgments as habitually as association uses its
laws to reproduce ideas. But because inference is an
inevitable, spontaneous, customary use of laws, it is not
on that account to be confused with association.

Hume made two very great blunders about inference:
he confused custom with association, and limited reasoning to deduction, or rather demonstration. But not all
custom is association: there are habits of conceiving,

of judging, of acting ; and analogy, induction, and deduction are habits of judging by inference, not habits
of conceiving by association. Again, all inference is
reasoning, because it advances from judgment to judgment ; reasoning does not begin with demonstration
from axioms; and there are three kinds of reasoning, all
ultimately founded on judgments of synthetic sense, all
inevitable, spontaneous and customary inferences by laws
of their forms, used without being known, except to the
science of logic :—these three types of inference are
analogical, inductive and deductive reasoning.

Reasoning is an instinct. The premises are acquired
from experience, and the conclusion is inferred ; but the
process of inferring is instinctive. It was probably
gradually acquired by the action of natural uniformity
on our organs : but it is used without presupposing any
axiom of natural uniformity as a major premise. This
instinctiveness of reason escapes the notice of philosophers and even of logicians. Hume, for example, postponed reasoning to association, because it is slow, because it does not appear during the first years of infancy,
because it is liable to error, and because nature has implanted in us the instinct of association.[1] But, in the
first place, nothing is more rapid than reasoning, which
goes through its trains of judgment as quickly as association through its trains of ideas ; secondly, it is an
adult prejudice to suppose that young infants are not
reasoning, because they are not talking, when they are
far better occupied in the sensible and rational discovery
of an internal and external world ; thirdly, reasoning is
liable to error, but association has no perception of truth;
fourthly, if association is an instinct, so is reasoning,
each spontaneously using its laws to proceed from expe-

[1] *Inquiry*, § 5.

rience, but the former to ideas. the latter to judgments.
So closely related are the instincts of association and
reasoning, yet so different, that, if association were not
the vaguest term in the vague vocabulary of mental
philosophy, I should have proposed to distinguish the
two successions of thought as the association of ideas
and the association of judgments.

Hume allowed the psychology of association to
blind him to the logic of reasoning. The consequence
was that he missed the whole origin of rational judgments and of rational ideas; thus defeating his own
object, which was to find the causes of ideas. The
origin of ideas is in reality a very complicated problem,
inseparable from that of judgments. We must distinguish productive and reproductive conception. The
sources of productive conception, which we have
reached so far, are simple sensations of sensible objects
producing sensible ideas, synthetic sense and judgment
of sensible relations producing ideas of relations, and
reasoning to rational judgments producing rational
conceptions; moreover, we have distinguished three
kinds of rational conception, answering to three kinds
of inference—analogous, inductive and deductive; and,
finally, deductive conception produces ideas not only of
the relation in the conclusion but of the insensible objects of that relation, e.g. the idea of corpuscles as well
as of their cohesion. Reproductive conception has two
main sources, both obeying the same laws—voluntary
recollection (ἀνάμνησις), analysed by Aristotle,[1] and
involuntary association, analysed by Hume; who proceeded to elevate a mere reproduction of ideas into a
substitute for the inference of judgments, and, when it
does not produce ideas at all, and is only one way of

[1] Ar. De Mem. ii.

X

reproducing them, positively made it the sole source of all belief in matters of fact. What a contrast there is between the analytic genius of Aristotle, giving each operation its due place, and the exaggerated scepticism of Hume, exalting the weakest over the strongest force in man's composition!

Hume invariably speaks as if all association of ideas were of one kind; so usually do his followers. It is because they have become enamoured of one power to the neglect of the rest. This kind I have ventured to call 'simple sensitive association,' because it starts with simple sensation and experience. But I have shown that Hume covertly introduces another kind, which I have called 'synthetic sensitive association,' because it starts with synthetic sense and experience. To this sort belongs the association used by him to explain the apprehension of causation; a process which, starting from the sense of sequence, and passing through the experience of constant conjunction, ends by the antecedent introducing the idea of the consequent, which he falsely supposed to be our judgment of a cause producing an effect. But, now that I have analysed reasoning, I am prepared to take a further step and say that reasoning, though never association, is the foundation of a third kind of association, which I shall call 'rational association.' When we have by any kind of inference inferred a relation, and by any kind of rational conception produced the ideas representing the relation and its objects, then, and not till then, rational association will enable us to reproduce the ideas by its own laws. Thus the contemplation of eye, which suggests to the ordinary man the idea of love or war, will to the optician reproduce the rational ideas of æther, of undulation, of

reflection and refraction. But it would be mere confusion to merge the reasoning by which he discovered these facts in the association of the ideas,
when the rational conception of the ideas intervenes
between the rational inference and the rational association. The optician first by reasoning judges the
existence of æther and its motions, then rationally
conceives what ideas of them he can, and finally is
reminded of them by association. Most associations
are post-rational.

The inference at the bottom of rational association
will be found to solve many unsolved problems. One
is the solubility of association. If we depended on association alone, an association acquired by a constant
experience could only be dissolved by one acquired by
a still more constant experience. But, as a fact, a
single instance will destroy the strongest association :
when the idea of the proverbial whiteness of swans was
dispelled by the discovery of a black swan, it was
reason which dissolved the association. Another problem is the origin of complex ideas of substance. The
theory of Associationists is that, having by sensation
acquired together the ideas of yellowness from sight,
smoothness from touch, sweetness from taste, association
recalls these ideas so constantly as to form one complex
idea of an orange. In this analysis the main elements
of the simple ideas, and the process between them and
the complex idea, are omitted. By sight we already see
a yellow, by touch a smooth, by taste a sweet substance ;
hence the simple ideas of substances ; by reasoning, we
infer that all these correspond in our senses to one
complex substance outside, represented by the yellow
in sight, the smooth in touch, the sweet in taste : and,
having thus inferred an external orange, we form a

rational complex idea of it, which we then reproduce, not produce, by rational association.

Another and somewhat different kind of problem is the origin of fictitious ideas, of the ideas of art, and of ideals. Hume truly said that an idea, such as that of a golden mountain, is ultimately made out of impressions, but falsely thought that it is produced by sensitive association, which by itself could only reproduce the sensible ideas of gold and of mountain. The reasoning of the possible intervenes. We infer that as a mountain is made of one material it might be made of another, and having judged the possibility, analogically conceive the idea of a golden mountain, which is only reproduced by association. Sometimes we infer the possibility of more, sometimes of less, than sense perceives; hence we multiply man and horse into centaur, or diminish man into ghost. Sometimes we infer the possibility of something better than ordinary, as Homer did Achilles; sometimes worse, as Shakespeare did Caliban. But in artistic idealisation there is always an inference of possibility, which is the foundation of all ideal conception. It is quite the same in philosophical ideals. Plato thought of the possibility of men becoming angels before he conceived his ideal state.

The final and most difficult problem is the influence of the association of ideas beyond ideas. Locke started this general problem in the 'Essay.' The following is an often quoted instance from his chapter on Association:—

'The *ideas* of *goblins* and *sprights* have really no more to do with darkness than light; yet let but a foolish maid inculcate these often on the mind of a child, and raise them there together, possibly he shall never be able to separate them again so long as he lives; but darkness shall ever afterwards bring with it these frightful *ideas*, and they shall be so joined that he can no more bear the one than the other.' [1]

Locke did not make so much of this effect of association as the followers of Hume, who often suppose that the association of the ideas of ghosts and the dark produces a belief which produces a fear. But the fear often follows the idea, without the belief. There are in reality two different cases, in one of which there is no belief, in the other a belief, but not caused by the association of ideas. In simple sensitive association, where there has been no judgment of the relation of a ghost with the dark, the idea of the dark mechanically recalls the idea of the ghost, and this the idea of pain which is sufficient to generate fear. In synthetic sensitive association, where there has been a judgment that a ghost appears in the dark arising from a child's belief in the narratives of its nurse, the association of ideas is accompanied by a belief that a ghost may possibly appear, which, however, does not arise from the association of ideas, but by parallel inference from the same judgment as that which produces the association. Sometimes this judgment of possibility may arise, even when the person is sceptical about the actuality of ghosts. Still more often it is a vague inference of some dreadful possibility, because the dark is mysterious to man.

Whenever, then, the association of ideas is of a simple kind, which has not arisen from a judgment, it is powerless to produce one ; and whenever it is accompanied by a judgment, they are joint effects of an original judgment, which produces on the one hand an inference at least of possibility, and on the other hand an association of ideas. At the same time there is an effect of association on belief, like the effect of volition.

[1] *Essay*, ii. 33, 10.

These two reproductive causes of ideas, by constantly promoting the same idea, challenge our attention not only to the idea but also to the parallel judgments. Thus a person, who constantly cherishes the idea of being wiser than others, will at last come to think he is so, not however from the association itself, but because his attention is thereby called towards the evidences which infer his superiority, and away from those which disprove it.

Hume's empirical theory consists in three propositions: (1) All perceptions are impressions and ideas or thoughts; (2) All ideas or thoughts are copies of impressions; (3) Association of ideas is the origin of all beliefs of facts, that is, ideas or thoughts. But it is one thing to assert an empirical theory in general, and another to fill in its details. Impressions, as Hume described them, are not by the process of association, as Hume described it, the origin of ideas, which are not, as Hume described them, all our thoughts. In the first place, the simplest sensation is merely an abstract attribute of a substantial subject apprehending a substantial object, and the simplest reflection an abstract attribute of that substantial subject apprehending himself. Secondly, sense is not only simple but synthetic; and synthetic sense is the immediate origin of sensitive judgment, which is not an idea, but the immediate apprehension of a relation of sensible objects. Thirdly, association is a reproduction, but it is not a production, of ideas, still less of beliefs, which are not ideas but judgments ultimately based on synthetic sense. Fourthly, reasoning is not an association of ideas, but of judgments; and there are three types of inference—analogical, inductive, and deductive—all starting from synthetic sense, and by their own laws instinctively inferring rational judgments

which are not impressions nor ideas, yet are thoughts.
Fifthly, the productive origin of ideas is simple sense
forming the first ideas of qualified substances, synthetic
sense forming the first ideas of relation, and reasoning
analogical, inductive and deductive, which forms ideas
not only of what is inferred to be actual, but also of
what is inferred to be possible, fictitious, ideal: the reproductive origin of ideas is passive association and
active volition. Sixthly, there are three species of association, simple and synthetic sensitive association, and
rational association. A philosopher who, like Hume,
does not understand reasoning, cannot understand ideas
and their association. Logic is necessary to psychology.
Empirical philosophy must comprise reason. If all
knowledge is from experience, it is certainly not acquired by association.

Hume concludes his 'Inquiry' with his Academical
Philosophy.[1] He starts with what he calls the instinct
by which men 'suppose the very images presented by
the senses to be the external objects;' on which he
makes the following comment :—

'But this universal and primary opinion of all men
is soon destroyed by the slightest philosophy, which
teaches us that nothing can ever be present to the
mind but an image or perception, and that the senses
are only the inlets through which these images are
conveyed without being able to produce any immediate
intercourse between the mind and the object.'

This most instructive passage shows, first, that idealism has a real advantage over intuitive realism, which
falsely accepts the perception of an external object,
and secondly, that idealists tend to beg that the representative image perceived is a perception by confusing

[1] *Inquiry.* § 12.

the object with the operation of sense.   Idealism is the
scientific truth that sensible objects are effects on
the senses, misinterpreted into the hypothesis that they
are 'perceptions in the mind,' as Hume calls them in
the same paragraph, without evidence.

Having now got himself into a self-made difficulty
about the data of sense, he proceeds to torture himself
with the following question :—

'By what argument can it be proved that the perceptions of the mind must be caused by external objects,
entirely different from them, though resembling them
(if that be possible), and could not arise either from the
energy of the mind itself, or from the suggestion of
some invisible and unknown spirit, or from some other
cause unknown to us ? '

This question is put with the logical power of
Berkeley, and is answered with even more logic :—

'It is a question of fact, whether the perceptions of
the senses be produced by external objects resembling
them : how shall this question be determined ? By
experience, surely, as all other questions of a like
nature. But here experience is, and must be, entirely
silent. The mind has never anything present to it but
the perceptions, and cannot possibly reach any experience of their connection with objects. The supposition
of such a connection is, therefore, without any foundation in reasoning.'

The fallacy of this argument consists in the assumption with which it begins. Really, we are conscious of
perceptions, or rather of ourselves perceiving ; but we
perceive not perceptions, but sensible objects, and not
in the mind, but in the nervous system ; and from these
physical objects within we infer physical objects without, different individually, but specifically similar to the

sensible objects from which they are inferred. But
though Hume's data were false, his conclusions were
logical. If all that we perceived were perceptions, they
would be entirely different from external objects; and
experience, being confined to perceptions, would have
no data to prove anything at all about objects, internal
or external. Moreover, if the data both of sensitive
and reflective perception were perceptions, qualities as
ideas of sensation, and operations as ideas of reflection,
as Locke and Berkeley formally stated, we should only
be able to infer perceptions. Hume has the best of the
logic when he refuses to follow either Locke in supposing matter, or Berkeley in supposing mind, seeing
that neither of these philosophers allowed matter and
mind in the data of sensation and reflection, when they
were delivering themselves *ex cathedra* on the subject of
sensible data. As Hume afterwards says, nothing remains but 'a certain unknown, inexplicable *something*,
as the cause of our perceptions.' Such is the false
though logical end of Hume's speculative philosophy.

He proceeds illogically to correct himself of his
Pyrrhonism by the old view of the Academy that 'all
human life must perish, were his principles universally
and steadily to prevail,' which is no answer to the
Pyrrhonist or to Berkeley, who would immediately
resolve our bodies, our clothes, our food, our estates,
into perceptions. But Hume valued common life too
highly, and natural philosophy too little. We are not
committed to the dilemma of thinking in one way and
living in another. The answer to his 'mitigated scepticism or academical philosophy' is the physical discoveries of natural philosophy. If, indeed, the objects
of perception were perceptions, we should never infer
anything but perceptions, with an unknown, inex-

plicable something. But natural philosophy has discovered imperceptible objects, substances qualified,
causing and receiving motions, in accordance with universal laws, and ultimately causing our perceptions.
Therefore, it is neither true that knowledge ends in an
unknown something, nor that the objects of perception
are perceptions, from which imperceptible objects of
science could not have been inferred. The slightest
philosophy teaches us that what is present to sense is an
image, but not that this image is a perception. Simple
sense perceives an object, internal but physical; synthetic sense and experience perceive the relations of
these physical objects within, and reason infers the
relations and existence of physical objects without.

Hume's philosophy is a *deductio ad absurdum* of
idealistic hypotheses. It is what was sure to follow if
Locke and Berkeley were taken at their word, no regard being paid to their admissions. As soon as the
Cartesian consciousness of the thinking subject had
been forgotten, all the data of sense were reduced by
Locke and Berkeley to ideas, qualities as ideas of sensation, and operations as ideas of reflection; and the
objects of understanding were logically inferred to be
also ideas. Locke illogically admitted the supposition
of substances, material and thinking; Berkeley dogmatically asserted the existence of mind as gathered from
its effects; and both ended by admitting the consciousness of one's own existence. Berkeley saw the inconsequence of Locke's supposition of material substance
beyond mere ideas of sensation, but he did not see
that he was with equal inconsequence introducing
mind, soul, spirit, directly after mere ideas of reflection.
Hume acutely detected the half measures of Berkeley,
but took the wrong alternative. Instead of going be-

hind both Locke and Berkeley to show that both sensation and reflection perceive qualified substances, he
banished the thinking to the limbo of the material
substance, and rigidly confined us to the abstract perceptions which form the sum of the data of perception
by the confession of both his predecessors. This conclusion is argued out in the 'Treatise' on the following
text: 'We have no perfect idea of anything but of a
perception. A substance is entirely different from a
perception. We have therefore no idea of a substance.' [1]
This logical syllogism, of which however the major is
quite false, is applied both to material and thinking
substance, in the 'Treatise.' In the 'Inquiry,' he became
silent on this point; but ignorance of substance is a
necessary consequence from the perception of perceptions, which is common to both books.

Hume may be said to have gathered the ideal theory
of perception into a focus which reveals to us its errors.
The supposition that sensible objects are psychical
operations deprives us of objects and physical objects
within, from which to infer physical objects without.
The supposition that sensible objects are qualities and
operations deprives us of the sense and inference of
substances; of the sensation and inference of material
substances, and of the consciousness and inference of
thinking substances, partly physical, partly psychical.
On every side he paraded the mere logic of idealism.
He was particularly attracted by Berkeley's philosophy;
for instance, by the theory of general ideas, and of
primary and secondary qualities. Berkeley's hypothesis,
in the 'Principles,' of the inactivity of ideas, anticipated Hume's scepticism about power in causation;
while, in the 'Theory of Vision,' the hypothesis that

[1] *Treatise*, iv. § 5.

visible ideas suggest tangible ideas, without any inference of an external object common to touch and vision, gave the first hint for Hume's substitution of association for reasoning. Hume's scepticism is the dark shadow of Berkeley's theosophy, giving us the logical warning— if no matter, then no spirit, and no God. He had no suspicion that Berkeley's so-called principles were hypotheses, any more than modern idealists have. Hence he says of Berkeley's arguments that ' *they admit of no answer, and produce no conviction.*' [1]

Here Hume missed an opportunity, such as seldom falls to the lot of a philosopher. Instead of being merely logical from the original hypotheses of his predecessors, he ought to have used their subsequent admissions for a new departure in philosophy. He should have returned to the Cartesian consciousness of a thinking subject. He should have shown that both Locke and Berkeley, after beginning with a reflection of mere ideas of operations, admitted at last a direct consciousness of one's own existence. He should have pointed out that this means a reflective consciousness of oneself as a thinking substance, and have similarly recognised sensations of qualified substances within oneself. From these data, together with the synthetic sense of relations, he could have proceeded to explain our inferences of external substances—bodies, thinkers, God. But he preferred not to answer his predecessors, to stick to the idealistic last, and to work on nothing but impressions of sensation and reflection.

To this scepticism about sense Hume added a scepticism about reason. Logic, through the process of being made into text-books for education, has been too much schematised. For example, Aristotle distinguished

[1] *Inquiry*, § 12, Part I., note.

simple from complex apprehension,[1] and names from propositions,[2] but did not co-ordinate reasoning with the two other apprehensions. St. Thomas Aquinas schematistically added reasoning as a third operation.[3] The moderns, by co-ordinating the three operations, have tended to lose sight of the process of reasoning at the back of conception and judgment, and many modern logicians speak as if there were three independent processes, conducted quite independently, each with its own independent laws. But reasoning is a process from judgment to judgment, producing new conceptions. Again, the conceptualistic view of logic intensified the mischief, by regarding judgment as apprehending, and therefore reasoning as inferring, relations of ideas. At the same time, Descartes exaggerated the power of ideas over knowledge.

These causes produced the exaggerated attention to ideas and their origin, their arbitrariness, and the postponement of reasoning in Locke's 'Essay' and Berkeley's 'Principles.' The disease came to a head in Hume's works. In the first part of his 'Treatise,' which is directly modelled on Locke's Second Book, Hume takes as his problem the mere origin of ideas. In the course of the same work he animadverts on the distinction of acts of the understanding into conception, judgment and reasoning, and the definitions given of them. 'Conception,' he says, 'is defined to be the simple survey of one or more ideas; judgment to be the separating or uniting of different ideas; reasoning to be the separating or uniting of different ideas by the interposition of others.'[1] But his animadversions on these purely conceptualistic definitions only end in his reducing all these

[1] Ar. *De An.* iii. 6.   [2] Id. *Periherm*, i.
[3] *Aquinas in Periherm*. i.   [4] *Treatise*, iii. § 7, note.

acts to conceptions. Hence his resolution of judgment
or belief into a vivid conception or idea, from which
the substitution of association of ideas for inference of
judgments immediately follows. The answer is that
judgment is an apprehension of relations, beginning
with the synthetic sense of the relations of sensible
objects, and reasoning an inference from sensitive to
rational judgments, culminating in the laws or uniform
relations of insensible objects. Judgment is not an
idea ; reasoning not an association of ideas.

Hume was misled by psychological idealism and
conceptualistic logic. Hence his scepticism about sense
and reason. His philosophy, after all, is only the most
conspicuous instance of four idealistic faults : the confusion of the operation and the object of sense, the invention of all sorts of out-of-the-way sources of ideas
which are all the time due to sense and inference, the
postponement of reasoning, and the conceptualistic
supposition that conception, judgment, and reasoning
are all equally concerned with ideas. The proper cor-
rective is the study of Aristotle's ' Organon,' Bacon's
' Novum Organum,' and Newton's ' Principia.' ' The
fame of Cicero,' says Hume, ' flourishes at present ; but
that of Aristotle is utterly decayed.' Deservedly did
Aristotle's fame decay in natural philosophy. But his
logic of reasoning, widened by Bacon's theory of induction and Newton's explanatory method, is necessary to
all mental philosophy. Logical reasoning from adequate data of sense is the main origin of knowledge,
and of ideas, and of their association.

CHAPTER X.

KANT's 'Critique of Pure Reason'[1] begins by assuming Hume's theory of impressions' :—

'That all our knowledge begins with experience there can be no doubt; for how should the faculty of knowledge be awakened into exercise otherwise than by means of objects which affect our senses, and partly of themselves produce representations, partly rouse our power of understanding into activity, to compare, to combine, or to separate these, and so to convert the raw material of our sensory impressions into a knowledge of objects, which is called experience? In respect of time, therefore, no knowledge of ours is antecedent to experience, and all begins with it.'

This passage contains the truth, which I have all along admitted to lie at the foundation of psychological idealism; that sense perceives not external things in themselves, but internal images representing them in our senses. But, like his predecessors, Kant went on to corrupt this truth by two assumptions. On the one hand, he supposed the operation of sense to be purely psychical; on the other hand, he confounded the representative image with the operation of representa-

---

[1] *Critique of Pure Reason*, ed. Hartenstein, p. 33 = Meiklejohn's translation (Bohn), p. 1.

Ueberweg's summary of the *Critique of Pure Reason* is printed in an Appendix at the end of this essay.

tion—a confusion constantly favoured by the vague abstractions of modern languages, in which representation means indiscriminately both the operation of representing and the representative object, sensation and the sensible, or, in Aristotelian language, *æsthesis* and *æsthema*.

Hence, he started with the assumption that the matter of sense is nothing but its own representations, which do not exist out of the mind, and are not sensibly apprehended as objects.[1] This mere assumption vitiates the whole work ; for, of course, if there is no sense of objects within, reason cannot infer objects without, and, to know objects, we must find some other origin of knowledge. Hence, also, in the absence of adequate data of inference, sense and reason are displaced and divorced from one another by the intervention of an independent understanding, on which the main stress is laid. Hence, finally, as understanding can act only on sensible representations, which are not sufficient data for a rational inference of external objects, knowledge is limited to sensible representations converted by understanding into objects of experience, or phænomena of the mind. This would have been tolerable, if Kant had started by proving that sense only apprehends its own representations. But he did not even make it a question. It never occurred to him that touch and vision are operations, but the hot felt and the red seen objects. He straightway begged that there is no such distinction in sense, and founded the ' Critique ' on a *petitio principii*. Why ? Because, uncritically, he accepted the hypothesis, that the matter of sense is impressions, from Hume.

[1] Cf. Hart. 111-20, 347 = Meik. 77-86, 307.

Of all the many errors of psychological idealism the worst is its sequacity. Even critical idealism begins by being uncritical. Kant seemed to delight in assuming as data the unproved assumptions of his predecessors, which have been already criticised in this essay. From Descartes he accepted the confusion of subject and soul, the imaginary power of eliciting ideas, and the supposed psychical object of sense; and from Locke the deduction that all objects of understanding are psychical, the hypothesis that outer sense is concerned with mere qualities and inner sense with mere operations, the neglect of logical reasoning, the consequent deduction of the false conclusion that relations are a work of understanding, and the unexplained supposition of an unknown thing as cause of the data of sense. After Berkeley, Kant surrendered the inconsequent deduction by Descartes, and the inconsistent admission by Locke, of a knowledge of physical objects, and accepted the logical conclusion that the objects of human knowledge, with all their qualities, primary as well as secondary, are psychical objects of perception, and the consequent but false identification of the perceptible and the real, so far as known.

But Hume was Kant's main authority. They rightly agreed in rejecting Berkeley's dogmatism about the existence of mind and the non-existence of matter, and in the revival of the real distinction made by Aristotle between sensation and conception, in Hume's terminology between impression and idea, in Kant's between intuition and conception. Along with these merits, the critic, without a word of criticism, accepted from the sceptic the extraordinary mass of paradoxes about sense and the sensible, by which idealism had become scepticism. What men call sensible objects,

and believe to be external, what we have found to be
internal but not psychical objects, are supposed by
Hume and Kant to be not only internal but in the mind,
not objects distinct from the operation of sensation or
sensory 'representation,' as Kant would say, not substantial, nor including any sensible relation of cause
and effect; in a word, impressions, nothing more.
Critical or transcendental idealism, and all the many
idealisms which have sprung from it, exist only under
the shadow and protection of Hume's scepticism; for
all of them, without exception, start with a sense of
sensations, which has no authority except idealistic
hypothesis ending in Hume's paradox of impressions.
But we must go behind both Hume and Kant for the
data of sense.

Kant even went beyond Hume's scepticism about
the matter, which the senses receive from without.
The sceptic had doubted a sense of anything spatial or
temporal, and had denied a sense of connection; but,
however informally, he allowed a sense of conjunction.
His critic, taking him at his word when he put forward
mere impressions as the data of sense, proceeded, logically but falsely, to separate space and time from the
matter of sense, to obliterate the last trace of sensible
relation, and to reduce the matter of sense to sensible
representations or impressions, only lasting for an instant. Moreover, Kant was the author of the paradox
that 'the apprehension of the apparent manifold is
always successive,' and 'the manifold of appearances is
always successively produced in the mind,'[1] not allowing that even coexistence is sensible. According to
him, the matter of sense received from without is

---

[1] *Critique of Pure Reason*, ed. Hartenstein, p. 175 – Meiklejohn's
translation (Bohn), pp. 142-43.

nothing but a manifold or aggregate of unrelated impressions, a mere play of representations,[1] a rhapsody
of perceptions.[2] One wonders at last that he did not
say at once that nothing is sensible. Meanwhile, this
emasculation of the senses is not a result of any independent examination, but simply the last step in the
imitation of one idealist by another. Yet it is necessary
to the argument of the 'Critique.' It is because the
matter of sense is presupposed to be mere impression
that our knowledge of objects is supposed to be due to
a priori sources. In short, Kant attempted a criticism
of pure reason without a previous criticism of the
matter of sense. After what I have said in this essay,
not against one but against all these idealistic assumptions, I cannot be expected to enter even the vestibule
of this uncritical philosophy.

The opening of the Introduction to the 'Critique'
carries us insensibly back to the last section of Hume's
'Inquiry':—'The mind,' says Hume, 'has never anything present to it but the perceptions, and cannot
possibly reach any experience of their connection with
objects.'[3] Hence we see the resemblance and difference
between the two philosophers. Both agree that the
senses perceive impressions or representations. But
the point of Hume's philosophy is: given impressions,
we have not the faculties to experience objects of any
kind. The point of Kant's philosophy is: given representations, the objects of knowledge require faculties to
convert the raw material of our sensory impressions
into a knowledge of objects called experience. The
difference, however, is by no means so great as it
appears at first sight: for Hume and Kant alike begin

[1] Hart. 178 = Meik. 115.   [2] Hart. 152 Meik. 118.
[3] *Inquiry*, 12, Part I.

by assuming that the matter of sense is mere impressions, and end by denying a knowledge of objects beyond experience.

How, then, from sensible representations, supposed to be the matter of sense, do we arrive at a knowledge of objects? The answer of Kant immediately follows the opening passage of the Introduction :—

' But, though all our knowledge begins *with* experience, it by no means follows that all arises *out of* experience. For it could well be that even our empirical knowledge is a compound of that which we receive through impressions, and that which our own power of knowledge (merely occasioned by sensible impressions) supplies from itself, an addition which we cannot distinguish from the original element given by sense, till long practice has made us attentive to, and skilful in separating it. It is, therefore, at least a question which requires close investigation, and is not to be answered at first sight; whether there exist a knowledge altogether independent of experience, and even of all impressions of sense? Knowledge of this kind is called *a priori*, in contradistinction to empirical knowledge, which has its sources *a posteriori*, that is, in experience.' [1]

By *a priori*, as he proceeds to explain, he does not mean merely deductive from the results of previous experience, though this, or rather deductive from the prior cause to the posterior effect, was the usual meaning of the phrase : what he calls knowledge *a priori* is 'absolutely independent of experience.' [2] It is nearly related to what Descartes called innate. But the novelty of Kant's theory is that even sense and experience contain *a priori* forms. Given that mere representations are the matter of sense received from with-

[1] Hart. 33 – Meik. 1.   [2] Ib. 34 – Meik. 2.

out, sense requires *a priori* forms or pure intuitions of space and time to receive representations in outer and inner sense; understanding requires *a priori* forms of thought, pure notions, or categories, to convert representations into a perception and experience of objects; and reason requires us to conceive *a priori* ideas beyond objects of sense, understanding, perception, experience, knowledge, but cannot enable us speculatively to know the unconditioned objects of those ideas. The Kantian *a priori* theory differs from the Cartesian theory of innate ideas by the assertion of *a priori* forms in empirical knowledge and by the denial of a knowledge through *a priori* ideas beyond experience.

I remarked in the first part of this essay that every theory of the origin of knowledge is an hypothesis, which must be tested by direct and indirect evidence; and that the indirect evidence must comprise both explanation of the known facts and elimination of other hypotheses; while of all things what must be avoided is synthetical hypothesis, which, starting from the supposed verity of putative principles, arbitrarily dictates and denies facts. It will be our task to apply these logical rules to Kant's *a priori* theory, comparing it with other theories of the origin of knowledge, as occasion may arise. In the treatment of this subject it is too often supposed that the alternative lies between Hume and Kant, and that an empirical origin of knowledge means association, from which the only refuge is transcendentalism. I shall avoid this danger, thinking that in philosophy, as elsewhere, this is a pretty safe rule: when opposite parties quarrel with one another more hotly than usual, the truth lurks elsewhere. Moreover, I have shown in the last chapter, first, that sense is a very different thing from mere impression, and, secondly, that the empirical association of ideas is quite different from, and insignificant compared with, the empirical inference of judgments and the consequent conception of ideas, analogical, inductive, and deductive; so that there are at least two empirical theories of the origin of knowledge and ideas, which we may distinguish as the imaginative and the inferential. Lastly, I pointed out that there are laws which our operations mechanically obey without knowing them, even in reasoning itself. It is evident that *causæ cognoscendi* are of a very complicated nature. The choice does not lie between Hume and Kant.

Transcendentalism has no direct evidence. It supposes what may be called, perhaps, a self-informing power, what Cudworth called a potential omniformity of the mind. But, however we name it, it is a power of which one is not conscious. In this respect it is inferior to all forms of empiricism, which assume only conscious powers, such as sense, imagination, association, memory, judgment, and reasoning. Kant, on the other hand, supposes a power of adding *a priori* to *a posteriori* elements for reasons of his own, not on account of, but rather in spite of, consciousness. I am not conscious, for example, when I put my hand on the table, that I apprehend something *a posteriori* as hard, and *a priori* as extended: rather, I seem, as Berkeley said, to be feeling the primary quality of extension inseparably united with the secondary quality of hardness. Moreover, there is an absence of any anatomical evidence for a self-informing power. Where is its nervous organ? Not the brain in particular, which is the general organ of sense, reasoning, will; not the nervous system as hereditarily adapted to perform its operations, for quick is not *a priori* apprehension. When Kant

says that we know because we have an *a priori* power,
it is suspiciously like saying we know because we have
an occult power of knowing. Direct evidence, however, is not absolutely necessary, and it may be urged
perhaps that the *a priori* stands on the same footing
as the æthereal hypothesis. But there is a decisive
difference. Æther is supposed to be moving according
to the known laws of motion of all bodies. But according to what laws does the supposed self-informing
power act? The only laws at all like it are those of
pure fancy, which supplements the adventitious by the
fictitious. But the laws of fancy will not suit the *a
priori* hypothesis, which demands not fiction but knowledge. The peculiarity of transcendentalism is that it
supposes a power and supposes it to obey laws of its
own. It is what Mill would call an hypothesis of both
cause and law.[1]

Transcendentalism really stands and falls on the
indirect evidence that the objects of knowledge cannot
be otherwise explained. Kant appeals, in the first place,
to necessary judgments. As experience examines only
many instances and not all, induction can conclude
only comparative universality, which is, after all, open
to exception. 'Necessity and strict universality,' he
concludes, 'are, therefore, sure signs of a knowledge
a priori.'[2] Now there are, according to him, necessary
judgments; for example, any proposition in mathematics, and the necessary connection of cause and effect in
the ordinary use of understanding. These necessary
judgments, then, will be not inductive but *a priori.*
Secondly, he argues that 'not only in judgments, but
even in universal conceptions, an *a priori* origin sometimes discovers itself;' take away from the empirical

[1] Mill, *Logic*, iii. 14.   [2] Hart. 35 = Meik. 3.

conception of a body everything empirical, it disappears, but the space it occupied remains; take away from the empirical universal conception of any object its empirical qualities, substance remains.[1] Thirdly, he points to universal conceptions, which have no object corresponding in experience, but belong to a suprasensible sphere, where experience can, as he thinks, give no guidance. 'These unavoidable problems of pure reason itself are,' he says, 'God, Freedom, and Immortality.'[2]

These three arguments for the *a priori* are stated in the Introduction, and are the gist of the 'Critique.' They have a common point: they all refer to objects, supposed to require an *a priori* or self-informing power. But the first appeals to necessary judgments about objects of science, the second to objects of common experience, and the third to objects beyond all experience in a suprasensible world. Again, the first challenges the limits of induction, the second the limits of sense, the third the limits of experience. To answer them, we have to ask ourselves, indeed, whether induction, sense, and experience are so limited; but also, whether, in each case, our apprehensions of the objects are *a priori*. It should be noticed that there are always two different questions to be answered, before we can draw the transcendental conclusion; there is the question what is not, and the question what is, the origin of our knowledge and ideas. The negative criticism of a given aspect of empiricism is not always a positive proof of transcendentalism.

The three arguments require different answers. The first is the most plausible. Induction is only probable; necessary judgments therefore are not merely inductive. But it does not follow that they are therefore *a priori*;

---

[1] Hart. 36 = Meik. 4.   [2] Ib. 37 = Meik. 4.

on the contrary, as we shall presently find, they are
analytical judgments *a posteriori*. The second argument
depends, not on the logical limits of induction, but on
Hume's hypothesis of the limits of sense, uncritically
adopted by Kant. But sense is not limited to representations; it perceives the extended, as we found in
examining Berkeley's 'Theory of Vision,' and substance,
as we found in discussing Locke's 'Essay'; whatever
extended substance is in experience is previously in
sense, and what is not in sense is inferred by logical
reasoning from sense. The third argument depends on
the kind of experience which would be possible, if it
were made out of representations by *a priori* notions of
understanding, and were, therefore, confined to sensible
phænomena, as Kant supposes. In that case, there
would be no logical reasoning from experience of
phænomena to non-phænomenal objects. But sense,
outer and inner, apprehends internal but substantial
objects, unthinking and thinking; experience is the sum
of sense; and, not sense and experience, but logical
reasoning from them infers *a posteriori* similar substantial objects beyond experience; God, nature made,
and man made, saved, and raised by Him. The whole
'Critique' is a depreciation of sense and reason; for,
if a philosopher denies the objects of sense, he destroys
the data of reason. Finally, to close this preliminary
sketch, even if we could give no positive answer to
Kant, we could at all events not accept his theory,
which confessedly limits our inferences of necessary
truths and extended substances to mere phænomena,
and our apprehension of God, freedom, and immortality
to bare ideas. He, at any rate, does not explain the
power, the extent, the grasp, of human reason, because
he has no adequate data of reasoning.

Of the three indirect arguments, which constitute the proof of transcendentalism, the first is further developed in the Introduction, and required throughout the sequel of the 'Critique.' It was derived from Leibnitz, who, in the Avant-propos of the 'Nouveaux Essais,' had argued that necessary truths, especially in pure mathematics, though they are occasioned by the senses, do not depend on their evidence, but are innate.[1] Hume had, moreover, called attention to the belief in the supposed necessary connection of cause and effect, which he had explained away by experience and association. Stimulated by the problem of Hume, and prepared by the theory of Leibnitz, Kant extended the hypothesis of an *a priori* origin of necessary judgments from mathematics to natural philosophy, with the special view of solving thereby the problem of causation. At the same time, he did more than extend the *a priori* theory; he altered its character. Leibnitz had held an *a priori* analytical theory of necessity, and thought that necessary truths are innate in the sense of an analysis of our conceptions. Kant, agreeing that they are not inductive but *a priori*, added the novel supposition that they are not analytical but synthetical, and therefore proposed the question: How are synthetical judgments *a priori* possible?

At the present day, it is frequently supposed that the question of necessary truths depends on a choice between two synthetical theories, the *a priori* view of Kant and the *a posteriori* view of Mill. Kant, in his day, was at all events free from this defect. He knew that he had to deal with Leibnitz as well as empiricists, and directed his theory, so far as synthetical against

[1] Leibnitz, *Opera* (ed. Erdmann), 195 A, 209 B.

the former, and, so far as *a priori* against the latter.
There are, therefore, at least three alternatives about
necessary truths : that they are synthetical *a posteriori* ;
that they are synthetical *a priori* ; that they are analytical *a priori*. There is one more alternative : they are
analytical *a posteriori*.

Having, in imitation of Leibnitz, eliminated the inductive theory, Kant proceeded to eliminate the analytical *a priori* theory of Leibnitz, in order to establish
his own conclusion that necessary truths are synthetical
a priori judgments. An analytical judgment he defines
as one which analyses a subject into its constituent
notions, *e.g.* all bodies are extended ; while a synthetical
judgment is one which adds a predicate to our notion of
the subject, *e.g.* all bodies are heavy.[1] Then he contends
that, though some necessary judgments are analytical,
all necessary principles are synthetical. He begins with
pure mathematics. From arithmetic, having selected the
sum $7 + 5 = 12$, he points out that the universal conception of twelve is by no means thought by thinking
the union of seven and five. Pure geometry seemed to
him to contain the judgment, that a straight line is the
shortest between two points, which, as he contended, is
synthetical, because the notion of straight contains
nothing of magnitude, but only a quality, and the
notion of shortest is added to, not extracted from, the
notion of a straight line.[2] 'Natural science (*Physica*)
contains synthetical judgments *a priori* as principles in
itself ; '[3] this is his next point. Finally, he concludes
that ' metaphysics, at least as regards its end, consists
of merely synthetical propositions *a priori* ; ' and asks
the question, How are synthetical judgments *a priori*

<hr>

[1] Hart. 40 = Meik. 7.   [2] Ib. 43 4 Meik. 10.
[3] Ib. 44 - Meik. 11.

possible? He even commits himself to the extraordinary paradox that the solution of this problem
must determine whether metaphysics is to stand or
fall.[1]

Now, to resume his whole argument from necessary
to synthetical *a priori* judgments: necessary judgments
are not inductive; they are, therefore, *a priori*: but
there are necessary judgments, *e.g.* in mathematics and
natural philosophy; they are, therefore, not inductive,
but *a priori*: again, they may be analytical or synthetical; now, analytical judgments are analyses of a subject
into its conceptions, and, though some necessary judgments *a priori* are of this kind, necessary principles,
e.g. in mathematics and natural philosophy, being
a priori additions of a predicate to a subject, are not
analytical but synthetical *a priori*. Such is the ingenious reasoning by which Kant tried to eliminate, first,
the inductive, and, secondly, the analytical theories of
the origin of necessary truths. It opens up a number
of questions; but, as it admits the existence of analytical judgments, and we have not as yet looked into
this aspect of analysis, our first anxiety must be to discover what is the nature and value of analytical judgment, and what its limit.

Aristotle laid the foundation of the distinction
between analytical and synthetical judgments by his
investigations about simple and complex being and
intelligence (νόησις), about the axioms of being and
knowing, about the self-evident principles of demonstration. In the 'Metaphysics' he discussed, as axioms
of being, the principles of contradiction and excluded
middle,[2] and distinguished simple and complex being,
remarking that things simple (τὰ ἀσύνθετα), such as a

---

[1] Hart. 45 = Meik. 12.   [2] Met. Γ. 3 seq.

unit, are objects about which we may be ignorant, but not deceived, and either understand them altogether or not at all; whereas about a combination, such as wood being white, we may make propositions either true or false.[1] In the 'De Anima,' after distinguishing simple and complex intelligence, he contended that the simple apprehension of the essence of a thing is always true, while the complex apprehension of something merely belonging to it may be either true or false, e.g. a white thing may or may not be a man.[2] In the 'Posterior Analytics' he insists that the principles of demonstration must be necessary, that is, self-evident,[3] that the axioms of being, though principles, are not the actual premises,[4] and that the principles of demonstration are acquired by a gradual process of sense, memory, experience, induction, and are recognised by intellect (νοῦς), of which the obvious function is to apprehend their necessity.[5]

I do not commit myself to the whole of this theory of the self-evident principles of demonstration. Aristotle did not successfully explain the power of intellect to apprehend the self-evident, and, though he founded the constituents, did not actually recognise the analytical judgment. Especially I take exception to his doctrine that the apprehension of an essence or definition is always true. There are really two ways of arriving at definitions, one of which I take to be on the whole that described by Aristotle, and exemplified in the simple definitions of mathematics; but the other is far more complicated, being an accumulation of facts, followed by an explanatory hypothesis of essence; a way which is exemplified in the explanation of the

[1] Met. O. 10.   [2] De An. iii. 6.   [3] Post. An. i. 4 6.
[4] Ib. i. 11.   [5] Ib. ii. 19.

facts of heat and light by defining them as undulations of æther. The omission of this second process
is a great blot in Aristotle's logic of science, which
is too much modelled on mathematics. It made him,
as Bacon remarked, fly to principles, think all scientific
principles simple and self-evident, and all science demonstrative, or deductive from the self-evident. Hence
his anticipation of nature in natural philosophy; for
example, his hypothesis that heat is a primary quality
of matter whose nature is simple and self-evident;
whereas it is a secondary quality, whose nature has
been discovered only after an indirect process of accumulating its properties, and then explaining them by
æthereal motion. But at the bottom of these exaggerations Aristotle was the discoverer of a great truth. There
are self-evident truths about things, simple not synthetic,
in accordance with the principles of contradiction and
excluded middle, yet not deduced from them, discovered
a posteriori, but recognised by some power of intellect,
and forming principles of demonstration. Aristotle's is
a realistic theory of self-evident truths. It has, moreover, exercised an immense influence on modern philosophy, though it has become corrupted by conceptualism
and nominalism.

Even empirical philosophers admit self-evident truths,
and some of them even adopt the analytical theory of
mathematics. Among the conceptualists, Locke, at the
beginning of the Fourth Book of his 'Essay,' recognised
self-evidence under the name of 'intuitive knowledge,'
which perceives the agreement or disagreement of ideas
by themselves, *e.g.* that white is not black, that a circle
is not a triangle, that three are more than two and
equal to one and two; he admitted that intuition is the
most certain kind of knowledge, and the foundation of

demonstration,[1] in mathematics. But he gave no proof
that it is limited to ideas, nor any explanation of its
operation. Similarly, Hume in the 'Treatise' admits
intuition. 'No one,' says he, 'can once doubt but
existence and non-existence destroy each other, and
are perfectly incompatible and contrary.'[2] In the
'Inquiry' he regards pure mathematics as consisting
of propositions, which express relations of ideas, either
intuitively or demonstratively certain, and discoverable
by the mere operation of thought.[3] 'The conclusions,'
says he, 'which it draws from considering one circle
are the same which it would form upon surveying all the
circles in the universe.'[4] But he confined the self-
evident and demonstrative to mathematics.[5] He
adopted from Locke the analytical theory of mathematics in a conceptualistic form, but neither of them
proved that self-evident truths express merely relations
of ideas. Mill differed on this subject from them in
two respects. In the first place, he adopted, from
Hobbes, a nominalistic view of self-evidence, regarding
all self-evident, analytical, identical, essential propositions as purely verbal, stating the meaning of a name
but giving no information about a thing.[6] Secondly,
he attempted to banish the self-evident entirely from
science, and went to a pitch of scepticism of which even
Hume hardly dreamt, by reducing mathematical necessity to probability, resulting from induction and association. In this respect he at the same time departed
from Hobbes, who had taken up the extraordinary position that, while self-evident propositions are merely
nominal, they are principles of science, which would
make truth and falsity purely arbitrary. Meanwhile,

---

[1] *Essay.* iv. 2, 1.   [2] *Treatise,* iii. § 1.   [3] *Inquiry,* § 4.
[4] Ib. § 5.   [5] Cf. ib. § 12, Part III.   [6] Mill, *Logic,* i. 6, 4.

Mill's nominalism did not rid him of self-evident propositions. He allowed that they are 'such as every
one assented to without proof the moment he comprehended the meaning of the words.'[1] Moreover, he
admitted 'the original inconceivability of a direct
contradiction,'[2] without, however, seeing that it is a
negative instance entirely disproving the reduction of
all necessity to association.

There are, therefore, three theories of self-evidence,
all admitting the self-evident : the realistic theory of
Aristotle, the conceptualistic of Locke and Hume, and
the nominalistic of Hobbes and Mill; and there are
two theories among modern empiricists about necessary
truths in mathematics, the older empiricists holding them
to be self-evident, while Mill thinks them mere results
of induction and association. But before going any
further, we must first say something about Leibnitz,
whose views about self-evidence, and the self-evident
character of the necessary truths of mathematics, were
the immediate occasion of Kant's distinction of analytical and synthetical judgments *a priori*.

Leibnitz, being, even more than Locke, under the
influence of Descartes, adopted the conceptualistic
theory that self-evident truths are founded on ideas.
But his originality appeared in his attempt for the first
time to explain in detail how we apprehend their necessity. In opposition to Locke's criticism, Leibnitz contended for innate ideas, in the form that, on the
occasion of sensation, the mind by reflection finds
certain ideas in itself, and for innate principles formed
out of these innate ideas. The axiom of identity, that
which is is, of difference, that which is the same thing
is not different, of contradiction, it is impossible that a

[1] Mill, *Logic*, i. 6, 4.   [2] *Examination of Hamilton's Phil.* chap vi.

thing should be and not be at the same time, were re-garded by him as innate identical principles, from which we deduce propositions such as, sweet is not bitter, and a square is not a circle. To the objection that men make such propositions without knowing the principles, he answers that they are like the majors suppressed in enthymemes. Finally, he regarded arithmetic and geometry as purely innate, consisting of necessary prin-ciples analysing our innate ideas by the principles of identity, difference, &c.[1]

Hence Kant's theory of analytical judgments. Ac-cording to him, an analytical judgment is obtained *a priori* from an analysis of a conception by means of the principle of contradiction, which he regards as the supreme principle *a priori* of all analytical judgments.[2] From Leibnitz he adopted the conceptualistic theory of the nature, and the *a priori* theory of the origin, of an analytical judgment. But he differed from his prede-cessor in thinking that the necessary principles of mathematics are not included among such analytical judgments, but are synthetical judgments *a priori*. We have, therefore, now to find a way, if we can, through a host of disputes, and to ask ourselves about the nature, origin, and limits of analytical judgments. Are they concerned with names, conceptions, or things? Are they *a priori* or *a posteriori*? Are they necessary principles?

To begin with the last point, mathematicians evi-dently use some analytical premises. The axiom, the whole is greater than its part, is confessedly an analytical judgment, which, according to Mill, would state the meaning of the name, and according to Leibnitz and

---

[1] Leibnitz, *Nouveaux Essais*, i. 1 (*Opera*, p. 204 *seq.* ed. Erdmann).
[2] Hart. 148–50 – Meik. 115 7.

Kant, the analysis of the conception, of a whole. Now, to take one instance out of many, it is used as a major premise in Euclid I. 7, twice over to prove that an angle is greater than an angle contained in it. Again, Kant confesses that the axioms of equality are analytical,[1] and the first of them is the major premise of the very first proposition in Euclid, while the third is the basis of the fifth proposition. The way of getting out of this objection in the 'Critique' is exceedingly lame. Kant, having to admit the use of these analytical judgments in geometry, maintains that they serve only 'for the chain of method, and not as principles.'[2] But in Euclid I. 7 the axiom, the whole is greater than its part, is used as a primary major premise, and, when it is combined with a minor premise, stating that a given angle is a whole of which the contained angle is a part, it produces the conclusion that the given angle is greater than the contained angle. A confessedly analytical axiom then is a primary major premise in a geometrical deduction; and it is a mere affair of words whether it is called a principle or not.

Analytical judgments, being scientific principles, in the sense of primary premises in mathematical reasoning, are not mere analyses of conceptions, nor meanings of names. Both Kant and Mill admit that mathematical truths apply beyond conceptions and names to sensations or phænomena, which they regard as facts, while mechanics and all mixed mathematics prove that they apply to the minutest particles, beyond our sensations, conceptions, and names. But if any premise in a mathematical deduction were about conceptions or names, it would be a fallacy to conclude about anything else. The demonstration in Euclid I. 7 would be

---

[1] Hart. 157 = Meik. 124.　　　　[2] Hart. 44 = Meik. 11.

a paralogism with a *quaternio terminorum*, if it stood in this form : the conception or the name, whole, is the conception or the name, of something greater than its part; but the angle ACD is a whole, of which the angle BCD is a part; and therefore, the angle ACD is greater than the angle BCD. The conception or the name would never prove that an actual whole includes its part, even among phænomena, much less that a whole body is greater than its particles. Since, then, this and other analytical axioms are principles, which enable us to come to conclusions beyond conceptions and names, they must themselves be concerned with something more than conceptions and names. That something more would, according to Kant and Mill, have to be phænomena ; but really, it includes insensible things beyond. The axiom of totality enables me, as I look at this paper and its ink-marks, to infer that the whole coloured surface must be greater than any one of its black parts; and it also enables science to infer that a whole drop of water must be greater than any one of its imperceptible particles. Every whole in the universe is a case of this analytical law. Hence the conceptualistic and nominalistic theories of analytic judgments are miserably narrow; for analytical judgments are principles of sensible and of insensible objects. We must return to Aristotle's realism of the self-evident.

The conceptualistic and nominalistic theories of analytical judgments have each its peculiar error. The former theory was caused by the Cartesian confusion of the sensible and conceivable. Since the objects of sense were supposed to be concerned with ideas, it followed that analytical judgments, requiring no new experience, could not go beyond our ideas. We have destroyed this error from the foundation by separating sensible objects from ideas. The latter theory, as it exists in Mill's 'Logic,' is founded on a false disjunction. He supposes that all propositions are either verbal or real, and finding that analytical judgments, often expressing the meaning of a name, are verbal, concludes that they are not real. But the division of propositions into verbal and real is defective. A verbal is not necessarily opposed to a real proposition, a predicate does not cease to be a characteristic of a thing by becoming the meaning of a name, and there are some propositions which are verbal and real, such as all bodies are extended, the whole is greater than its part. Mill pokes fun at such a proposition as *Omnis homo est rationalis*, which expresses part of the meaning of the name, man. But does that prevent men from being rational? Again, his remark that analytical judgments convey no information about the thing, betrays a sad ignorance of human nature; for most men's simple apprehensions are miserably confused, as you may find by asking them what is a substance, an attribute, a body, a unit, a whole, a circle; and one of the main uses of analytical judgments is to make a confused apprehension distinct by dividing it into a subject and the predicates contained in it. In short, the division into analytical and synthetical does not correspond to the imperfect distinction of verbal and real; analytical judgments are sometimes about names, sometimes about conceptions, but also sometimes about objects distinct from both; and these latter are real. Sometimes the same analytical judgment is at once real, notional, and verbal, *e.g.* the whole is, is conceived, and means, that which is the sum of its parts.

So far, then, we have ascertained that analytical judgments, such as the whole is greater than its part, are principles of science, and are accordingly not limited to names and conceptions, but are concerned with sensible and insensible objects of science. Our next step must be to find their origin. Mill has no theory on the subject. Leibnitz and Kant have a theory, the common point of which is that we deduce the analysis of our conceptions from the principle of contradiction *a priori*.[1] As Kant merely followed Leibnitz in this respect, it will be best to criticise the original authority, in accordance with the method of this essay, which always contemplates the discovery of idealistic errors at their first source.

Descartes had, as we found, a confused notion of an innate power discovering ideas in ourselves, which Locke showed to be nothing but inner sense or reflection. It is an extraordinary thing that in the 'Nonveaux Essais,' which is an elaborate criticism of Locke's 'Essay,' Leibnitz knew Locke's theory of reflection, and yet coolly repeats that the ideas derived from it are innate, without taking any notice of the sensible and presentative origin of such ideas from inner sense. 'Perhaps,' he says, 'our able author will not be entirely removed from my sentiments ; for, after having employed all his first book in rejecting innate lights, taken in a certain sense, he avows at the commencement of the second and in the sequel, that ideas which have not their origin from sensation come from reflection. Now reflection is nothing but attention to that which is in us, and the senses do not give us that which we already possess. This being so, can it be denied that there is much that is innate since we are innate, so to speak, to ourselves ; and that there is in us Being, Unity, Substance, Duration, Change, Action, Perception, Pleasure,

---

[1] Hart. 39–42, 148–50 = Meik. 7–9, 115–17.

and a thousand other objects of our intellectual ideas?'[1] Locke's answer would have been simple and conclusive. Admitting that we derive all these ideas, except that of substance, by attention to what is in us, which is reflection and not sensation, he had shown that this reflection is a sense, which notices our being, unity, &c., only because they are there to be noticed, and are presented to it, precisely as sensation notices white or hot when presented. To call these results of inner sense innate is to confuse the intuitive and presentative with the *a priori* and elicited.

Leibnitz made a second mistake about innate ideas, in which Locke himself perhaps encouraged him. He put ideas down to reflection which are not confined to it. The correction of this mistake is of consequence, because Locke's exaggeration of the sphere of reflection, and the conversion of its ideas by Leibnitz into innate ideas, gave occasion to Kant's hypothesis that time is the mere form of inner sense and similar errors. Now, in the list of ideas quoted above, and supposed by Leibnitz to be innate, perception and pleasure are pure data of reflection, but being and unity belong to all data of sense, and to all things. Not being confined to reflection, they are not innate ideas, in the Leibnitzian meaning of this phrase. He made the same mistake about numbers, which he supposed to be purely innate ideas, giving rise to innate truths.[2] But, as the very hairs of our heads, so are the data of sense, and the particles of matter, all numbered. His theory, therefore, that number and its truths are innate, because they are results of reflection, is not adequate to our knowledge of universal number.

To come now to the bearing of the theory of innate

[1] Leib. *Opera* (ed. Erdmann), 196 A.   [2] Ib. 210 A, 212 A.

ideas on the origin of analytical judgments. If analytical judgments were formed out of ideas, they would be concerned with ideas, and, as we have already found, they would not in that case be applied to the sensible and insensible beyond ideas, and therefore could not be principles of science. But Leibnitz admitted, or rather contended, that they are the principles of science. It follows that an analytical judgment, such as a square is not a circle, cannot be formed, as Leibnitz thought, purely from innate ideas, because it is applicable to sense. In fact, it was the adoption of this theory of analytical judgments from Leibnitz that made Kant refuse to analytical judgments the title of principles. But the right alternative would have been to conclude that, since analytical judgments are universal principles of science beyond conceptions, they are not derived from mere conceptions.

But the most fundamental error of Leibnitz, which Kant shared with him, was the supposed deduction of analytical judgments from metaphysical principles *a priori*. Leibnitz supposed that, in order to say a square is not a circle, or bitter is not sweet, we must already be in possession of the general axioms, A is A, A is not non-A, A is not B, and so forth, which are therefore innate principles of analytical judgments. It is better to have no theory than a bad one; and Locke, though he did not probe the origin of an analytical judgment, such as white is not black, at all events divined that it cannot be derived by deduction from principles, because men make such judgments in entire ignorance of the principles. 'Who perceives not,' he asks, ' that a child certainly knows that a stranger is not its mother: that its sucking-bottle is not the rod,

long before he knows that 'tis impossible for the same
thing to be, and not to be ?'[1]

Leibnitz replies that ' one founds oneself on these
general maxims, as one founds oneself on the majors,
which are suppressed in reasoning by enthymemes.'[2]
But in an enthymeme we apprehend the major in
thought and suppress it in speech, usually because
the hearer will supply it himself, though sometimes because we know it to be doubtful, and hope that it will
escape his notice ; moreover, we recognise the major
when expressed. On the other hand, it can hardly be
maintained that a young child apprehends but sup-
presses the principle of contradiction : and it is certainly false that he would recognise it when expressed.
It needs a considerable education to recognise such
principles ; and, indeed, they were rejected over and
over again by philosophers until the genius of Aristotle
established their metaphysical formulæ. That same
genius established them without exaggerating them.
He pointed out that the principle of contradiction is
a condition, but not a premise of any deduction, unless
it has been denied in a particular case.[3] Leibnitz, on
the other hand, and Kant after him, fell into the error
of confusing the man with the metaphysician, when
they supposed that we deduce analytical judgments
from the principle of contradiction *a priori*.

It does not follow that we must commit ourselves
wholly to Locke's view about the principle of contradiction. This and similar axioms put us in a kind
of dilemma. On the one hand, Locke shows that they
are not known *a priori* ; on the other, Leibnitz as
clearly shows that they are required to make any

---

[1] Locke, *Essay*, iv. 7, 9.   [2] *Opera* (ed. Erd.), 211 A.
[3] Ar. *Post. An.* i. 11.

analytical judgment. The way out of this difficulty may be found by combining the hint of Aristotle, that they are conditions, not premises, with the last chapter, in which I pointed out that the laws of association, and the axioms obeyed by reasoning, analogical, inductive and deductive, are not premises of association and reasoning. Now, as, when the sight of a dog recalls the idea of his master, I use the law of association by contiguity; as, when I reason from the earth to Mars, I use the axiom of analogy; as, when I reason from dead men to the mortality of man, I use the axiom of uniformity; as, when I reason in the first figure, I use the *dictum de omni*, in the second the *dictum de diverso*, in the third the *dictum de exemplo*; but in no case deduce either my idea in association, or my judgment in reasoning, from the law, axiom, or *dictum* which governs the process; so do I use the axioms of identity, difference, contradiction, &c.. when I make an analytical judgment, such as the whole is greater than its part, or white is not black, or a square is not a circle; but I do not deduce any of these analytical judgments from these axioms, which are the spontaneous laws of the form of analytical judgments, not known premises to deduce them *a priori*.

The arguments of Leibnitz prove this and no more. He admitted that they are not universally known, but rejoined that 'one employs them without envisaging them expressly,' that 'they are necessary as muscles and tendons are necessary to walk,' and that they are like veins in marble before they are discovered.[1] But these arguments and analogies only prove, not that the principle of contradiction and similar axioms are innate major premises, but that they are laws which

[1] *Opera* (ed. Erd.), 207 B, 211 B, 213 A.

regulate the operation of analytical judgment. The
ordinary man knows nothing about them: the metaphysician has often denied them, Plato only caught
glimpses of them, and they were never extended to the
whole universe of being and thinking, until Aristotle
established them. In metaphysics, indeed, they are
themselves analytical judgments, and are a justification of the self-evidence of other analytical judgments,
but in ordinary thinking they are laws spontaneously
governing analysis, without being known.

If, then, we frame analytical judgments not from,
but only by, the axioms of identity, &c., from what
source do we derive them? Ultimately, by general
reasoning from sense, inductive and deductive. The
axioms alone, even if they were known *a priori*, would
be powerless: as it is, being only used, they are not
even major premises. Without sense and reasoning,
we should never know of anything being one and
many, whole and part, white or black, sweet or bitter,
square or round, or solid. By general reasoning we
infer that there are classes of these objects, and also
that a body moves its places in time, that a solid
body is of three dimensions, that things are one and
many, that a whole thing is greater than its parts. It
is thus we get the content of all our general judgments.
But I have confessed that induction and deduction from
induction are only probable. How, then, do we pass
from the probability of general reasoning to the necessity of analytical judgment? By the perfection of
rational abstraction.

There is another power in man, discovered by
Aristotle—abstraction. Abstraction has already been
mentioned in this essay. I have admitted, in the
chapter on Locke, that abstraction from sense may

conceive general ideas ; and in the chapter on Berkeley, that abstraction is a kind of attention, which does not form a merely abstract general idea. I have contended, against Locke and Berkeley alike, that it forms a general idea of a miscellaneous assemblage of similar individuals. But, without reasoning, such abstraction is limited merely to a general idea of sensible objects ; it is general, not universal. I added that there is a rational abstraction, such that, when reasoning infers a class of objects, e.g. of corpuscles, and rational conception forms a general idea of them, abstraction is capable of attending to them. Now, because it is attention, abstraction is not limited to ideas, but attends also to their objects. We may attend to names, to ideas, and to objects of sense and reason ; and it is no easier to attend to ideas than it is to objects. Abstraction, like other powers, has suffered at the hands of modern conceptualists.

Abstraction, as Aristotle was aware, neglects the other characteristics of a complex object for the purpose of isolating one characteristic, or rather the object as so characterised. For example, there is no such thing as a whole ; but we can neglect the other characteristics of an object, which is, among other things, a whole, and attend to it so far as it is a whole. Hence we often use the formula, ' as a whole,' or ' qui whole '—the Latin ' qui ' being a translation of the Aristotelian " ῇ ." The value of this operation, which the moderns ridicule as metaphysicians but use as men, is that we get rid of the complexity of general reasoning, and are able, by attention, to isolate a simple kind of object ; and all abstract sciences take advantage of this isolation. Now, not in all cases, but in those objects which are peculiarly susceptible of isolation, there is a further effect : we are able so far to isolate a simple kind of object, that we get rid of the synthesis of general reasoning, attend to a simple object in its completeness, and apprehend its nature or essence. Thus, general reasoning infers that a whole thing is greater than its part ; but this conclusion is liable to exceptions, for the thing may be absolutely simple, in which case it has no part to be exceeded by the whole. Again, general reasoning infers that one thing is undivided in quantity ; but, if it is a complex body, it is also many corpuscles in quantity, divided from one another. But by rational abstraction we are so far able to isolate the wholeness of a thing as to apprehend a thing *quâ* whole as that which is nothing but a sum of its parts ; and so far able to isolate the unity of a thing as to apprehend a thing *quâ* one as the undivided in quantity, and nothing more.

This perfect abstraction is the foundation of exact science. The perfect abstractions of arithmetic have just .been given. In the same way in geometry, general reasoning tells us that bodies are extended in three dimensions, but perfect abstraction is required to isolate the solidity of body and apprehend body *quâ* solid as that which is long, broad, and deep, and nothing more. Similarly, in abstract mechanics, it is not till we have regarded a body *quâ* moving as simply changing place during time, and not as possessing any particular structure, that we can strictly apply to it the laws of motion. There is, then, in exact sciences, a perfect abstraction, not *a priori*, but founded on general reasoning, inductive and deductive, from sense, consisting of attention, not to an abstract idea, but to a simple object in the abstract, and the apprehension of its nature, to the neglect of its synthesis with other characteristics or with other objects. This power is sometimes called intuition. But it is not intuitive any more than *a priori*. It requires sense, general reasoning, and rational abstraction ; nor is this rational abstraction always perfect ; but when it is perfect it is a simple apprehension of the nature of the object.

An analytical judgment is one which divides a simple object of perfect abstraction into subject and predicate. When we have thus got the entire content from general reasoning, and have abstracted simple objects, an affirmative analytical judgment simply divides the same simple object into subject and predicate by, not from, the principle of identity—a thing is the same as itself. This operation must be carefully guarded from misapprehension : there is no mystery about it. In the first place, it is not merely concerned with a common name, nor with an abstract idea, but with an object in the abstract, discovered by reasoning, isolated by perfect abstraction, and divided into subject and predicate by analysis. Secondly, it is not, as usually described, an analysis of the subject of the judgment into the predicate, which would deprive the latter of its content, but an analysis of the simple object isolated by perfect abstraction into subject and predicate, as the object and its nature. Thirdly, it adds nothing to the abstraction, but, as the abstraction isolates the simple object from the synthesis of general reasoning, so the analysis divides this simple object into subject and predicate. For example, having discovered that things which are wholes contain their parts, and having by perfect abstraction isolated a thing *quâ* whole as merely a sum of its parts, the analytical judgment simply asserts this result of perfect abstraction in the form of a judgment, for the purpose of making demon-

strations from it. Indeed, Aristotle was not wrong in
saying that there is a simple apprehension of simple
objects, though he ought to have added the analytical
judgment, because it is as a judgment that the apprehension becomes a principle of demonstration. Fourthly,
the analytical judgment is made spontaneously by the
principle of identity, which is the law of its form, but
not deduced from the principle as a premise. It has
nothing *a priori* about it, being derived from sense and
general reasoning, through perfect abstraction, by analysis, adding nothing but the division into subject and
predicate, not independent of experience, but only requiring no new experience ; in short, *a priori* only in
the old sense of indirectly *a posteriori*.

A negative analytical judgment is of the same kind, but
one degree more complicated. General reasoning from
sense infers that white objects are not black, that sweet
objects are not bitter, that square objects are not round,
and so forth. Perfect abstraction isolates the different
objects and causes a simple apprehension of their
natures as different. In the case of simple objects of
sense, such as sensibly white and sensibly black, perfect
abstraction is applicable, because the objects are so
simple, and the abstraction simply apprehends the sensibly white as containing nothing black, and *vice versâ*.
In the case of other objects, such as things which are
square or round, the abstraction, to become perfect,
requires the neglect of many extraneous circumstances,
in order to apprehend a thing *qui* square containing
nothing round, and *vice versâ*. A negative analytical
judgment, thereupon, divides the objects differentiated
in the abstract as subject and predicate of a negative
judgment, a sensible object *qui* white is never black, a
thing *qui* square is never round. Its principle is that

of difference, that which is the same thing is not different, or two different things are not the same, or, in its more developed form, the principle of contradiction. But this law of the form of a negative analytical judgment is not an *a priori* major premise from which any analytical judgment is deduced, except in metaphysics and logic as sciences.

Perfect abstraction and analytical judgments are not unlimited. Quantitative objects are more capable of abstract isolation than qualitative, in the narrow sense of this word. Perhaps no precise limit can be marked out, but we may lay down the general rules, that with the power of isolating a simple kind of object and apprehending its nature, abstraction ceases to be perfect, and, when perfect abstraction fails, analytical judgment is no longer possible. Thus we can perfectly abstract a thing *qua* whole, and judge analytically that so far it is greater than its part; perfectly abstract the sensibly white from the sensibly black, and judge analytically that so far one is not the other. On the other hand, when we come to so complicated an object as external light, we can no longer apprehend in isolation what light is as light, but must accumulate its facts and infer that its nature is undulative by the method of explanation. Hence two origins of definition : perfect abstraction in exact science, explanation of properties in other sciences. An abstract science is one which attends to an object, so far as characterised in some particular manner : an exact science is one in which this abstract attention is perfect.

An analytical is the same as a self-evident judgment, and its necessity is self-evidence. If all other things are possible, it is at least impossible that a thing should not be the same as itself, or be the same as something

different. Not metaphysics but perfect abstraction
gives this internal necessity to analytical judgments.
But metaphysics justifies it by analysing the analytical
axioms of identity and difference, and affords a technical
description, by which, if we are asked why a whole,
for example, is greater than its part, we can answer
because a thing *quâ* whole is the same as the sum of
its parts, because otherwise it would not be a whole,
and because to deny it would be a contradiction in
terms. But such a deduction is purely metaphysical.
Nor is it a valid objection that the ordinary man could
not apprehend the necessity of his analytical judgments
unless he knows the axioms, for he is in the same
position about ordinary deduction, where he plainly
knows the logical necessity of the inference, without
knowing the axioms which it requires. Analytical
judgments, then, are self-evident, without being deduced
a priori from their axioms.

This self-evidence has several special characteristics.
In the first place, we have no apprehension of it till
we apprehend the objects, but directly we apprehend
them in the abstract we at once accept the analytical
judgment. Hence it is that there are many men, and
even nations, who have never heard of the very judgments which to others are self-evident. The former
have not, the latter have, performed the necessary
abstraction. A man who has not thought of a thing as
a whole has no acquaintance with the judgment, the
whole is greater than its part; no sooner has he thought
of it *quâ* whole, than he asks for no proof of the axiom.
The analytical theory of principles is the only one
which accounts for this extreme contrast between
ignorance and certainty. Secondly, self-evidence gives
to analytical judgments a universal applicability. They

are not liable to the difficulty of synthesis, that an exception may be found to the combination of two kinds of objects; a difficulty which, Kant confesses, applies even to *a priori* synthesis beyond objects of experience. In an analytical judgment there is only one kind of object, which must be the same as itself and different from other things, wherever it is found. Thus the synthetical judgment, a whole thing is greater than its part, is liable to the exception that a thing may sometimes have no parts; but the analytical judgment, a thing so far as it is a whole is greater than its part, can have no exception, because *quâ* whole it is only a sum of parts. Thirdly, self-evidence makes analytical judgments convertible or coextensive; so long as a thing is a whole it is greater than its part, and as soon as it ceases to be greater than its part it ceases to be a whole. We can even say that such a judgment is of eternal application; for, even if things ceased to be wholes, it would still be true that they would be greater than their parts if there were wholes. Hence, there could not be another world in which a whole would not be greater than its part, for it could not be a whole; nor can any really self-evident or analytical judgment be reversed.

Such is the outline of a realistic theory of self-evident analytical judgments *a posteriori*, of which the points are, first, that such judgments are not always about names and conceptions, but also about objects of sense and reason; secondly, that we discover the objects by general reasoning from sense, by perfect abstraction apprehend a simple kind of object, and analyse it into subject and predicate by, not from, the principles of identity and difference, or contradiction, *a posteriori*; thirdly, that analytical judgments are self-evident to one who has abstracted the objects, universal without exception, and convertible ; and, fourthly, that analytical judgments about objects of reason in the abstract are sometimes principles of science.

As analytical principles are self-evident, conclusions logically deduced from them are necessary, though not self-evident, and the process of deduction from self-evident principles is demonstrative. There are two kinds of necessary truths : self-evident principles and demonstrative conclusions. Again, there are two kinds of deduction, which may be distinguished as empirical and demonstrative, provided we remember that demonstration is indirectly empirical. In the last chapter we discussed empirical deduction from induction, which, though formally necessary, is materially only as probable as the induction on which it is founded. In the present chapter we have added that deduction is not always limited by the probabilities of induction, but, when mediated by perfect abstraction, and starting from analytical self-evident principles *a posteriori*, is demonstrative of necessary conclusions. There are, therefore, two kinds of knowledge : one consisting of induction and deduction, combined together in circumstantial evidence, with various degrees of probability up to approximate certainty ; while the other starts in the same manner, but by the perfect abstraction of a simple, non-synthetic object, such as a thing *quâ* whole, a body *quâ* solid, a body *quâ* moving, &c., obtains self-evident analytical judgments, from which deduction demonstrates conclusions, materially as well as formally necessary. The former is science ; but the latter is exact science.

Kant in the ' Critique,' and Mill in his ' Logic,' both recognised analytical judgments and their self-evidence, but the former was deceived by conceptualism and the latter by nominalism, and accordingly both fell into the common error of excluding analytical judgments from principles of science. In order to answer them, we have only to remember that the axiom, the whole is greater than its part, is confessedly an analytical judgment, and certainly a primary major premise in mathematical demonstrations. Hence it is not a mere analysis of conceptions, still less the mere meaning of a name. It is the analysis of an object of general reasoning isolated by a perfect abstraction of a thing *quâ* whole as a sum of its parts. This analytical *a posteriori* axiom, being a real principle, is a sufficient contradictory instance to destroy both the theory in Kant's 'Critique' that all mathematical principles are synthetical *a priori*, and the synthetical *a posteriori* theory in Mill's 'Logic.' *Major est vis instantiæ negativæ.*

We found that Kant starts his argument by the position that necessity and strict universality are not inductive. This position is common ground. After and beyond induction, Aristotle introduced an intelligent understanding of principles, purposely to explain their necessity. 'Neque tamen,' says Bacon, 'etiam in universalibus istis propositionibus exactam aut absolutam affirmationem vel abnegationem requirimus.'[1] Newton, in the fourth 'Regula Philosophandi,' with which he opens the Third Book of the 'Principia,' acknowledges that induction is only valid 'donec alia occurrerint phænomena.' Similarly, all that Mill contends is that ' whatever has been found true in innumerable instances, and never found to be false in any, we are safe in acting on as universal provisionally until an undoubted exception appears ; provided the nature of the case be such that a real exception could scarcely have escaped notice.'[2] More-

---

[1] *Nov. Org.* ii. 38. [2] Mill, *Logic*, iii. 21, 4.

over, it is patent, from the limitation of human experience to some instances out of all, that the induction of
all must end in probability, however great.

The difference between Kant and Mill begins with
the contention of the latter that there are no truths
more necessary than those mere probabilities of induction which seem necessary to us only through inseparable association. But, in the first place, Mill is not true to
his own position, because, as we saw before, he acknowledges ' the original inconceivability of a contradiction ';
though, like other philosophers, he passes lightly over
this negative instance destructive of his theory that
association is the origin of all ideas of necessity.
Secondly, he ought to have gone further than mere
inconceivability. Analytical principles of science are
such that the contradictory is not only inconceivable in
idea but impossible in belief, because it is incredible
that a thing should not be the same as itself. Now
Mill admits, on the one hand, that the impossible is
different from the inconceivable, and, on the other
hand, that association is limited to the inconceivable.
As, then, association is no origin of principles, whose
contradictions are impossible, and as self-evident analytical judgments are such principles, it follows that
their necessity cannot be due to association of ideas.
Moreover, if the axiom, the whole is greater than its
part, were a synthetical *a posteriori* judgment, discovered by mere induction, with a mere idea of necessity
due to association, there would be two ideas, one of
which would suggest the other ; but there is only one
idea of one kind of object which is analytically judged
to be identically a whole and greater than its part.
Association, in fact, is no origin of the real and identical necessity of an analytical principle, which is self-

evident. There are, then, necessary truths of which the opposites are neither mere improbabilities of induction nor mere inconceivabilities of association, but incredible impossibilities of existence; namely, self-evident analytical judgments.

Kant then was right in repeating after Leibnitz that there are necessary judgments in the sciences; thereby he eliminated their synthetical *a posteriori* origin. But he did not thereby eliminate their analytical *a posteriori* origin 'Necessity and strict universality are, therefore,' says he, 'sure signs of a knowledge *a priori*.' That 'therefore' is a rash word. 'Baculus stat in angulo; ergo pluit.' There is another alternative. Because the necessary is not inductive, it does not follow that it is straightway *a priori*. Necessity is a soluble and not an infallible sign, because there is another source of necessity, namely, self-evident analytical judgments *a posteriori*. But Kant was misled by Leibnitz into thinking that analytical judgments were *a priori*. Hence his *non sequitur* from the inductive to the *a priori*. Hence also the importance of showing, as I have attempted to do, that analytical judgments are *a posteriori*, real, and necessary principles. It is to found a theory of necessity without mysticism.

Kant, in fact, eliminated analytical judgments from the position of scientific principles, only in the conceptualistic *a priori* shape into which, under Cartesian influences, they had been thrown by Leibnitz. He did not eliminate them in the realistic *a posteriori* light in which they were rightly regarded by Aristotle. Not all necessary truths are *a priori*, because self-evident necessary truths are *a posteriori*. Not all necessary principles of science are synthetical judgments *a priori*, because some analytical judgments *a posteriori* are necessary principles of science. The analytical axioms, the whole is greater than the part, if equals be added to equals the wholes are equal, if equals be taken from equals the remainders are equal, have a reality in things, and an *a posteriori* origin, and a position among Euclid's principles, which contradict the fundamental hypothesis of Kant's 'Critique,' that all necessary principles of science are synthetical judgments *a priori*.

Kant might reply that, though some analytical judgments may be principles, they do not carry us far; and that most principles at all events are synthetical judgments *a priori*; such as $7 + 5 = 12$ in arithmetic, and a straight line is the shortest between two points. But Kant was, to say the least of it, unfortunate in his instances. The proposition, $7 + 5$ are 12, is not an arithmetical principle, but a demonstrative conclusion; and the shortest distance between two points is so far from being the geometrical definition of a straight line that it is not geometrical at all, being merely that property of a straight line which is of most importance in mechanics.

The definition of a straight line would require an investigation of space and geometry. I will only remark at present that Euclid's definition is at all events geometrical, and it is unsatisfactory only because he attempted to define a line without a superficies, committing a blunder common with systematisers of previous discoveries, that of beginning too synthetically. A point is only definable by abstraction from a line; and similarly, a line from a surface, a surface from a solid, in the manner indicated, though not completely developed, by Dr. Simson in his Notes to the First Book of Euclid. A straight line also requires this analytical treatment. It has been for centuries perfectly abstracted; but, as often happens, it has been over-abstracted, and will never be successfully defined until it is analytically approached from its place in a superficies. But arithmetic comes before geometry: a unit is simpler than a point, a number than a magnitude. As Aristotle remarked, and Comte repeated, a science from fewer data precedes a science which adds more.[1] Accordingly, the question of necessary truths ought to be contested in the simpler and more universal science of arithmetic.

The arithmetical principle concerned with the number 12 is 11 + 1, which is its sole and sufficient definition. If we were to take 7 + 5 for a definition, 12 would have infinite definitions by the addition and subtraction of other numbers, none of which would be of any further use, because to use a number in a sum we must know out of what number it is formed by the addition of a unit. In the case of 12, 11 is that number which by the addition of 1 makes 12, as 10 is the number which by the addition of 1 makes 11, and so on till we come back to 1 + 1 are 2. All those arithmetical principles, which are definitions of numbers, are founded on the units added together; as the Greeks knew perfectly well when they said that the unit is the origin of number, and number is multitude composed of units.[2]

The discovery of abstract numbers is a good instance of the process of abstraction and analysis I have been describing in this chapter. By sense and reason we find that objects are one and many and wholes, among other of their attributes, and infer that one object is always undivided, many are divided into units, and a whole is greater than its part. We thus discover truths of number. But how do we apprehend their necessity? By perfect abstraction we isolate an object *qua* one as undi-

---

[1] Ar. *Post. An.* i. 27.   [2] *Eucl.* VII. Def. 2.

vided in quantity, objects *quâ* two as one + one, &c., &c.
This abstraction is necessary to the science of arithmetic.
As Plato, though he did not understand abstraction,
long ago pointed out,[1] concrete units are not altogether
undivided; a man, for example, is many in his members
and only one on the whole; but an arithmetical unit is
absolutely undivided. Why? Simply because the thing
as divided is neglected, and attended to only as undivided, by perfect abstraction. On this abstraction of
the unit, not as a mere conception, but as a simple
object of attention, we have, not *a priori*, but by *a
posteriori* analysis, the analytical judgment, which is
the definition of a unit: not, be it remarked, the contingent proposition, one thing is the undivided in
quantity, which is not always true; but a thing *quâ*
one is the undivided in quantity, which is self-evidently
necessary. So far as a thing is one, it is undivided in
quantity, and so far as it is divided in quantity, it is no
longer one. This analytical definition is the foundation
of all arithmetical definitions, all of which are merely
analyses of numbers into units; thus $1 + 1$ are 2; $2 + 1$
are 3, and so forth; every one of which are analytical
definitions. Hence, though $7 + 5$ is not, $11 + 1$ is, the
analytical definition of 12. All things, *quâ* $11 + 1$ are 12,
and *quâ* 12 are $11 + 1$.

Mill, indeed, contends that there is a difference
between $2 + 1$ and 3, because 'three pebbles in two
separate parcels, and three pebbles in one parcel, do
not make the same impression on our senses.'[2] But he
overlooks the fact that, when three pebbles are in two
separate parcels, if they give us the impression $2 + 1$,
this is the impression 3 without any comparison with
three pebbles in one parcel; and conversely, when three

pebbles are in one parcel, if they give us the impression
3, this is the impression 2 + 1, without any comparison
with three pebbles in two parcels. We do not require two
sets of three objects each to count 2 and 1 are 3. The
truth is that he was deceived by the formula 2 + 1 = 3,
in which, for mere convenience, we apply to number the
geometrical sign for equality of two magnitudes ; but
we must not allow this mere symbol to make us think
that we are always comparing different quantities on
each side of it ; in arithmetic, equality means identity,
and the correct arithmetical formula is 2 + 1 *are* 3.

Kant, on the other hand, did not even take the
definition of the number 12, which, as we have seen, is
11 + 1, but one of its many properties, 7 + 5. He rightly
says that the proposition, 7 + 5 are 12, is not analytical :
12 is not the selfsame thing as 7 + 5, because it is
8 + 4, &c. But this proposition, though not analytical,
is also not a principle, but a demonstrative conclusion
from principles which are analytical, the definition of
the unit and the definitions of the numbers up to 12, as
11 + 1 ; and we are able from these analytical to demonstrate synthetical judgments, by that combination which
we found in the last chapter to be the essence of syllogism
or deduction. Kant's attempt to prove that the principles of arithmetical demonstration are not analytical
by the instance 7 + 5 are 12, is an *ignoratio elenchi*, because this proposition is not a principle, but a demonstrative conclusion from analytical principles, including
11 + 1 are 12.

It is curious what a cursory attention is paid to
arithmetic in Kant's 'Critique' and Mill's 'Logic.' But by
looking a little more closely into this most fundamental
of all special sciences, we have found that it contains
analytical principles *a posteriori* both in the axiom, the

whole is greater than its part, and in its definitions.
Thus we can destroy both the synthetical theories. On
the one hand, as these principles, being self-evident,
are such that the contradictory is impossible, Mill is
wrong in reducing arithmetic to the mere probability of
induction and association. He quotes, indeed, with
approval a supposition that there might be a world,
in which, whenever two pairs of things are contemplated together, a fifth thing is brought within contemplation. and the result to the mind of contemplating
two two's would be to count five.[1] But it is absurd
to suppose minds contemplating a fifth thing without
counting it in the enumeration, and yet to end the sum,
as if they had counted it, with the number 5. Either
one would count the fifth thing, in which case the sum
would be $2+2+1$ are 5, or one would not, in which
case the sum would be $2+2$ are 4. There can be no
world in which the result to the mind of contemplating
two two's would be to count five, because $2+2$ are de-
monstrably 4, and $4+1$ are identically the same as 5.
On the other hand, as necessary arithmetical principles
are *a posteriori* analytical judgments, we cannot follow
Kant in passing from the synthetical *a posteriori* to the
a priori synthetical theory ; for a definition, such as
$11+1$ are 12, is discovered by empirical reasoning, and
by perfect abstraction and analysis becomes a self-evident principle, whereby $7+5$ is 12 are demonstrated.

Finally, if we were to surrender entirely the analytical *a posteriori* origin of necessary truths, yet the
synthetical *a priori* origin is an untenable hypothesis,
because it does not explain the facts. Let us take for
granted the Kantian series of arguments : the necessary is not inductive, therefore it is *a priori* ; there are

[1] *Examination of Hamilton's Philosophy*, chap. vi. note.

necessary principles in the sciences, therefore they are
a priori; analytical judgments are merely *a priori* analyses of conceptions, but principles of science are true
beyond conceptions, therefore they are never analytical
judgments: but if they are neither synthetical *a posteriori*, nor analytical *a priori*, all principles of science are
synthetical *a priori*.   Now, everywhere throughout the
'Critique,' Kant confesses that the *a priori* is contributed by mind to mental representations, and that the
data of mental representations, without which the *a
priori* is mere conception, are sensations, which the *a
priori* converts into objects of knowledge.   Hence he
concludes that perception, experience, understanding,
reasoning, knowledge, science are all confined to
sensible representations informed by *a priori* elements.
Hence, according to him, necessary principles of science,
being synthetical *a priori*, are necessary within, but
impossible without, the sphere of sense and experience.
Kant everywhere accepts this consequence : synthetical
principles *a priori* are necessary, and apply, only within
the limits of phænomena.[1]

This corollary of transcendentalism may be illustrated
by its application to arithmetic.   According to Kant,
arithmetic will contain analytical *a priori* axioms —
for example, the whole is greater than its part — which,
however, will not be principles ; and synthetical prin
ciples *a priori*, an example of which will be 7 + 5 are 12.
He did not, indeed, leave a satisfactory theory of the
place of number in his system.   There is a sentence in
the 'Critique'[2] in which he says 'that number is nothing but the unity of the synthesis of the manifold of
a homogeneous intuition in general, gained by my gene-

[1] Hart. 57, 152 3, 208   Meik. 44, 119, 177.
[2] Hart. 144   Meik. 110.

rating time itself in the apprehension of the intuition ;'
that is, apparently, by generating a successive addition
of units in time. The same view is confirmed by a passage
in the 'Prolegomena to all Future Metaphysics.' 'Geometry,' says he, 'is based upon the pure intuition of
space. Arithmetic accomplishes its concept of number
by the successive addition of unities in time.'[1] This,
however, is a conclusion so paradoxical, that we may
in charity suppose him to concede that we also apprehend
contiguous units in space. But even so, space and time
alike are regarded by him merely as *a priori* forms of
sense and of sensible phænomena. Moreover, the categories, schemata, and principles of quantity are all
confined by him to phænomena. The consequence is
that number is strictly limited to phænomena, and even
the synthetical principles *a priori* of arithmetic are regarded by Kant himself as necessarily true of phænomena
of sense, and no more. Hence his extraordinary statements, '*numerus* est quantitas phænomenon,' and
'*æternitas, necessitas*, phænomena,' &c.[2]

But is it true that the laws of number are limited
to the phænomena of sense? The very first definitions
of Newton's 'Principia' disprove such a narrow theory.
'The quantity of matter is the measure of the same
arising from its density and magnitude conjointly :' this
is the first definition, which is immediately illustrated by
the arithmetical proposition that 'air of a double density
in a double space is quadruple, in a triple space sex-
tuple,' while this quantity of matter is identified with
its mass. 'The quantity of motion is the measure of
the same arising from the velocity and quantity of
matter conjointly :' this is the second definition, which

---

[1] *Prolegomena* (translated by Mahaffy), p. 45.
[2] Hart. 146 = Meik. 113.

is again elucidated by the arithmetical illustration, that 'in a body, double in quantity, motion with equal velocity is double, with double velocity quadruple.' If, now, arithmetic were limited to the phænomena of sense, the laws of mass and motion would either have to be limited to the phænomena of sense, or, beyond the phænomena of sense, contain no quantity of matter or of motion, no measure, no numerical proportion ; both of which alternatives are absurd.

The truth is that the laws of mass and motion carry us far beyond the phænomena of sense into a nonphænomenal yet scientific world of material particles, and carry the laws of arithmetic with them. The law of gravitation is a law of motion by numerical proportion. All the particles of matter gravitate to one another with a force directly as their mass, and inversely to the square of the distance ; on the one hand, this gravitation is inferred to be in numerical proportion both to the quantity of matter and to the distances of the particles ; on the other hand, every particle of matter in the universe is inferred to gravitate with this numerical proportion, in times, places, and circumstances, wholly inaccessible to any possible senses of living beings. In the laws too of the structures and motions of imperceptible particles, all the definitions and axioms of arithmetic are employed. For example, in a drop of water, every thousand of the imperceptible particles with another particle makes one thousand and one, and is a whole including every one of these particles as parts. 'In rebus enim,' says Bacon, 'quæ per numeros transiguntur, tam facile quis posuerit aut cogitaverit millenarium, quam unum ; aut millesimam partem unius, quam unum integrum.'[1] As Mill remarks, 'the

---

[1] Bacon. *Nov. Org.* ii. 8.

great agent for transforming experimental into deductive sciences is the science of number.'[1] We can neither allow that these deductive sciences, which measure the structures and motions of imperceptible particles, are limited to phænomena of sense, nor that there is any measure of quantity available except number.

But we need not go beyond the 'Critique' itself to see the impossibility of limiting number, the quantitative categories of unity plurality and totality, and arithmetical principles, to phænomena. One of the points of the 'Critique' is that God is not a phænomenon. But God is one. Therefore unity is not limited to phænomena. Kant also assures us that we have a unity of apperception, an identical self, which is supposed by him to be not a phænomenon, but that which unites phænomena. Lest we should suppose that these objections prove only unity and not number beyond phænomena, he distinguishes for us the human understanding with its unity of apperception to combine sensible representations from the divine understanding, which does not require it.[2] There are, therefore, according to Kant, who was innocent of the Hegelian identification of similars and confusion of divine and human, two understandings, the divine and the human, numerically different, yet neither a phænomenon. God, he also tells us, does not make a whole with the world; there are, therefore, three things—God, the world, and human understanding; none of them phænomena.

All things are at least numbered, whether they be material or spiritual; hence the dispute, whether Kant ought to have made number belong to space or to time, is completely beside the mark, for it belongs to everything whatever. It is impossible, therefore, to confine

[1] Mill, *Logic*, ii. 4, 7.   [2] Hart. 119, 123 = Meik. 85. 89.

number, arithmetic, or arithmetical necessity to phænomena of sense. What is the consequence? Not all
necessary principles are limited to phænomena. Consequently, again, they cannot be synthetical judgments
a priori, which, on Kant's own confession, would limit
them to phænomena. In other words, the synthetical
a priori theory does not account for arithmetical necessity, the simplest and best instance of scientific necessity, beyond phænomena in an imperceptible world.

Arithmetical principles apply to everything whatever. After all, there is only one theory which can
account for this absolute universality of arithmetic, which
counts subjects as well as sensations, men, bodies, corpuscles, and God Himself. There is not one arithmetical
judgment limited to phænomena any more than to ideas.
Now, this could not be, if they were analytical *a priori*,
which would limit them to ideas, nor synthetical *a posteriori*, which would make them contingent, nor synthetical *a priori*, which would make them necessary
only within the limits of phænomena. But it can be,
if they are analytical *a posteriori* judgments about
simple objects of reasoning in the abstract. Either,
then, this theory must be accepted, or some new theory
found. But where?

When we look back on the whole discussion of this
difficult subject, we shall find that there is no evidence
for the Kantian hypothesis of *a priori* synthetical judgments, as the origin of necessary truths, except its
advantage over the synthetical *a posteriori* and the
analytical *a priori* theories. It has no direct evidence,
either from consciousness or from anatomy, and it is
not only that we are unconscious of *a priori* necessity,
but that we are unconscious of any *a priori* power, or
of anything like it. In indirect evidence it also fails. It

does not attempt to eliminate an analytical *a posteriori* theory, although such a theory, as I have shown, can readily be developed from the works of Aristotle. But what finally condemns it, and makes it quite impossible, is its confessed inability to explain even the logical inference, much more the scientific knowledge, of necessary truths beyond the phænomena of sense; when, as a matter of fact, in all the sciences, and not only in mechanics and all natural philosophy, but also in psychology and theology itself, insensible and imperceptible objects are logically inferred and known to obey the necessary laws of unity, plurality, and totality. Everything known is one; not everything a phænomenon.

What makes so many philosophers at this moment cling to an hypothesis so utterly wanting in verification, elimination, and explanation? Partly, no doubt, its superiority to the hypothesis of Mill. But two blacks do not make a white; and it makes little difference whether we say that association makes us necessarily conceive, or *a priori* synthesis necessarily believe, the necessity of principles within the phænomena of sense, when the real question is how we infer their necessity in insensible and imperceptible nature, and in the supernatural world. Partly, it is thought that the Kantian theory of necessity must be accepted, because other parts of the 'Critique' seem to support religion. But we must beware of building the house of religion on the sand; and religion can hardly be supported by a philosophy, which makes it a fallacy to say that God is one. The main cause of the popularity of Kant's philosophy, however, seems to be founded on the vague use of the term 'phænomena,' which suggests to the unwary all the facts in heaven and earth, sensible, insensible, and imperceptible. But this is not what Kant

meant, nor what he could mean, by phænomena, and
it would be a sad pity to rest the reputation of a
philosophy on an equivocation.

As Leibnitz before him spoke of '*phænomena* sive
apparitiones quæ in mente mea existunt,'[1] so Kant
always speaks of them as sensible representations which
cannot exist out of our mind; opposing them to nou-
mena, or things of which we must form ideas, but
which as objects are unknown.   He was aware that his
philosophy compelled him to make these sensible representations the limit of knowledge, not merely because
they are the matter of sense, but also because *a priori*
forms of mind cannot be valid beyond *a posteriori* data
of mind.   Moreover, as we find from the Preface to the
Second Edition,[2] he looked upon it as one of the advantages of his 'Critique of Pure Reason,' so to limit
speculative knowledge to phænomena that 'we can have
knowledge of no object as a thing in itself, but only so
far as it is an object of sensory intuition, *i.e.* as manifes-
tation,' because thereby he thought to make room for a
practical proof of the freedom of the will beyond the
area of phænomena.

Kant, then, in limiting all speculative knowledge to
phænomena, meant that necessary truths, being synthetical judgments *a priori*, are only necessary about the
a priori forms of sensible representations and about
sensible representations converted into objects of knowledge by these *a priori* forms.   Such a limitation to
things of sense, Sinnenwesen, phænomena, is far too
narrow, because arithmetical necessity applies to every
imperceptible object of logical reasoning and scientific
knowledge.   His fundamental position, that necessity is

[1] Leibnitz, *Op.* (ed. Erdmann), p. 442, A.
[2] Hart. 22 *seq.*—Meik. xxxii. *seq.*

an infallible sign of *a priori* knowledge, must be traversed by this still more fundamental position : imperceptibility is an infallible sign of a logical inference and a scientific knowledge which is neither phænomenal nor *a priori*.

Kant's 'Critique of Pure Reason' is a conspicuous instance of the failure of the synthetic method, and indeed of the impossibility of carrying it out consistently. He supposes himself to use the origin of knowledge to determine the limits of the objects known. Accordingly, on this synthetic method, he begins with sense, at once begs a sense of sensible representations, and thus founds his philosophy on an hypothesis which dictates the conclusion that knowledge is limited to phænomena. On the other hand, every one of his main arguments takes a premise from the other end of knowledge, its objects, and, by an analytic method, uses the objects to infer an *a priori* origin of knowledge. Thus, in the Introduction, necessary truths about objects of science are used to deduce the theory of synthetic judgments *a priori*; in the 'Transcendental Æsthetic,' from their known properties space and time are inferred to be *a priori* forms of sense; in the 'Transcendental Analytic,' a definition of the objects of knowledge is used to prove that they contain *a priori* categories of understanding. Nor is this all. Having taken as much about an object as he wants for his *a priori* theory, Kant then, by his synthetic method, uses his *a priori* theory to dispose of the rest of the object. Thus, he argues that necessity requires synthetical judgments *a priori*, which again prove necessity phænomenal ; that the properties of time and space require *a priori* forms of sense, which again prove time and space phænomenal; that known objects require *a priori* categories, *e.g.* substance and cause, which again prove known objects, *e.g.* substances and causes, phænomenal.[1]

The 'Critique' is a perpetual see-saw between two methods; the professed from the origin to the objects, and the concealed from the objects to the origin of knowledge. It is first synthetical, then analytical, and finally synthetical. It assumes as a principle that the matter of sense is representations. But this synthetic beginning would not justify transcendentalism. It then argues that the objects of knowledge require *a priori* elements. Now, this analytical procedure gives transcendentalism a momentary plausibility. It finally contends that *a posteriori* representations converted into objects by *a priori* elements are the objects of experience, and that all objects of logical inference and knowledge are phænomena. But this synthetical ending brings transcendentalism into conflict with a characteristic of the objects of knowledge, omitted in the analysis; namely, that they are not limited to phænomena. It is as if a natural philosopher should show that the theory of emission explains reflection and refraction, and then deny the interference of polarised light. So Kant shows that the *a priori* theory explains the necessity of synthetical truths, and then denies their universal applicability; shows that it explains the properties of time and space in, and then denies them beyond, sense; shows that it explains the experience of objects, and then denies the knowledge of objects beyond experience. He arbitrarily appeals to some of the characteristics, but neglects the insensibility, of objects of science. His whole method is *ad placitum*. He makes origin and objects, objects and origin, origin and objects, reciprocally determine one another, in a perpetual circle.

[1] Hart. 22, 80, 123–4, 133–4, &c. = Meik. xxxiii. 44, 90, 100, &c.

The analytic method, used consistently, makes complete havoc of the 'Critique.' 'Tempus, spatium, locus, et motus sunt omnibus notissima. Notandum tamen, quod vulgus quantitates hasce non aliter quam ex relatione ad sensibilia concipiat.'[1] In this passage, Newton points out that the limitation of the objects of science to the sensible is a vulgar error. Yet it is a constant error of mental philosophers, who think that, when they have considered only objects of sense, they have solved the secret of the scientific universe. It was the very error of Kant when he called time and space forms of sense, and therefore limited motion to sense ; when heenunciated the extraordinary series of paradoxes: '*numerus* est quantitas phænomenon, *sensatio* realitas phænomenon, *constans* et perdurabile rerum substantia phænomenon, *æternitas*, *necessitas*, phæno- mena, &c.'[2] ; when he concluded that whatever is known is a phænomenon, and what is not a phænomenon can be conceived by pure reason, but neither inferred by logical reason nor scientifically known. This philosophy, *secun- dum sensum*, was an hypothetical corollary from the theory that all objects of experience are sensible repre- sentations informed by *a priori* intuitions and notions of mind. But as certainly it is false, because it cannot explain a millionth, nor even an infinitesimal, part of the insensible objects of science.

Let us return from the 'Critique of Pure Reason' to the 'Philosophiæ Naturalis Principia Mathematica,' and enlarge our thoughts, not to the immensity of the unknown, but to the extent of the objects of science, such as was made known by Newton,

Felix, qui potuit rerum cognoscere causas.

Insensible corpuscles of matter are scientifically inferred

[1] Newton, *Principia, Def. Scholium.*   [2] Hart. 146 = Meik. 113.

to be each one, many and numbered, and to obey the
necessary laws of number; to be in insensible time and
space, and to obey the necessary laws of magnitude; to
be insensible substances, and move according to the laws
of motion; to be insensible causes of insensible motions,
and to be insensible causes of sensible objects. They
are actual, but they are not actual phænomena of sense,
but insensible external causes of internal sensible effects. Nor, being actual, are they possible phænomena;
for possible, which are not actual, phænomena are
nothing at present, whereas the insensible particles of a
drop of water, now gravitating towards my hand, are
actual at present, real because causal of effects in my
senses, and at the same time not only insensible but
imperceptible; so far from possibilities, impossibilities of
sensation; yet actual objects of science. The irresistible
conclusion of this consistent and thorough appeal to
the objects of knowledge, is that not all of them are
phænomena, actual or possible, but far the larger part
non-phænomenal, noumenal in the sense of rationally
inferred, known things in themselves, as apart from our
senses, though not as apart from their relations to one
another.

The weight of natural philosophy is destined to
destroy all that mental philosophy of the present day
which begins from a sense of sensations, even if it
makes a vain effort to recover its false start by catching
at the shadow of *a priori* mysticism. When Kant pro-
poses to convert sensible representations of minds into
objects of knowledge by *a priori* intuitions and notions
of minds, he all the more limits scientific inference to
phænomena. But, as we have just seen, the objects of
scientific inference include insensible and imperceptible
things, which are not phænomena, actual or possible.

Therefore, in the first place, the ' Critique ' is incredibly narrow and absolutely false in limiting scientific inference to phænomena, actual and possible ; and secondly, the data of scientific inference cannot be sensible representations, even sublimated by *a priori* forms, which all the more surely would condemn science to the narrow limits of phænomena.

Finally, we must apply consistent analysis to the Kantian arguments in detail. Thus, if necessary truths were synthetical judgments *a priori*, they would be limited to phænomena ; but science extends them to all particles of matter ; therefore, they are not limited to phænomena, and therefore are not synthetical judgments *a priori*. Secondly, if time and space were such as to be necessarily *a priori* forms of sense, they would be limited to phænomena ; but science infers that they are forms of every particle of matter in the universe ; therefore, they are not limited to phænomena, and therefore they are not *a priori* forms of sense. Thirdly, if objects were such as to require *a priori* categories of substance and cause, they would be limited to phænomenal substances and causes ; but science infers that all particles of matter are substantial bodies, causing and receiving motions, acting and reacting on one another, inert until moved or resisted by one another, and, among countless effects, producing sensible objects in us ; therefore, objects scientifically inferred are not phænomenal substances and causes, and, therefore, substance and cause are not *a priori* categories. In short, objects of scientific inference are not phænomena, and could not be inferred from *a posteriori* sensations converted into objects by *a priori* forms. Critical idealism is a false philosophy, both of the limits and of the origin of knowledge.

The one beacon of the present day is scientific discovery and invention: it was lighted by the principles of the Newtonian philosophy. But though natural philosophy will reveal to us nature, and provide us external goods, it will not alone produce philosophical wisdom or constitute essential happiness. What we want is principles in general philosophy. When such principles have been found, it will be discovered that there was a time when the details of nature were not so well known, but the general relation of God, nature, and man was much better understood than at present. We may laugh at the want of knowledge, but we must never forget the wisdom of the ancients. The stream of human discovery has been like a river, part of which escapes into marshes, while the main channel flows on into the sea: so philosophy, the perennial sources of which are to be found in Greek philosophy and sciences, speculative and practical, has in modern times been partly diverted into the marshes of idealism, while the main stream has expanded into the natural philosophy of Copernicus and Kepler, Bacon and Galileo, Descartes and Newton, and perpetually issues in discoveries and inventions.

Can we bring mental philosophy back into the main stream of discovery? We can, by using the discoveries of natural philosophy as objects of science to discover the data of sense. Idealism has failed because it has used a wrong method, and begun at an unknown beginning. It has taken psychical data of sense for principles, which are really hypotheses, and has used them to dictate the objects of knowledge. As it has found new difficulties, it has feigned new hypotheses, until it has culminated in the absolute idealism of Hegel, who, by heaping hypothesis on hypothesis,—sensible representations, *a priori* categories, one spiritual subject in God and all men, of which nature is a system of objective thoughts—compiled a system of philosophy which is as cumbrous a mass of hypotheses as the Ptolemaic system of astronomy. But the truth is, that, like the old hypothesis of planetary circles round the earth, the modern idealistic hypothesis of a sense of psychical data, whether called ideas or impressions, representations or sensations, is a false beginning, and could never lead to scientific knowledge.

Modern astronomers succeeded by reversing the method of astronomy. They gave up reasoning synthetically from hypotheses of planetary circles to the details of planetary motion, and began with the planetary motions as facts. Copernicus found that the planets move round the sun, and Kepler that they move not in circles but in ellipses: proceeding from these facts, Newton inquired analytically what simple motions were required to explain such elliptical motions : this was the analytical method which ended in Newton's discovery of astronomical principles. In the same way mental philosophy should reverse its method. Instead of reasoning synthetically from hypotheses of sensible data to what objects we can and must know, we should find what we do infer and know in the sciences, and then inquire analytically what sensible data are required to explain our inference and science. In this way, and no other, as Newton by an analysis of elliptical motions discovered the principles of astronomy, so may we by an analysis of the objects of scientific reasoning discover the principles of mental philosophy.

There is one characteristic of objects scientific, which is at once a positive instance to bring us to principles of mental philosophy, and a negative instance to destroy all psychological idealism : it is the insensibility of corpuscles. Corpuscles, insensible and imperceptible substances in time and space, moving according to laws of motion, are physical objects of science, requiring physical data of sense. On the one hand, consider this analytical deduction destructively. In the first place, it follows that these insensible and imperceptible objects of scientific inference are not sensible ideas, not perceptions, not phænomena, nor unknown things. This consequence destroys the idealisms of Berkeley, Hume, and Kant. Secondly, these insensible and imperceptible objects of scientific inference could not be logically inferred from ideas, nor from impressions, nor from sensible representations converted into phænomenal objects by *a priori* forms. This destroys the idealisms I have examined, from Descartes to Kant. Nor could they be inferred from any sense of sensations, however elaborated. This destroys the idealisms of our own day. On the other hand, consider this analytical deduction constructively. These insensible and imperceptible objects of scientific inference require a sense, from which reason may infer them by parity of reasoning. Hence, in the first place, sense is simple and synthetic ; perceiving substantial objects, which are internal but physical, durable, extended, and related to one another, within our nervous systems. Secondly, reason infers similar objects and relations in external nature. There are three types of inference, analogical, inductive and deductive, each mechanically obeying its own laws, and primarily from judgments of synthetic sense inferring judgments about objects insensible and imperceptible. General reasoning, inductive and deductive, used circumstantially, produces a knowledge and science with an approximate always tending to an absolute certainty. After sense and general reasoning, perfect abstraction by attention, mechanically obeying the laws of identity and difference, makes us apprehend a kind of object as simply the same with itself, and frame analytical judgments of what it must be and not be, in the abstract. These analytical judgments are self-evident principles of demonstration, producing exact science, but *a posteriori*. This is a general outline of the analytical philosophy attempted in this essay.

Among many difficulties, which may occur to others, I anticipate three main lines of objection to this essay. In the first place, it may be thought that, whatever value physical realism may have in dealing with nature as an object of scientific knowledge, idealism retains an advantage of its own in its treatment of man as a spiritual subject. On the contrary, against Descartes and all his followers, but from the consilience of consciousness, observation, and reasoning about myself, I contend that man is an organism, partly body and partly soul; who knows of himself, on the one hand, that he is an animal, inhabiting the surface of no very large planet in a considerable solar system, which is only one among countless stellar worlds, in a stupendous immeasurable universe; and, on the other hand, that, infinitesimally little as he is in himself, by sense and reason he is great, in his knowledge and power over nature, which make him like even to God. But, reasonable as is this realistic, but not materialistic, conclusion, the idealists more and more tend to the hypothesis, that man is a purely psychical self, while his own body is not an integral part of himself, as subject, but is one among all other known bodies, which, as objects, are either all alike inferred from, or all alike identical with, his sensations or thoughts in general.

Now, the former of these alternatives leaves out half the man; the latter inverts man and nature; while both idealistic theories of personal identity, by drawing the line of self at spirit, or between soul and body instead of between man and nature, contradict the consilience of consciousness, observation, and reasoning : a combined evidence not to be parted, because man is a complex being, mainly imperceptible to himself, who by night falls asleep and becomes oblivious of his being, by day does not remember his infancy, never can remember nor as yet be conscious of his future career, and, therefore, is not aware of his personal identity throughout life by retentive consciousness alone. Why, then, does modern thought tend towards idealistic spiritualism? Partly from a want of simplicity and a certain vanity of man, who in his rationality would fain forget he is an animal; mainly from a confusion of idealism and spiritualism with Christianity. But we have the best possible authority on the Christian doctrine of man himself: the words of Christ incarnate. 'And He said unto them, why are ye troubled? and wherefore do reasonings arise in your heart? See My hands and My feet, that it is I Myself: handle Me, and see; for a spirit hath not flesh and bones, as ye behold Me having.'[1]

Secondly, it will be doubted whether my general theory can be worked out in detail. I feel the full force of this difficulty. When this essay was mapped out it was to include many more details. Starting from Newton's 'Principia,' I had hoped to include a theory, long cherished, that the properties of time and space, enunciated by him in the 'Scholium to the Definitions,' can only be explained by defining time and space as

---

[1] St. Luke xxiv. 38–39 (Revised Version).

the continuance and continuity of the universe, the former being the continual duration, the latter the continuous extension, of the universe as one substance including many substances, from a star to an atom. From the same starting-point, I hoped to show that a necessary physical cause of motion is any body which displaces or resists any other body, as demonstratively following from the impenetrability of matter, by which two bodies cannot at the same time occupy the same place in space, and that again from the analytical judgment that a body as solid is extended in three dimensions. Moreover, I had hoped to apply the analytical *a posteriori* theory of necessity to geometry by starting from the definition of a solid. I have also written chapters, which are in print, on possible phænomena, and on actual realities, in order to show at length that scientific objects cannot be resolved into the former. These were to be followed by a discussion of ideas, including a criticism of Hegelianism, written but not printed. I have in print chapters on touch and on vision, directed against the doctrines of 'local signs,' further developing the views in my criticism of Berkeley's 'Theory of Vision,' and also based on the argument that a sense of place is necessary to a sense of motion. Finally, I meant to have revived the logic of a method, which appears in Aristotle, but has fallen out of logic. I mean the analytical deduction from effect to cause, which appears to me to be the commonest method of science, because man knows facts before and better than causes. But seeing that all these matters would have made at least another volume, and fearful of becoming tedious, I also felt that I had already claimed as much attention as could be hoped by an untried author.

Thirdly, it will be said that I have exaggerated the power of sense. This is a difficulty I do not feel or allow. The emasculation of sense, which is the most fundamental defect of modern philosophy, is a result of a bygone anatomy. It was formerly thought that the five senses were inlets, passages, or pores through which sensible effects were received within us, according to some, to the heart, according to others, to the head. In these circumstances, it was excusable to suppose that such poverty-stricken organs contributed nothing but isolated data, which the soul worked up within into all sorts of relations. But all that is changed now. It has been discovered that the senses are highly complicated nervous structures ending in the brain, that the brain is an integral organ of sense as well as of reason, and that the whole nervous system has been for countless generations hereditarily modified by its operations, and, on the whole, better adapted to perform more and more complex operations. Since these discoveries, I submit that there is no bar to supposing that so wondrous a sensitive structure, as a brain and a system of sensory nerves has become, is an organ of simple and synthetic sense of objects and relations, internal and physical, as I have suggested. But I do not merely rely on anatomy.

My main trust is in the philosophy of science. Science proves the power of man to know nature. But logic also proves the weakness of mere reason, which, without adequate data of sense, is consistency, not science. Reason cannot logically infer insensible objects and relations in external nature, unless there are sensible objects and relations in our internal nature for sense to perceive. Hence, to provide adequate data for the parity of reasoning, I suppose a simple and synthetic sense of physical objects and relations within the nervous system. I hope, by this means, to have done what I could to physic two diseases of modern idealism —the separation of reason from nature, and the divorce of reason from sense. The real problem of philosophy is not how to form ideas, nor how to escape from them to things; it is not to start with sensations, and ask how much, by association, we can conceive but not know, nor how much, by *a priori* elements, we can know, of mere phænomena. What are the adequate data of sense, and what the logical processes of reasoning, which enable science to infer an insensible and imperceptible world. These are the questions for psychology and logic to ask about sense and reason. 'Itaque,' in the words of Bacon, 'ex harum facultatum, Experimentalis scilicet et Rationalis, arctiore et sanctiore fœdere (quod adhuc factum non est) bene sperandum est.' [1]

----

[1] *Nov. Org.* i. 95.

APPENDIX.

—— ✦ ——

By the critique of the reason Kant understands the examination of the origin, extent, and limits of human knowledge. Pure reason is his name for reason independent of all experience. The 'Critique of the Pure Reason' subjects the pure speculative reason to a critical scrutiny. Kant holds that this scrutiny must precede all other philosophical procedures. Kant terms every philosophy, which transcends the sphere of experience without having previously justified this act by an examination of the faculty of knowledge, a form of 'Dogmatism'; the philosophical limitation of knowledge to experience he calls 'Empiricism'; philosophical doubt as to all knowledge transcending experience, in so far as this doubt is grounded on the insufficiency of all existing attempts at demonstration, and not on an examination of the human faculty of knowledge in general, is termed by him 'Skepticism,' and his own philosophy, which makes all further philosophising dependent on the result of such an examination, 'Criticism.' Criticism is 'transcendental philosophy' or 'transcendental idealism' in so far as it inquires into and then denies the possibility of a transcendent knowledge, *i.e.* of knowledge respecting what lies beyond the range of experience.

Kant sets out in his critique of the reason with a twofold division of judgments (in particular, of categorical judgments). With reference to the relation of the predicate to the subject, he divides them into analytical or elucidating judgments—where the predicate can be found in the conception of the subject by simple analysis of the latter or is identical with it (in which latter case the analytical judgment is an identical one)—and synthetic or amplifi-

[1] Ueberweg's *Hist. of Phil.* (English Trans.), vol. ii. pp. 154–58 (§ 122).

cative judgments—where the predicate is not contained in the
concept of the subject, but is added to it. The principle of analytical judgments is the principle of identity and contradiction ; a
synthetic judgment, on the contrary, cannot be formed from the
conception of its subject on the basis of this principle alone. Kant
further discriminates, with reference to their origin as parts of
human knowledge, between judgments *a priori* and judgments *a
posteriori* ; by the latter he understands judgments of experience,
but by judgments *a priori*, in the absolute sense, those which
are completely independent of all experience, and in the relative sense,
those which are based indirectly on experience, or in which the conceptions employed, though not derived immediately from experience, are
deduced from others that were so derived. As absolute judgments
a priori Kant regards all those which have the marks of necessity
and strict universality, assuming (what he does not prove, but
simply posits as self-evident, although his whole system depends
upon it) that necessity and strict universality are derivable from
no combination of experiences, but only independently of all experience. All analytical judgments are judgments *a priori* ; for
although the subject-conception may have been obtained through
experience, yet to its analysis, from which the judgment results, no
further experience is necessary. Synthetic judgments, on the contrary, fall into two classes. If the synthesis of the predicate with
the subject is effected by the aid of experience, the judgment is
synthetic *a posteriori* ; if it is effected apart from all experience, it
is synthetic *a priori*. Kant holds the existence of judgments of
the latter class to be undeniable ; for among the judgments which
are recognised as strictly universal and apodictical, and which are
consequently, according to Kant's assumption, judgments *a priori*,
he finds judgments which must at the same time be admitted to be
synthetic. Among these belong, first of all, most mathematical
judgments. Some of the fundamental judgments of arithmetic
(*e.g.* a=a) are, indeed, according to Kant, of an analytical nature ;
but the rest of them, together with all geometrical judgments, are,
in his view, synthetic, and, since they have the marks of strict
universality and necessity, are synthetic judgments *a priori*. The
same character pertains, according to Kant, to the most general
propositions of physics, such as, for example, that in all the changes
of the material world the quantity of matter remains unchanged.
These propositions are known to be true apart from all experience,
since they are universal and apodictical judgments ; and yet they
are not obtained through a mere analysis of the conceptions of their
subjects, for the predicate adds something to those conceptions. In

like manner, finally, are all metaphysical principles, at least in their tendency, synthetic judgments *a priori*, *e.g.* the principle, that every event must have a cause. And if the principles of metaphysics are not altogether incontrovertible, yet those of mathematics at least are established beyond all dispute. There exist, therefore, concludes Kant, synthetic judgments *a priori* or judgments of the pure reason. The fundamental question of his Critique becomes, then : How are synthetic judgments *a priori* possible ?

The answer given is : Synthetic judgments *a priori* are possible, because man brings to the material of knowledge, which he acquires empirically in virtue of his receptivity, certain pure forms of knowledge, which he himself creates in virtue of his spontaneity and independently of all experience, and into which he fits all given material. These forms, which are the conditions of the possibility of all experience, are at the same time the conditions of the possibility of the objects of experience, because whatever is to be an object for me, must take on the forms through which the *Ego*, my original consciousness, or the 'transcendental unity of apperception,' shapes all that is presented to it ; they have, therefore, objective validity in a synthetic judgment *a priori*. But the objects, with reference to which they possess this validity, are not the things-in-themselves or transcendental objects, *i.e.* objects as they are in themselves, apart from our mode of conceiving them ; they are only the empirical objects or the phænomena which exist in our consciousness in the form of mental representations. The things-in-themselves are unknowable for man. Only a creative, divine mind, that gives them reality at the same time that it thinks them, can have power truly to know them. Things-in-themselves do not conform themselves to the forms of human knowledge, because the human consciousness is not creative, because human perception is not free from subjective elements, is not 'intellectual intuition.' Nor do the forms of human knowledge conform themselves to things-in-themselves ; otherwise all our knowledge would be empirical and without necessity and strict universality. But all empirical objects, since they are only representations in our minds, do conform themselves to the forms of human knowledge. Hence we can know empirical objects or phænomena, but only these. All valid *a priori* knowledge has respect only to phænomena, hence to objects of real or possible experience.

The forms of knowledge are forms either of intuition or of thought. The 'Transcendental Æsthetic' treats of the former, the 'Transcendental Logic' of the latter.

The forms of intuition are space and time. Space is the form of external sensibility, time is the form of internal and indirectly of external sensibility. On the *a priori* nature of space depends the possibility of geometrical and on the *a priori* nature of time depends the possibility of arithmetical judgments. Things-in-themselves or transcendental objects are related neither to space nor to time ; all co-existence and succession are only in phænomenal objects, and consequently only in the perceiving Subject.

The forms of thought are the twelve categories or original conceptions of the understanding, on which all the forms of our judgments are conditioned. They are : unity, plurality, totality,—reality, negation, limitation,—substantiality, causality, reciprocal action,—possibility, existence, necessity. On their *a priori* nature depends the validity of the most general judgments, which lie at the foundation of all empirical knowledge. The things-in-themselves or transcendental objects have neither unity nor plurality ; they are not substances, nor are they subject to the causal relation, or to any of the categories ; the categories are applicable only to the phænomenal objects which are in our consciousness.

The reason strives to rise above and beyond the sphere of the understanding, which is confined to the finite and conditioned, to the unconditioned. It forms the idea of the soul, as a substance which ever endures ; of the world, as an unlimited causal series ; and of God, as the absolute substance and union of all perfections, or as the 'most perfect being.' Since these ideas relate to objects which lie beyond the range of all possible experience, they have no theoretic validity ; if the latter is claimed for them (in dogmatic metaphysics) this is simply the result of a misleading logic founded on appearances, or of dialectic. The psychological paralogism confounds the unity of the I—which can never be conceived as a predicate, but only and always as a subject—with the simplicity and absolute permanence of a psychical substance. Cosmology leads to antinomies, whose mutually contradictory members are each equally susceptible of indirect demonstration, if the reality of space, time and the categories be presupposed, but which with the refutation of this supposition cease to exist. Rational theology, in seeking by the ontological, cosmological, and physico-theological arguments to prove the existence of God, becomes involved in a series of sophistications. Still these ideas of the reason are in two respects of value : (1) theoretically, when viewed not as constitutive principles through which a real knowledge of things-in-themselves can be obtained, but as regulative principles, which affirm that, however far empirical investigation may at any time have advanced, the sphere of objects of possible experience can never be regarded as fully exhausted, but that there will always be room for further investigation ; (2) practically, in so far as they render conceivable suppositions, to which the practical reason conducts with moral necessity.

In the 'Metaphysical Principles of Physics,' Kant seeks, by reducing matter to forces, to justify a dynamical explanation of nature.

PRINTED BY
SPOTTISWOODE AND CO., NEW-STREET SQUARE
LONDON

Catalogue of Books

PUBLISHED BY

MESSRS. LONGMANS, GREEN, & CO.

39 PATERNOSTER ROW, LONDON, E.C.

Abbey.—*THE ENGLISH CHURCH AND ITS BISHOPS*, 1700–1800. By CHARLES J. ABBEY, Rector of Checkendon. 2 vols. 8vo. 24s.

Abbey and Overton.—*THE ENGLISH CHURCH IN THE 'EIGHTEENTH CENTURY.* By CHARLES J. ABBEY, Rector of Checkendon, and JOHN H. OVERTON, Rector of Epworth and Canon of Lincoln. Crown 8vo. 7s. 6d.

Abbott.—*THE ELEMENTS OF LOGIC.* By T. K. ABBOTT, B.D. 12mo. 3s.

Acton. — *MODERN COOKERY FOR PRIVATE FAMILIES.* By ELIZA ACTON. With 150 Woodcuts. Fcp. 8vo. 4s. 6d.

Adams.—*PUBLIC DEBTS:* an Essay on the Science of Finance. By HENRY C. ADAMS, Ph.D. 8vo. 12s. 6d.

A. K. H. B.—*THE ESSAYS AND CON-TRIBUTIONS OF A. K. H. B.*—Uniform Cabinet Editions in crown 8vo.
Autumn Holidays of a Country Parson, 3s. 6d.
Changed Aspects of Unchanged Truths, 3s. 6d.
Commonplace Philosopher, 3s. 6d.
Counsel and Comfort from a City Pulpit, 3s. 6d.
Critical Essays of a Country Parson, 3s. 6d.
Graver Thoughts of a Country Parson. Three Series, 3s. 6d. each.
Landscapes, Churches, and Moralities, 3s. 6d.
Leisure Hours in Town, 3s. 6d.
Lessons of Middle Age, 3s. 6d.
Our Little Life. Two Series, 3s. 6d. each.
Our Homely Comedy and Tragedy, 3s. 6d.
Present Day Thoughts, 3s. 6d.
Recreations of a Country Parson. Three Series, 3s. 6d. each.
Seaside Musings, 3s. 6d.
Sunday Afternoons in the Parish Church of a Scottish University City, 3s. 6d.

Amos.—*WORKS BY SHELDON AMOS.*
A PRIMER OF THE ENGLISH CON-STITUTION AND GOVERNMENT. Crown 8vo.
A SYSTEMATIC VIEW OF THE SCIENCE OF JURISPRUDENCE. 8vo. 18s.

Aristotle.—*THE WORKS OF.*
THE POLITICS, G. Bekker's Greek Text of Books I. III. IV. (VII.) with an English Translation by W. E. BOLLAND, M.A.; and short Introductory Essays by A. LANG, M.A. Crown 8vo. 7s. 6d.

THE POLITICS: Introductory Essays. By ANDREW LANG. (From Bolland and Lang's 'Politics.') Crown 8vo. 2s. 6d.

THE ETHICS; Greek Text, illustrated with Essays and Notes. By Sir ALEXANDER GRANT, Bart. M.A. LL.D. 2 vols. 8vo. 32s.

THE NICOMACHEAN ETHICS, Newly Translated into English. By ROBERT WILLIAMS, Barrister-at-Law. Crown 8vo. 7s. 6d.

Armstrong.— *WORKS BY GEORGE FRANCIS ARMSTRONG, M.A.*
POEMS: Lyrical and Dramatic. Fcp. 8vo. 6s.
KING SAUL. (The Tragedy of Israel, Part I.) Fcp. 8vo. 5s.
KING DAVID. (The Tragedy of Israel, Part II.) Fcp. 8vo. 6s.
KING SOLOMON. (The Tragedy of Israel, Part III.) Fcp. 8vo. 6s.
UGONE: A Tragedy. Fcp. 8vo. 6s.
A GARLAND FROM GREECE; Poems. Fcp. 8vo. 9s.
STORIES OF WICKLOW; Poems. Fcp. 8vo. 9s.
VICTORIA REGINA ET IMPERATRIX: a Jubilee Song from Ireland, 1887. 4to. 5s. cloth gilt.
THE LIFE AND LETTERS OF EDMUND J. ARMSTRONG. Fcp. 8vo. 7s. 6d.

Armstrong.— *WORKS BY EDMUND J. ARMSTRONG.*
POETICAL WORKS. Fcp. 8vo. 5s.
ESSAYS AND SKETCHES. Fcp. 8vo. 5s.

A

Arnold. — *Works by Thomas Arnold, D.D. Late Head master of Rugby School.*

Introductory Lectures on Modern History, delivered in 1841 and 1842. 8vo. 7s. 6d.

Sermons Preached mostly in the Chapel of Rugby School. 6 vols. crown 8vo. 30s. or separately, 5s. each.

Miscellaneous Works. 8vo. 7s. 6d.

Arnold.—*A Manual of English Literature,* Historical and Critical. By Thomas Arnold, M.A. Crown 8vo. 7s. 6d.

Arnott.—*The Elements of Physics or Natural Philosophy.* By Neil Arnott, M.D. Edited by A. Bain, LL.D. and A. S. Taylor, M.D. F.R.S. Woodcuts. Crown 8vo. 12s. 6d.

Ashby. — *Notes on Physiology for the Use of Students Preparing for Examination.* With 120 Woodcuts. By Henry Ashby, M.D. Lond. Fcp. 8vo. 5s.

Atelier (The) du Lys; or, an Art Student in the Reign of Terror. By the Author of ' Mademoiselle Mori.' Crown 8vo. 2s. 6d.

Bacon.—*The Works and Life of.*

Complete Works. Edited by R. L. Ellis, M.A. J. Spedding, M.A. and D. D. Heath. 7 vols. 8vo. £3. 13s. 6d.

Letters and Life, including all his Occasional Works. Edited by J. Spedding. 7 vols. 8vo. £4. 4s.

The Essays ; with Annotations. By Richard Whately, D.D., 8vo. 10s. 6d.

The Essays; with Introduction, Notes, and Index. By E. A. Abbott, D.D. 2 vols. fcp. 8vo. price 6s. Text and Index only, without Introduction and Notes, in 1 vol. fcp. 8vo. 2s. 6d.

Bagehot. — *Works by Walter Bagehot, M.A.*

Biographical Studies. 8vo. 12s.

Economic Studies. 8vo. 10s. 6d.

Literary Studies. 2 vols. 8vo. 28s.

The Postulates of English Political Economy. Crown 8vo. 2s. 6d.

The BADMINTON LIBRARY, edited by the Duke of Beaufort, K.G. assisted by Alfred E. T. Watson.

Hunting. By the Duke of Beaufort, K.G. and Mowbray Morris. With Contributions by the Earl of Suffolk and Berkshire, Rev. E. W. L. Davies, Digby Collins, and Alfred E. T. Watson. With Coloured Frontispiece and 53 Illustrations by J. Sturgess, J. Charlton, and Agnes M. Biddulph, Crown 8vo. 10s. 6d.

Fishing. By H. Cholmondeley-Pennell. With Contributions by the Marquis of Exeter, Henry R. Francis, M.A., Major John P. Traherne, G. Christopher Davies, R. B. Marston, &c.

Vol. I. Salmon, Trout, and Grayling. With 150 Illustrations. Cr. 8vo. 10s. 6d.

Vol. II. Pike and other Coarse Fish. With 58 Illustrations. Cr. 8vo. 10s. 6d.

Racing and Steeplechasing. By the Earl of Suffolk and Berkshire, W. G. Craven, The Hon. F. Lawley, A. Coventry, and A. E. T. Watson. With Coloured Frontispiece and 56 Illustrations by J. Sturgess. Cr. 8vo. 10s. 6d.

Shooting. By Lord Walsingham and Sir Ralph Payne-Gallwey, Bart. with Contributions by Lord Lovat, Lord Charles Lennox Kerr, The Hon. G. Lascelles, and Archibald Stuart Wortley. With 21 full-page Illustrations and 149 Woodcuts by A. J. Stuart-Wortley, C. Whymper, J. G. Millais, &c.

Vol. I. Field and Covert. Cr. 8vo. 10s. 6d.

Vol. II. Moor and Marsh. Cr. 8vo. 10s. 6d.

Cycling. By Viscount Bury, K.C.M.G. and G. Lacy Hillier. With 19 Plates and 61 Woodcuts by Viscount Bury and Joseph Pennell. Cr. 8vo. 10s. 6d.

Athletics and Football. By Montague Shearman. With Introduction by Sir Richard Webster, Q.C. M.P. With 6 full-page Illustrations and 45 Woodcuts from Drawings by Stanley Berkeley, and from Instantaneous Photographs by G. Mitchell. Cr. 8vo. 10s. 6d.

*** Other volumes in preparation.

Bagwell. — *Ireland under the Tudors,* with a Succinct Account of the Earlier History. By Richard Bagwell, M.A. Vols. I. and II. From the first invasion of the Northmen to the year 1578. 2 vols. 8vo. 32s.

Bain. — *WORKS BY ALEXANDER BAIN, LL.D.*

MENTAL AND MORAL SCIENCE; a Compendium of Psychology and Ethics. Crown 8vo. 10s. 6d.

THE SENSES AND THE INTELLECT. 8vo. 15s.

THE EMOTIONS AND THE WILL. 8vo. 15s.

PRACTICAL ESSAYS. Cr. 8vo. 4s. 6d.

LOGIC, DEDUCTIVE AND INDUCTIVE. PART I. *Deduction,* 4s. PART II. *Induction,* 6s. 6d.

JAMES MILL; a Biography. Cr. 8vo. 2s.

JOHN STUART MILL; a Criticism, with Personal Recollections. Cr. 8vo. 1s.

Baker. — *WORKS BY SIR SAMUEL W. BAKER, M.A.*

EIGHT YEARS IN CEYLON. Crown 8vo. Woodcuts. 5s.

THE RIFLE AND THE HOUND IN CEYLON. Crown 8vo. Woodcuts. 5s.

Bale. — *A HANDBOOK FOR STEAM USERS;* being Notes on Steam Engine and Boiler Management and Steam Boiler Explosions. By M. POWIS BALE, M.I.M.E. A.M.I.C.E. Fcp. 8vo. 2s. 6d.

Ball. — *THE REFORMED CHURCH OF IRELAND* (1537–1886). By the Right Hon. J. T. BALL, LL.D. D.C.L. 8vo. 7s. 6d.

Barker. — *A SHORT MANUAL OF SURGICAL OPERATIONS,* having Special Reference to many of the Newer Procedures. By A. E. J. BARKER, F.R.C.S. Surgeon to University College Hospital. With 61 Woodcuts. Crown 8vo. 12s. 6d.

Barrett. — *ENGLISH GLEES AND PART-SONGS.* An Inquiry into their Historical Development. By WILLIAM ALEXANDER BARRETT. 8vo. 7s. 6d.

Beaconsfield. — *WORKS BY THE EARL OF BEACONSFIELD, K.G.*

NOVELS AND TALES. The Hughenden Edition. With 2 Portraits and 11 Vignettes. 11 vols. Crown 8vo. 42s.

Endymion.
Lothair.   Henrietta Temple.
Coningsby.   Contarini Fleming, &c.
Sybil.   Alroy, Ixion, &c.
Tancred   The Young Duke, &c.
Venetia.   Vivian Grey.

NOVELS AND TALES. Cheap Edition, complete in 11 vols. Crown 8vo. 1s. each; boards; 1s. 6d. each, cloth.

THE WIT AND WISDOM OF THE EARL OF BEACONSFIELD. Crown 8vo. 1s. boards, 1s. 6d. cloth.

Becker. — *WORKS BY PROFESSOR BECKER, translated from the German by the Rev. F. METCALF.*

GALLUS; or, Roman Scenes in the Time of Augustus. Post 8vo. 7s. 6d.

CHARICLES; or, Illustrations of the Private Life of the Ancient Greeks. Post 8vo. 7s. 6d.

Bentley. — *A TEXT-BOOK OF ORGANIC MATERIA MEDICA.* Comprising a Description of the VEGETABLE and ANIMAL DRUGS of the BRITISH PHARMACOPŒIA, with some others in common use. Arranged Systematically and especially Designed for Students. By ROBT. BENTLEY, M.R.C.S. Eng. F.L.S. With 62 Illustrations. Crown 8vo. 7s. 6d.

Boultbee. — *A COMMENTARY ON THE* 39 *ARTICLES* of the Church of England. By the Rev. T. P. BOULTBEE, LL.D. Crown 8vo. 6s.

Bourne. — *WORKS BY JOHN BOURNE, C.E.*

CATECHISM OF THE STEAM ENGINE in its various Applications in the Arts, to which is now added a chapter on Air and Gas Engines, and another devoted to Useful Rules, Tables, and Memoranda. Illustrated by 212 Woodcuts. Crown 8vo. 7s. 6d.

HANDBOOK OF THE STEAM ENGINE; a Key to the Author's Catechism of the Steam Engine. With 67 Woodcuts. Fcp. 8vo. 9s.

RECENT IMPROVEMENTS IN THE STEAM ENGINE. With 124 Woodcuts. Fcp. 8vo. 6s.

Bowen. — *HARROW SONGS AND OTHER VERSES.* By EDWARD E. BOWEN. Fcp. 8vo. 2s. 6d.; or printed on hand-made paper, 5s.

Brassey. — *WORKS BY LADY BRASSEY.*

A VOYAGE IN THE 'SUNBEAM,' OUR HOME ON THE OCEAN FOR ELEVEN MONTHS.

Library Edition. With 8 Maps and Charts, and 118 Illustrations, 8vo. 21s.

Cabinet Edition. With Map and 66 Illustrations, crown 8vo. 7s. 6d.

School Edition. With 37 Illustrations, fcp. 2s. cloth, or 3s. white parchment with gilt edges.

Popular Edition. With 60 Illustrations, 4to. 6d. sewed, 1s. cloth.

[Continued on next page.

Brassey. — *WORKS BY LADY BRASSEY—continued.*

SUNSHINE AND STORM IN THE EAST.
Library Edition. With 2 Maps and 114 Illustrations, 8vo. 21s.
Cabinet Edition. With 2 Maps and 114 Illustrations, crown 8vo. 7s. 6d.
Popular Edition. With 103 Illustrations, 4to. 6d. sewed, 1s. cloth.

IN THE TRADES, THE TROPICS, AND THE 'ROARING FORTIES.'
Cabinet Edition. With Map and 220 Illustrations, crown 8vo. 7s. 6d.
Popular Edition. With 183 Illustrations, 4to. 6d. sewed, 1s. cloth.

THREE VOYAGES IN THE 'SUNBEAM.'
Popular Edition. With 346 Illustrations, 4to. 2s. 6d.

Browne. — *AN EXPOSITION OF THE 39 ARTICLES,* Historical and Doctrinal. By E. H. BROWNE, D.D., Bishop of Winchester. 8vo. 16s.

Bryant. — *EDUCATIONAL ENDS;* or, the Ideal of Personal Development. By SOPHIE BRYANT, D.Sc.Lond. Crown 8vo. 6s.

Buckle. — *WORKS BY HENRY THOMAS BUCKLE.*

HISTORY OF CIVILISATION IN ENGLAND AND FRANCE, SPAIN AND SCOTLAND. 3 vols. crown 8vo. 24s.

MISCELLANEOUS AND POSTHUMOUS WORKS. A New and Abridged Edition. Edited by GRANT ALLEN. 2 vols. crown 8vo. 21s.

Buckton. — *WORKS BY MRS. C. M. BUCKTON.*

FOOD AND HOME COOKERY. With 11 Woodcuts. Crown 8vo. 2s. 6d.

HEALTH IN THE HOUSE. With 41 Woodcuts and Diagrams. Crown 8vo. 2s.

OUR DWELLINGS. With 39 Illustrations. Crown 8vo. 3s. 6d.

Bull. — *WORKS BY THOMAS BULL, M.D.*

HINTS TO MOTHERS ON THE MANAGEMENT OF THEIR HEALTH during the Period of Pregnancy and in the Lying-in Room. Fcp. 8vo. 1s. 6d.

THE MATERNAL MANAGEMENT OF CHILDREN IN HEALTH AND DISEASE. Fcp. 8vo. 1s. 6d.

Bullinger. — *A CRITICAL LEXICON AND CONCORDANCE TO THE ENGLISH AND GREEK NEW TESTAMENT.* Together with an Index of Greek Words and several Appendices. By the Rev. E. W. BULLINGER, D.D. Royal 8vo. 15s.

Burrows. — *THE FAMILY OF BROCAS OF BEAUREPAIRE AND ROCHE COURT,* Hereditary Masters of the Royal Buckhounds. With some account of the English Rule in Aquitaine. By MONTAGU BURROWS, M.A. F.S.A. With 26 Illustrations of Monuments, Brasses, Seals, &c. Royal 8vo. 42s.

Cabinet Lawyer, The; a Popular Digest of the Laws of England, Civil, Criminal, and Constitutional. Fcp. 8vo. 9s.

Canning. — *SOME OFFICIAL CORRESPONDENCE OF GEORGE CANNING.* Edited, with Notes, by EDWARD J. STAPLETON. 2 vols. 8vo. 28s.

Carlyle. — *THOMAS AND JANE WELSH CARLYLE.*

THOMAS CARLYLE, a History of the first Forty Years of his Life, 1795-1835. By J. A. FROUDE, M.A. With 2 Portraits and 4 Illustrations, 2 vols. 8vo. 32s.

THOMAS CARLYLE, a History of his Life in London : from 1834 to his death in 1881. By J. A. FROUDE, M.A. 2 vols. 8vo. 32s.

LETTERS AND MEMORIALS OF JANE WELSH CARLYLE. Prepared for publication by THOMAS CARLYLE, and edited by J. A. FROUDE, M.A. 3 vols. 8vo. 36s.

Cates. — *A DICTIONARY OF GENERAL BIOGRAPHY.* Fourth Edition, with Supplement brought down to the end of 1884. By W. L. R. CATES. 8vo. 28s. cloth ; 35s. half-bound russia.

Clerk. — *THE GAS ENGINE.* By DUGALD CLERK. With 101 Illustrations and Diagrams. Crown 8vo. 7s. 6d.

Clodd. — *THE STORY OF CREATION:* a Plain Account of Evolution. By EDWARD CLODD, Author of 'The Childhood of the World' &c. With 77 Illustrations. Crown 8vo. 6s.

Coats. — *A MANUAL OF PATHOLOGY.* By JOSEPH COATS, M.D. Pathologist to the Western Infirmary and the Sick Children's Hospital, Glasgow. With 339 Illustrations engraved on Wood. 8vo. 31s. 6d.

Colenso.—*THE PENTATEUCH AND BOOK OF JOSHUA CRITICALLY EXAMINED.* By J. W. COLENSO, D.D. late Bishop of Natal. Crown 8vo. 6s.

Comyn.—*ATHERSTONE PRIORY:* a Tale. By L. N. COMYN. Crown 8vo. 2s. 6d.

Conder. — *A HANDBOOK TO THE BIBLE*, or Guide to the Study of the Holy Scriptures derived from Ancient Monuments and Modern Exploration. By F. R. CONDER, and Lieut. C. R. CONDER, R.E. Post 8vo. 7s. 6d.

Conington. — *WORKS BY JOHN CONINGTON, M.A.*

THE ÆNEID OF VIRGIL. Translated into English Verse. Crown 8vo. 9s.

THE POEMS OF VIRGIL. Translated into English Prose. Crown 8vo. 9s.

Conybeare & Howson. — *THE LIFE AND EPISTLES OF ST. PAUL.* By the Rev. W. J. CONYBEARE, M.A. and the Very Rev. J. S. HOWSON, D.D.

Library Edition, with Maps, Plates, and Woodcuts. 2 vols. square crown 8vo. 21s.

Student's Edition, revised and condensed, with 46 Illustrations and Maps. 1 vol. crown 8vo. 7s. 6d.

Cooke. — *TABLETS OF ANATOMY.* By THOMAS COOKE, F.R.C.S. Eng. B.A. B.Sc. M.D. Paris. Fourth Edition, being a selection of the Tablets believed to be most useful to Students generally. Post 4to. 7s. 6d.

Cox. — *THE FIRST CENTURY OF CHRISTIANITY.* By HOMERSHAM COX, M.A. 8vo. 12s.

Cox.—*A GENERAL HISTORY OF GREECE:* from the Earliest Period to the Death of Alexander the Great; with a Sketch of the History to the Present Time. By the Rev. Sir G. W. Cox, Bart., M.A. With 11 Maps and Plans. Crown 8vo. 7s. 6d.

*** For other Works by Sir G. Cox, *see* 'Epochs of History,' p. 24.

Creighton. — *HISTORY OF THE PAPACY DURING THE REFORMATION.* By the Rev. M. CREIGHTON, M.A. 8vo. Vols. I. and II. 1378-1464, 32s.; Vols. III. and IV. 1464-1518, 24s.

Crookes. — *SELECT METHODS IN CHEMICAL ANALYSIS* (chiefly Inorganic). By WILLIAM CROOKES, F.R.S. V.P.C.S. With 37 Illustrations. 8vo. 24s.

Crozier.—*CIVILIZATION AND PROGRESS.* By JOHN BEATTIE CROZIER. New and Cheaper Edition. 8vo. 5s.

Crump.—*A SHORT ENQUIRY INTO THE FORMATION OF POLITICAL OPINION,* from the Reign of the Great Families to the Advent of Democracy. By ARTHUR CRUMP. 8vo. 7s. 6d.

Culley.—*HANDBOOK OF PRACTICAL TELEGRAPHY.* By R. S. CULLEY, M. Inst. C.E. Plates and Woodcuts. 8vo. 16s.

Dante.—*THE DIVINE COMEDY OF DANTE ALIGHIERI.* Translated verse for verse from the Original into Terza Rima. By JAMES INNES MINCHIN. Crown 8vo. 15s.

Davidson.—*AN INTRODUCTION TO THE STUDY OF THE NEW TESTAMENT,* Critical, Exegetical, and Theological. By the Rev. S. DAVIDSON, D.D. LL.D. Revised Edition. 2 vols. 8vo. 30s.

Davidson.—*WORKS BY WILLIAM L. DAVIDSON, M.A.*

THE LOGIC OF DEFINITION EXPLAINED AND APPLIED. Crown 8vo. 6s.

LEADING AND IMPORTANT ENGLISH WORDS EXPLAINED AND EXEMPLIFIED. Fcp. 8vo. 3s. 6d.

Decaisne & Le Maout. — *A GENERAL SYSTEM OF BOTANY.* Translated from the French of E. LE MAOUT, M.D., and J. DECAISNE, by Mrs. HOOKER; with Additions by Sir J. D. HOOKER, C.B. F.R.S. Imp. 8vo. with 5,500 Woodcuts, 31s. 6d.

De Salis. — *WORKS BY MRS. DE SALIS.*

SAVOURIES À LA MODE. Fcp. 8vo. 1s. boards.

ENTRÉES À LA MODE. Fcp. 8vo. 1s. 6d. boards.

SOUPS AND DRESSED FISH À LA MODE. Fcp. 8vo. 1s. 6d. boards.

OYSTERS À LA MODE. Fcp. 8vo. 1s. 6d. boards.

SWEETS AND SUPPER DISHES À LA MODE. Fcp. 8vo. 1s. 6d. boards.

De Tocqueville.—*DEMOCRACY IN AMERICA.* By ALEXIS DE TOCQUEVILLE. Translated by HENRY REEVE, C.B. 2 vols. crown 8vo. 16s.

Dickinson. — *ON RENAL AND URINARY AFFECTIONS.* By W. HOWSHIP DICKINSON, M.D. Cantab. F.R.C.P. &c. With 12 Plates and 122 Woodcuts. 3 vols. 8vo. £3. 4s. 6d.

Dixon.—*RURAL BIRD LIFE;* Essays on Ornithology, with Instructions for Preserving Objects relating to that Science. By CHARLES DIXON. With 45 Woodcuts. Crown 8vo. 5s.

Dove.—*DOMESDAY STUDIES:* being the Papers read at the Meetings of the Domesday Commemoration 1886. With a Bibliography of Domesday Book and Accounts of the MSS. and Printed Books exhibited at the Public Record Office and at the British Museum. Edited by P. EDWARD DOVE, of Lincoln's Inn, Barrister-at-Law, Honorary Secretary of the Domesday Commemoration Committee. Vol. I. 4to. 18s.; Vol. II. 4to. 18s.

Dowell.—*A HISTORY OF TAXATION AND TAXES IN ENGLAND FROM THE EARLIEST TIMES TO THE YEAR 1885.* By STEPHEN DOWELL, Assistant Solicitor of Inland Revenue. Second Edition, Revised and Altered. (4 vols. 8vo.) Vols. I. and II. The History of Taxation, 21s. Vols. III. and IV. The History of Taxes, 21s.

Doyle.—*THE OFFICIAL BARONAGE OF ENGLAND.* By JAMES E. DOYLE. Showing the Succession, Dignities, and Offices of every Peer from 1066 to 1885. Vols. I. to III. With 1,600 Portraits, Shields of Arms, Autographs, &c. 3 vols. 4to. £5. 5s.

Large-paper Edition, 3 vols. £15. 15s.

Doyle.—*WORKS BY J. A. DOYLE,* Fellow of All Souls College, Oxford.

THE ENGLISH IN AMERICA: VIRGINIA, MARYLAND, AND THE CAROLINAS. 8vo. 18s.

THE ENGLISH IN AMERICA: THE PURITAN COLONIES. 2 vols. 8vo. 36s.

Dublin University Press Series (The): a Series of Works undertaken by the Provost and Senior Fellows of Trinity College, Dublin.

Abbott's (T. K.) Codex Rescriptus Dublinensis of St. Matthew. 4to. 21s.

——————— Evangeliorum Versio Antehieronymiana ex Codice Usseriano (Dublinensi). 2 vols. crown 8vo. 21s.

Burnside (W. S.) and Panton's (A. W.) Theory of Equations. 8vo. 12s. 6d.

Casey's (John) Sequel to Euclid's Elements. Crown 8vo. 3s. 6d.

——————— Analytical Geometry of the Conic Sections. Crown 8vo. 7s. 6d.

Davies's (J. F.) Eumenides of Æschylus. With Metrical English Translation. 8vo. 7s.

Dublin Translations into Greek and Latin Verse. Edited by R. Y. Tyrrell. 8vo. 12s. 6d.

Graves's (R. P.) Life of Sir William Hamilton. (3 vols.) Vols. I. and II. 8vo. each 15s.

Griffin (R. W.) on Parabola, Ellipse, and Hyperbola, treated Geometrically. Crown 8vo. 6s.

Haughton's (Dr. S.) Lectures on Physical Geography. 8vo. 15s.

Hobart's (W. K.) Medical Language of St. Luke. 8vo. 16s.

Leslie's (T. E. Cliffe) Essays in Political and Moral Philosophy. 8vo. 10s. 6d.

Macalister's (A.) Zoology and Morphology of Vertebrata. 8vo. 10s. 6d.

MacCullagh's (James) Mathematical and other Tracts. 8vo. 15s.

Maguire's (T.) Parmenides of Plato, Greek Text with English Introduction, Analysis, and Notes. 8vo. 7s. 6d.

Monck's (W. H. S.) Introduction to Logic. Crown 8vo. 5s.

Purser's (J. M.) Manual of Histology. Fcp. 8vo. 5s.

Roberts's (R. A.) Examples in the Analytic Geometry of Plane Curves. Fcp. 8vo. 5s.

Southey's (R.) Correspondence with Caroline Bowles. Edited by E. Dowden. 8vo. 14s.

Thornhill's (W. J.) The Æneid of Virgil, freely translated into English Blank Verse. Crown 8vo. 7s. 6d.

Tyrrell's (R. Y.) Cicero's Correspondence. Vols. I. and II. 8vo. each 12s.

————————— The Acharnians of Aristophanes, translated into English Verse. Crown 8vo. 2s. 6d.

Webb's (T. E.) Goethe's Faust, Translation and Notes. 8vo. 12s. 6d.

————————, The Veil of Isis: a Series of Essays on Idealism. 8vo. 10s. 6d.

Wilkins's (G.) The Growth of the Homeric Poems. 8vo. 6s.

Edersheim.—*WORKS BY THE REV. ALFRED EDERSHEIM, D.D.*

THE LIFE AND TIMES OF JESUS THE MESSIAH. 2 vols. 8vo. 24s.

PROPHECY AND HISTORY IN RELATION TO THE MESSIAH: the Warburton Lectures, delivered at Lincoln's Inn Chapel, 1880-1884. 8vo. 12s.

Ellicott. — *WORKS BY C. J. ELLICOTT, D.D.* Bishop of Gloucester and Bristol.

A CRITICAL AND GRAMMATICAL COMMENTARY ON ST. PAUL'S EPISTLES. 8vo.

I. CORINTHIANS. 16s.
GALATIANS. 8s. 6d.
EPHESIANS. 8s. 6d.
PASTORAL EPISTLES. 10s. 6d.
PHILIPPIANS, COLOSSIANS, and PHILEMON. 10s. 6d.
THESSALONIANS. 7s. 6d.

HISTORICAL LECTURES ON THE LIFE OF OUR LORD JESUS CHRIST. 8vo. 12s.

English Worthies. Edited by ANDREW LANG, M.A. Fcp. 8vo. 2s. 6d. each.

DARWIN. By GRANT ALLEN.
MARLBOROUGH. By G. SAINTSBURY.
SHAFTESBURY (The First Earl). By H. D. TRAILL.
ADMIRAL BLAKE. By DAVID HANNAY.
RALEIGH. By EDMUND GOSSE.
STEELE. By AUSTIN DOBSON.
BEN JONSON. By J. A. SYMONDS.
CANNING. By FRANK H. HILL.
CLAVERHOUSE. By MOWBRAY MORRIS.

Epochs of Ancient History. 10 vols. fcp. 8vo. 2s. 6d. each. *See* p. 24.

Epochs of Church History. 8 vols. fcp. 8vo. 2s. 6d. each. *See* p. 24.

Epochs of Modern History. 18 vols. fcp. 8vo. 2s. 6d. each. *See* p. 24.

Erichsen.—*WORKS BY JOHN ERIC ERICHSEN, F.R.S.*

THE SCIENCE AND ART OF SURGERY: Being a Treatise on Surgical Injuries, Diseases, and Operations. With 984 Illustrations. 2 vols. 8vo. 42s.

ON CONCUSSION OF THE SPINE, NERVOUS SHOCKS, and other Obscure Injuries of the Nervous System. Cr. 8vo. 10s. 6d.

Ewald. — *WORKS BY PROFESSOR HEINRICH EWALD,* of Göttingen.

THE ANTIQUITIES OF ISRAEL. Translated from the German by H. S. SOLLY, M.A. 8vo. 12s. 6d.

THE HISTORY OF ISRAEL. Translated from the German. 8 vols. 8vo. Vols. I. and II. 24s. Vols. III. and IV. 21s. Vol. V. 18s. Vol. VI. 16s. Vol. VII. 21s. Vol. VIII. with Index to the Complete Work. 18s.

Fairbairn.—*WORKS BY SIR W. FAIRBAIRN, BART. C.E.*

A TREATISE ON MILLS AND MILLWORK, with 18 Plates and 333 Woodcuts. 1 vol. 8vo. 25s.

USEFUL INFORMATION FOR ENGINEERS. With many Plates and Woodcuts. 3 vols. crown 8vo. 31s. 6d.

Farrar. — *LANGUAGE AND LANGUAGES.* A Revised Edition of *Chapters on Language and Families of Speech.* By F. W. FARRAR, D.D. Crown 8vo. 6s.

Firbank.—*THE LIFE AND WORK OF JOSEPH FIRBANK, J.P. D.L.* Railway Contractor. By FREDERICK McDERMOTT, Barrister-at-Law. 8vo. 5s.

Fitzwygram. — *HORSES AND STABLES.* By Major-General Sir F. FITZWYGRAM, Bart. With 19 pages of Illustrations. 8vo. 5s.

Forbes.—*A COURSE OF LECTURES ON ELECTRICITY,* delivered before the Society of Arts. By GEORGE FORBES, M.A. F.R.S. (L. & E.) With 17 Illustrations. Crown 8vo. 5s.

Ford.—*THE THEORY AND PRACTICE OF ARCHERY.* By the late HORACE FORD. New Edition, thoroughly Revised and Re-written by W. BUTT, M.A. With a Preface by C. J. LONGMAN, M.A. F.S.A. 8vo. 14s.

Fox.—*THE EARLY HISTORY OF CHARLES JAMES FOX.* By the Right Hon. Sir G. O. TREVELYAN, Bart. Library Edition, 8vo. 18s. Cabinet Edition, cr. 8vo. 6s.

Francis.—*A BOOK ON ANGLING;* or, Treatise on the Art of Fishing in every branch; including full Illustrated Lists of Salmon Flies. By FRANCIS FRANCIS. Post 8vo. Portrait and Plates, 15s.

Freeman.—*The Historical Geography of Europe.* By E. A. Freeman, D.C.L. With 65 Maps. 2 vols. 8vo. 31s. 6d.

Froude.—*Works by James A. Froude, M.A.*

The History of England, from the Fall of Wolsey to the Defeat of the Spanish Armada.
Cabinet Edition, 12 vols. cr. 8vo. £3. 12s.
Popular Edition, 12 vols. cr. 8vo. £2. 2s.

Short Studies on Great Subjects. 4 vols. crown 8vo. 24s.

Cæsar : a Sketch. Crown 8vo. 6s.

The English in Ireland in the Eighteenth Century. 3 vols. crown 8vo. 18s.

Oceana ; or, England and Her Colonies. With 9 Illustrations. Crown 8vo. 2s. boards, 2s. 6d. cloth.

The English in the West Indies; or, The Bow of Ulysses. With 9 Illustrations. 8vo. 18s.

Thomas Carlyle, a History of the first Forty Years of his Life, 1795 to 1835. 2 vols. 8vo. 32s.

Thomas Carlyle, a History of His Life in London from 1834 to his death in 1881. With Portrait engraved on steel. 2 vols. 8vo. 32s.

Galloway. — *The Fundamental Principles of Chemistry Practically Taught by a New Method.* By Robert Galloway, M.R.I.A. F.C.S. Crown 8vo. 6s. 6d.

Ganot. — *Works by Professor Ganot.* Translated by E. Atkinson, Ph.D. F.C.S.

Elementary Treatise on Physics. With 5 Coloured Plates and 923 Woodcuts. Crown 8vo. 15s.

Natural Philosophy for General Readers and Young Persons. With 2 Plates, 518 Woodcuts, and an Appendix of Questions. Cr. 8vo. 7s. 6d.

Gardiner. — *Works by Samuel Rawson Gardiner, LL.D.*

History of England, from the Accession of James I. to the Outbreak of the Civil War, 1603-1642. Cabinet Edition, thoroughly revised. 10 vols. crown 8vo. price 6s. each.

A History of the Great Civil War, 1642-1649. (3 vols.) Vol. 1. 1642-1644. With 24 Maps. 8vo. 21s.
[*Continued above.*]

Gardiner.—*Works by S. R. Gardiner, LL.D.—continued.*

Outline of English History, B.C. 55-A.D. 1886. With 96 Woodcuts, fcp. 8vo. 2s. 6d.

*** For other Works, *see* 'Epochs of Modern History,' p. 24.

Garrod.—*Works by Sir Alfred Baring Garrod, M.D. F.R.S.*

A Treatise on Gout and Rheumatic Gout (Rheumatoid Arthritis). With 6 Plates, comprising 21 Figures (14 Coloured), and 27 Illustrations engraved on Wood. 8vo. 21s.

The Essentials of Materia Medica and Therapeutics. New Edition, revised and adapted to the New Edition of the British Pharmacopoeia, by Nestor Tirard, M.D. Crown 8vo. 12s. 6d.

Gilkes.—*Boys and Masters:* a Story of School Life. By A. H. Gilkes, M.A. Head Master of Dulwich College. Crown 8vo. 3s. 6d.

Goethe.—*Faust.* A New Translation, chiefly in Blank Verse ; with Introduction and Notes. By James Adey Birds, B.A. F.G.S. Crown 8vo. 12s. 6d.

Faust. The German Text, with an English Introduction and Notes for Students. By Albert M. Selss, M.A. Ph.D. Crown 8vo. 5s.

Goodeve.—*Works by T. M. Goodeve, M.A.*

Principles of Mechanics. With 253 Woodcuts. Crown 8vo. 6s.

The Elements of Mechanism. With 342 Woodcuts. Crown 8vo. 6s.

A Manual of Mechanics : an Elementary Text-Book for Students of Applied Mechanics. With 138 Illustrations and Diagrams, and 141 Examples. Fcp. 8vo. 2s. 6d.

Grant.—*The Ethics of Aristotle.* The Greek Text illustrated by Essays and Notes. By Sir Alexander Grant, Bart. LL.D. D.C.L. &c. 2 vols. 8vo. 32s.

Gray. — *Anatomy, Descriptive and Surgical.* By Henry Gray, F.R.S. late Lecturer on Anatomy at St. George's Hospital. With 569 Woodcut Illustrations, a large number of which are coloured. Re-edited by T. Pickering Pick, Surgeon to St. George's Hospital. Royal 8vo. 36s.

Green.—*THE WORKS OF THOMAS HILL GREEN*, late Fellow of Balliol College, and Whyte's Professor of Moral Philosophy in the University of Oxford. Edited by R. L. NETTLESHIP, Fellow of Balliol College, Oxford (3 vols.) Vols. I. and II.—Philosophical Works. 8vo. 16s. each.

Greville.—*A JOURNAL OF THE REIGNS OF KING GEORGE IV. KING WILLIAM IV. AND QUEEN VICTORIA.* By the late CHARLES C. F. GREVILLE, Esq. Clerk of the Council to those Sovereigns. Edited by HENRY REEVE, C.B. D.C.L. Corresponding Member of the Institute of France. 8 vols. Crown 8vo. 6s. each. (*In course of Publication in Monthly Volumes.*)

Grove.—*THE CORRELATION OF PHYSICAL FORCES.* By the Hon. Sir W. R. GROVE, F.R.S. &c. 8vo. 15s.

Gwilt.—*AN ENCYCLOPÆDIA OF ARCHITECTURE.* By JOSEPH GWILT, F.S.A. Illustrated with more than 1,100 Engravings on Wood. Revised, with Alterations and Considerable Additions, by WYATT PAPWORTH. 8vo. 52s. 6d.

Haggard.—*WORKS BY H. RIDER HAGGARD.*

SHE: A HISTORY OF ADVENTURE. Crown 8vo. 6s.

ALLAN QUATERMAIN. With 31 Illustrations by C. H. M. KERR. Crown 8vo. 6s.

Halliwell-Phillipps.—*OUTLINES OF THE LIFE OF SHAKESPEARE.* By J. O. HALLIWELL-PHILLIPPS, F.R.S. 2 vols. Royal 8vo. 10s. 6d.

Harte.—*NOVELS BY BRET HARTE.*

IN THE CARQUINEZ WOODS. Fcp. 8vo. 1s. boards; 1s. 6d. cloth.

ON THE FRONTIER. Three Stories. 16mo. 1s.

BY SHORE AND SEDGE. Three Stories. 16mo. 1s.

Hartwig.—*WORKS BY DR. G. HARTWIG.*

THE SEA AND ITS LIVING WONDERS. With 12 Plates and 303 Woodcuts. 8vo. 10s. 6d.

THE TROPICAL WORLD. With 8 Plates, and 172 Woodcuts. 8vo. 10s. 6d.

THE POLAR WORLD. With 3 Maps, 8 Plates, and 85 Woodcuts. 8vo. 10s. 6d.

[*Continued above.*]

Hartwig.—*WORKS BY DR. G. HARTWIG.—continued.*

THE SUBTERRANEAN WORLD. With 3 Maps and 80 Woodcuts. 8vo. 10s. 6d.

THE AERIAL WORLD. With Map, 8 Plates, and 60 Woodcuts. 8vo. 10s. 6d.

The following books are extracted from the foregoing works by Dr. HARTWIG :—

HEROES OF THE ARCTIC REGIONS. With 19 Illustrations. Crown 8vo. 2s. cloth extra, gilt edges.

WONDERS OF THE TROPICAL FORESTS. With 40 Illustrations. Crown 8vo. 2s. cloth extra, gilt edges.

WORKERS UNDER THE GROUND; or, Mines and Mining. With 29 Illustrations. Crown 8vo. 2s. cloth extra, gilt edges.

MARVELS OVER OUR HEADS. With 29 Illustrations. Crown 8vo. 2s. cloth extra, gilt edges.

MARVELS UNDER OUR FEET. With 22 Illustrations. Crown 8vo. 2s. cloth extra, gilt edges.

DWELLERS IN THE ARCTIC REGIONS. With 29 Illustrations. Crown 8vo. 2s. 6d. cloth extra, gilt edges.

WINGED LIFE IN THE TROPICS. With 55 Illustrations. Crown 8vo. 2s. 6d. cloth extra, gilt edges.

VOLCANOES AND EARTHQUAKES. With 30 Illustrations. Crown 8vo. 2s. 6d. cloth extra, gilt edges.

WILD ANIMALS OF THE TROPICS. With 66 Illustrations. Crown 8vo. 3s. 6d. cloth extra, gilt edges.

SEA MONSTERS AND SEA BIRDS. With 75 Illustrations. Crown 8vo. 2s. 6d. cloth extra, gilt edges.

DENIZENS OF THE DEEP. With 117 Illustrations. Crown 8vo. 2s. 6d. cloth extra, gilt edges.

Hassall.—*THE INHALATION TREATMENT OF DISEASES OF THE ORGANS OF RESPIRATION,* including Consumption. By ARTHUR HILL HASSALL, M.D. With 19 Illustrations of Apparatus. Cr. 8vo. 12s. 6d.

Havelock.—*MEMOIRS OF SIR HENRY HAVELOCK, K.C.B.* By JOHN CLARK MARSHMAN. Crown 8vo. 3s. 6d.

Hearn.—*THE GOVERNMENT OF ENGLAND;* its Structure and its Development. By WILLIAM EDWARD HEARN, Q.C. 8vo. 16s.

Helmholtz.—*WORKS BY PROFESSOR HELMHOLTZ.*

ON THE SENSATIONS OF TONE AS A PHYSIOLOGICAL BASIS FOR THE THEORY OF MUSIC. Royal 8vo. 28s.

POPULAR LECTURES ON SCIENTIFIC SUBJECTS. With 68 Woodcuts. 2 vols. Crown 8vo. 15s. or separately, 7s. 6d. each.

Herschel.—*OUTLINES OF ASTRONOMY.* By Sir J. F. W. HERSCHEL, Bart. M.A. With Plates and Diagrams. Square crown 8vo. 12s.

Hester's Venture : a Novel. By the Author of 'The Atelier du Lys.' Crown 8vo. 2s. 6d.

Hewitt. — *THE DIAGNOSIS AND TREATMENT OF DISEASES OF WOMEN, INCLUDING THE DIAGNOSIS OF PREGNANCY.* By GRAILY HEWITT, M.D. With 211 Engravings. 8vo. 24s.

Historic Towns. Edited by E. A. FREEMAN, D.C.L. and Rev. WILLIAM HUNT, M.A. With Maps and Plans. Crown 8vo. 3s. 6d. each.

LONDON. By W. E. LOFTIE.

EXETER. By E. A. FREEMAN.

BRISTOL. By W. HUNT.

OXFORD. By C. W. BOASE.

*** Other Volumes are in preparation.

Hobart.—*SKETCHES FROM MY LIFE.* By Admiral HOBART PASHA. With Portrait. Crown 8vo. 7s. 6a.

Holmes.—*A SYSTEM OF SURGERY,* Theoretical and Practical, in Treatises by various Authors. Edited by TIMOTHY HOLMES, M.A. and J. W. HULKE, F.R.S. 3 vols. royal 8vo. £4. 4s.

Homer.—*THE ILIAD OF HOMER,* Homometrically translated by C. B. CAYLEY. 8vo. 12s. 6d.

THE ILIAD OF HOMER. The Greek Text, with a Verse Translation, by W. C. GREEN, M.A. Vol. I. Books I.-XII. Crown 8vo. 6s.

Hopkins.—*CHRIST THE CONSOLER;* a Book of Comfort for the Sick. By ELLICE HOPKINS. Fcp. 8vo. 2s. 6d.

Howitt.—*VISITS TO REMARKABLE PLACES,* Old Halls, Battle-Fields, Scenes illustrative of Striking Passages in English History and Poetry. By WILLIAM HOWITT. With 80 Illustrations engraved on Wood. Crown 8vo. 5s.

Hudson & Gosse.—*THE ROTIFERA OR 'WHEEL-ANIMALCULES.'* By C. T. HUDSON, LL.D. and P. H. GOSSE, F.R.S. With 30 Coloured Plates. In 6 Parts. 4to. 10s. 6d. each. Complete in 2 vols. 4to. £3. 10s.

Hullah.—*WORKS BY JOHN HULLAH, LL.D.*

COURSE OF LECTURES ON THE HISTORY OF MODERN MUSIC. 8vo. 8s. 6d.

COURSE OF LECTURES ON THE TRANSITION PERIOD OF MUSICAL HISTORY. 8vo. 10s. 6d.

Hume.—*THE PHILOSOPHICAL WORKS OF DAVID HUME.* Edited by T. H. GREEN, M.A. and the Rev. T. H. GROSE, M.A. 4 vols. 8vo. 56s. Or separately, Essays, 2 vols. 28s. Treatise of Human Nature. 2 vols. 28s.

Huth.—*THE MARRIAGE OF NEAR KIN,* considered with respect to the Law of Nations, the Result of Experience, and the Teachings of Biology. By ALFRED H. HUTH. Royal 8vo. 21s.

In the Olden Time : a Tale of the Peasant War in Germany. By the Author of 'Mademoiselle Mori.' Crown 8vo. 2s. 6d.

Ingelow.—*WORKS BY JEAN INGELOW.*

POETICAL WORKS. Vols. 1 and 2 Fcp. 8vo. 12s.

LYRICAL AND OTHER POEMS. Selected from the Writings of JEAN INGELOW. Fcp. 8vo. 2s. 6d. cloth plain ; 3s. cloth gilt.

Jackson.—*AID TO ENGINEERING SOLUTION.* By LOWIS D'A. JACKSON, C.E. With 111 Diagrams and 5 Woodcut Illustrations. 8vo. 21s.

James.—*THE LONG WHITE MOUNTAIN;* or, a Journey in Manchuria, with an Account of the History, Administration, and Religion of that Province. By H. E. JAMES, of Her Majesty's Bombay Civil Service. With Illustrations and a Map. 1 vol. 8vo. 24s.

Jameson.—*WORKS BY MRS JAMESON.*

LEGENDS OF THE SAINTS AND MARTYRS. With 19 Etchings and 187 Woodcuts. 2 vols. 31s. 6d.

LEGENDS OF THE MADONNA, the Virgin Mary as represented in Sacred and Legendary Art. With 27 Etchings and 165 Woodcuts. 1 vol. 21s.

[Continued on next page.

Jameson.—*WORKS BY MRS. JAME-SON—continued.*

LEGENDS OF THE MONASTIC ORDERS.
With 11 Etchings and 88 Woodcuts.
1 vol. 21s.

HISTORY OF THE SAVIOUR, His Types
and Precursors. Completed by Lady
EASTLAKE. With 13 Etchings and 281
Woodcuts. 2 vols. 42s.

Jeans.—*WORKS BY J. S. JEANS.*

ENGLAND'S SUPREMACY: its Sources,
Economics, and Dangers. 8vo. 8s. 6d.

RAILWAY PROBLEMS: An Inquiry
into the Economic Conditions of Railway Working in Different Countries.
8vo. 12s. 6d.

Jenkin. — *PAPERS, LITERARY,
SCIENTIFIC, &c.* By the late FLEEMING
JENKIN, F.R.S.S. L. & E. Professor of
Engineering in the University of Edin-
burgh. Edited by SIDNEY COLVIN, M.A.
and J. A. EWING, F.R.S. With Memoir
by ROBERT LOUIS STEVENSON, and
Facsimiles of Drawings by Fleeming
Jenkin. 2 vols. 8vo. 32s.

Johnson.—*THE PATENTEE'S MAN-
UAL;* a Treatise on the Law and Practice
of Letters Patent. By J. JOHNSON and
J. H. JOHNSON. 8vo. 10s. 6d.

Johnston.—*A GENERAL DICTION-
ARY OF GEOGRAPHY,* Descriptive, Physical, Statistical, and Historical ; a complete Gazetteer of the World. By KEITH
JOHNSTON. Medium 8vo. 42s.

Johnstone.—*A SHORT INTRODUC-
TION TO THE STUDY OF LOGIC.* By
LAURENCE JOHNSTONE. Crown 8vo.
2s. 6d.

Jordan. — *WORKS BY WILLIAM
LEIGHTON JORDAN, F.R.G.S.*

THE OCEAN: a Treatise on Ocean
Currents and Tides and their Causes.
8vo. 21s.

*THE NEW PRINCIPLES OF NATURAL
PHILOSOPHY.* With 13 plates. 8vo. 21s.

THE WINDS : an Essay in Illustration
of the New Principles of Natural Philosophy. Crown 8vo. 2s.

THE STANDARD OF VALUE. Crown
8vo. 5s.

Jukes.—*WORKS BY ANDREW JUKES.*

*THE NEW MAN AND THE ETERNAL
LIFE.* Crown 8vo. 6s.

THE TYPES OF GENESIS. Crown
8vo. 7s. 6d.

*THE SECOND DEATH AND THE RE-
STITUTION OF ALL THINGS.* Crown 8vo.
3s. 6d.

THE MYSTERY OF THE KINGDOM.
Crown 8vo. 2s. 6d.

Justinian. — *THE INSTITUTES OF
JUSTINIAN;* Latin Text, chiefly that of
Huschke, with English Introduction,
Translation, Notes, and Summary. By
THOMAS C. SANDARS, M.A. 8vo. 18s.

Kalisch. — *WORKS BY M. M.
KALISCH, M.A.*

BIBLE STUDIES. Part I. The Pro-
phecies of Balaam. 8vo. 10s. 6d. Part
II. The Book of Jonah. 8vo. 10s. 6d.

*COMMENTARY ON THE OLD TESTA-
MENT;* with a New Translation. Vol. I.
Genesis, 8vo. 18s. or adapted for the
General Reader, 12s. Vol. II. Exodus,
15s. or adapted for the General Reader,
12s. Vol. III. Leviticus, Part I. 15s. or
adapted for the General Reader, 8s.
Vol. IV. Leviticus, Part II. 15s. or
adapted for the General Reader, 8s.

HEBREW GRAMMAR. With Exercises. Part I. 8vo. 12s. 6d. Key, 5s.
Part II. 12s. 6d.

Kant.—*WORKS BY EMMANUEL KANT.*

CRITIQUE OF PRACTICAL REASON.
Translated by Thomas Kingsmill Abbott,
B.D. 8vo. 12s. 6d.

*INTRODUCTION TO LOGIC, AND HIS
ESSAY ON THE MISTAKEN SUBTILTY
OF THE FOUR FIGURES.* Translated by
Thomas Kingsmill Abbott, B.D. With
a few Notes by S. T. Coleridge. 8vo. 6s.

Kendall.—*WORKS BY MAY KEN-
DALL.*

FROM A GARRET. Crown 8vo. 6s.

DREAMS TO SELL; Poems. Fcp.
8vo. 6s.

Killick. — *HANDBOOK TO MILL'S
SYSTEM OF LOGIC.* By the Rev. A. H.
KILLICK, M.A. Crown 8vo. 3s. 6d.

Kirkup.—*AN INQUIRY INTO SOCIAL-
ISM.* By THOMAS KIRKUP, Author of
the Article on 'Socialism' in the 'Encyclopædia Britannica.' Crown 8vo. 5s.

Knowledge Library. (*See* PROCTOR'S
Works, p. 17.)

Kolbe.—*A Short Text-book of Inorganic Chemistry.* By Dr. HERMANN KOLBE. Translated from the German by T. S. HUMPIDGE, Ph.D. With a Coloured Table of Spectra and 66 Illustrations. Crown 8vo. 7s. 6d.

Ladd. — *Elements of Physiological Psychology:* a Treatise of the Activities and Nature of the Mind from the Physical and Experimental Point of View. By GEORGE T. LADD. With 113 Illustrations and Diagrams. 8vo. 21s.

Lang.—*Works by Andrew Lang.*

Myth, Ritual, and Religion. 2 vols. crown 8vo. 21s.

Custom and Myth; Studies of Early Usage and Belief. With 15 Illustrations. Crown 8vo. 7s. 6d.

Letters to Dead Authors. Fcp. 8vo. 6s. 6d.

Books and Bookmen. With 2 Coloured Plates and 17 Illustrations. Cr. 8vo. 6s. 6d.

Johnny Nut and the Golden Goose. Done into English by ANDREW LANG, from the French of CHARLES DEULIN. Illustrated by Am. Lynen. Royal 8vo. 10s. 6d. gilt edges.

Ballads of Books. Edited by ANDREW LANG. Fcp. 8vo. 6s.

Larden.—*Electricity for Public Schools and Colleges.* With numerous Questions and Examples with Answers, and 214 Illustrations and Diagrams. By W. LARDEN, M.A. Crown 8vo. 6s.

Laughton.—*Studies in Naval History;* Biographies. By J. K. LAUGHTON, M.A. Professor of Modern History at King's College, London. 8vo. 10s. 6d.

Lecky.—*Works by W. E. H. Lecky.*

History of England in the Eighteenth Century. 8vo. Vols. I. & II. 1700–1760. 36s. Vols. III. & IV. 1760–1784. 36s. Vols. V. & VI. 1784–1793. 36s.

The History of European Morals from Augustus to Charlemagne. 2 vols. crown 8vo. 16s.

History of the Rise and Influence of the Spirit of Rationalism in Europe. 2 vols. crown 8vo. 16s.

Lewes.—*The History of Philosophy,* from Thales to Comte. By GEORGE HENRY LEWES. 2 vols. 8vo. 32s.

Lindt.—*Picturesque New Guinea.* By J. W. LINDT, F.R.G.S. With 50 Full-page Photographic Illustrations reproduced by the Autotype Company. Crown 4to. 42s.

Liveing.— *Works by Robert Liveing, M.A. and M.D. Cantab.*

Handbook on Diseases of the Skin. With especial reference to Diagnosis and Treatment. Fcp 8vo. 5s.

Notes on the Treatment of Skin Diseases. 18mo. 3s.

Lloyd.—*A Treatise on Magnetism,* General and Terrestrial. By H. LLOYD, D.D. D.C.L. 8vo. 10s. 6d.

Lloyd.—*The Science of Agriculture.* By F. J. LLOYD. 8vo. 12s.

Longman.—*History of the Life and Times of Edward III.* By WILLIAM LONGMAN, F.S.A. With 9 Maps, 8 Plates, and 16 Woodcuts. 2 vols. 8vo. 28s.

Longman.—*Works by Frederick W. Longman, Balliol College, Oxon.*

Chess Openings. Fcp. 8vo. 2s. 6d.

Frederick the Great and the Seven Years' War. With 2 Coloured Maps. 8vo. 2s. 6d.

A New Pocket Dictionary of the German and English Languages. Square 18mo. 2s. 6d.

Longman's Magazine. Published Monthly. Price Sixpence.
Vols. 1–10, 8vo. price 5s. each.

Longmore.— *Gunshot Injuries;* Their History, Characteristic Features, Complications, and General Treatment. By Surgeon-General Sir T. LONGMORE, C.B., F.R.C.S. With 58 Illustrations. 8vo. 31s. 6d.

Loudon.—*Works by J. C. Loudon, F.L.S.*

Encyclopædia of Gardening; the Theory and Practice of Horticulture, Floriculture, Arboriculture, and Landscape Gardening. With 1,000 Woodcuts. 8vo. 21s.

Encyclopædia of Agriculture; the Laying-out, Improvement, and Management of Landed Property; the Cultivation and Economy of the Productions of Agriculture. With 1,100 Woodcuts. 8vo. 21s.

Encyclopædia of Plants; the Specific Character, Description, Culture, History, &c. of all Plants found in Great Britain. With 12,000 Woodcuts. 8vo. 42s.

Lubbock.—*THE ORIGIN OF CIVILIZATION AND THE PRIMITIVE CONDITION OF MAN.* By Sir J. LUBBOCK, Bart. M.P. F.R.S. With Illustrations. 8vo. 18s.

Lyall.—*THE AUTOBIOGRAPHY OF A SLANDER.* By EDNA LYALL, Author of 'Donovan,' 'We Two,' &c. Fcp. 8vo. 1s. sewed.

Lyra Germanica ; Hymns Translated from the German by Miss C. WINKWORTH. Fcp. 8vo. 5s.

Macaulay.—*WORKS AND LIFE OF LORD MACAULAY.*

HISTORY OF ENGLAND FROM THE ACCESSION OF JAMES THE SECOND:
Student's Edition, 2 vols. crown 8vo. 12s.
People's Edition, 4 vols. crown 8vo. 16s.
Cabinet Edition, 8 vols. post 8vo. 48s.
Library Edition, 5 vols. 8vo. £4.

CRITICAL AND HISTORICAL ESSAYS, with LAYS of ANCIENT ROME, in 1 volume :
Authorised Edition, crown 8vo. 2s. 6d. or 3s. 6d. gilt edges.
Popular Edition, crown 8vo. 2s. 6d.

CRITICAL AND HISTORICAL ESSAYS:
Student's Edition, 1 vol. crown 8vo. 6s.
People's Edition, 2 vols. crown 8vo. 8s.
Cabinet Edition, 4 vols. post 8vo. 24s.
Library Edition, 3 vols. 8vo. 36s.

ESSAYS which may be had separately price 6d. each sewed, 1s. each cloth :
Addison and Walpole.
Frederick the Great.
Croker's Boswell's Johnson.
Hallam's Constitutional History.
Warren Hastings. (3d. sewed, 6d. cloth.)
The Earl of Chatham (Two Essays).
Ranke and Gladstone.
Milton and Machiavelli.
Lord Bacon.
Lord Clive.
Lord Byron, and The Comic Dramatists of the Restoration.

The Essay on Warren Hastings annotated by S. HALES, 1s. 6d.
The Essay on Lord Clive annotated by H. COURTHOPE BOWEN, M.A. 2s. 6d.

SPEECHES:
People's Edition, crown 8vo. 3s. 6d.

MISCELLANEOUS WRITINGS :
Library Edition, 2 vols. 8vo. 21s.
People's Edition, 1 vol. crown 8vo. 4s. 6d.
[Continued above.]

Macaulay—*WORKS AND LIFE OF LORD MACAULAY*—continued.
LAYS OF ANCIENT ROME, &c.
Illustrated by G. Scharf, fcp. 4to. 10s. 6d.
———————— Popular Edition, fcp. 4to. 6d. sewed, 1s. cloth.
Illustrated by J. R. Weguelin, crown 8vo. 3s. 6d. cloth extra, gilt edges.
Cabinet Edition, post 8vo. 3s. 6d.
Annotated Edition, fcp. 8vo. 1s. sewed 1s.6d. cloth, or 2s. 6d. cloth extra, gilt edges.

SELECTIONS FROM THE WRITINGS OF LORD MACAULAY. Edited, with Occasional Notes, by the Right Hon. Sir G. O. TREVELYAN, Bart. Crown 8vo. 6s.

MISCELLANEOUS WRITINGS AND SPEECHES:
Student's Edition, in ONE VOLUME, crown 8vo. 6s.
Cabinet Edition, including Indian Penal Code, Lays of Ancient Rome, and Miscellaneous Poems, 4 vols. post 8vo. 24s.

THE COMPLETE WORKS OF LORD MACAULAY. Edited by his Sister, Lady TREVELYAN.
Library Edition, with Portrait, 8 vols. demy 8vo. £5. 5s.
Cabinet Edition, 16 vols. post 8vo. £4. 16s.

THE LIFE AND LETTERS OF LORD MACAULAY. By the Right Hon. Sir G. O. TREVELYAN, Bart.
Popular Edition, 1 vol. crown 8vo.
Cabinet Edition, 2 vols. post 8vo.
Library Edition, 2 vols. 8vo. 36s.

Macdonald.—*WORKS BY GEORGE MACDONALD, LL.D.*
UNSPOKEN SERMONS. First Series. Crown 8vo. 3s. 6d.
UNSPOKEN SERMONS. Second Series. Crown 8vo. 3s. 6d.
THE MIRACLES OF OUR LORD. Crown 8vo. 3s. 6d.
A BOOK OF STRIFE, IN THE FORM OF THE DIARY OF AN OLD SOUL: Poems. 12mo. 6s.

Macfarren.—*WORKS BY SIR G. A. MACFARREN.*
LECTURES ON HARMONY. 8vo. 12s.
ADDRESSES AND LECTURES. Crown 8vo. 6s. 6d.

Macleod.—*WORKS BY HENRY D. MACLEOD, M.A.*
THE ELEMENTS OF ECONOMICS. In 2 vols. Vol. I. crown 8vo. 7s. 6d. Vol. II. PART 1, crown 8vo. 7s. 6d.
THE ELEMENTS OF BANKING. Crown 8vo. 5s.
THE THEORY AND PRACTICE OF BANKING. Vol. I. 8vo. 12s. Vol. II. 14s.

McCulloch. — *THE DICTIONARY OF COMMERCE AND COMMERCIAL NAVIGATION* of the late J. R. McCULLOCH, of H.M. Stationery Office. Latest Edition, containing the most recent Statistical Information by A. J. WILSON. 1 vol. medium 8vo. with 11 Maps and 30 Charts, price 63s. cloth, or 70s. strongly half-bound in russia.

Mademoiselle Mori: a Tale of Modern Rome. By the Author of 'The Atelier du Lys.' Crown 8vo. 2s. 6d.

Mahaffy. — *A HISTORY OF CLASSICAL GREEK LITERATURE.* By the Rev. J. P. MAHAFFY, M.A. Crown 8vo. Vol. I. Poets, 7s. 6d. Vol. II. Prose Writers, 7s. 6d.

Malmesbury. — *MEMOIRS OF AN EX-MINISTER:* an Autobiography. By the Earl of MALMESBURY, G.C.B. Crown 8vo. 7s. 6d.

Manning. — *THE TEMPORAL MISSION OF THE HOLY GHOST;* or, Reason and Revelation. By H. E. MANNING, D.D. Cardinal-Archbishop. Crown 8vo. 8s. 6d.

Martin. — *NAVIGATION AND NAUTICAL ASTRONOMY.* Compiled by Staff-Commander W. R. MARTIN, R.N. Instructor in Surveying, Navigation, and Compass Adjustment; Lecturer on Meteorology at the Royal Naval College, Greenwich. Sanctioned for use in the Royal Navy by the Lords Commissioners of the Admiralty. Royal 8vo. 18s.

Martineau — *WORKS BY JAMES MARTINEAU, D.D.*
HOURS OF THOUGHT ON SACRED THINGS. Two Volumes of Sermons. 2 vols. crown 8vo. 7s. 6d. each.
ENDEAVOURS AFTER THE CHRISTIAN LIFE. Discourses. Crown 8vo. 7s. 6d.

Maunder's Treasuries.
BIOGRAPHICAL TREASURY. Reconstructed, revised, and brought down to the year 1882, by W. L. R. CATES. Fcp. 8vo. 6s.
TREASURY OF NATURAL HISTORY; or, Popular Dictionary of Zoology. Fcp. 8vo. with 900 Woodcuts, 6s.
TREASURY OF GEOGRAPHY, Physical, Historical, Descriptive, and Political. With 7 Maps and 16 Plates. Fcp. 8vo. 6s.
HISTORICAL TREASURY: Outlines of Universal History, Separate Histories of all Nations. Revised by the Rev. Sir G. W. Cox, Bart. M.A. Fcp. 8vo. 6s.
[*Continued above.*]

Maunder's Treasuries—*continued.*
TREASURY OF KNOWLEDGE AND LIBRARY OF REFERENCE. Comprising an English Dictionary and Grammar, Universal Gazetteer, Classical Dictionary, Chronology, Law Dictionary, &c. Fcp. 8vo. 6s.
SCIENTIFIC AND LITERARY TREASURY: a Popular Encyclopædia of Science, Literature, and Art. Fcp. 8vo. 6s.
THE TREASURY OF BIBLE KNOWLEDGE; being a Dictionary of the Books, Persons, Places, Events, and other matters of which mention is made in Holy Scripture. By the Rev. J. AYRE, M.A. With 5 Maps, 15 Plates, and 300 Woodcuts. Fcp. 8vo. 6s.
THE TREASURY OF BOTANY, or Popular Dictionary of the Vegetable Kingdom. Edited by J. LINDLEY, F.R.S. and T. MOORE, F.L.S. With 274 Woodcuts and 20 Steel Plates. Two Parts, fcp. 8vo. 12s.

Max Müller. — *WORKS BY F. MAX MÜLLER, M.A.*
BIOGRAPHICAL ESSAYS. Crown 8vo. 7s. 6d.
SELECTED ESSAYS ON LANGUAGE, MYTHOLOGY AND RELIGION. 2 vols. crown 8vo. 16s.
LECTURES ON THE SCIENCE OF LANGUAGE. 2 vols. crown 8vo. 16s.
INDIA, WHAT CAN IT TEACH US? A Course of Lectures delivered before the University of Cambridge. 8vo. 12s. 6d.
HIBBERT LECTURES ON THE ORIGIN AND GROWTH OF RELIGION, as illustrated by the Religions of India. Crown 8vo. 7s. 6d.
INTRODUCTION TO THE SCIENCE OF RELIGION: Four Lectures delivered at the Royal Institution. Crown 8vo. 7s. 6d.
THE SCIENCE OF THOUGHT. 8vo. 21s.
BIOGRAPHIES OF WORDS, AND THE HOME OF THE ARYAS. Crown 8vo. 7s. 6d.
A SANSKRIT GRAMMAR FOR BEGINNERS. New and Abridged Edition, accented and transliterated throughout, with a chapter on Syntax and an Appendix on Classical Metres. By A. A. MACDONELL, M.A. Ph.D. Crown 8vo. 6s.

May. — *WORKS BY THE RIGHT HON. SIR THOMAS ERSKINE MAY, K.C.B.*
THE CONSTITUTIONAL HISTORY OF ENGLAND SINCE THE ACCESSION OF GEORGE III. 1760-1870. 3 vols. crown 8vo. 18s.
DEMOCRACY IN EUROPE; a History. 2 vols. 8vo. 32s.

Meath.—*WORKS BY THE EARL OF MEATH (Lord Brabazon).*

SOCIAL ARROWS: Reprinted Articles on various Social Subjects. Crown 8vo. 1s. boards, 5s. cloth.

PROSPERITY OR PAUPERISM? Physical, Industrial, and Technical Training. (Edited by the EARL OF MEATH). 8vo. 5s.

Melville.—*NOVELS BY G. J. WHYTE MELVILLE.* Crown 8vo. 1s. each, boards; 1s. 6d. each, cloth.

The Gladiators.	Holmby House.
The Interpreter.	Kate Coventry.
Good for Nothing.	Digby Grand.
The Queen's Maries.	General Bounce.

Mendelssohn.—*THE LETTERS OF FELIX MENDELSSOHN.* Translated by Lady WALLACE. 2 vols. crown 8vo. 10s.

Merivale.—*WORKS BY THE VERY REV. CHARLES MERIVALE, D.D. Dean of Ely.*

HISTORY OF THE ROMANS UNDER THE EMPIRE. 8 vols. post 8vo. 48s.

THE FALL OF THE ROMAN REPUBLIC: a Short History of the Last Century tury of the Commonwealth. 12mo. 7s. 6d.

GENERAL HISTORY OF ROME FROM B.C. 753 TO A.D. 476. Crown 8vo. 7s. 6d.

THE ROMAN TRIUMVIRATES. With Maps. Fcp. 8vo. 2s. 6d.

Meyer.—*MODERN THEORIES OF CHEMISTRY.* By Professor LOTHAR MEYER. Translated, from the Fifth Edition of the German, by P. PHILLIPS BEDSON, D.Sc. (Lond.) B.Sc. (Vict.) F.C.S.; and W. CARLETON WILLIAMS, B.Sc. (Vict.) F.C.S. 8vo. 18s.

Mill.—*ANALYSIS OF THE PHENOMENA OF THE HUMAN MIND.* By JAMES MILL. With Notes, Illustrative and Critical. 2 vols. 8vo. 28s.

Mill.—*WORKS BY JOHN STUART MILL.*

PRINCIPLES OF POLITICAL ECONOMY. Library Edition, 2 vols. 8vo. 30s. People's Edition, 1 vol. crown 8vo. 5s.

A SYSTEM OF LOGIC, Ratiocinative and Inductive. Crown 8vo. 5s.

ON LIBERTY. Crown 8vo. 1s. 4d.

ON REPRESENTATIVE GOVERNMENT. Crown 8vo. 2s.

UTILITARIANISM. 8vo. 5s.

EXAMINATION OF SIR WILLIAM HAMILTON'S PHILOSOPHY. 8vo. 16s.

NATURE, THE UTILITY OF RELIGION, AND THEISM. Three Essays. 8vo. 5s.

Miller.—*WORKS BY W. ALLEN MILLER, M.D. LL.D.*

THE ELEMENTS OF CHEMISTRY, Theoretical and Practical. Re-edited, with Additions, by H. MACLEOD, F.C.S. 3 vols. 8vo.

Vol. I. CHEMICAL PHYSICS, 16s.
Vol. II. INORGANIC CHEMISTRY, 24s.
Vol. III. ORGANIC CHEMISTRY, 31s. 6d.

AN INTRODUCTION TO THE STUDY OF INORGANIC CHEMISTRY. With 71 Woodcuts. Fcp. 8vo. 3s. 6d.

Mitchell.—*A MANUAL OF PRACTICAL ASSAYING.* By JOHN MITCHELL, F.C.S. Revised, with the Recent Discoveries incorporated. By W. CROOKES, F.R.S. 8vo. Woodcuts, 31s. 6d.

Molesworth.—*MARRYING AND GIVING IN MARRIAGE:* a Novel. By Mrs. MOLESWORTH. Fcp. 8vo. 2s. 6d.

Monsell.—*WORKS BY THE REV. J. S. B. MONSELL, LL.D.*

SPIRITUAL SONGS FOR THE SUNDAYS AND HOLYDAYS THROUGHOUT THE YEAR. Fcp. 8vo. 5s. 18mo. 2s.

THE BEATITUDES. Eight Sermons. Crown 8vo. 3s. 6d.

HIS PRESENCE NOT HIS MEMORY. Verses. 16mo. 1s.

Mulhall.—*HISTORY OF PRICES SINCE THE YEAR 1850.* By MICHAEL G. MULHALL. Crown 8vo. 6s.

Munk.—*EUTHANASIA;* or, Medical Treatment in Aid of an Easy Death. By WILLIAM MUNK, M.D. F.S.A. Fellow and late Senior Censor of the Royal College of Physicians, &c. Crown 8vo. 4s. 6d.

Murchison.—*WORKS BY CHARLES MURCHISON, M.D. LL.D. &c.*

A TREATISE ON THE CONTINUED FEVERS OF GREAT BRITAIN. Revised by W. CAYLEY, M.D. Physician to the Middlesex Hospital. 8vo. with numerous Illustrations, 25s.

CLINICAL LECTURES ON DISEASES OF THE LIVER, JAUNDICE, AND ABDOMINAL DROPSY. Revised by T. LAUDER BRUNTON, M.D. and Sir JOSEPH FAYRER, M.D. 8vo. with 43 Illustrations, 24s.

Napier. *THE LIFE OF SIR JOSEPH NAPIER, BART. EX-LORD CHANCELLOR OF IRELAND.* From his Private Correspondence. By ALEX. CHARLES EWALD, F.S.A. With Portrait on Steel, engraved by G. J. Stodart, from a Photograph. 8vo. 15s.

Nelson.—*LETTERS AND DESPATCHES OF HORATIO, VISCOUNT NELSON.* Selected and arranged by JOHN KNOX LAUGHTON, M.A. 8vo. 16s.

Nesbit.—*LAYS AND LEGENDS.* By E. NESBIT. Crown 8vo. 5s.

Newman.— *WORKS BY CARDINAL NEWMAN.*

APOLOGIA PRO VITÂ SUÂ. Crown 8vo. 6s.

THE IDEA OF A UNIVERSITY DEFINED AND ILLUSTRATED. Crown 8vo. 7s.

HISTORICAL SKETCHES. 3 vols. crown 8vo. 6s. each.

THE ARIANS OF THE FOURTH CENTURY. Crown 8vo. 6s.

DISCUSSIONS AND ARGUMENTS ON VARIOUS SUBJECTS. Crown 8vo. 6s.

AN ESSAY ON THE DEVELOPMENT OF CHRISTIAN DOCTRINE. Crown 8vo. 6s.

CERTAIN DIFFICULTIES FELT BY ANGLICANS IN CATHOLIC TEACHING CONSIDERED. Vol. 1, crown 8vo. 7s. 6d.; Vol. 2, crown 8vo. 5s. 6d.

THE VIA MEDIA OF THE ANGLICAN CHURCH, ILLUSTRATED IN LECTURES &c. 2 vols. crown 8vo. 6s. each.

ESSAYS, CRITICAL AND HISTORICAL. 2 vols. crown 8vo. 12s.

ESSAYS ON BIBLICAL AND ON ECCLESIASTICAL MIRACLES. Crown 8vo. 6s.

AN ESSAY IN AID OF A GRAMMAR OF ASSENT. 7s. 6d.

THE DREAM OF GERONTIUS. 16mo. 6d. sewed.

Noble.—*HOURS WITH A THREE-INCH TELESCOPE.* By Captain W. NOBLE, F.R.A.S. &c. With a Map of the Moon. Crown 8vo. 4s. 6d.

Northcott.—*LATHES AND TURNING*, Simple, Mechanical, and Ornamental. By W. H. NORTHCOTT. With 338 Illustrations. 8vo. 18s.

O'Hagan. — *SELECTED SPEECHES AND ARGUMENTS OF THE RIGHT HONOURABLE THOMAS BARON O'HAGAN.* Edited by GEORGE TEELING. With a Portrait. 8vo. 16s.

Oliphant.—*NOVELS BY MRS. OLIPHANT.*

MADAM. Crown 8vo. 1s. boards; 1s. 6d. cloth.

IN TRUST.—Crown 8vo. 1s. boards; 1s. 6d. cloth.

Oliver. — *ASTRONOMY FOR AMATEURS:* a Practical Manual of Telescopic Research adapted to Moderate Instruments. Edited by J. A. WESTWOOD OLIVER, with the assistance of E. W. MAUNDER, H. GRUBB, J. E. GORE, W. F. DENNING, W. S. FRANKS, T. G. ELGER, S. W. BURNHAM, J. R. CAPRON, T. W. BACKHOUSE, and others. With several Illustrations. Crown 8vo. 7s. 6d.

Overton.—*LIFE IN THE ENGLISH CHURCH* (1660–1714). By J. H. OVERTON, M.A. Rector of Epworth. 8vo. 14s.

Owen. — *THE COMPARATIVE ANATOMY AND PHYSIOLOGY OF THE VERTEBRATE ANIMALS.* By Sir RICHARD OWEN, K.C.B. &c. With 1,472 Woodcuts. 3 vols. 8vo. £3. 13s. 6d.

Paget. — *WORKS BY SIR JAMES PAGET, BART. F.R.S. D.C.L. &c.*

CLINICAL LECTURES AND ESSAYS. Edited by F. HOWARD MARSH, Assistant-Surgeon to St. Bartholomew's Hospital. 8vo. 15s.

LECTURES ON SURGICAL PATHOLOGY. Re-edited by the AUTHOR and W. TURNER, M.B. 8vo. with 131 Woodcuts, 21s.

Pasteur.—*LOUIS PASTEUR*, his Life and Labours. By his SON-IN-LAW. Translated from the French by Lady CLAUD HAMILTON. Crown 8vo. 7s. 6d.

Payen.—*INDUSTRIAL CHEMISTRY;* a Manual for Manufacturers and for Colleges or Technical Schools; a Translation of PAYEN'S 'Précis de Chimie Industrielle.' Edited by B. H. PAUL. With 698 Woodcuts. Medium 8vo. 42s.

Payn.—*NOVELS BY JAMES PAYN.*

THE LUCK OF THE DARRELLS. Crown 8vo. 1s. boards; 1s. 6d. cloth.

THICKER THAN WATER. Crown 8vo. 1s. boards; 1s. 6d. cloth.

Pears.—*THE FALL OF CONSTANTINOPLE:* being the Story of the Fourth Crusade. By EDWIN PEARS, LL.B. Barrister-at-Law, late President of the European Bar at Constantinople, and Knight of the Greek Order of the Saviour. 8vo. 16s.

Pennell.—*OUR SENTIMENTAL JOURNEY THROUGH FRANCE AND ITALY.* By JOSEPH and ELIZABETH ROBINS PENNELL. With a Map and 120 Illustrations by Joseph Pennell. Crown 8vo. 6s. cloth or vegetable vellum.

Perring.—*HARD KNOTS IN SHAKESPEARE.* By Sir PHILIP PERRING, Bart. 8vo. 7s. 6d.

Piesse.—*THE ART OF PERFUMERY,* and the Methods of Obtaining the Odours of Plants; with Instructions for the Manufacture of Perfumes, &c. By G. W. S. PIESSE, Ph.D. F.C.S. With 96 Woodcuts, square crown 8vo. 21*s.*

Pole.—*THE THEORY OF THE MODERN SCIENTIFIC GAME OF WHIST.* By W. POLE, F.R.S. Fcp. 8vo. 2*s.* 6*d.*

Prendergast.—*IRELAND,* from the Restoration to the Revolution, 1660–1690. By JOHN P. PRENDERGAST. 8vo. 5*s.*

Proctor.—*WORKS BY R. A. PROCTOR.*

THE ORBS AROUND US; a Series of Essays on the Moon and Planets, Meteors and Comets. With Chart and Diagrams, crown 8vo. 5*s.*

OTHER WORLDS THAN OURS; The Plurality of Worlds Studied under the Light of Recent Scientific Researches. With 14 Illustrations, crown 8vo. 5*s.*

THE MOON; her Motions, Aspects, Scenery, and Physical Condition. With Plates, Charts, Woodcuts, and Lunar Photographs, crown 8vo. 6*s.*

UNIVERSE OF STARS; Presenting Researches into and New Views respecting the Constitution of the Heavens. With 22 Charts and 22 Diagrams, 8vo. 10*s.* 6*d.*

LARGER STAR ATLAS for the Library, in 12 Circular Maps, with Introduction and 2 Index Pages. Folio, 15*s.* or Maps only, 12*s.* 6*d.*

NEW STAR ATLAS for the Library, the School, and the Observatory, in 12 Circular Maps (with 2 Index Plates). Crown 8vo. 5*s.*

LIGHT SCIENCE FOR LEISURE HOURS; Familiar Essays on Scientific Subjects, Natural Phenomena, &c. 3 vols. crown 8vo. 5*s.* each.

CHANCE AND LUCK; a Discussion of the Laws of Luck, Coincidences, Wagers, Lotteries, and the Fallacies of Gambling &c. Crown 8vo. 5*s.*

STUDIES OF VENUS-TRANSITS; an Investigation of the Circumstances of the Transits of Venus in 1874 and 1882. With 7 Diagrams and 10 Plates. 8vo. 5*s.*

OLD AND NEW ASTRONOMY.

*** In course of publication, in twelve monthly parts and a supplementary section. In each there will be 64 pages, imp. 8vo. many cuts, and 2 plates, or one large folding plate. The price of each part will be 2*s.* 6*d.*; that of the supplementary section, containing tables, index, and preface, 1*s.* The price of the complete work, in cloth, 36*s.*

The 'KNOWLEDGE' LIBRARY. Edited by RICHARD A. PROCTOR.

HOW TO PLAY WHIST: WITH THE LAWS AND ETIQUETTE OF WHIST. By R. A. PROCTOR. Crown 8vo. 5*s.*

HOME WHIST: an Easy Guide to Correct Play. By R. A. PROCTOR. 16mo. 1*s.*

THE POETRY OF ASTRONOMY. A Series of Familiar Essays. By R. A. PROCTOR. Crown 8vo. 6*s.*

NATURE STUDIES. By GRANT ALLEN, A. WILSON, T. FOSTER, E. CLODD, and R. A. PROCTOR. Crown 8vo. 6*s.*

LEISURE READINGS. By E. CLODD, A. WILSON, T. FOSTER, A. C. RUNYARD, and R. A. PROCTOR. Crown 8vo. 6*s.*

THE STARS IN THEIR SEASONS. An Easy Guide to a Knowledge of the Star Groups, in 12 Large Maps. By R. A. PROCTOR. Imperial 8vo. 5*s.*

STAR PRIMER. Showing the Starry Sky Week by Week, in 24 Hourly Maps. By R. A. PROCTOR. Crown 4to. 2*s.* 6*d.*

THE SEASONS PICTURED IN 48 SUN-VIEWS OF THE EARTH, and 24 Zodiacal Maps, &c. By R. A. PROCTOR. Demy 4to. 5*s.*

STRENGTH AND HAPPINESS. By R. A. PROCTOR. Crown 8vo. 5*s.*

ROUGH WAYS MADE SMOOTH. Familiar Essays on Scientific Subjects. By R. A. PROCTOR. Crown 8vo. 5*s.*

OUR PLACE AMONG INFINITIES. A Series of Essays contrasting our Little Abode in Space and Time with the Infinities Around us. By R. A. PROCTOR. Crown 8vo. 5*s.*

THE EXPANSE OF HEAVEN. Essays on the Wonders of the Firmament. By R. A. PROCTOR. Crown 8vo. 5*s.*

THE GREAT PYRAMID, OBSERVATORY TOMB, AND TEMPLE. With Illustrations. Crown 8vo. 6*s.*

PLEASANT WAYS IN SCIENCE. By R. A. PROCTOR. Crown 8vo. 6*s.*

MYTHS AND MARVELS OF ASTRONOMY. By R. A. PROCTOR. Cr. 8vo. 6*s.*

Prothero.—*THE PIONEERS AND PROGRESS OF ENGLISH FARMING.* By ROWLAND E. PROTHERO. Crown 8vo. 5*s.*

Pryce.—*THE ANCIENT BRITISH CHURCH:* an Historical Essay. By JOHN PRYCE, M.A. Canon of Bangor. Crown 8vo. 6*s.*

Quain's Elements of Anatomy.

The Ninth Edition. Re-edited by ALLEN THOMSON, M.D. LL.D. F.R.S.S. L. & E. EDWARD ALBERT SCHÄFER, F.R.S. and GEORGE DANCER THANE. With upwards of 1,000 Illustrations engraved on Wood, of which many are Coloured. 2 vols. 8vo. 18s. each.

Quain.—*A Dictionary of Medicine.* By Various Writers. Edited by R. QUAIN, M.D. F.R.S. &c. With 138 Woodcuts. Medium 8vo. 31s. 6d. cloth, or 40s. half-russia; to be had also in 2 vols. 34s. cloth.

Reader.—*Works by Emily E. Reader.*

The Ghost of Brankinshaw and other Tales. With 9 Full-page Illustrations. Fcp. 8vo. 2s. 6d. cloth extra, gilt edges.

Voices from Flower-Land, in Original Couplets. A Birthday-Book and Language of Flowers. 16mo. 1s. 6d. limp cloth; 2s. 6d. roan, gilt edges, or in vegetable vellum, gilt top.

Fairy Prince Follow-my-Lead ; or, the *Magic Bracelet.* Illustrated by WM. READER. Crown 8vo. 2s. 6d. gilt edges; or 3s. 6d. vegetable vellum, gilt edges.

The Three Giants &c. Royal 16mo. 1s. cloth.

The Model Boy &c. Royal 16mo. 1s. cloth.

Be Yt Hys who Fynds Yt. Royal 16mo. 1s. cloth.

Reeve. — *Cookery and Housekeeping.* By Mrs. HENRY REEVE. With 8 Coloured Plates and 37 Woodcuts. Crown 8vo. 5s.

Rich.—*A Dictionary of Roman and Greek Antiquities.* With 2,000 Woodcuts. By A. RICH, B.A. Cr. 8vo. 7s. 6d.

Richardson.—*Works by Benjamin Ward Richardson, M.D.*

The Health of Nations: a Review of the Works—Economical, Educational, Sanitary, and Administrative—of EDWIN CHADWICK, C.B. With a Biographical Dissertation by BENJAMIN WARD RICHARDSON, M.D. F.R.S. 2 vols. 8vo. 28s.

The Commonhealth : a Series of Essays on Health and Felicity for Every-Day Readers. Crown 8vo. 6s.

Richey.—*A Short History of the Irish People*, down to the Date of the Plantation of Ulster. By the late A. G. RICHEY, Q.C. LL.D. M.R.I.A. Edited, with Notes, by ROBERT ROMNEY KANE, LL.D. M.R.I.A. 8vo. 14s.

Riley.—*Athos;* or, the Mountain of the Monks. By ATHELSTAN RILEY, M.A. F.R.G.S. With Map and 29 Illustrations. 8vo. 21s.

Rivers. — *Works by Thomas Rivers.*

The Orchard-House. With 25 Woodcuts. Crown 8vo. 5s.

The Miniature Fruit Garden; or, the Culture of Pyramidal and Bush Fruit Trees, with Instructions for Root Pruning. With 32 Illustrations. Fcp. 8vo. 4s.

Roberts.—*Greek the Language of Christ and His Apostles.* By ALEXANDER ROBERTS, D.D. 8vo. 18s.

Robinson. — *The New Arcadia,* and other Poems. By A. MARY F. ROBINSON. Crown 8vo. 6s.

Roget.—*Thesaurus of English Words and Phrases,* Classified and Arranged so as to facilitate the Expression of Ideas and assist in Literary Composition. By PETER M. ROGET. Crown 8vo. 10s. 6d.

Ronalds. — *The Fly-Fisher's Entomology.* By ALFRED RONALDS. With 20 Coloured Plates. 8vo. 14s.

Saintsbury.—*Manchester :* a Short History. By GEORGE SAINTSBURY. With 2 Maps. Crown 8vo. 3s. 6d.

Schäfer. — *The Essentials of Histology, Descriptive and Practical.* For the use of Students. By E. A. SCHÄFER, F.R.S. With 281 Illustrations. 8vo. 6s. or Interleaved with Drawing Paper, 8s. 6d.

Schellen. — *Spectrum Analysis in its Application to Terrestrial Substances,* and the Physical Constitution of the Heavenly Bodies. By Dr. H. SCHELLEN. Translated by JANE and CAROLINE LASSELL. Edited by Capt. W. DE W. ABNEY. With 14 Plates (including Angström's and Cornu's Maps) and 291 Woodcuts. 8vo. 31s. 6d.

Scott.—*Weather Charts and Storm Warnings.* By ROBERT H. SCOTT, M.A. F.R.S. With numerous Illustrations. Crown 8vo. 6s.

Seebohm.—*WORKS BY FREDERIC SEEBOHM.*

THE OXFORD REFORMERS — JOHN COLET, ERASMUS, AND THOMAS MORE; a History of their Fellow-Work. 8vo. 14s.

THE ENGLISH VILLAGE COMMUNITY Examined in its Relations to the Manorial and Tribal Systems, &c, 13 Maps and Plates. 8vo. 16s.

THE ERA OF THE PROTESTANT REVOLUTION. With Map. Fcp. 8vo. 2s. 6d.

Sennett. — *THE MARINE STEAM ENGINE;* a Treatise for the use of Engineering Students and Officers of the Royal Navy. By RICHARD SENNETT, Engineer-in-Chief of the Royal Navy. With 244 Illustrations. 8vo. 21s.

Sewell. — *STORIES AND TALES.* By ELIZABETH M. SEWELL. Crown 8vo. 1s. each, boards ; 1s. 6d. each, cloth plain ; 2s. 6d. each, cloth extra, gilt edges :—

Amy Herbert.	Margaret Percival.
The Earl's Daughter.	Laneton Parsonage.
The Experience of Life.	Ursula.
A Glimpse of the World.	Gertrude.
Cleve Hall.	Ivors.
Katharine Ashton.	

Shakespeare. — *BOWDLER'S FAMILY SHAKESPEARE.* Genuine Edition, in 1 vol. medium 8vo. large type, with 36 Woodcuts, 14s. or in 6 vols. fcp. 8vo. 21s.

OUTLINES OF THE LIFE OF SHAKESPEARE. By J. O. HALLIWELL-PHILLIPPS, F.R.S. 2 vols. Royal 8vo. 10s. 6d.

Shilling Standard Novels.

BY THE EARL OF BEACONSFIELD.

Vivian Grey.	The Young Duke, &c.
Venetia.	Contarini Fleming, &c.
Tancred.	Henrietta Temple.
Sybil.	Lothair.
Coningsby.	Endymion.
Alroy, Ixion, &c.	

Price 1s. each, boards ; 1s. 6d. each, cloth.

BY G. J. WHYTE-MELVILLE.

The Gladiators.	Holmby House.
The Interpreter.	Kate Coventry.
Good for Nothing.	Digby Grand.
Queen's Maries.	General Bounce.

Price 1s. each, boards; 1s. 6d. each, cloth.

BY ROBERT LOUIS STEVENSON.

The Dynamiter.
Strange Case of Dr. Jekyll and Mr. Hyde.
Price 1s. each, sewed ; 1s. 6d. each, cloth.
[*Continued above.*]

Shilling Standard Novels—*contd.*

BY ELIZABETH M. SEWELL.

Amy Herbert.	A Glimpse of the World.
Gertrude.	Ivors.
Earl's Daughter.	Katharine Ashton.
The Experience of Life.	Margaret Percival.
	Laneton Parsonage.
Cleve Hall.	Ursula.

Price 1s. each, boards ; 1s. 6d. each, cloth, plain ; 2s. 6d. each, cloth extra, gilt edges.

BY ANTHONY TROLLOPE.

The Warden. | Barchester Towers.
Price 1s. each, boards ; 1s. 6d. each, cloth.

BY BRET HARTE.

In the Carquinez Woods. 1s. boards ; 1s. 6d. cloth.
On the Frontier (Three Stories). 1s. sewed.
By Shore and Sedge (Three Stories). 1s. sewed.

BY MRS. OLIPHANT.

In Trust. | Madam.

BY JAMES PAYN.

Thicker than Water.
The Luck of the Darrells.
Price 1s. each, boards ; 1s. 6d. each, cloth.

Short.—*SKETCH OF THE HISTORY OF THE CHURCH OF ENGLAND TO THE REVOLUTION OF* 1688. By T. V. SHORT, D.D. Crown 8vo. 7s. 6d.

Smith.—*LIBERTY AND LIBERALISM;* a Protest against the Growing Tendency toward Undue Interference by the State with Individual Liberty, Private Enterprise, and the Rights of Property. By BRUCE SMITH, of the Inner Temple, Barrister-at-Law. Crown 8vo. 6s.

Smith, H. F.—*THE HANDBOOK FOR MIDWIVES.* By HENRY FLY SMITH, M.B. Oxon. M.R.C.S. late Assistant-Surgeon at the Hospital for Sick Women, Soho Square. With 41 Woodcuts. Crown 8vo. 5s.

Smith, R. Bosworth. - - *CARTHAGE AND THE CARTHAGINIANS.* By R. BOSWORTH SMITH, M.A. Maps, Plans, &c. Crown 8vo. 10s. 6d.

Smith, Rev. Sydney.— *THE WIT AND WISDOM OF THE REV. SYDNEY SMITH.* Crown 8vo. 1s. boards ; 1s. 6d. cloth.

Smith, T.—*A MANUAL OF OPERATIVE SURGERY ON THE DEAD BODY.* By THOMAS SMITH, Surgeon to St. Bartholomew's Hospital. A New Edition, re-edited by W. J. WALSHAM. With 46 Illustrations. 8vo. 12s.

Southey.—*THE POETICAL WORKS OF ROBERT SOUTHEY*, with the Author's last Corrections and Additions. Medium 8vo. with Portrait, 14s.

Stanley. — *A FAMILIAR HISTORY OF BIRDS.* By E. STANLEY, D.D. Revised and enlarged, with 160 Woodcuts. Crown 8vo. 6s.

Steel.—*WORKS BY J. H. STEEL, M.R.C.V.S.*

A TREATISE ON THE DISEASES OF THE DOG; being a Manual of Canine Pathology. Especially adapted for the Use of Veterinary Practitioners and Students. With 88 Illustrations. 8vo. 10s. 6d.

A TREATISE ON THE DISEASES OF THE OX; being a Manual of Bovine Pathology specially adapted for the use of Veterinary Practitioners and Students. With 2 Plates and 117 Woodcuts. 8vo. 15s.

Stephen. — *ESSAYS IN ECCLESIASTICAL BIOGRAPHY.* By the Right Hon. Sir J. STEPHEN, LL.D. Crown 8vo. 7s. 6d.

Stevenson.—*WORKS BY ROBERT LOUIS STEVENSON.*

A CHILD'S GARDEN OF VERSES. Small fcp. 8vo. 5s.

THE DYNAMITER. Fcp. 8vo. 1s. swd. 1s. 6d. cloth.

STRANGE CASE OF DR. JEKYLL AND MR. HYDE. Fcp. 8vo. 1s. sewed; 1s. 6d. cloth.

'Stonehenge.' — *THE DOG IN HEALTH AND DISEASE.* By 'STONEHENGE.' With 84 Wood Engravings. Square crown 8vo. 7s. 6d.

THE GREYHOUND. By 'STONEHENGE.' With 25 Portraits of Greyhounds, &c. Square crown 8vo. 15s.

Stoney. — *THE THEORY OF THE STRESSES ON GIRDERS AND SIMILAR STRUCTURES.* With Practical Observations on the Strength and other Properties of Materials. By BINDON B. STONEY, LL.D. F.R.S. M.I.C.E. With 5 Plates, and 143 Illustrations in the Text. Royal 8vo. 36s.

Sully.—*WORKS BY JAMES SULLY.*

OUTLINES OF PSYCHOLOGY, with Special Reference to the Theory of Education. 8vo. 12s. 6d.

THE TEACHER'S HANDBOOK OF PSYCHOLOGY, on the Basis of 'Outlines of Psychology.' Crown 8vo. 6s. 6d.

Supernatural Religion ; an Inquiry into the Reality of Divine Revelation. Complete Edition, thoroughly revised. 3 vols. 8vo. 36s.

Swinburne. — *PICTURE LOGIC;* an Attempt to Popularise the Science of Reasoning. By A. J. SWINBURNE, B.A. Post 8vo. 5s.

Taylor. — *STUDENT'S MANUAL OF THE HISTORY OF INDIA*, from the Earliest Period to the Present Time. By Colonel MEADOWS TAYLOR, C.S.I. Crown 8vo. 7s. 6d.

Taylor.—*AN AGRICULTURAL NOTE-BOOK:* to Assist Candidates in Preparing for the Science and Art and other Examinations in Agriculture. By W. C. TAYLOR. Crown 8vo. 2s. 6d.

Thompson.—*WORKS BY D. GREENLEAF THOMPSON.*

THE PROBLEM OF EVIL: an Introduction to the Practical Sciences. 8vo. 10s. 6d.

A SYSTEM OF PSYCHOLOGY. 2 vols. 8vo. 36s.

Thomson's Conspectus.—Adapted to the British Pharmacopœia of 1885. Edited by NESTOR TIRARD, M.D. Lond. F.R.C.P. New Edition, with an Appendix containing notices of some of the more important non-official medicines and preparations. 18mo. 6s.

Thomson.—*AN OUTLINE OF THE NECESSARY LAWS OF THOUGHT ;* a Treatise on Pure and Applied Logic. By W. THOMSON, D.D. Archbishop of York. Crown 8vo. 6s.

Three in Norway. By Two of THEM. With a Map and 59 Illustrations on Wood from Sketches by the Authors. Crown 8vo. 2s. boards; 2s. 6d. cloth.

Todd.—*ON PARLIAMENTARY GO-VERNMENT IN ENGLAND:* its Origin, Development, and Practical Operation. By ALPHEUS TODD, LL.D. C.M.G. Librarian of Parliament for the Dominion of Canada. Second Edition, by his SON. In Two Volumes—VOL. I. 8vo. 24*s.*

Trevelyan.—*WORKS BY THE RIGHT HON. SIR G.O.TREVELYAN, BART.*

THE LIFE AND LETTERS OF LORD MACAULAY.
> LIBRARY EDITION, 2 vols. 8vo. 36*s.*
> CABINET EDITION, 2 vols. crown 8vo. 12*s.*
> POPULAR EDITION, 1 vol. crown 8vo. 6*s.*

THE EARLY HISTORY OF CHARLES JAMES FOX. Library Edition, 8vo. 18*s.* Cabinet Edition, crown 8vo. 6*s.*

Trollope.—*NOVELS BY ANTHONY TROLLOPE.*

THE WARDEN. Crown 8vo. 1*s.* boards; 1*s. 6d.* cloth.
BARCHESTER TOWERS. Crown 8vo. 1*s.* boards; 1*s. 6d.* cloth.

Twiss.—*WORKS BY SIR TRAVERS TWISS.*

THE RIGHTS AND DUTIES OF NA-TIONS, considered as Independent Communities in Time of War. 8vo. 21*s.*
THE RIGHTS AND DUTIES OF NATIONS IN TIME OF PEACE. 8vo. 15*s.*

Tyndall.—*WORKS BY JOHN TYNDALL, F.R.S. &c.*

FRAGMENTS OF SCIENCE. 2 vols. crown 8vo. 16*s.*
HEAT A MODE OF MOTION. Crown 8vo. 12*s.*
SOUND. With 204 Woodcuts. Crown 8vo. 10*s. 6d.*
ESSAYS ON THE FLOATING-MATTER OF THE AIR in relation to Putrefaction and Infection. With 24 Woodcuts. Crown 8vo. 7*s. 6d.*
LECTURES ON LIGHT, delivered in America in 1872 and 1873. With 57 Diagrams. Crown 8vo. 5*s.*
LESSONS IN ELECTRICITY AT THE ROYAL INSTITUTION, 1875 76. With 58 Woodcuts. Crown 8vo. 2*s. 6d.*
NOTES OF A COURSE OF SEVEN LECTURES ON ELECTRICAL PHENO-MENA AND THEORIES, delivered at the Royal Institution. Crown 8vo. 1*s.* sewed, 1*s. 6d.* cloth.
[*Continued above.*

Tyndall.—*WORKS BY JOHN TYN-DALL, F.R.S. &c.—continued.*

NOTES OF A COURSE OF NINE LEC-TURES ON LIGHT, delivered at the Royal Institution. Crown 8vo. 1*s.* sewed, 1*s. 6d.* cloth.
FARADAY AS A DISCOVERER. Fcp. 8vo. 3*s. 6d.*

Ville.—*ON ARTIFICIAL MANURES,* their Chemical Selection and Scientific Application to Agriculture. By GEORGES VILLE. Translated and edited by W. CROOKES, F.R.S. With 31 Plates. 8vo. 21*s.*

Virgil.—*PUBLI VERGILI MARONIS BUCOLICA, GEORGICA, ÆNEIS;* the Works of VIRGIL, Latin Text, with English Commentary and Index. By B. H. KENNEDY, D.D. Crown 8vo. 10*s. 6d.*

THE ÆNEID OF VIRGIL. Translated into English Verse. By JOHN CONING-TON, M.A. Crown 8vo. 9*s.*
THE POEMS OF VIRGIL. Translated into English Prose. By JOHN CONING-TON, M.A. Crown 8vo. 9*s.*

Vitzthum.—*ST. PETERSBURG AND LONDON IN THE YEARS 1852–1864:* Reminiscences of Count CHARLES FRED-ERICK VITZTHUM VON ECKSTOEDT, late Saxon Minister at the Court of St. James'. Edited, with a Preface, by HENRY REEVE, C.B. D.C.L. 2 vols. 8vo. 30*s.*

Walker.—*THE CORRECT CARD;* or, How to Play at Whist; a Whist Catechism. By Major A. CAMPBELL-WALKER, F.R.G.S. Fcp. 8vo. 2*s. 6d.*

Walpole.—*HISTORY OF ENGLAND FROM THE CONCLUSION OF THE GREAT WAR IN 1815.* By SPENCER WALPOLE. 5 vols. 8vo. Vols. I. and II. 1815–1832, 36*s.*; Vol. III. 1832–1841, 18*s.*; Vols. IV. and V. 1841–1858, 36*s.*

Waters.—*PARISH REGISTERS IN ENGLAND:* their History and Contents. With Suggestions for Securing their better Custody and Preservation. By ROBERT E. CHESTER WATERS, B.A. 8vo. 5*s.*

Watson.—*MARAHUNA:* a Romance. By H. B. MARRIOTT WATSON. Crown 8vo. 6*s.*

Watts.—*A DICTIONARY OF CHEMIS-TRY AND THE ALLIED BRANCHES OF OTHER SCIENCES.* Edited by HENRY WATTS, F.R.S. 9 vols. medium 8vo. £15. 2*s. 6d.*

Webb.—*CELESTIAL OBJECTS FOR COMMON TELESCOPES.* By the Rev. T. W. WEBB. Map, Plate, Woodcuts. Crown 8vo. 9s.

Wellington.—*LIFE OF THE DUKE OF WELLINGTON.* By the Rev. G. R. GLEIG, M.A. Crown 8vo. Portrait, 6s.

West.—*WORKS BY CHARLES WEST, M.D. &c.* Founder of, and formerly Physician to, the Hospital for Sick Children.

LECTURES ON THE DISEASES OF INFANCY AND CHILDHOOD. 8vo. 18s.

THE MOTHER'S MANUAL OF CHILDREN'S DISEASES. Crown 8vo. 2s. 6d.

Whately. — *ENGLISH SYNONYMS.* By E. JANE WHATELY. Edited by her Father, R. WHATELY, D.D. Fcp. 8vo. 3s.

Whately.—*WORKS BY R. WHATELY, D.D.*

ELEMENTS OF LOGIC. Crown 8vo. 4s. 6d.

ELEMENTS OF RHETORIC. Crown 8vo. 4s. 6d.

LESSONS ON REASONING. Fcp. 8vo. 1s. 6d.

BACON'S ESSAYS, with Annotations. 8vo. 10s. 6d.

White and Riddle.—*A LATIN-ENGLISH DICTIONARY.* By J. T. WHITE, D.D. Oxon. and J. J. E. RIDDLE, M.A. Oxon. Founded on the larger Dictionary of Freund. Royal 8vo. 21s.

White.—*A CONCISE LATIN-ENGLISH DICTIONARY,* for the Use of Advanced Scholars and University Students By the Rev. J. T. WHITE, D.D. Royal 8vo. 12s.

Whiteing.—*THE ISLAND:* an Adventure of a Person of Quality; a Novel. By RICHARD WHITEING. Crown 8vo. 6s.

Wilcocks.—*THE SEA FISHERMAN.* Comprising the Chief Methods of Hook and Line Fishing in the British and other Seas, and Remarks on Nets, Boats, and Boating. By J. C. WILCOCKS. Profusely Illustrated. Crown 8vo. 6s.

Wilkinson.—*THE FRIENDLY SOCIETY MOVEMENT:* Its Origin, Rise, and Growth; its Social, Moral, and Educational Influences.—*THE AFFILIATED ORDERS.* —By the Rev. JOHN FROME WILKINSON, M.A. Crown 8vo. 2s. 6d.

Williams.—*PULMONARY CONSUMPTION;* its Etiology, Pathology, and Treatment. With an Analysis of 1,000 Cases to Exemplify its Duration and Modes of Arrest. By C. J. B. WILLIAMS, M.D. LL.D. F.R.S. F.R.C.P. and CHARLES THEODORE WILLIAMS, M.A. M.D. Oxon. F.R.C.P. With 4 Coloured Plates and 10 Woodcuts. 8vo. 16s.

Williams. — *MANUAL OF TELEGRAPHY.* By W. WILLIAMS, Superintendent of Indian Government Telegraphs. Illustrated by 93 Wood Engravings. 8vo. 10s. 6d.

Willich. — *POPULAR TABLES* for giving Information for ascertaining the value of Lifehold, Leasehold, and Church Property, the Public Funds, &c. By CHARLES M. WILLICH. Edited by H. BENCE JONES. Crown 8vo. 10s. 6d.

Wilson.—*A MANUAL OF HEALTH-SCIENCE.* Adapted for Use in Schools and Colleges, and suited to the Requirements of Students preparing for the Examinations in Hygiene of the Science and Art Department, &c. By ANDREW WILSON, F.R.S.E. F.L.S. &c. With 74 Illustrations. Crown 8vo. 2s. 6d.

Witt.—*WORKS BY PROF. WITT.* Translated from the German by FRANCES YOUNGHUSBAND.

THE TROJAN WAR. With a Preface by the Rev. W. G. RUTHERFORD, M.A. Head-Master of Westminster School. Crown 8vo. 2s.

MYTHS OF HELLAS; or, Greek Tales. Crown 8vo. 3s. 6d.

THE WANDERINGS OF ULYSSES. Crown 8vo. 3s. 6d.

Wood.—*WORKS BY REV. J. G. WOOD.*

HOMES WITHOUT HANDS; a Description of the Habitations of Animals, classed according to the Principle of Construction. With 140 Illustrations. 8vo. 10s. 6d.

INSECTS AT HOME; a Popular Account of British Insects, their Structure, Habits, and Transformations. With 700 Illustrations. 8vo. 10s. 6d.

INSECTS ABROAD; a Popular Account of Foreign Insects, their Structure, Habits, and Transformations. With 600 Illustrations. 8vo. 10s. 6d.

[Continued on next page.

Wood.—*WORKS BY REV. J. G. WOOD—continued.*

BIBLE ANIMALS; a Description of every Living Creature mentioned in the Scriptures. With 112 Illustrations. 8vo. 10s. 6d.

STRANGE DWELLINGS; a Description of the Habitations of Animals, abridged from 'Homes without Hands.' With 60 Illustrations. Crown 8vo. 5s. Popular Edition, 4to. 6d.

HORSE AND MAN: their Mutual Dependence and Duties. With 49 Illustrations. 8vo. 14s.

ILLUSTRATED STABLE MAXIMS. To be hung in Stables for the use of Grooms, Stablemen, and others who are in charge of Horses. On Sheet, 4s.

OUT OF DOORS; a Selection of Original Articles on Practical Natural History. With 11 Illustrations. Crown 8vo. 5s.

PETLAND REVISITED. With 33 Illustrations. Crown 8vo. 7s. 6d.

The following books are extracted from the foregoing works by the Rev. J. G. WOOD:

SOCIAL HABITATIONS AND PARASITIC NESTS. With 18 Illustrations. Crown 8vo. 2s. cloth extra, gilt edges.

THE BRANCH BUILDERS. With 28 Illustrations. Crown 8vo. 2s. 6d. cloth extra, gilt edges.

WILD ANIMALS OF THE BIBLE. With 29 Illustrations. Crown 8vo. 3s. 6d. cloth extra, gilt edges.

DOMESTIC ANIMALS OF THE BIBLE. With 23 Illustrations. Crown 8vo. 3s. 6d. cloth extra, gilt edges.

BIRD-LIFE OF THE BIBLE. With 32 Illustrations. Crown 8vo. 3s. 6d. cloth extra, gilt edges.

WONDERFUL NESTS. With 30 Illustrations. Crown 8vo. 3s. 6d. cloth extra, gilt edges.

HOMES UNDER THE GROUND. With 28 Illustrations. Crown 8vo. 3s. 6d. cloth extra, gilt edges.

Wood-Martin. — *THE LAKE DWELLINGS OF IRELAND:* or Ancient Lacustrine Habitations of Erin, commonly called Crannogs. By W. G. WOOD-MARTIN, M.R.I.A. Lieut.-Colonel 8th Brigade North Irish Division, R.A. With 50 Plates. Royal 8vo. 25s.

Wright.—*HIP DISEASE IN CHILDHOOD,* with Special Reference to its Treatment by Excision. By G. A. WRIGHT, B.A. M.B.Oxon. F.R.C.S.Eng. With 48 Original Woodcuts. 8vo. 10s. 6d.

Wylie. — *HISTORY OF ENGLAND UNDER HENRY THE FOURTH.* By JAMES HAMILTON WYLIE, M.A. one of Her Majesty's Inspectors of Schools. (2 vols.) Vol. 1, crown 8vo. 10s. 6d.

Wylie. — *LABOUR, LEISURE, AND LUXURY;* a Contribution to Present Practical Political Economy. By ALEXANDER WYLIE, of Glasgow. Crown 8vo. 1s.

Youatt. — *WORKS BY WILLIAM YOUATT.*

THE HORSE. Revised and enlarged by W. WATSON, M.R.C.V.S. 8vo. Woodcuts, 7s. 6d.

THE DOG. Revised and enlarged. 8vo. Woodcuts. 6s.

Younghusband.—*THE STORY OF OUR LORD, TOLD IN SIMPLE LANGUAGE FOR CHILDREN.* By FRANCES YOUNGHUSBAND. With 25 Illustrations on Wood from Pictures by the Old Masters, and numerous Ornamental Borders, Initial Letters, &c. from Longmans' Illustrated New Testament. Crown 8vo. 2s. 6d. cloth plain; 3s. 6d. cloth extra, gilt edges.

Zeller. — *WORKS BY DR. E. ZELLER.*

HISTORY OF ECLECTICISM IN GREEK PHILOSOPHY. Translated by SARAH F. ALLEYNE. Crown 8vo. 10s. 6d.

THE STOICS, EPICUREANS, AND SCEPTICS. Translated by the Rev. O. J. REICHEL, M.A. Crown 8vo. 15s.

SOCRATES AND THE SOCRATIC SCHOOLS. Translated by the Rev. O. J. REICHEL, M.A. Crown 8vo. 10s. 6d.

PLATO AND THE OLDER ACADEMY. Translated by SARAH F. ALLEYNE and ALFRED GOODWIN, B.A. Crown 8vo. 18s.

THE PRE-SOCRATIC SCHOOLS: a History of Greek Philosophy from the Earliest Period to the time of Socrates. Translated by SARAH F. ALLEYNE. 2 vols. crown 8vo. 30s.

OUTLINES OF THE HISTORY OF GREEK PHILOSOPHY. Translated by SARAH F. ALLEYNE and EVELYN ABBOTT. Crown 8vo. 10s. 6d.

EPOCHS OF ANCIENT HISTORY.

Edited by the Rev. Sir G. W. Cox, Bart. M.A. and by C. SANKEY, M.A.   10 volumes,
fcp. 8vo. with Maps, price 2s. 6d. each.

THE GRACCHI, MARIUS, AND SULLA. By
A. H. BEESLY, M.A. With 2 Maps.

THE EARLY ROMAN EMPIRE. From the
Assassination of Julius Cæsar to the Assassination
of Domitian. By the Rev. W. WOLFE CAPES, M.A.
With 2 Maps.

THE ROMAN EMPIRE OF THE SECOND CEN-
tury, or the Age of the Antonines. By the Rev.
W. WOLFE CAPES, M.A. With 2 Maps.

THE ATHENIAN EMPIRE FROM THE FLIGHT
of Xerxes to the Fall of Athens. By the Rev.
Sir G. W. Cox, Bart. M.A. With 5 Maps.

THE RISE OF THE MACEDONIAN EMPIRE.
By ARTHUR M. CURTEIS, M.A. With 8 Maps.

THE GREEKS AND THE PERSIANS. By the
Rev. Sir G. W. Cox, Bart. M.A. With 4 Maps.

ROME TO ITS CAPTURE BY THE GAULS.
By WILHELM IHNE. With a Map.

THE ROMAN TRIUMVIRATES. By the Very
Rev. CHARLES MERIVALE, D.D. Dean of Ely.
With a Map.

THE SPARTAN AND THEBAN SUPREMACIES.
By CHARLES SANKEY, M.A. With 5 Maps.

ROME AND CARTHAGE, THE PUNIC WARS.
By R. BOSWORTH SMITH, M.A. With 9 Maps
and Plans.

EPOCHS OF MODERN HISTORY.

Edited by C. COLBECK, M.A.   18 volumes, fcp. 8vo. with Maps, price 2s. 6d. each.

THE BEGINNING OF THE MIDDLE AGES.
By the Very Rev. RICHARD WILLIAM CHURCH,
M.A. &c. Dean of St. Paul's. With 3 Maps.

THE NORMANS IN EUROPE. By Rev. A.
H. JOHNSON, M.A. With 3 Maps.

THE CRUSADES. By the Rev. Sir G. W.
Cox, Bart. M.A. With a Map.

THE EARLY PLANTAGENETS. By the
Right Rev. W. STUBBS, D.D. Bishop of Chester.
With 2 Maps.

EDWARD THE THIRD. By the Rev. W.
WARBURTON, M.A. With 3 Maps and 3 Genealogical Tables.

THE HOUSES OF LANCASTER AND YORK;
with the Conquest and Loss of France. By
JAMES GAIRDNER. With 5 Maps.

THE EARLY TUDORS. By the Rev. C. E.
MOBERLY, M.A.

THE ERA OF THE PROTESTANT REVOLU-
tion. By F. SEEBOHM. With 4 Maps and 12
Diagrams.

THE AGE OF ELIZABETH. By the Rev. M.
CREIGHTON, M.A. LL.D. With 5 Maps and
4 Genealogical Tables.

THE FIRST TWO STUARTS AND THE PURI-
tan Revolution, 1603-1660. By SAMUEL RAWSON
GARDINER. With 4 Maps.

THE FALL OF THE STUARTS; AND WESTERN
Europe from 1678 to 1697. By the Rev. EDWARD
HALE, M.A. With 11 Maps and Plans.

THE AGE OF ANNE. By E. E. MORRIS,
M.A. With 7 Maps and Plans.

THE THIRTY YEARS' WAR, 1618-1648. By
SAMUEL RAWSON GARDINER. With a Map.

THE EARLY HANOVERIANS. By E. E.
MORRIS, M.A. With 9 Maps and Plans.

FREDERICK THE GREAT AND THE SEVEN
Years' War. By F. W. LONGMAN. With 2 Maps.

THE WAR OF AMERICAN INDEPENDENCE,
1775-1783. By J. M. LUDLOW. With 4 Maps.

THE FRENCH REVOLUTION, 1789-1795. By
Mrs. S. R. GARDINER. With 7 Maps.

THE EPOCH OF REFORM, 1830-1850. By
JUSTIN MCCARTHY, M.P.

EPOCHS OF CHURCH HISTORY.

Edited by the Rev. MANDELL CREIGHTON. Fcp. 8vo. price 2s. 6d. each.

THE ENGLISH CHURCH IN OTHER LANDS.
By the Rev. H. W. TUCKER, M.A.

THE HISTORY OF THE REFORMATION IN
England. By the Rev. GEORGE G. PERRY, M.A.

THE CHURCH OF THE EARLY FATHERS.
By ALFRED PLUMMER, D.D.

THE EVANGELICAL REVIVAL IN THE
Eighteenth Century. By the Rev. J. H. OVER-
TON, M.A.

THE HISTORY OF THE UNIVERSITY OF
Oxford. By the Hon. G. C. BRODRICK, D.C.L.

THE CHURCH AND THE ROMAN EMPIRE.
By the Rev. A. CARR.

THE CHURCH AND THE PURITANS, 1570-
1660. By HENRY OFFLEY WAKEMAN, M.A.

THE CHURCH AND THE EASTERN EMPIRE.
By the Rev. H. F. TOZER, M.A.

HILDEBRAND AND HIS TIMES. By the
Rev. W. R. W. STEPHENS, M.A.

** Other Volumes are in preparation.

Spottiswoode & Co. Printers, New-street Square, London.